WAR AND TRAUMA

SOLDIERS & AMBULANCES
1914-1918 In Flanders Fields Museum Ypres

SOLDIERS & PSYCHIATRISTS
1914-2014 Dr Guislain Museum Ghent

VREDESSTAD IEPER
IN FLANDERS FIELDS MUSEUM

MUSEUM DR.GUISLAIN

HANNIBAL

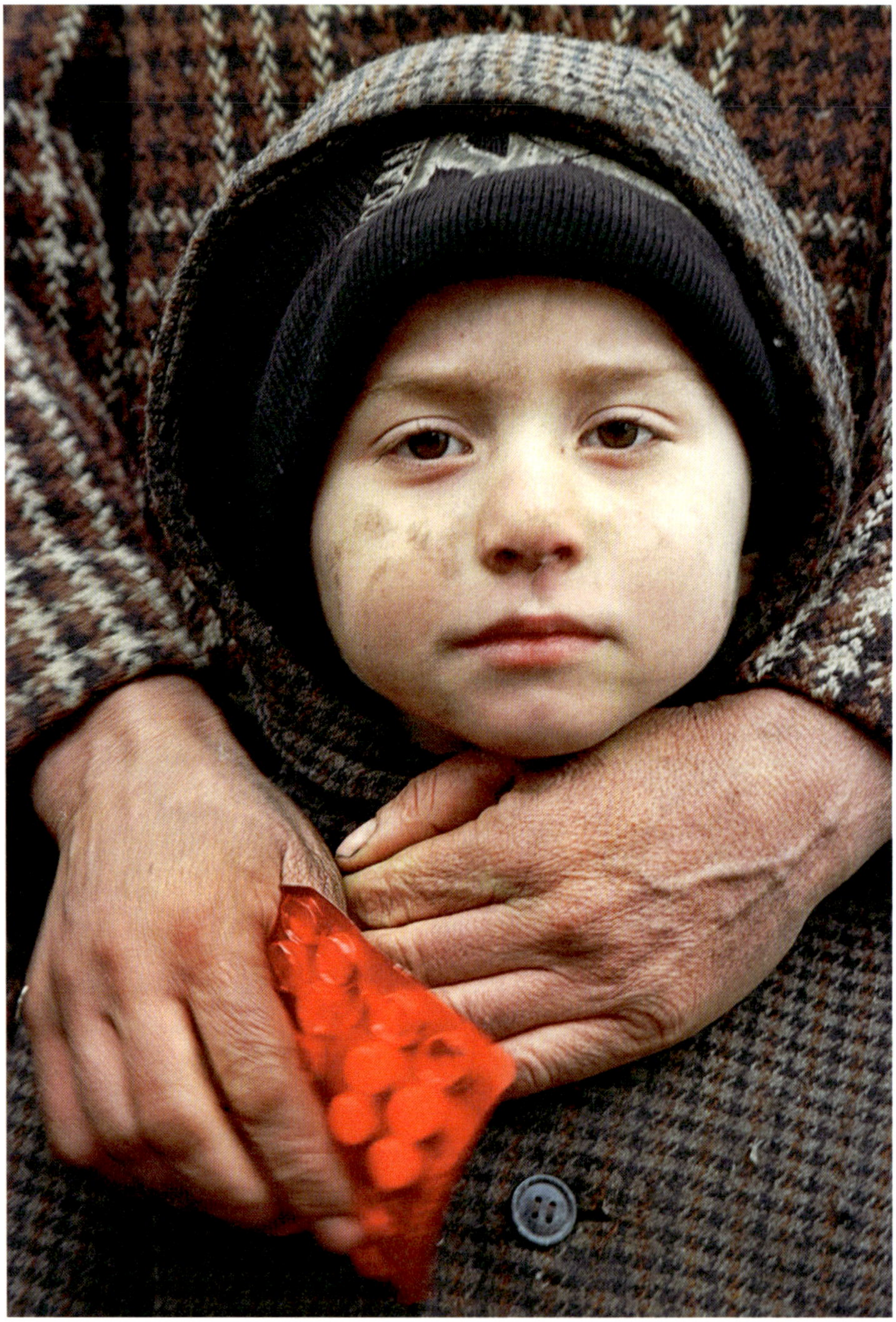

Sergey Maximishin (1964) served as a photographer in Cuba for the Soviet Army from 1985 to 1987. He then put his camera aside and studied physics. For some time Maximishin worked in the scientific and technical laboratory of the Hermitage Museum, until he started studying photo journalism in 1996. For the series *Chechnya, Winter 2000,* he took depressing photos of the war in Chechnya. He also worked on reports in, among other places, Russia, Iraq, Afghanistan and North Korea.
Sergey Maximishin, **Grozny**, Chechnya, 2000, photo. Courtesy of RTR Gallery, Paris

WAR AND TRAUMA

4)

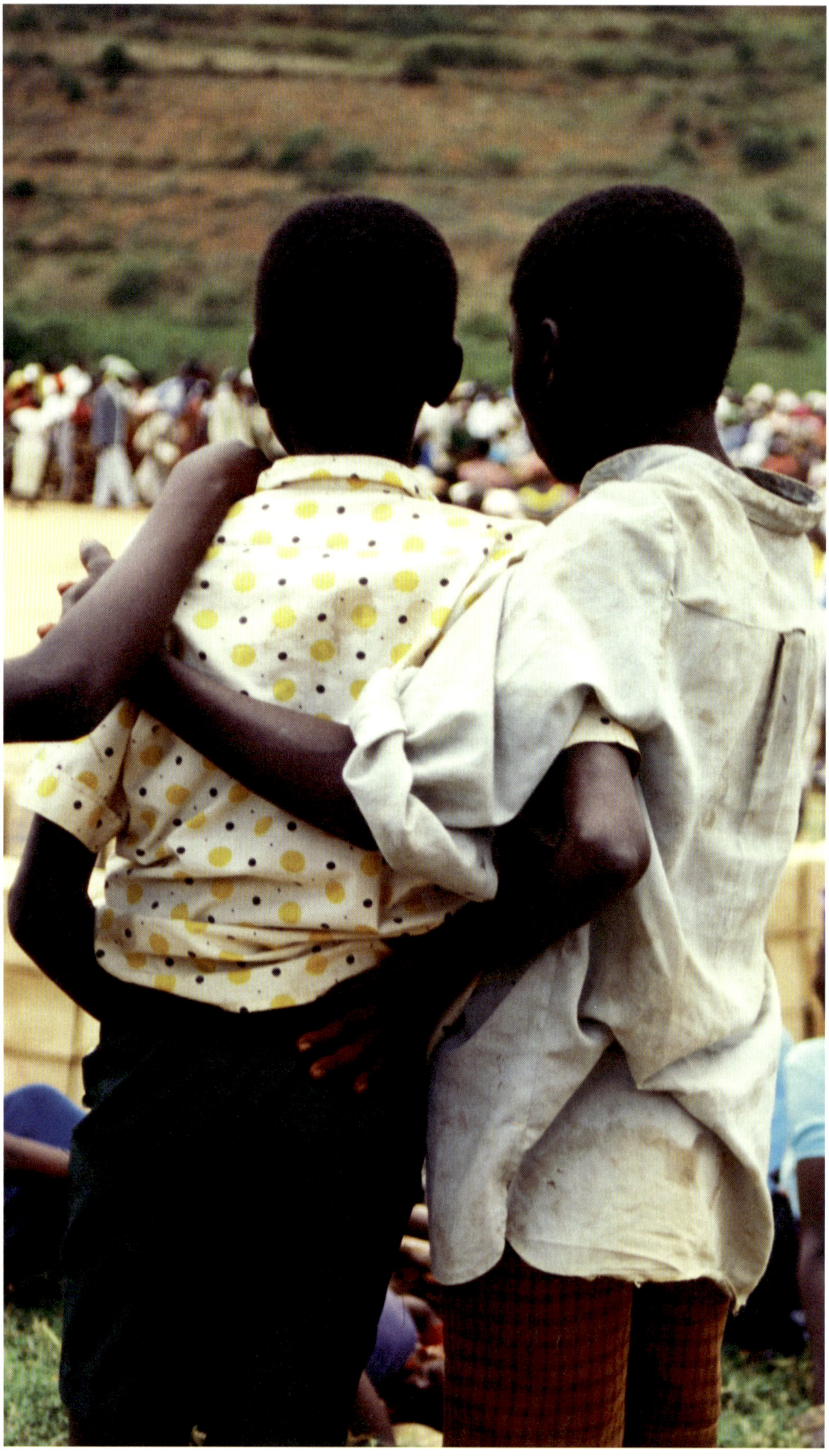

BR DR RENÉ STOCKMAN & JEF VERSCHOORE

Foreword

A hundred years ago, a conflict broke out that would affect many millions of people. Life no longer seemed to have value and many youngsters were sacrificed in a war that seemed as hopeless as absurd. The suffering was proportional: unprecedented numbers of victims, for many aid providers a situation they had absolutely no experience with. Even now this hopeless misery, physical as well as mental, renders us speechless.

A century later, we want to commemorate this terrible period and give it prominence to our time. We find it very appropriate that in the two museums, on two very symbolic *lieux de mémoires*, World War I forms the starting point for the double exhibition *War & Trauma*.

Like nothing else, the In Flanders Fields Museum in Ypres symbolises the great wound which this world war brought along with it: town and region were reshaped in a pool of human suffering. Ambulances drove to and fro: medical aid was barely organised, as everyone was taken by surprise by the enormous scale of the war. At the same time, the museum is also the pre-eminent place that urges people and politicians to want to learn from the horrors of history.

The Dr Guislain Museum in Ghent embodies the 'birth of the institution': psychiatry, which had originated in the 19th century, was confronted during World War I with a 'new type of sick military personnel and civilians' as, for the first time – albeit reluctantly and definitely also ambiguously – it recognised that situations of war brought people to and beyond the edge of insanity. This forms the beginning of a century during which the focus on psychological traumas in situations of war was increasingly recognised. What's more, in psychiatry the concept of 'trauma' was expanded to crisis situations and conflicts that also occur in everyday life: victims of abuse and rape confront psychiatrists with almost identical symptoms as seriously traumatised soldiers returning from the front.

The double exhibition *War & Trauma* wants to show the physical and mental consequences of the war and the organisation – or often disorganisation – of aid. It also wants to shed light on the discussions between physicians amongst themselves, physicians and servicemen, servicemen amongst themselves, political leaders, media, scientists and artists. But above all, it wants to request empathy for the way in which people attempted to relieve all the suffering that affected so many.

Undignified by the lack of media attention at the beginning of the conflict in Rwanda and the bombardment of meaningless media images that followed, artist, architect and filmmaker Alfredo Jaar (1956) created the three-part work *The Rwanda Project*. Irritated by the clichéd portrayal of Africa in the media, Jaar bars images in his work. The artist believes a flood of images leads to indifference. An important image that *is* part of his project is the video *Embrace*, in which two boys alternately embrace each other while staring at a crowd. With this video, Jaar shows the hidden stories behind the images: the pain and suffering that is hard to grasp, representing the non-representable.
Alfredo Jaar, **Embrace**, 1995, video, colour, 60". Courtesy of the artist, NY

6)

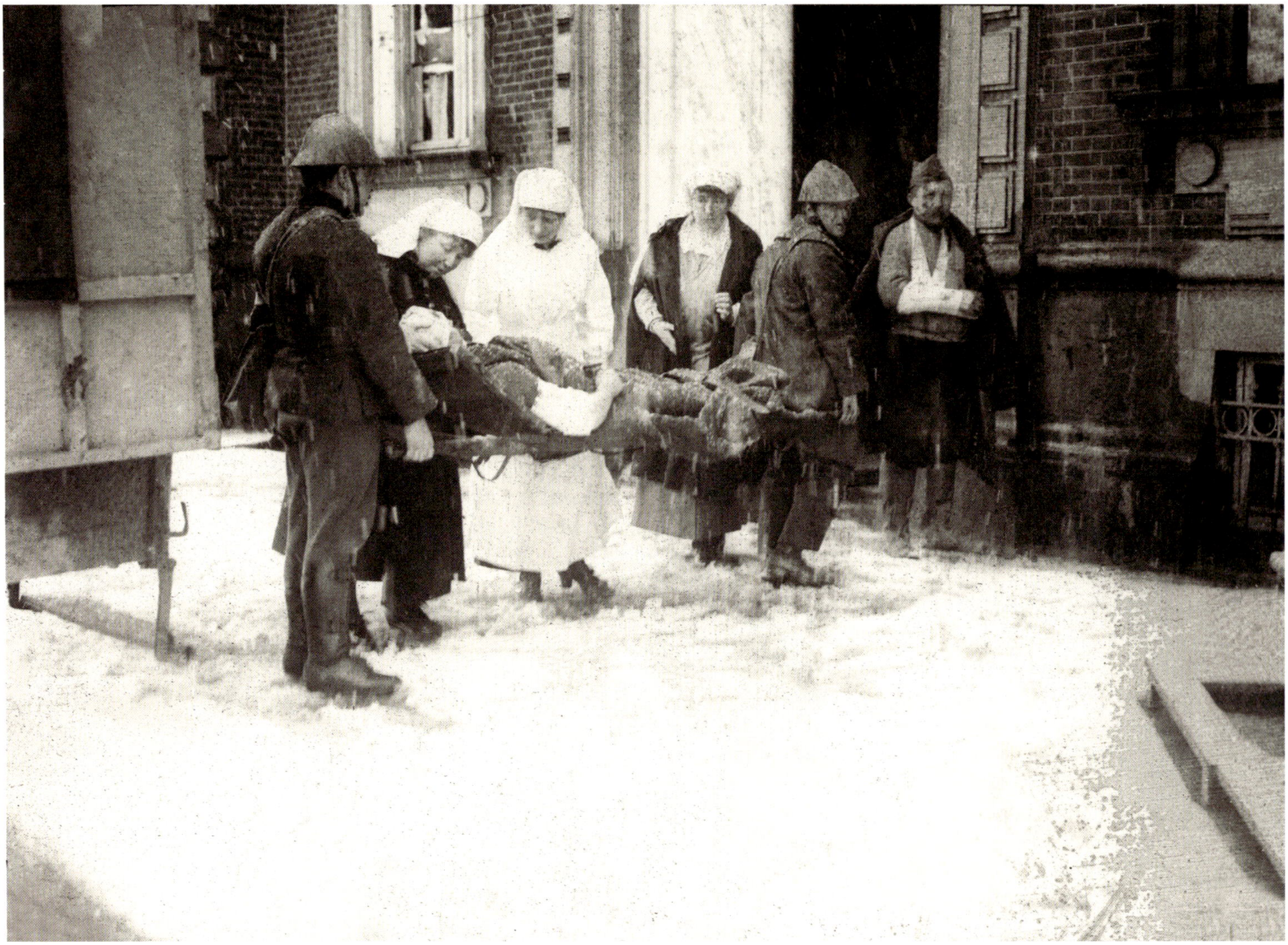

PATRICK ALLEGAERT & PIET CHIELENS

War & Trauma

During my training, I'd heard stories about soldiers who'd suddenly gone mad and consequently lost their speech or had started to wander, but in most cases the insanity had apparently been fabricated in order to escape the war and the soldiers had been court-martialled for treason or cowardice.
Stefan Brijs, *Post voor mevrouw Bromley*, 2011, p. 404

In the first few months, I had tried to bring order to the war, a pattern in the events by marking the cell walls each time a memory surfaced – with the intention of linking all these marks into a coherent whole later on, a story with an explanatory value.
Kevin C. Powers, *The Yellow Birds*, 2012, p. 224

In their recent novels, Flemish author Stefan Brijs and American Iraq veteran Kevin Powers each have given shape to the horrible impact of war on man's existence, both in his physical integrity as in his mental well-being. Brijs deals with this subject in a compelling story about the front in Flanders during World War I, and Powers has written a 'definitive' novel about the war in Iraq. His novel is bracketed together with *Im Westen nichts Neues* by Erich Maria Remarque and *Catch-22* by Joseph Heller, about the First and the Second World War respectively. The war in Powers' novel stands for death, destruction, boredom and psychological desperation. These novels express the endless fascination for stories that try to shed light on, explain and represent the essence of war on humanity.

On the eve of the remembrance of World War I, the In Flanders Fields Museum in Ypres and the Dr Guislain Museum in Ghent want to make clear with the double exhibition *War & Trauma* that the focus, also a hundred years later, should be on the fate of people. The In Flanders Fields Museum deals with the organisation of general medical care at the front in 1914–1918. The events at the front in Flanders teach us that no one could cope with the huge stream of victims of the first industrialised war.

As the armies invested too little in the relief of victims, during the first year of the war a lot of care was provided through philanthropy, private initiative and the heroic efforts of a few individuals. A striking amount of this effort has been preserved in diaries, letters, literature, photography and objects. When, by 1917 and 1918, the organisation and relief was going far more smoothly, this was not a major revolution, but what should be expected from a modern army.

The only revolution in the medical field that can be attributed to World War I is the (gradual) recognition and description of shell shock. The Dr Guislain Museum departs from this 'discovery of the omnipresence of mental suffering' during World War I. The Ghent-based exhibition zooms in on the various conflicts from the 20th century to now, but with an emphasis on a specific branch of medicine: psychiatry. It shows the history from shell shock to posttraumatic stress disorder.

SOLDIERS AND AMBULANCES

Shell shock was recognised in the midst of a deep-rooted distrust of slackers and cowardice. As was customary in the military world, this mainly gave cause for disciplinary action. Dramatic, inhuman circumstances seemingly required dramatic, inhuman measures. In the documents of a court-martial, in the field in the British Army, that ended in the death penalty, but where the court itself asked for mercy from the higher army command, "Owing to the intense bombardment to which the accused had been subjected ", Field Marshal Sir Douglas Haig wrote: "How can we ever win, if this plea is allowed?"

A wounded Belgian soldier is dropped off by an ambulance at the Elisabeth Hospital that was situated in *Château D'Hondt* in Poperinghe, winter 1915–1916. The hospital, which mainly took care of civilian casualties until the early summer of 1915, was run by Countess Maria van den Steen de Jehay, Valentine Terlinden and Louise d'Ursel. After the Second Battle of Ypres, the last civilians were systematically evacuated to the hinterland. A small Belgian medical unit stayed behind at Château D'Hondt. Photo, In Flanders Fields Museum, Ypres

In times of war, army commanders behave like managers of death. Here, the fate of the individual is always subordinate to that of the group. Consequently, psychological trauma was almost exclusively approached as a disciplinary problem, like venereal disease in the ranks or the behaviour of soldiers in a gas attack. Those who weren't hygienic were punished; running away during a gas attack was not allowed, even if you had so-called shell shock. Those who disobeyed orders were punished. Finding a suitable punishment was the solution.

However, it became clear that the number of traumatic reactions did not decrease in the slightest – and also frequently occurred in officers and in previously exemplary soldiers. This is why so-called shell shock was gradually left to the medical service, albeit not wholeheartedly. As late as 10 December 1916, in the British army Second Lieutenant E.S. Poole was executed (in the courtyard of the town hall of Poperinge), although a Medical Board had diagnosed shell shock and had prescribed care. However, as Haig wrote in his diary: "Such an event is more serious in the case of an officer than a man, and it is also highly important that all ranks should realise that the law is the same for an officer as a private." Another six months on, Corps Commander Lieutenant-General Sir Richard Haking imparted that mental cases also had to appear before a court-martial, but that a medical examining board first had to determine whether they were insane at the moment of their criminal offence (usual desertion). If this was the case, they still had to appear before a court-martial if they were seen as fit for trial.

Just like self-inflicted injuries, in the case of

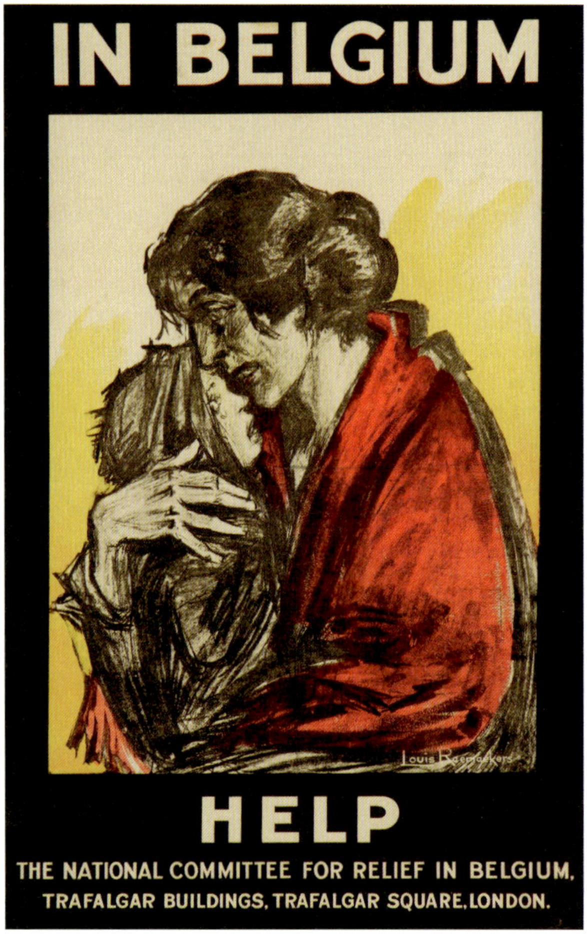

Louis Raemaekers, **In Belgium**,
s.d., paper, canvas. Historial de la Grande Guerre, Péronne (Somme)

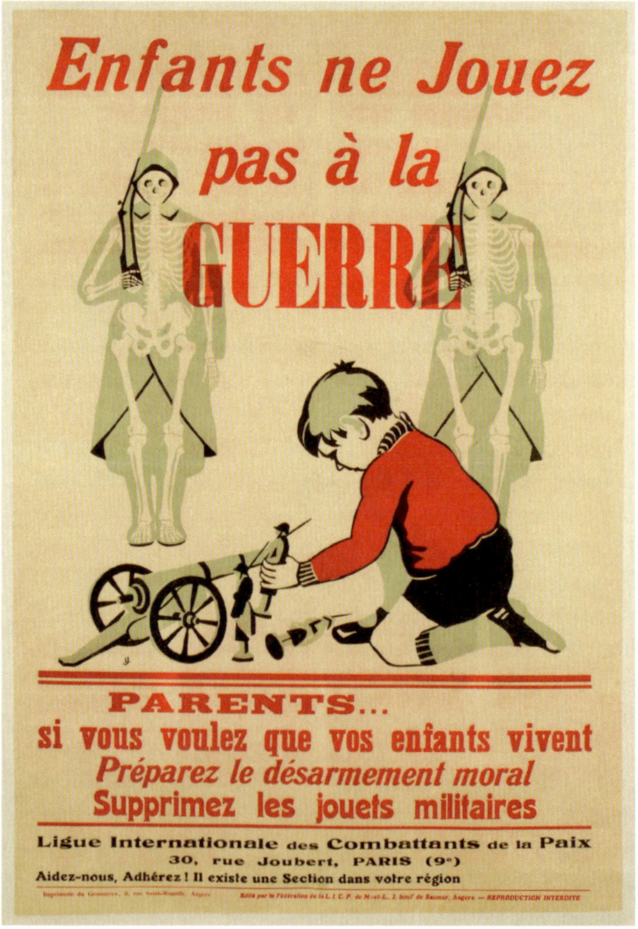

Enfants ne jouez pas à la guerre,
s.d., paper, canvas. Historial de la Grande Guerre, Péronne (Somme)

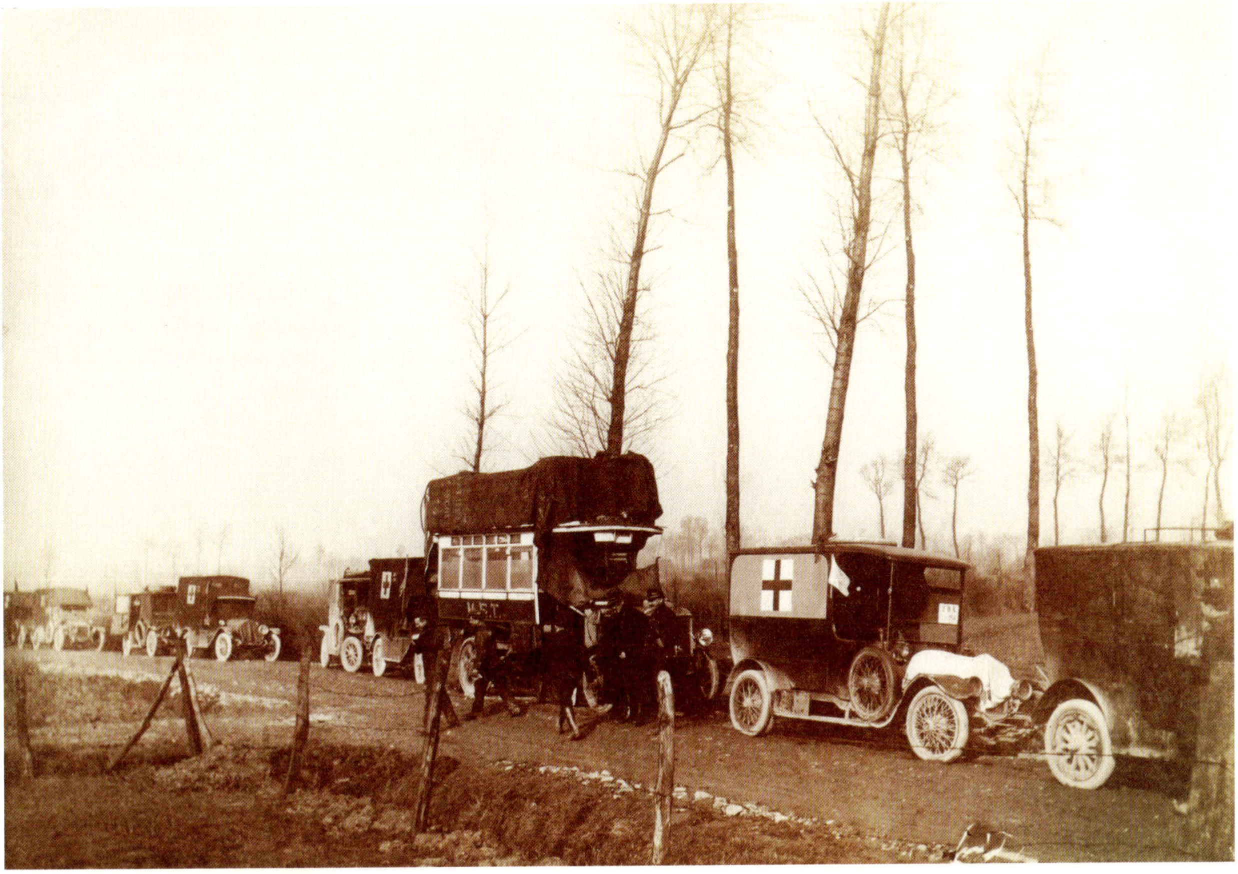

traumatic stress reactions, it was expected that the medical service would play detective. This was the crux of the problem of the medical-military dilemma. "A civil physician takes care of his patients. An army physician does not take care of the ill, he evacuates them!" said Max Deauville, pseudonym of battalion physician Dr Maurice Duwez, frankly. An army physician had to first and foremost think of the organisation, ensure that the war machine operates smoothly, while the civil physician always has to think of his patients. Deauville's irony is sharp: "By auscultating, sounding and examining his patient the physician creates a certain bond, a vague relationship based on trust that does not benefit discipline. In his contact with an army physician, the soldier soon realises that even his illness is regulated. As soon as he has discovered this and it has properly sunken in, he is saved. From this day on, he has discipline in his blood. To the death."

NO PRIORITY

Almost everything in the army structure indicates management and efficiency, obtained and assured by hierarchy and discipline. Calculated and planned in the smallest detail. This is why it is as yet so remarkable and disgraceful to have to determine that in preparation of World War I none of the participating armies seriously considered the evacuation of victims. In the quarter of a century before the beginning of the war, the fire power of the armies seriously increased, but the care for victims lagged far behind. With one doctor [*Medical Officer* (British Expeditionary Force - BEF), bataljonsarts/*médecin de bataillon* (Armée Belg(e) isch Leger - ABL), *Sanitätsoffizier* (Deutsches Reich) or *médecin aide-major* (France)] for about 1,000 men, with a motorised ambulance fleet that had to be more or less stolen ('requisitioned') at the outbreak of the war,

The *Colonne Automobile d'Ambulances et Brancards* (C.A.A.B.) of the 2nd Belgian Army Division, founded by doctor Albert De Moor, is stationed by the side of the road, in front of the farm of Mayor Mahieu in Sint-Rijkers, 1915. Note the large London double-decker bus that Dr De Moor used as an ambulance. Photo, De Moor Collection, In Flanders Fields Museum, Ypres

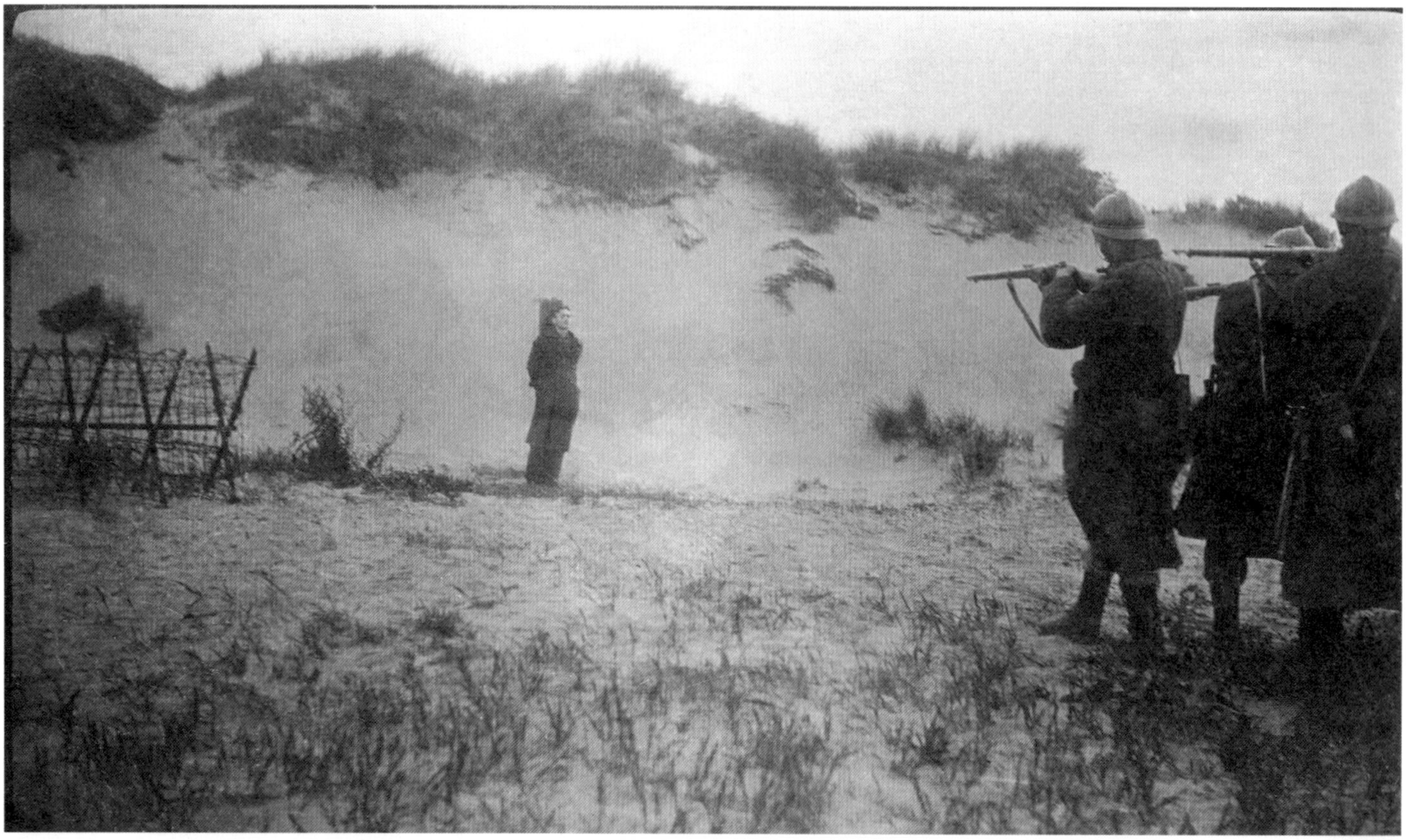

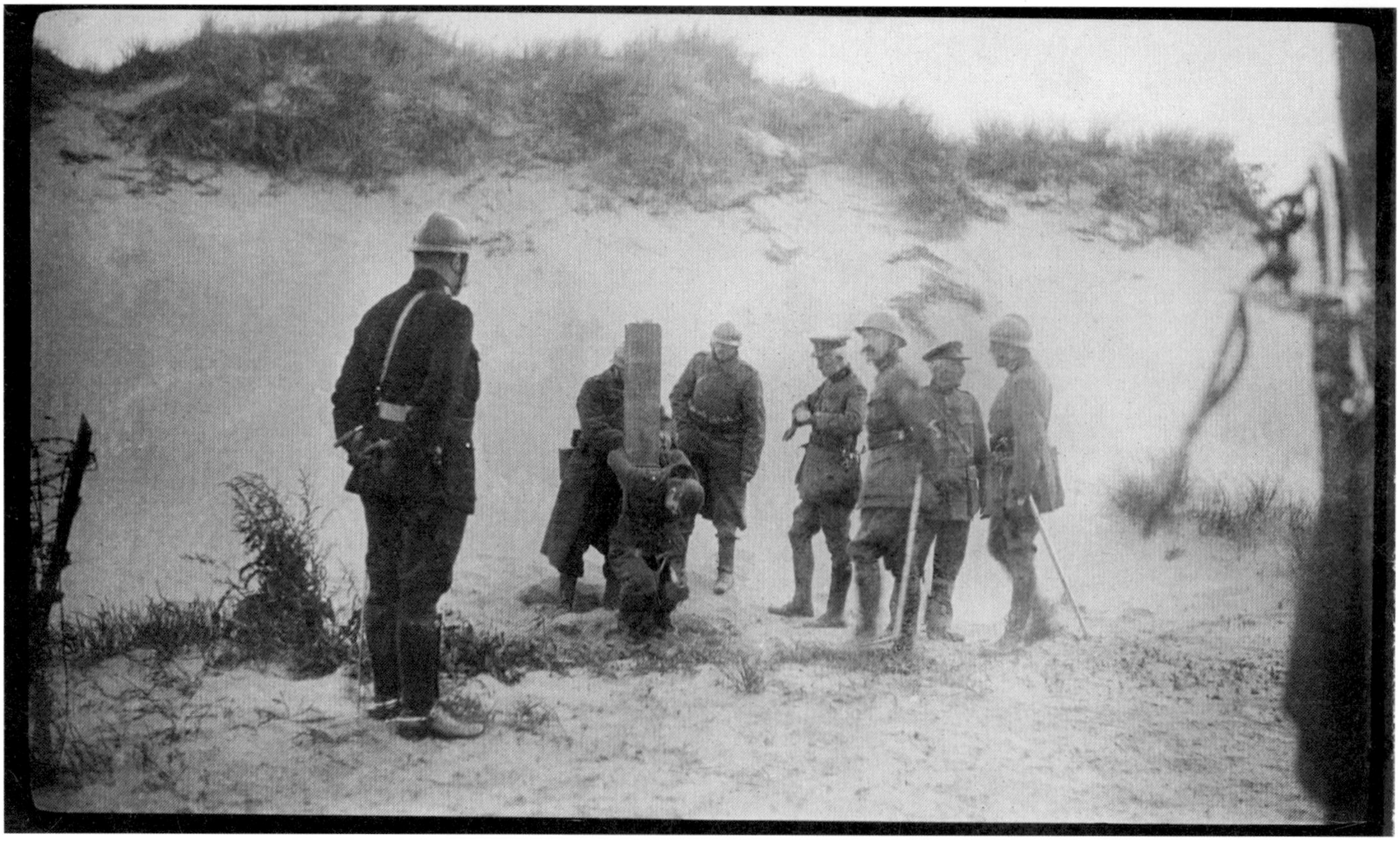

with other – horse-drawn – evacuation units who were grouped in the transport corps and stood at the back of the line, with units of stretcher-bearers who barely had any training, let alone medical or psychological guidance. It is clear that the physical and mental consequences of warfare were at the bottom of the military priority list for its participants.

This realisation determines the outlook of the exhibition, in Ghent as well as in Ypres. The idea of progress is that war, any war, causes a major breakthrough. During World War I, considerable progress was indeed made in almost every medical field, as will be seen later on. However, the fundamental conclusion then still applies: everything could have been developed far sooner, parallel to the technical developments in arming and defence. The idea of progress, which is applied in warfare all too soon and all too slowly, should be dealt with critically. Progress was at least in part simply catching up with what had previously unjustifiably been neglected.

If there was a breakthrough in the field of medical care during World War I, then this is, as said earlier, undoubtedly the recognition of the massive impact of psychological trauma. Although we should for the sake of honesty add that this was done reluctantly, that it was not unlike a procession of Echternach: thinking you see something and then trying to forget it as soon as possible.

These thoughts and findings were important in the development of the concept for the exhibition of *War & Trauma, Soldiers and Ambulances, 1914–1918* in the In Flanders Fields Museum in Ypres.

SOLDIERS AND PSYCHIATRISTS

For the other part of the exhibition, *War & Trauma, Soldiers and Psychiatrists 1914–2014*, the Dr Guislain Museum in Ghent departs from the omnipresence of shell shock during World War I.

The exhibition begins with the situation of psychiatry in the year 1914. There is a focus on the work of Jean-Martin Charcot, La Salpêtrière and the glory time of (exclusively) female hysteria. Charcot was a *visuel*: he recorded symptoms without any interest in the inner life of the patients. Charcot's followers such as Pierre Janet on the one hand, and Sigmund Freud and Joseph

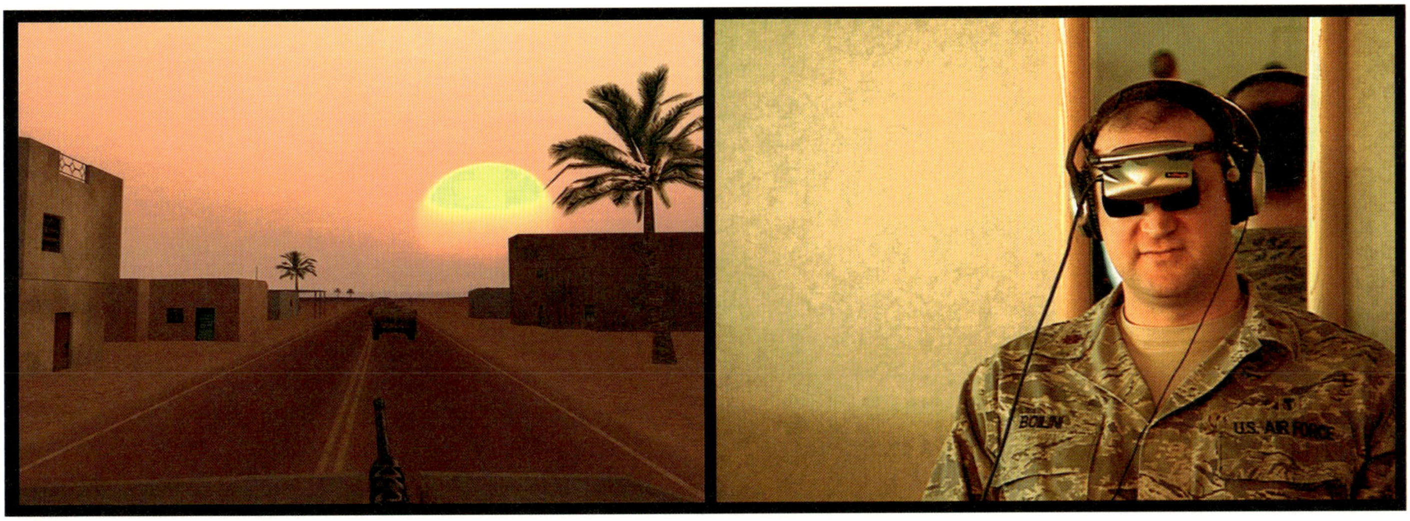

Aloïs Wulput was the last of 12 Belgian servicemen who stood before the firing squad during World War I. He was executed on 3 June 1918 in the dunes between Coxide and Oostduinkerke.
Photos, in Flanders Fields Museum, Ypres

In 2009 and 2010 German filmmaker and artist Harun Farocki (1944) worked on the *Serious Games* project, which consists of four video films in which the influence of gaming technology and role-play in the army is illustrated. For instance, during training of the soldiers, video games are often used or possible situations are simulated through role-play. The third part of *Serious Games*, *Immersion* shows a workshop in Fort Lewis, near Seattle, in which therapists demonstrate to their military colleagues how to use *Virtual Iraq* in the treatment of posttraumatic stress disorder in soldiers. This computer programme, which looks like a video game, lets the soldier relive the traumatising event. In a virtual reality where the circumstances are imitated as much as possible, from the sound of helicopters and explosions to simulating day and night, the soldier confronts his trauma. The extremely realistic testimonies make the therapists seem like real soldiers rather than just therapists giving a demonstration.
Harun Farocki, **Serious Games III**: **Immersion**. © Harun Farocki (2009)

Breuer on the other, each indicated separately in the mid-1890s that hysteria was caused by a psychological trauma. Janet spoke of 'dissociation': a changed state of consciousness that aroused symptoms of hysteria, as a consequence of unbearable emotional reactions to a traumatic event.

In turn, Freud turned away from his own findings when, by listening to his female patients, it turned out that the 'perverse actions' towards children and women were 'endemic', not only within the proletariat but also in decent civilian families. The foundations, he claimed, were not actual experiences, but 'imaginings' that came from feelings of lust. Today this change in Freud's thinking is branded as a scandal and a form of cowardice. Freud came up with a development theory in which the falseness and inferiority of women played a substantial part. Janet, once a rival of Freud, remained convinced of the traumatic foundations of hysteria. He did not distance himself, unlike Freud, from his hysterical female patients. During his lifetime he had to live through the fact that his work was forgotten and ignored. Freud's theory, psychoanalysis, was a hit and flourished. Janet was only 'rediscovered' in the 1980s.

MEN AS HYSTERICAL WOMEN

But the reality of psychological traumas would once again undisputedly force itself on the general public due to the horrors of World War I. Millions of men lost their lives:

"One of the many things that were lost in the acts of war was the illusion that men could obtain honour and fame in the battlefield. When men were continuously exposed to the horrors of trench war, a disturbingly large number of them broke down. Many soldiers who, in a state of forced helplessness, were constantly threatened with destruction and without the prospect of any respite had to see how their mates were mutilated or killed, started to behave like hysterical women. They started screaming and suffered from uncontrollable fits of weeping. Their limbs stiffened, so they could no longer move. They lost their speech and no longer reacted to their environment. They suffered from memory loss and became numb."

Thus argues Judith Lewis Herman, Professor of Psychiatry at the Harvard Medical School, in her classic *Trauma and Recovery. The Aftermath of Violence - From Domestic Abuse to Political Terror* (1993). There were a large number of victims of such nervous breakdowns. Hospitals were commanded to accommodate them. Herman states that forty per cent of British losses were due to nervous breakdowns. The military commanders were seriously bothered by the situation. They feared demoralisation among the militaries and the population.

Charles Myers, a British psychologist who examined some of the first victims, attributed their disorder to physical causes, particularly the shock effect of exploding grenades. The term 'shell shock' was born.

Gradually, soldiers and psychiatrists had to admit that the symptoms of shell shock were caused by a psychological trauma. The discussions continued: some servicemen also believed that soldiers should not be allowed to show emotions at the front, and were certainly not allowed to fall victim to terror. Those who did, were inferior creatures, simulants or cowards. More progressive doctors realised that the so-called war neurosis was a real mental disorder that could occur in all soldiers. They pleaded for humane treatment based on psychoanalytic principles.

This humane approach was at odds with the traditional military attitude that centred around punishment and where the aim was to prepare the patient for warfare again as soon as possible. In the post-war period, there was less attention to psychological traumas in medical and military circles. War veterans were hidden in mental institutions and had become a burden. In Germany, people cynically spoke of *Rentenneurose*: cowardice, weakness and abuse were suggested to go hand in hand, and there was little empathy for those affected. The first part of the exhibition concentrates on the 'knowing and forgetting' of shell shock. How did psychiatrists, servicemen and victims deal with this?

INSANITY AS DEGENERATION

But the hardness of military logic also shed light on another aspect: the conviction that the obliteration of mental illness was an objective to strive for socially. The

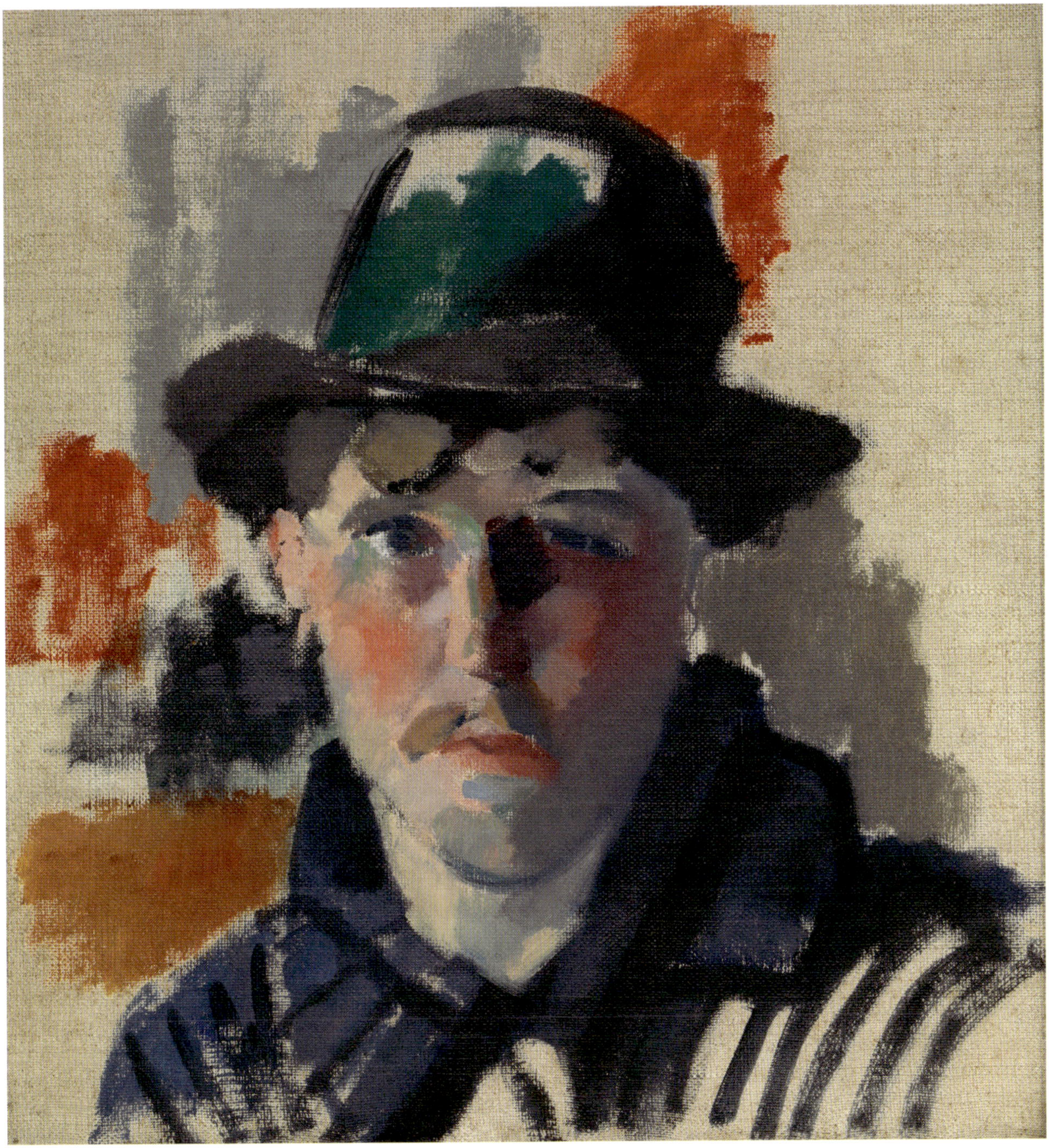

On 30 July 1914, Rik Wouters (1882–1916) was called up to fight in Liège against the German force invading the Belgian countryside. The artist saw horror, death and hell in Liège: "The horrific sight of all those young dead drove me mad." Liège fell ten days later and Wouters escaped from the front in all the chaos. After being advised by friends, who pointed out the severe penalties for desertion, he returned to his platoon. In the months that followed, the artist, together with other soldiers, was relocated to the encampments in Lier, Antwerp, Zeist and eventually in the safety of Amsterdam. Although the artist was in safe places, he was no longer the same. Rik Wouters was seriously marked by the traumatic experiences in Liège. Rik Wouters, **Self Portrait in Green Hat**, 1915, oil on canvas. Royal Museum of Fine Arts Antwerp © Lukas-Art in Flanders vzw, photo Hugo Maertens

second part of the exhibition focuses on this extraordinarily dark chapter in the history of psychiatry. This culminated in the way in which Nazism, as a totalitarian ideology, supported by a hard military conviction, dealt with mental illness.

A direct link can be made to the age-old 'degeneration hypothesis' (Morel, 1857) (the mentally ill are degenerates) about the *Entartung* (1892) of Max Nordau (degeneration as a central concept in the rejection of everything that is 'different', both the mentally ill as avant-garde artists). Still the Nazi ideology went furthest with regard to sterilising the mentally ill against their will and murdering them. It turned out to be a grim prelude to the even more severe massacres during World War II.

The Holocaust was increasingly described as an excessive psychological trauma. The extreme world of destruction in the concentration camps comprises all elements of the contemporary view of trauma, its causes and consequences. From the mid-1950s, psychiatrists and psychologists became increasingly interested in this group of camp survivors: the holocaust syndrome is almost an enlargement of all aspects of psychological trauma.

PHOTOGRAPHERS AND ARTISTS AT THE FRONT

After World War II, doctors described the limited impact of classic hypnosis or medicinal treatment: real catharsis or cure was rarely achieved. Together with a critical counterculture in the 1960s and 1970s the interests of groups, such as veterans, but also other parties involved, were increasingly recognised. This had a dual effect: on the one hand they offered help to the traumatised, because they were allowed to express their experiences and feelings in a group, on the other hand they made the general public aware of the traumatic consequences of war.

This is the subject of the third part of the exhibition: how is war perceived at home? What is the role of reporters and photographers? How do artists depict the madness of war? Each of them represents the conflict in their own way and tries to find a way to deal with all this violence.

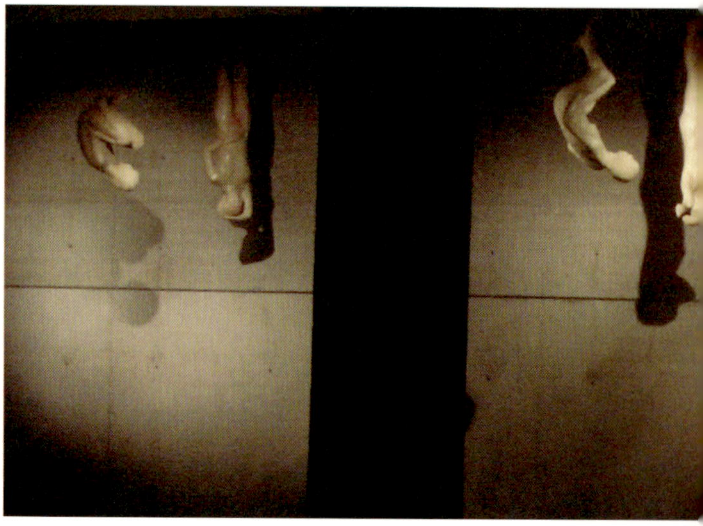

Just think of the war in Vietnam and the traumatic return of war veterans. How does a veteran feel when he comes home after the misery of war to an atmosphere of protest? Is he regarded as a hero or a criminal? Is there support and understanding? Is he helped or is there dread? Do people want to 'forget' the soldier or veteran because he stands for a painful – traumatic – reminder of a recent public past? The role of documentary photography is very significant in all this: images, and therefore also corresponding feelings, are part of how people will experience a war: as 'just' or as 'wrong'. This in turn had a major impact on anyone who was directly involved in that war.

BROAD CONCEPT OF TRAUMA

Since 1980 the concept of posttraumatic stress disorder (PTSD) has been included in the list of disorders in the leading *DSM*, the bible of modern-day psychiatrists. Thanks to the activities of war veterans and the Women's Movement, an increasing number of parallels were found between both groups of victims. It became clear that the psychological syndrome found in victims of rape, domestic violence and incest was in essence the same as the syndrome found in survivors of war. Judith Lewis Herman: "Its implications are currently equally horrific as a century ago: the subordinate position of women is maintained and enforced by the hidden

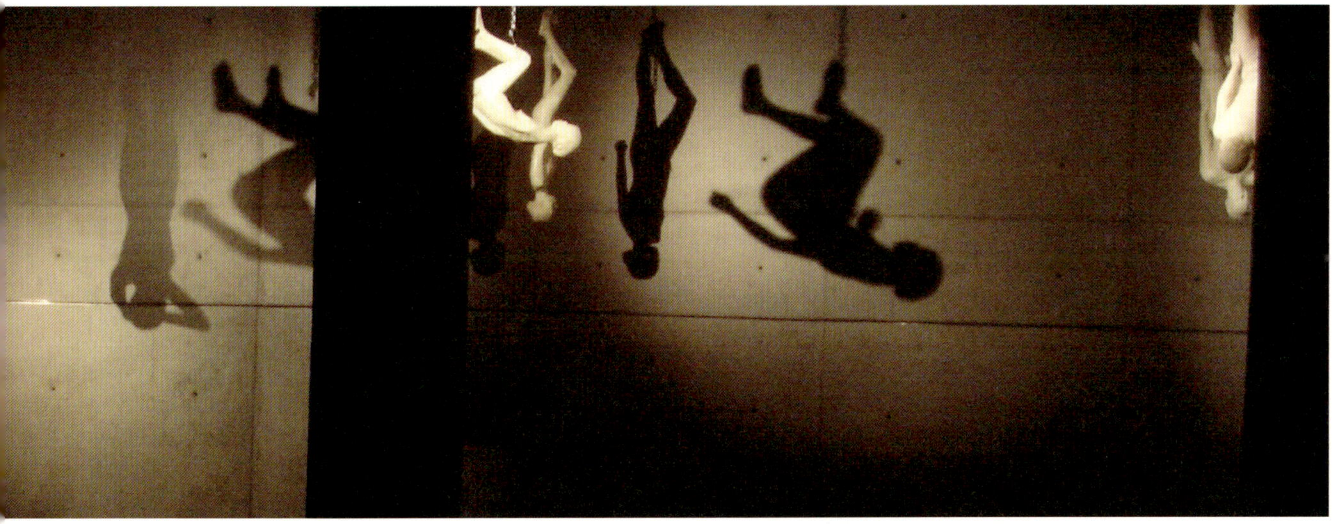

violence of men. A war is raging between the sexes. Raped or abused women and sexually abused children are the victims of this war. Hysteria is the war neurosis of the battle between the sexes."

Thus the exhibition ends with a fourth part, which focuses on the broadening of the concept of trauma. This also means that many psychiatric syndromes are understood in the framework of 'trauma'. Current figures indicate that 50 to 60 per cent of psychiatric patients are in fact dealing with the consequences of trauma. We partly see this translated in the latest version of DSM, DSM V (2013), which includes reactive attachment, acute stress, posttraumatic stress, adaptation disorders and *'disinhibited social engagement disorders'* under trauma and stress-related disorders.

1914–1918 TO 2014

The history of hysteria, shell shock and posttraumatic stress disorder reveals an important aspect of the development of society from the 20th century until now: how the subordinate position of women led to the cause of trauma being banished to the world of female imagination, how soldiers with shell shock became a forgotten group during and definitely after the war. Currently the social debate and research into psychological traumas seem to be strongly embedded as a legitimate item in modern-day psychiatry. The area of research has experienced a spectacular expansion. History teaches us, however, that this knowledge can also be lost. Searching for the impact of psychological traumas must be supported by society on a broader level.

Realising the true consequences of warfare and equality between the sexes are two sides of the same coin in this history. How can psychological trauma be given the place it deserves, so the victims of war, rape or domestic violence get more attention?

Soon the centenary of World War I will form the cause for an extensive symbolic confirmation of being in the right, national interest, the brilliance of leaders and the necessity of legitimised violence. The victims, the so-called centre of attention, will only be pretexts. With this exhibition, the In Flanders Fields Museum and Dr Guislain Museum hope to give visitors the same

With *Chinese Offspring,* Chinese artist Zhang Dali (1963) wants to give attention to the immigrants who are currently working on construction in China. Although he believes they are shaping China's physical reality, they are an invisible group with a low social status. By depicting these immigrants in waxwork, the artist not only wants to acknowledge their existence but also to express appreciation for their contribution to society. In total, Zhang Dali created a hundred immigrants in a variety of shapes and sizes, always carrying a tattoo of a number, the artist's signature and the project's title. These life-size portraits are often hung upside down to represent their vulnerability, their uncertain existence and their impotence against their own fate. Their personal trauma is in stark contrast to the anonymity in which they are forced.
Zhang Dali, **Chinese Offspring**, 2003–2005, resin, glass fibre.
Collection Adrian David Gallery, Knokke

warning: do not forget that what is shown and what happened first and foremost bears witness to the acts of violence, ranging from domestic abuse to the acts of war, and recognise that they are related in one way or another, then as well as now.

From their own viewpoint both museums zoom in on various periods: In Flanders Fields Museum focuses on *Soldiers and Ambulances 1914–1918*, Dr Guislain Museum is about *Soldiers and Psychiatrists 1914–2014*. Both museums, however, request the same social alertness and watchfulness towards the trauma of violence. In Flanders Fields Museum concentrates on the historic documentation of a period that is typical of the former front, and still characterises many war relics. Most cemeteries are after all directly linked to medical evacuation. The Ghent Museum focuses on aspects of the history of psychiatry and psychology in relation to war and trauma. They also show how artists and documentary photographers depict these extreme experiences.

We regard the differences between both exhibitions as an added value: they broaden the horizon of dealing with what happened in our country, in Flanders, in the period 1914–1918. They also offer the possibility of linking what happened 'then and there' to what can also occur in everyday life in extreme circumstances. Seeing this connection, in spite of possible differences, can be highly valuable in the exploration into the further refinement of the impact of trauma on the lives of so many victims.

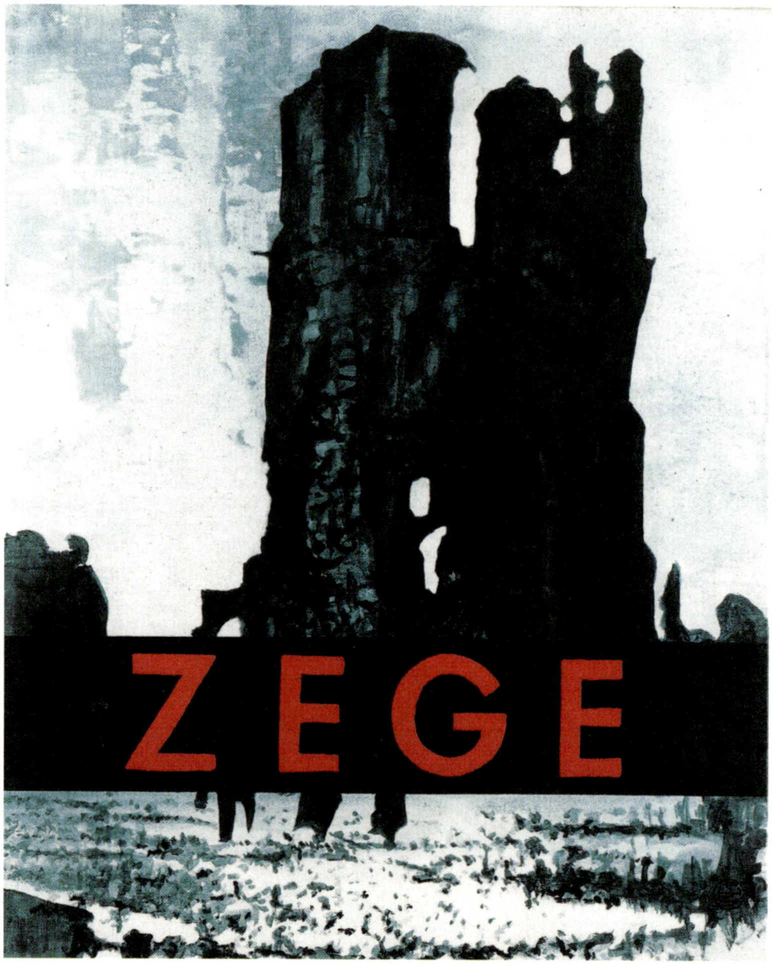

With the series *Are those misleading You deceiving Themselves?*, Belgian painter Gery De Smet (1961) seeks a new visual language of ideologies. This series includes large paintings in bluish shades, each with a bright-red slogan referring to war propaganda and slogans. De Smet seeks the contrast between image and text. Inspired by photographic material from the interbellum, he paints recognisable images of people and locations. For instance, in this painting, "zege" (victory) is written in big letters on top of the image of the ruin of a belfry. With this painting, *Zege*, De Smet questions the ideological messages of nationalist regimes.
Gery De Smet, **Zege**, 1992, acrylic paint on canvas. Private collection PhD

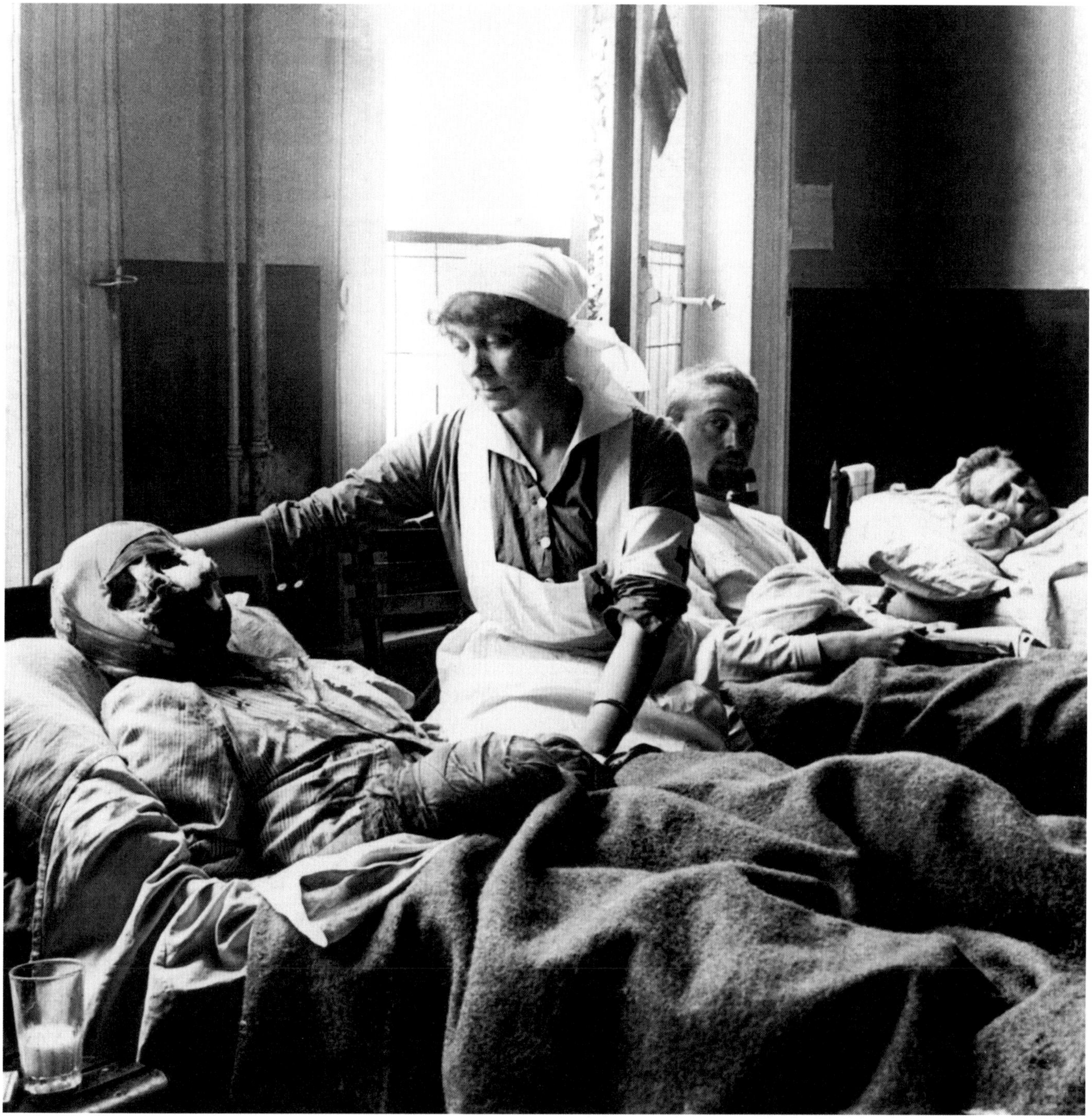

Inside view of a ward of the *Belgian Field Hospital* in Antwerp, circa September 1914. A heavily injured soldier is assisted by a nurse. Photo, In Flanders Fields Museum, Ypres

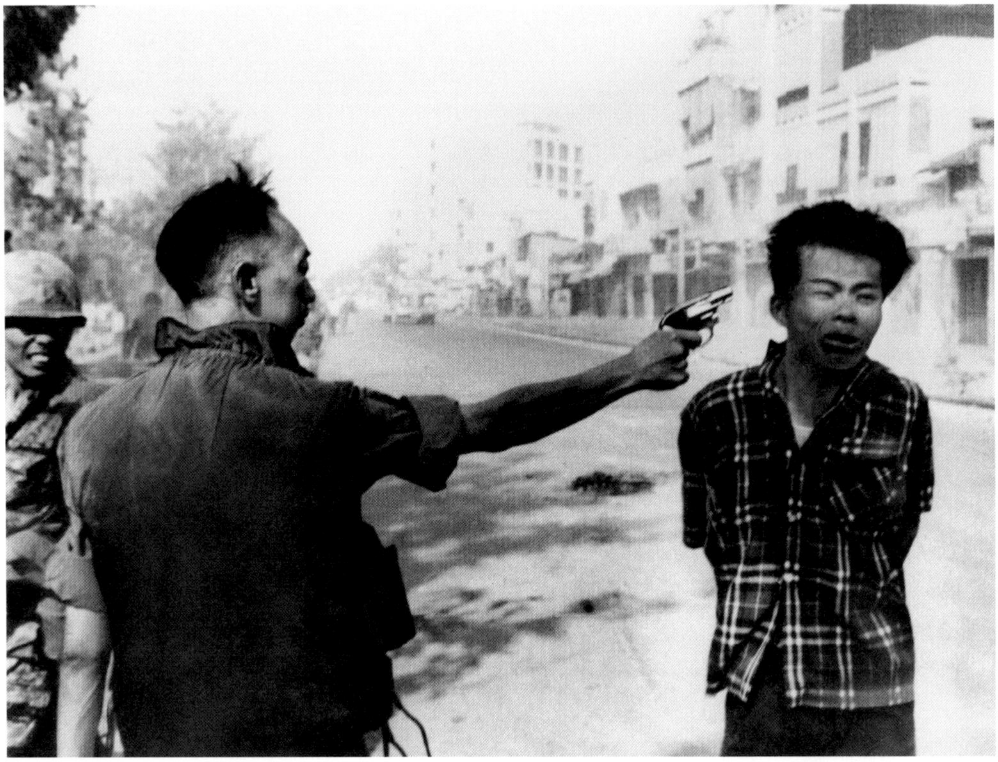

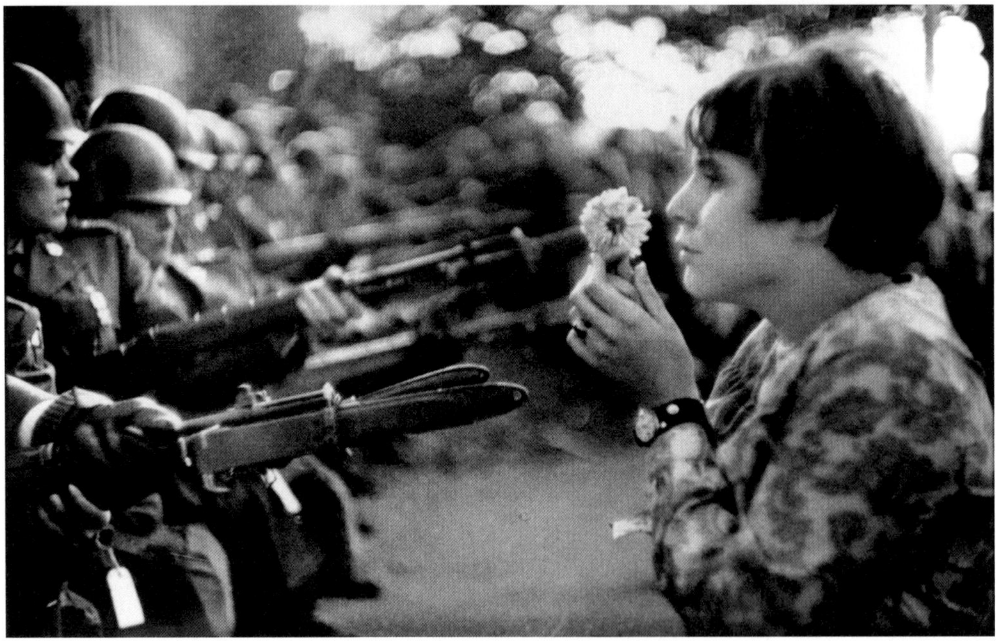

In 1968, Eddie Adams (1933–2004), war photographer in Vietnam, captured an execution that went around the world. The photo indicates the brutality and horror of war. A Vietnamese general is shooting a man, apparently in civilian clothing, through the head. Eddie Adams knew the true story. He proclaimed: the executed man was a murderer, responsible for a failed attack on the general. The image is, however, easily taken out of context: the photo made the front pages of many newspapers as the execution of a civilian and thus kindled the anti-war sentiment. Eddie Adams: "The general killed the Vietcong; I killed the general with my camera. Photos are the world's most powerful weapons. People believe them; but photos lie, even without manipulation. They are merely half-truths. ..." *(Time)*

Eddie Adams, **Moments of Execution. Vietnam 1968**, photo. Fondation Francès, Senlis

The invisible tunnel system of the Vietnamese resistance fighters provided an enemy that was difficult to quantify. The war in Vietnam, which was intended as a short war, became a tough and unwinnable fight between the US and the Vietcong. The high rates of victims among American soldiers flared up the protests. An iconic image is the photo *Anti-Vietnam* by Marc Riboud (1923). In 1967 American Jan Rose Kasmir put a flower in the barrel of a gun during the anti-Vietnam demonstration at the Pentagon. Riboud captured it and thus created a symbol for the many protests that would eventually herald the end of the Vietnam War.

Marc Riboud, **Jan Rose Kasmir. Protest Against The War In Vietnam**, Washington 21 October 1967, gelatin silver print. Musée de la Photographie, Charleroi © Marc Riboud

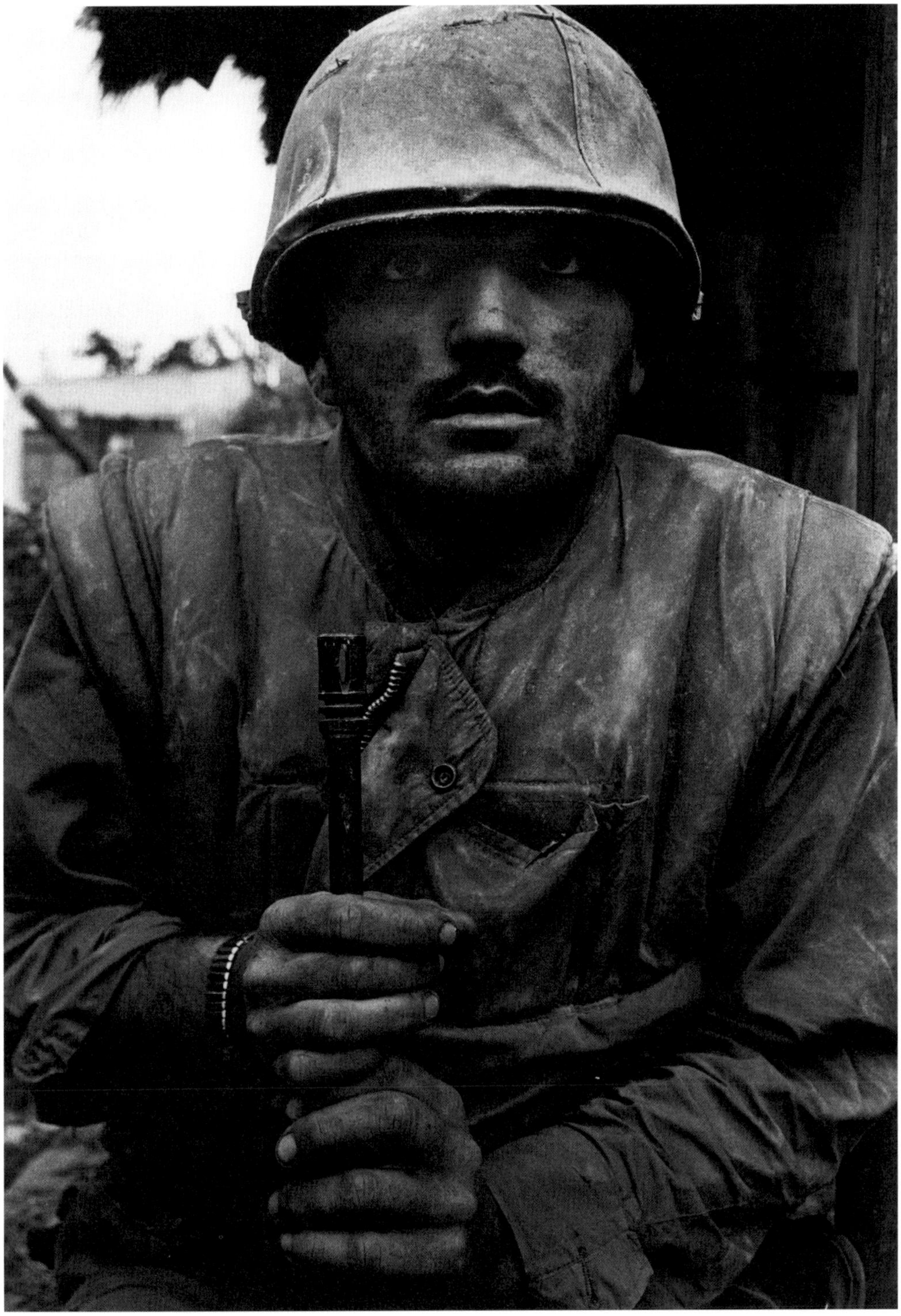

The best-known picture of American war photographer Don McCullin shows a Vietnam soldier staring vacantly into space. McCullin took the photograph in 1968 during the battle of Hue, when he stayed with the US Navy unarmed. This town had fallen into the hands of North-Vietnamese soldiers. The Americans suffered many losses and the town was destroyed. The marine, immortalised by McCullin, is not looking into the lens but to something next to it. Or is he looking at nothing, is he staring? McCullin's soldier is in shock and his thoughts are clearly somewhere else. Although this picture does not explicitly show the horror of war as the equally well-known *Saigon Execution* by Eddie Adams or *Napalm Girl* by Nick Ut, the marine's gaze tells us just as much. The portrait of the traumatised Vietnam soldier became iconic and became a symbol of the untold human damage of war.

Don McCullin, **Shell-Shocked US Soldier Awaiting Transportation Away From The Frontline,**
Tet Offensive, Hue, South Vietnam, 1968, photo. © Don McCullin (courtesy of Contact Press Images)

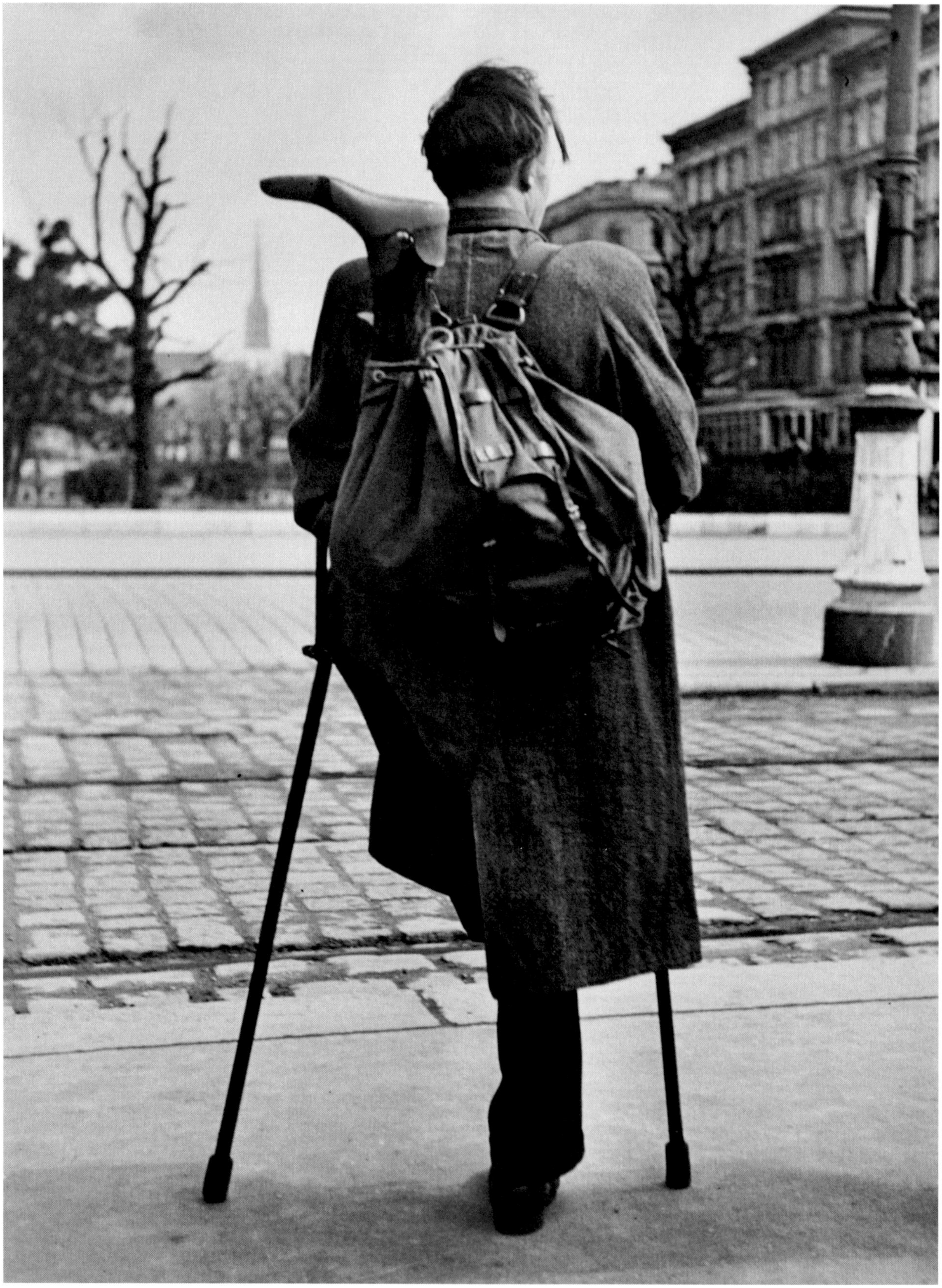

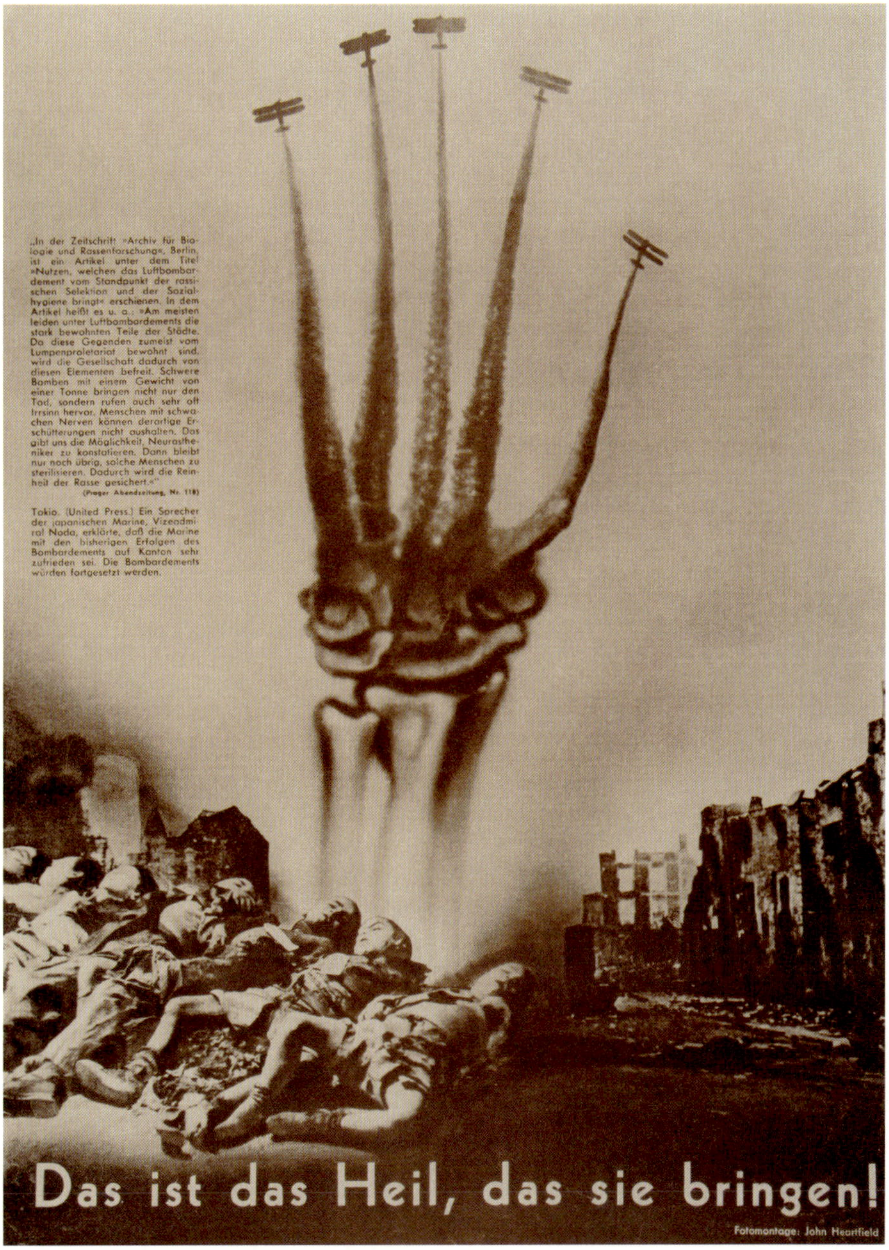

Austrian Magnum photographer Ernst Haas (1921–1986) is considered as one of the pioneers of colour photography. He started photographing just after World War II and was noted by *Life* magazine for his black-and-white series about returning Austrian prisoners of war. In 1953, the magazine published a 24-page colour photo essay about New York, and its retrospective in 1962 was the first exhibition of colour photography in the Museum of Modern Art in New York. When Robert Capa died in Indochina in 1954, Haas travelled there himself to continue to cover the war.
Ernst Haas, **Homecoming Prisoner**,
Vienna, 1946–1948, silver bromide print.
FotoMuseum Province of Antwerp

John Heartfield (1891–1968) was a German Dadaist artist. He was actually called Helmut Herzfeld, but changed his name as a protest against German militarism. He left Berlin in 1933 after the SS had broken into his apartment. He did not return until 1950. Heartfield made world famous posters with clear political, mainly anti-fascist messages. He later also opposed the Vietnam War. He is known for his photo montages, for which he never made images but used prints from magazines, which he processed and combined into new ones. For John Heartfield, art was a powerful weapon against the insanity of war.
John Heartfield, **Das ist das Heil, das sie bringen!**
1938, offset. FotoMuseum Province of Antwerp, © SABAM Belgium 2013

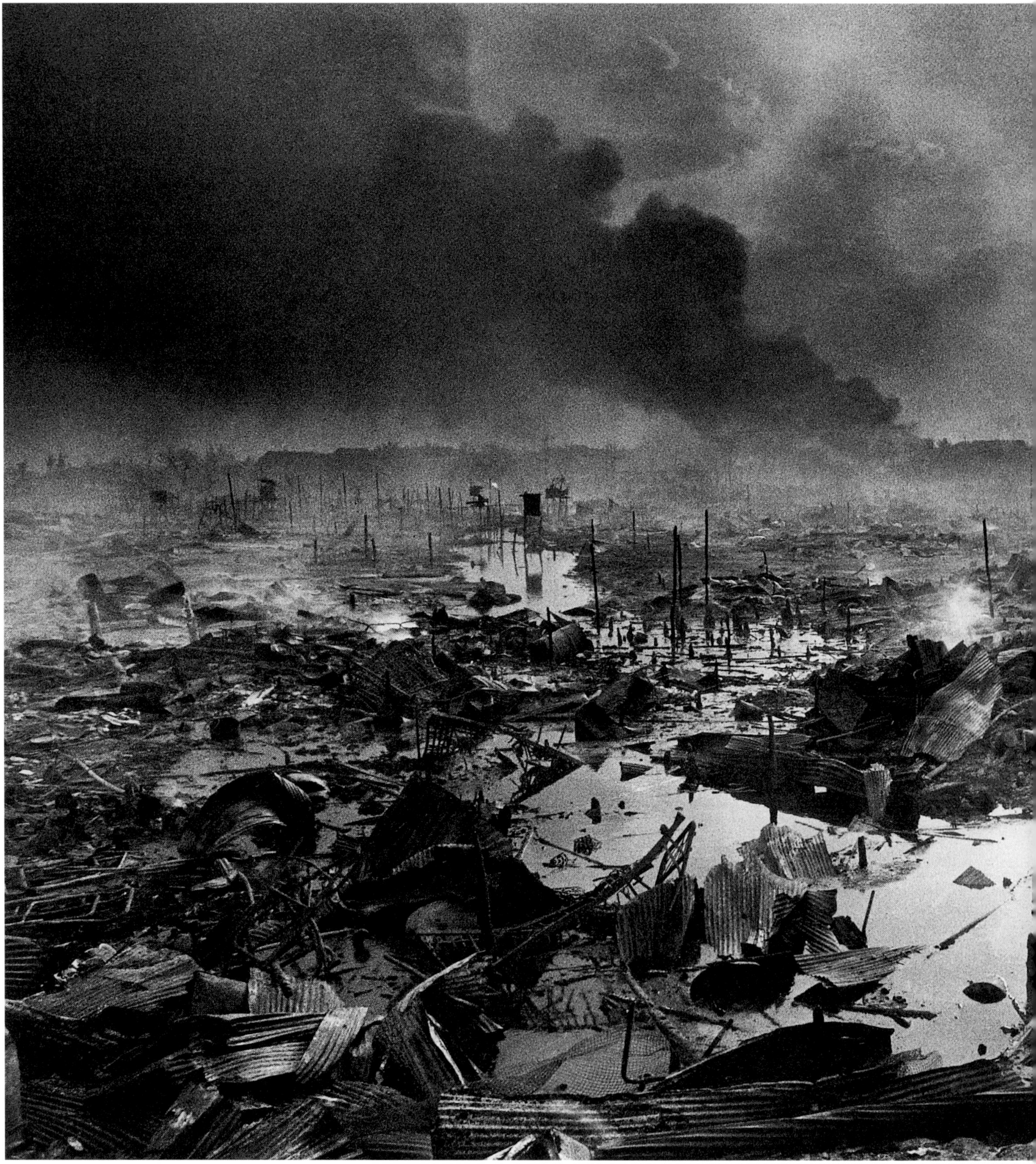

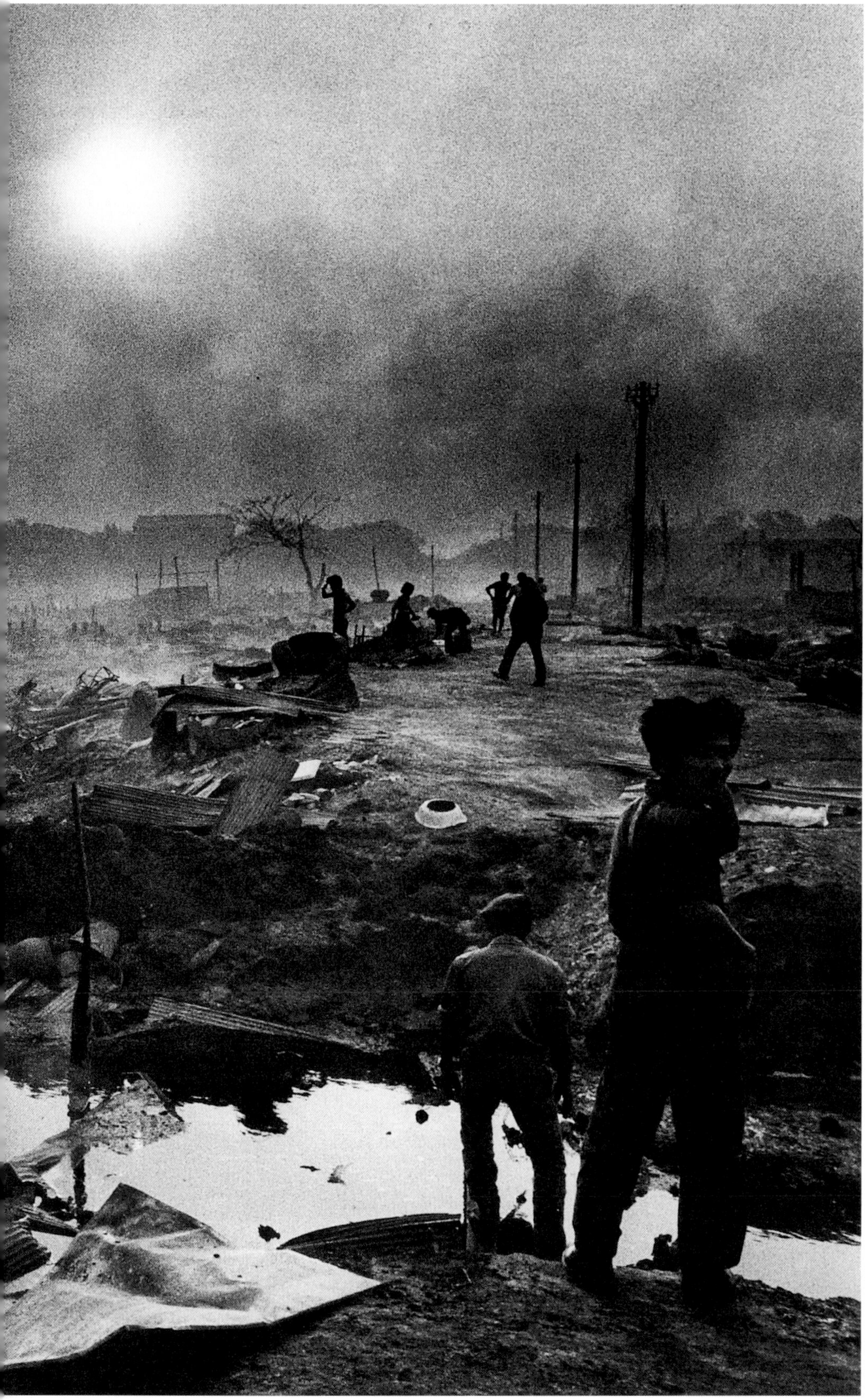

Christine Spengler's (1945) photo of the bombardments of Phnom Penh (Cambodia) in 1975 captured the horror of destruction in an aesthetic photo. Spengler rarely shows the injured, the dead, blood or explicit violence. We see people continue their lives in misery or at least try to lead a normal life amongst the rubble. These are often images from the point of view of women and children. Her photography isn't typical anti-war photography. Although she does not want to aestheticize the horror, her work has a great sense of drama that is reminiscent of paintings such as those of Velázquez and Goya.
Christine Spengler,
Phnom-Penh Bombardment,
photo. Fondation Francès, Senlis

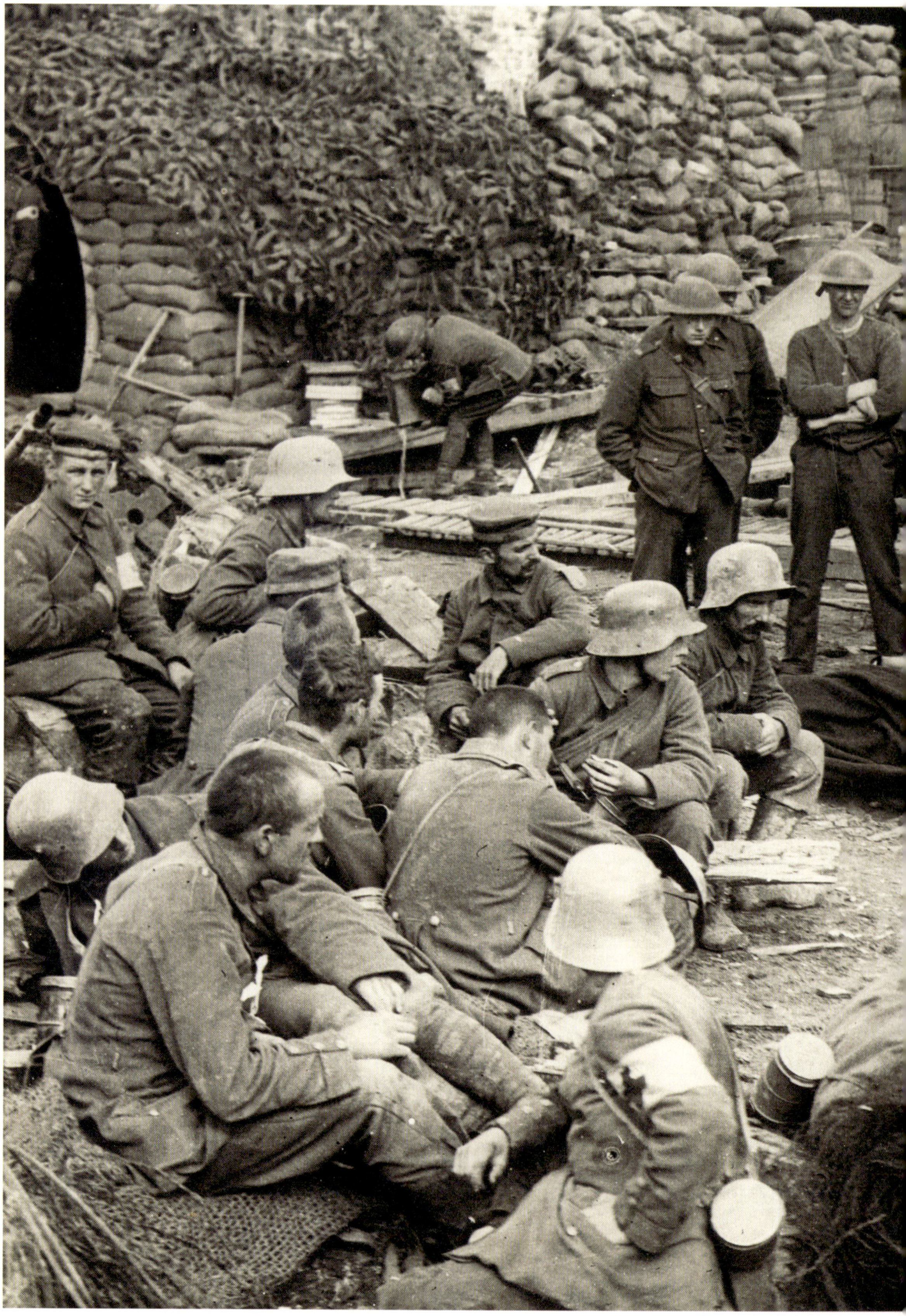

20 September 1917, the first day of the Battle of the Menin Road. British aid providers and wounded soldiers wait together with German prisoners of war, whether or not wounded, for treatment or evacuation at the British first-aid station that was set up in *Potyze Château*. Today the castle has disappeared and the former presence of medical activities is reflected in three cemeteries around the site: *Potijze Chateau Grounds Cemetery*, *Potijze Chateau Lawn Cemetery* and *Potijze Chateau Wood Cemetery*.
Photo, Imperial War Museum, London (Q02850)

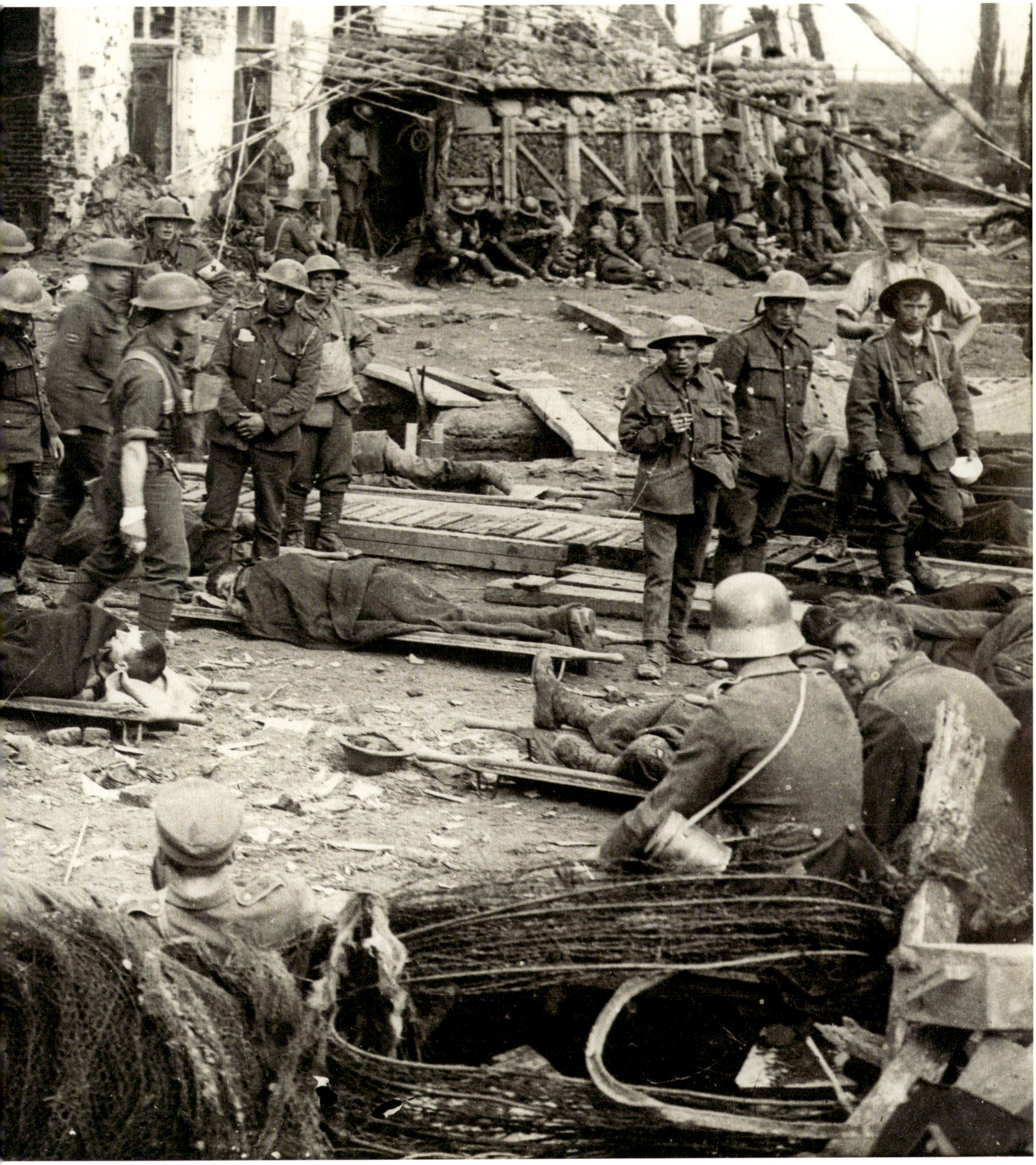

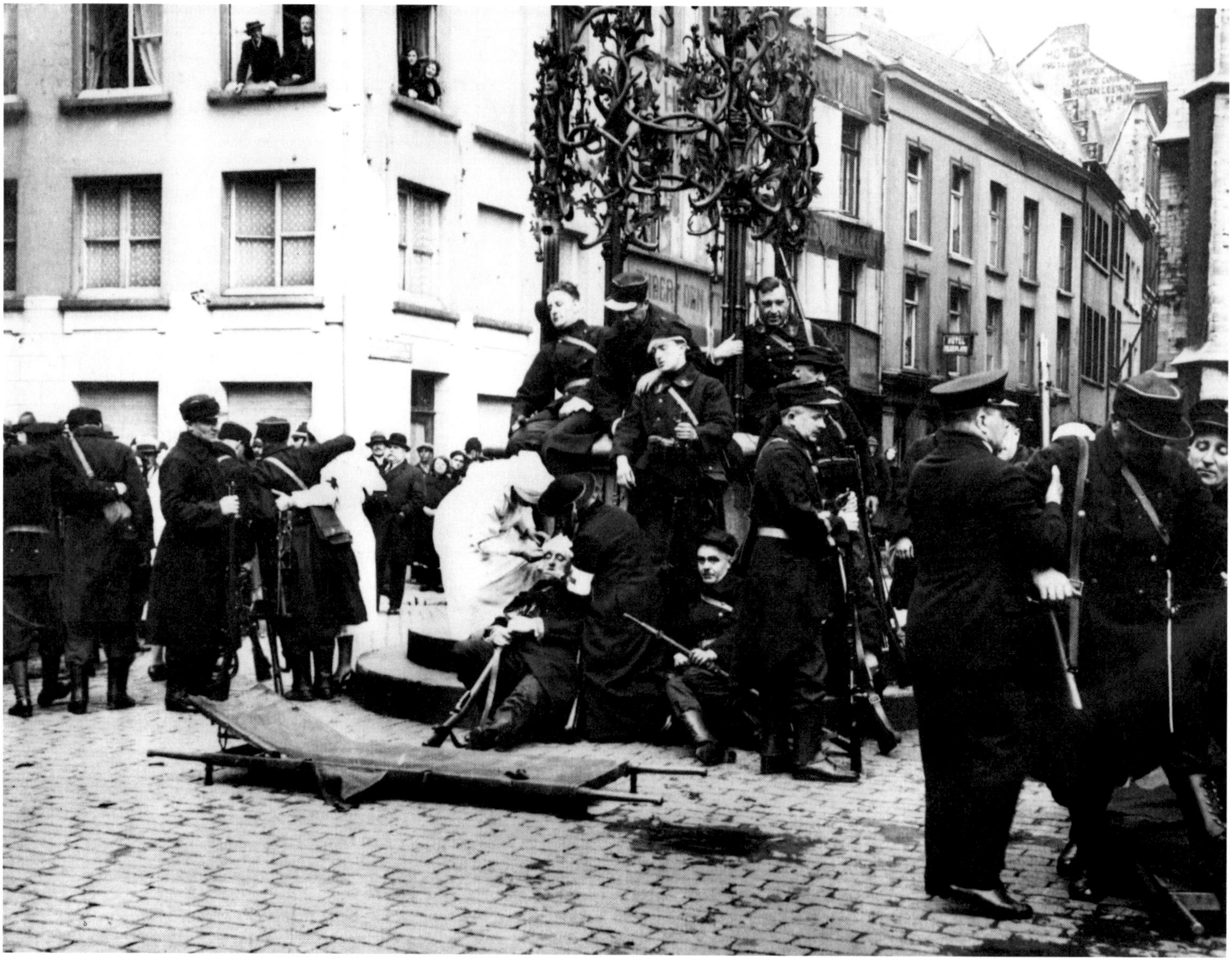

PIET CHIELENS & PIETER TROGH

Soldiers and Ambulances

"There are two groups of people in warfare – those organized to inflict and those organized to repair wounds – and there is little doubt that in all wars, and in this one particular, the former have been better prepared for their jobs."
Harvey Cushing, *From a Surgeon's Diary*

PERSONAL STORY **PIET CHIELENS**

One of my great-uncles was a stretcher-bearer, one of those who walked in a soutane with a Red Cross armband behind a column of ambulances drawn by horses in August 1914. This took him to Antwerp. And Aarschot. And straight into the Battle of the Yser. It all became too much for him later on. I couldn't find any details, but he wrote to a cousin that he could no longer bear to watch it. So he ran away, twice, and was court-martialled. Thankfully, by that time (November 1915), the Belgian army had slightly adjusted its attitude towards 'scaredy-cats' and 'cowards' (posttraumatic stress disorder?). Shooting them as in the first ten months was no longer allowed, but punishment was. My great-uncle, Herman Pieter, was imprisoned for five years in the prison of Dijon (Burgundy). When, however, they realised that the defaulters were in fact escaping danger this way, which suited them, an arrangement was developed where a convict could rehabilitate via a regimental company – which suited the army.

My great-uncle 'accepted' – what else? After a year's imprisonment in Dijon he was transferred to the regimental company on the punishment island of Cézembre, near the coast of Saint-Malo, where he had to stay for three months. Inspector-General Selliers de Moranville had come up with the system. It was said that this was at the request of the King and Queen. Others said the executions caused too much rebellion among the convicts' mates. In any case, Selliers had not come up with it himself.

He had been a public prosecutor before the court martial for Private Henri Reyns from Daknam. After an illness had taken him from the turmoil of battle at the end of September 1914, Reyns had come to the front early in April 1915, in the period when the Belgian troops were heavily attacked along the Ypres–Yser canal. The first time he was in the trenches 25 of his mates fell during the battle. Out of fear, Reyns ran away from his post four times. Or more accurately: after this first time he had not returned to the trenches. *"Je n'ose plus aller aux tranchées, j'ai peur."* "Desertion", said Selliers and he demanded the death penalty. The court accorded the penalty and Henri Reyns was shot dead at 8 a.m. on 17 May, 800 metres north of the Church of Oostvleteren. It was the last time, except for in the case of murder or manslaughter, that a Belgian soldier was executed during World War I.

In his clarification of the punishment reform of the Belgian army in July 1915, Selliers de Moranville described his punishment island:

"The island of Cézembre is out at sea one mile from the coast. It is only connected to the mainland via a ferryboat that comes from Saint-Malo for provisions once a day. It is a deserted rock, from where there is no escape. The accommodation is extremely gloomy and a punishment in itself; but to increase the grimness, the prisoners are deprived of any view of the sea, due to a long palisade of more than two metres high that is connected to the buildings, which forms a fully enclosed square in which the defaulters are accommodated. They cannot leave or look over it. Their shifts have been arranged in such a way that they develop a burning longing to rejoin their own unit and behave like dutiful soldiers, even if it was just for the prospect of another stay. After two or three months at Cézembre, defaulters may get permission from the Inspector

Chaos at the Antwerp Handschoenenmarkt, end of September – beginning of October 1914. From the crossroads of Jan Blomstraat and Blauwmoezelstraat, civilians see how exhausted and injured Belgian soldiers gather around the Quinten Metsysput. At the time, the city was being sieged by and under fire from the Germans. Some injured people are being helped by nurses in white uniforms, central is a priest-stretcher-bearer taking care of the head wound of an injured Belgian. Photo, Royal Army Museum, Brussels.

General to join the rehabilitation company of their army division. Many have moments of weakness and despair, but still nevertheless remain susceptible to proper treatment and are feeling fine. All of them are dying to see the ocean again, whose waves they hear breaking on the island's rocks, and behind which are their families and their fatherland. They all want to be good soldiers and good Belgians again. At the time of their discharge, they all ask whether they can take a walk on the island, from where there is a wonderful view. Everyone is granted this favour, and it is moving to see these soldiers free once more before they leave Cézembre, where they have lived for so long and repented."

Did the sea air reform them? I don't know. The fact is that my great-uncle Herman Pieter then accomplished a period without new punishments, as a second-class stretcher-bearer in the 7th line regiment. First six months in the rehabilitation company and then another 11 months of normal service. He was mortally wounded on the second day of the final offensive, during the attack on the Keiberg (Moorslede). He was in a bad state: "*fractures multiples par éclat d'obus*". His mates evacuated him to the aid station, then to the car ambulance and to the l'Océan 2 Hospital in Vinkem. It was a route that he knew at least partially from his own journeys with the injured. Now it was his evacuation route. He lived for another two days, until 1 October 1918. When I requested the documents of his court-martial from the military tribunal I was not allowed to see them; after all, in the eyes of the army, he had been fully rehabilitated.

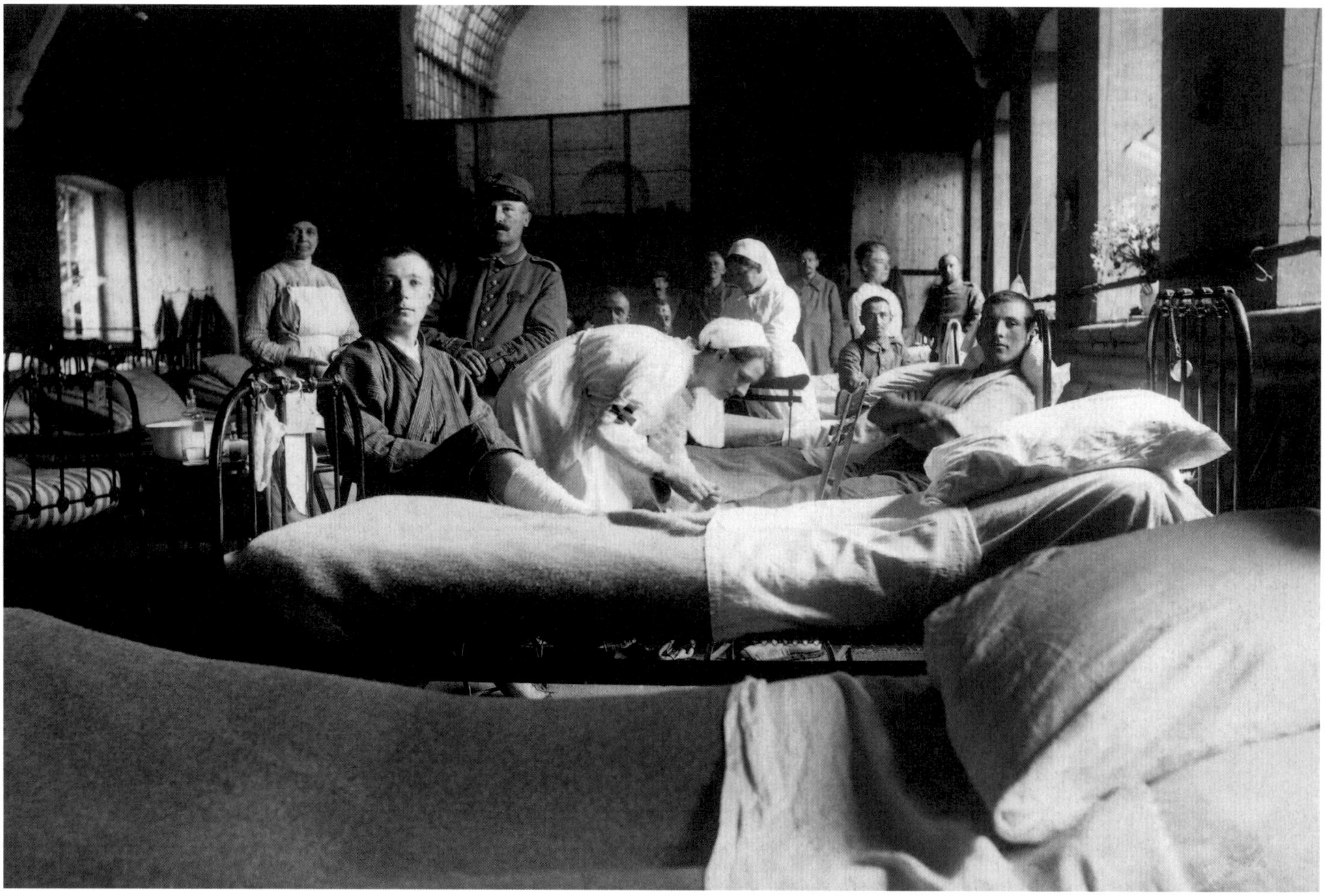

Inside view of a German hospital ward that was set up in one of the buildings of the castle grounds in Morlanwelz-Mariemont (Henegouwen). Wounded German soldiers are taken care of by professional German Red Cross nurses. Photo, In Flanders Fields Museum, Ypres.

THE FIRST YEAR OF THE WAR

When Europe went to war in August 1914, not a single army was equipped for the evacuation and relief of the many hundreds of thousands of victims who fell almost immediately. However, an analysis of the weaponry and the scope of the armies could have predicted the number of victims and thus indicate the need for considerable investment in evacuation and care. Yet neither the army medical services, nor the various national divisions of the Red Cross that were ordered to assist the army, were prepared for an armed conflict between the world's greatest nation states. Military development had barely paid attention to this aspect.

Classic historiography claims that war itself causes major changes, and that this is always the case. This reasoning slightly holds true for World War I. Progress was made quite quickly in all areas of the medical field. But the conclusion remains that in most areas action could have been taken a lot sooner, even before the war; that the medical organisations could have at least been aligned with the military-technical evolution and with the scale increase of the armies. The fact that this was not done is proved by the problems that arose during the first year of the war.

MOTOR AMBULANCES

For a long time, the industrial world had counted on the evacuation of victims by rail. Stretcher-bearers and horse-drawn ambulances had to be deployed from the battlefield to the railway. This 19th century model still applied in 1914. Yet motorised ambulances had been around since the end of the 19th century and in the first years of the 20th century, Red Cross services in several countries were already using motor ambulances, but were not mobilised en masse in the armies. In August 1914, the British Expeditionary Force (BEF) had one or two motor ambulances per division, all in all just a few dozen for more than 100,000 men. By the end of November 1914, this was already 150. In the entire French army, originally 450 motor ambulances were in use, compared to over 5,700 by the end of the war. In 1914 all German armies together had about 5,000 motor vehicles: we could not trace the division between trucks, staff vehicles, tractors for heavy artillery and *Sanitätsfahrzeuge*, but it could not have been more than several hundred motor ambulances.

Naturally, Belgium, with its dense railway network, also took on the idea of evacuation by rail. Lieutenant-General (Doctor) Leopold Melis, Inspector-General of the Health Department of the Belgian army, nonetheless understood that in modern warfare, fast evacuation had a major role to play. Apart from the seven CABs *(columns d'ambulances et de brancardiers)* that existed in the six infantry divisions and the cavalry division, all with horse-drawn ambulances, Melis decided to set up CAABs *(columns d'ambulances automobiles et de brancardiers)* for the general mobilisation. The Chief Physician was ordered to set up a CAAB for his division, i.e. requisitioning vehicles from the civilian population, and received an envelope with money to try to convert these cars into motor ambulances as effectively as possible. This way, Doctor Albert De Moor, Head of the CAAB of the Second Army Division, managed to prepare a fleet of 60 motor vehicles *and* a double-decker bus (!) in just a few weeks and – more importantly – to let this unit operate separately from the transport corps as an independent evacuation unit. During the sorties from Antwerp, the CAAB of the second Army Division evacuated more than a thousand injured soldiers and later on, during the Battle of the Yser, more than 1,700 (including numerous French troops).

This of course required considerable initiative and a huge effort from those responsible in the rigid military organisation. Apart from Doctor De Moor in the Second Army Division, Doctor Molhant in the Third Army Division also proved the efficiency of the car ambulances of his division. Stretcher-bearer/teacher Armand Luchies in the Sixth Army Division described how the stretcher-bearers were also taken to the injured by car. However, where this initiative was lacking, the system turned out not to be able to cope with the greatest needs. Legendary is the work of Doctor Munro's Flying Ambulance Corps. This British voluntary department of motor ambulances, in which women played a principal role, had already reached Ghent at the end of September 1914. From the Battle of the Yser on, they operated in the area of the First Belgian Army Division, which had apparently not managed to mobilise the CAAB

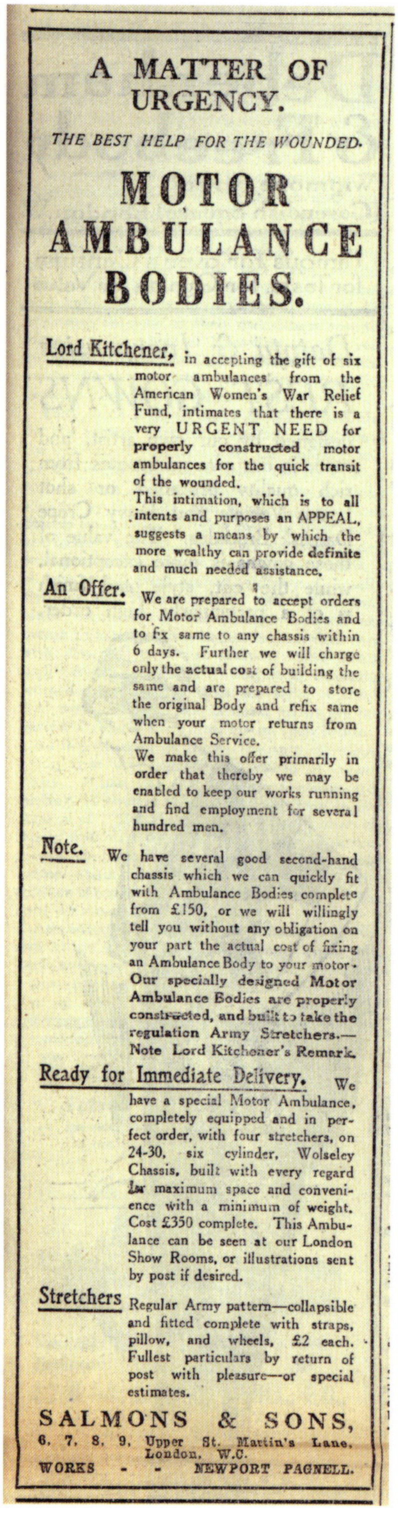

during the moving warfare, so the British motor ambulances of Elsie and Mairi and their colleagues were more than welcome. The detailed and, for reasons of fund-raising, sometimes embroidered stories of these *Angels of Pervyse* appealed and still appeal to the imagination, but undeservedly overshadow the professional work of a number of soldiers in the various armies.

PRIVATE INITIATIVE

The significant structural shortcomings in the military medical departments during the first year of the war enabled the various Red Cross departments and a lot of private initiatives to offer a necessary addition during the evacuation, relief and care of the large number of wounded and sick. Most of the help came from circles that weren't exactly regarded as important in military headquarters: conscientious objectors, women, committed artists and intellectuals, etc.

Many initiatives of this kind are mentioned in relation to the Belgian front. Probably because this front was opened last, the need was exceptional here. What the armies had with regard to medical relief had been brought into action previously, and because it had turned out to be inadequate, the help offered was (usually) accepted with gratitude. On the other hand, many Anglo-Saxon initiative takers also wanted do to their bit for suffering Belgium. Allied propaganda had strongly emphasised that it had all started for *brave little Belgium*.

BELGIAN FIELD HOSPITAL

In the wake of British participation in the war the commitment of the Red Cross in Belgium and Northern France also came to the fore. One of the leading figures of the British Division, Sir Alfred Keogh, dedicated himself to the fast evacuation via motor ambulances. Sending these ambulances to the front was one thing, but forcing up its production and the philanthropy in this area was another matter.

Columns of motor ambulances were deployed, departments in Belgium and France were approached, and independent aid organisations such as the (Order of) St. John's Ambulances were involved and

The British Red Cross service soon realised that modern warfare required rapid evacuation of the wounded by motor ambulances. On 2 October 1914, the *British Red Cross Society* launched an appeal to the population via *The Times* in order to raise funds that would enable setting up columns of motorised ambulances and sending them to Belgium and France. *The Times* would remain an important partner of the British division throughout the war. The Times spontaneously supported private initiatives. As an organisation, the British Red Cross provided accommodation for this initiative of British Surgeon H.S. Souttar and a team of seven doctors and 20 nurses, which became known under the name Belgian Field Hospital. On 4 September 1914, they set up a field hospital in Antwerp with 150 beds. After the fall of Antwerp, they returned via London back to the hinterland of the Yser front. On 23 October 1914, they settled in the Episcopal College of Veurne and became the Belgian Army's Advanced Field Hospital at the Yser. Four doctors from Munro's corps came to reinforce after a few days. In Veurne, patients were operated on in order to stabilise their condition and then be sent on to the base hospitals, which were situated in Calais for Belgian soldiers and in Dunkirk for the equally large number of French who had been deployed at the Yser front. The Belgian Field Hospital moved to the more southerly Hoogstade in January 1915. In May 1916, the hospital was completely taken over by the Belgian Medical Corps, and only the British nurses remained active.

NURSES AND NUNS

This also became a constant. While in Belgium and France, care for the sick was still often the domain of nuns, this care had for some time been laicised and professionalised in Great Britain, the US and Germany. Nurse training as it existed in Belgium, like in Brussels, had been organised according to the English model. At the request of Doctor Antoine Depage of the Red Cross, British nurse Edith Cavell was in charge as of 1907. On 12 October 1915, she was executed by the German occupier as a spy in Brussels. Laicised nurse training in France and Belgium did not result in enough registered nurses, because of which British nurses were more than welcome. The British Red Cross detached qualified nurses of the VAD (Voluntary Aid Detachment) and QAIMNS (Queen Alexandra's Imperial Military Nursing Service) to Red Cross hospitals, such as L'Océan in De Panne. In occupied Belgium, most hospitals functioned for civilians but often also for German servicemen. Sometimes convent orders took on this task, also if they hadn't carried out any tasks in hospitals previously. In the front region many schools and convents were claimed as *Feldlazarett*. This was the case in, for instance, Wervik, Geluwe, Dadizele, Menen and Sint-Eloois-Winkel. In Moorslede, some of the sisters of O.L.V.-ten-Bunderen took care of the German wounded in their school buildings from November 1914 to September 1917. In Roeselare relief had been organised for Allied prisoners of war in the Redemptorist Monastery from October 1914. In 1915 they took care of an international company of victims of the Second Battle of Ypres.

EVEN MORE MOTOR AMBULANCES

The Friends' Ambulance Unit (FAU) turned up on the Allied side of the front at the end of October 1914. This ambulance service was founded by former reporter Geoffrey Winthrop Young, with the help of Arthur Stanley (British Red Cross) and several important Quaker families (Baker, Cadbury, etc.). This voluntary aid organisation consisted of Quakers, who refused to carry arms. The service provided independent aid to all those suffering, friend and foe, but mainly to civilians. The *Friends* joined the Battle of the Yser via Dover and Dunkirk. After the relief of military victims who had been waiting for care for days, 20 ambulances went to the scene of action in Ypres. In accordance with their religious convictions they concerned themselves with everyone, so also wounded German prisoners of war. Their main contribution was, however, provided in the evacuation of typhoid victims. The *Friends* remained active in the Ypres-Poperinghe region until May 1916.

NOBLE LADIES

In Poperinghe, for many months, the *Friends* brought civilians and militaries to the Elisabeth hospital, one of the few field hospitals where civilians as well as soldiers were welcome. The person in charge was Countess Maria van den Steen de Jehay, who had already set up her place of residence, Chevetogne Castle (Ciney), as a Red Cross post in August 1914. At the time, mainly French military personnel from the *Bataille des Frontières* were taken care of there. When her home lay behind German lines, she still managed to reach the unoccupied part of Belgium via the Netherlands, England and Northern France. Her main objective was to again be involved in health care. She succeeded in this via the establishment of the Aide Civile Belge and of the Elisabeth Hospital in Poperinghe. *Sisters in Arms* were Valentine Terlinden, with whom she had established the Catholic nursing school of Saint-Camille in Uccle in 1907, and Countess Louise d'Ursel, a lady-in-waiting of Queen Elisabeth.

Millicent, Duchess of Sutherland, had decided shortly after the British declaration of war to enter into service with *Secours aux Blessés*, a department of the French Red Cross, run by an aristocratic girlfriend. She ended up in Brussels mid-August where she met Dr Depage, who encouraged her to set up an independent operational hospital unit. The duchess withdrew from the French Red Cross and joined the Belgian Health Service. Her capital and network in high society enabled a surgeon (O.G. Morgan), a stretcher-bearer and eight professional nurses to quickly come from England on 16 August 1914 and form the Millicent Sutherland Ambulance Unit. The unit first took care of the injured of the Siege of Namur. After the Germans had conquered the city the duchess stayed behind German lines and was active for another three weeks. She mainly treated the Belgian, British and French injured. In September, her unit came under German supervision in Brussels. However, Millicent Sutherland wanted to get back to the field with her ambulance as soon as possible. As the Duchess of Sutherland she had already enjoyed pre-war fame in high-class European circles, so also among the Germans. After long insistence she was given permission to go to the Netherlands. From there she went to England, where she reorganised the ambulance. From 27 October her team evacuated Belgian and French injured soldiers from the Battle of the Yser to the hospitals in Dunkirk. She had eight motor ambulances, nurses, drivers and two surgeons at her disposal. In Malo-les-Bains a temporary hospital was set up in Café Belle Vue, with a hundred beds. Private capital enabled the best guarantee for quick action in these chaotic conditions. In the spring and autumn of 1915, Millicent Sutherland led a hospital in Bourbourg that came under the French Service, the *Santé de l'Armée*. Several victims of the Second Battle of Ypres came to her.

MARY BORDEN

Rich American Mary *'May'* Borden had already voluntarily come to work behind the front as a nurse in 1914, for the French in Dunkirk. However, due to

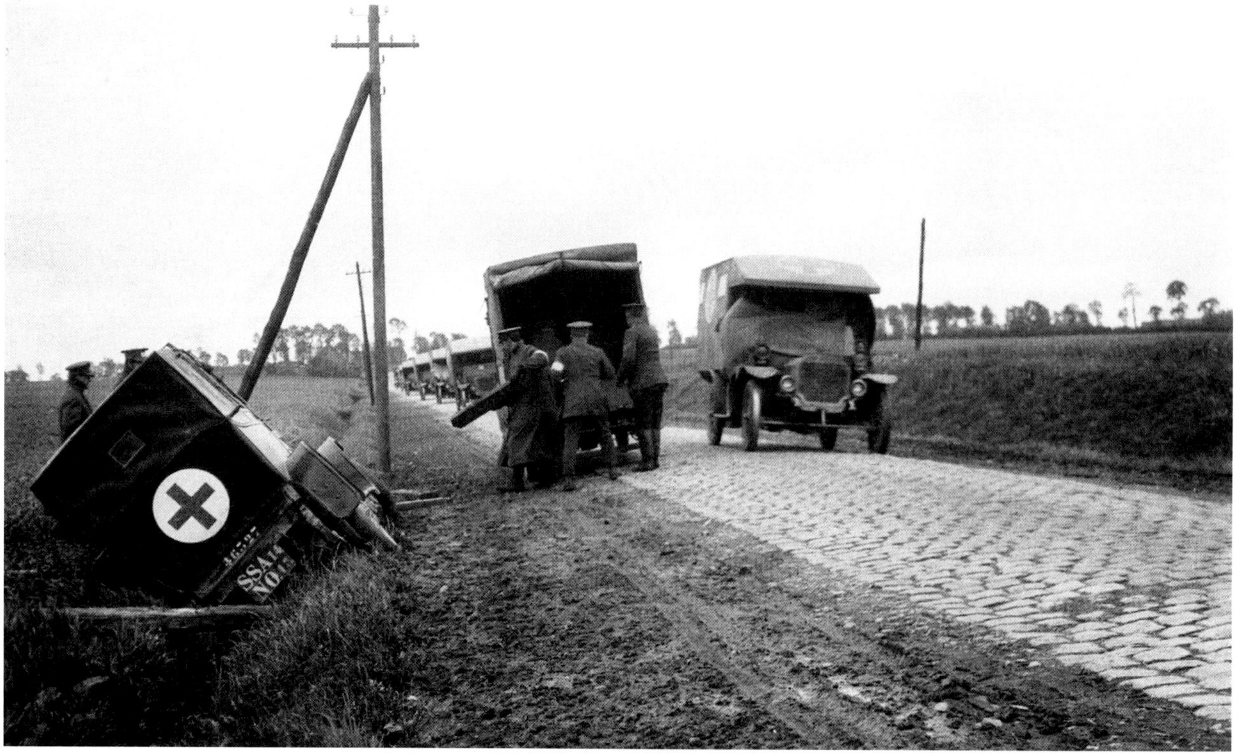

Columns of ambulances of the Friends' Ambulance Unit, somewhere in the Westhoek, 1915. The ambulances that were part of the *Section Sanitaire Anglaise* (see the number plate of the vehicle that has ended up in the ditch), were used in the French sector. Photo, Paul Handford, Birmingham

the anti-female situation in the French Health Department, she decided to set up her own field hospital. This was still for the French army, i.e. with French military doctors, but also with an international group of nurses under her own management. On 25 July 1915, the *Service de Santé* of the 45th (Algerian) Division at the front near Steenstrate noted: "Since 22 July, we have also started evacuating patients to the mobile army surgical hospital in Beveren (Mrs Turner)." Turner was the name of May Borden's husband, Scottish missionary George Douglas Turner, whom she divorced after she met British Liaison Officer Edward Louis Spears. In 1916, the unit moved to the Somme, then to Champagne, to end up in Belgium again at the end of the war. Borden had already been literarily active before the war. About her period in the mobile army surgical hospital in Beveren (Hoge Seine), she published *The Forbidden Zone* in 1929. Another American nurse in Beveren was Ellen N. La Motte. She had already published the sensational *The Backwash of War* in 1916 about her time in Mary Borden's field hospital, which was banned in France and later also in the US due to the raw but especially critical description of the suffering of the injured. Flemish novelist Erwin Mortier published wonderful translations of both accounts in 2009 and 2010.

INTERNATIONAL RED CROSS

Apart from the Americans, Australian and British nurses also worked in Beveren. In this sense, the Red Cross was also a truly supranational organisation, where nursing staff of the British, American, Canadian or Australian Red Cross were deployed in institutes run by the Belgian or the French Red Cross. One example among thousands: in 1914, husband and wife Charles and Ellen Hawes believed they had to contribute to the war effort. He was a GP in Reading (Berkshire); she had been trained as a nurse at the VAD. In November 1914, they started working for the French at Nevers English Hospital, set up in a building of the French railways. In the spring of 1915, the number of injured people dropped and Charles offered his services to the British Army. He became a doctor with the RAMC (Royal Army Medical Corps) and worked on the hospital ships in Gallipoli, in the Irish Sea during the Easter Rising and on the channel between Le Havre and Southampton. In April 1917, he drowned after a double collision with German sea mines in the Seine Estuary. Ellen had returned to England after Nevers, but was already working abroad in November 1915. This time as a nurse in *L'Océan*, in the now beautifully furnished

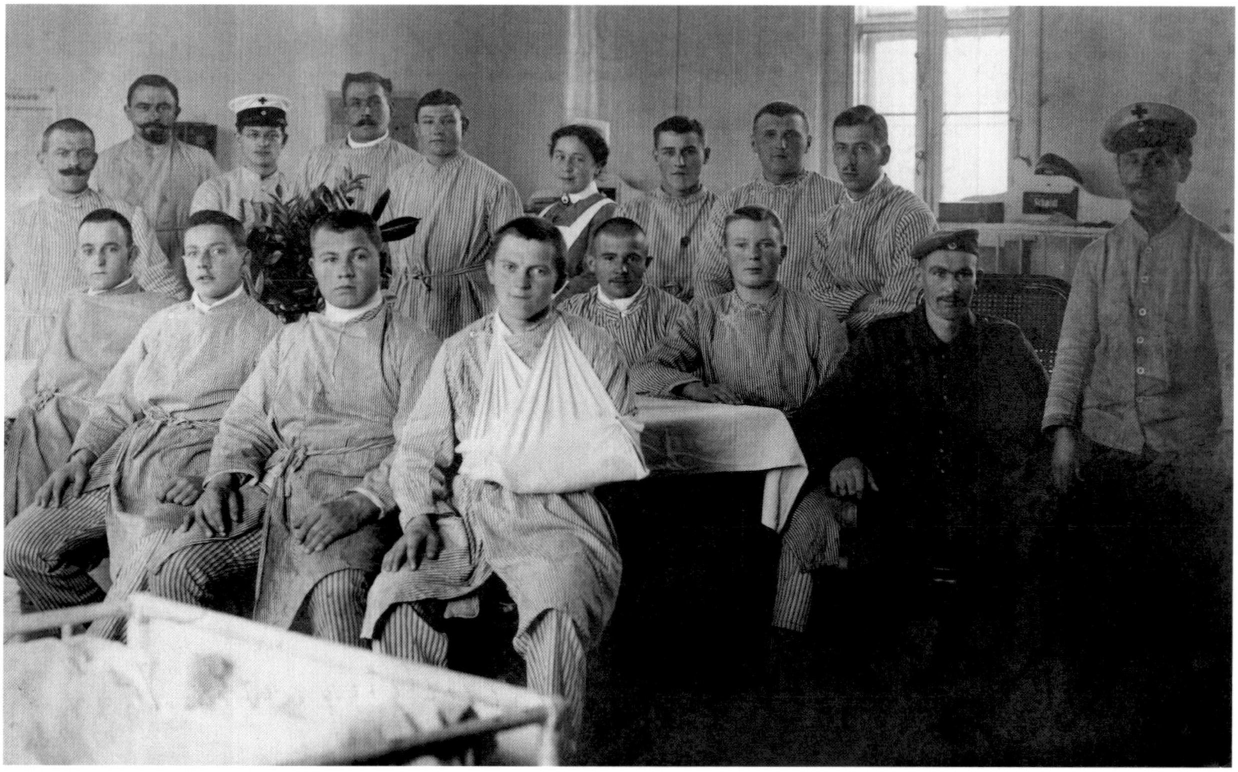

Inside view of a German hospital ward, with wounded Germans wearing typical pyjamas. The carers are all volunteers: in the middle are nurses, on the far right and standing third from left are *Kriegsfreiwillige Sanitäter*. In a similar capacity, German expressionist artist Max Beckmann (1884 – 1950) was present in 1915 in hospitals in, among other places, Courtrai and Wervik.
Photo, In Flanders Fields Museum, Ypres

hospital of the Belgian Red Cross in De Panne. She returned to England in 1916. First she was a staff nurse, but according to her grandson, British artist Stephen Hurst, she had in the meantime been so overwhelmed by her own suffering in the war – she had lost two of her brothers as well as her husband – that she could cope with the war less and less. She ended her war efforts, still in voluntary service, as a chef and help in a canteen. She'd had enough.

STRETCHER-BEARERS, SCHOOLTEACHERS AND CLERGYMEN

Many testified the fact that it was hard to be prepared for the horrors of war. In his first letter to his brother, who had fled to the Netherlands, stretcher-bearer novice Lode(wijk) Van Eyck wrote the following shortly after the Battle of the Yser:

"We see thousands and thousands of fit boys in their oblivious youth head for the battlefield and behind them we see Death as an image closing the ranks... An hour later, sometimes even earlier, we are called to make away with those poor fallen, riddled and red of blood, unconscious, those same boys, bandage them up while they groan and this groaning cuts through you like a knife and then a word of semi-despair escapes them: 'Oh, to have known this my sweet wife, to have known this my dear child!' How many injured volunteers have I not heard groan: 'If only I had listened to my mother who wanted to stop me.' No one can imagine such a war!"

Hundreds of clergymen and novices filled the ranks of stretcher-bearers and nurses. The holy commandment – 'Thou shalt not kill' – in mind, clergymen in times of peace had been exempt from military service. As part of the political balance between believers and non-believers, this favour had also been attributed to teachers. This was also the case in France, at least until the separation of Church and State in 1905. During the first year of the war, schoolteachers and clergymen together formed the Belgian and French columns of ambulances and stretcher-bearers. Also in Germany and the British Empire, clergymen were originally often assigned to the medical service. It was presumed due to their vocation that they cared for their fellow man, and numerous testimonies indicate that many offered words of consolation that others may not have had. But at first they received little help and barely any training.

POSITIVE COMMITMENT

It is striking how many artists and intellectuals, apart from doctors, teachers and clergymen, could be found in the medical services of World War I. There was barely an alternative: those who did not want to kill and still wanted to participate, tried to make themselves useful in the medical service. This required courage and commitment, but at least it seemed to be positive commitment. The work in the medical service gave an insight into the high toll of the war, which was often crueller than being present among the dead in the battlefield. They saw less shocking trauma, but more

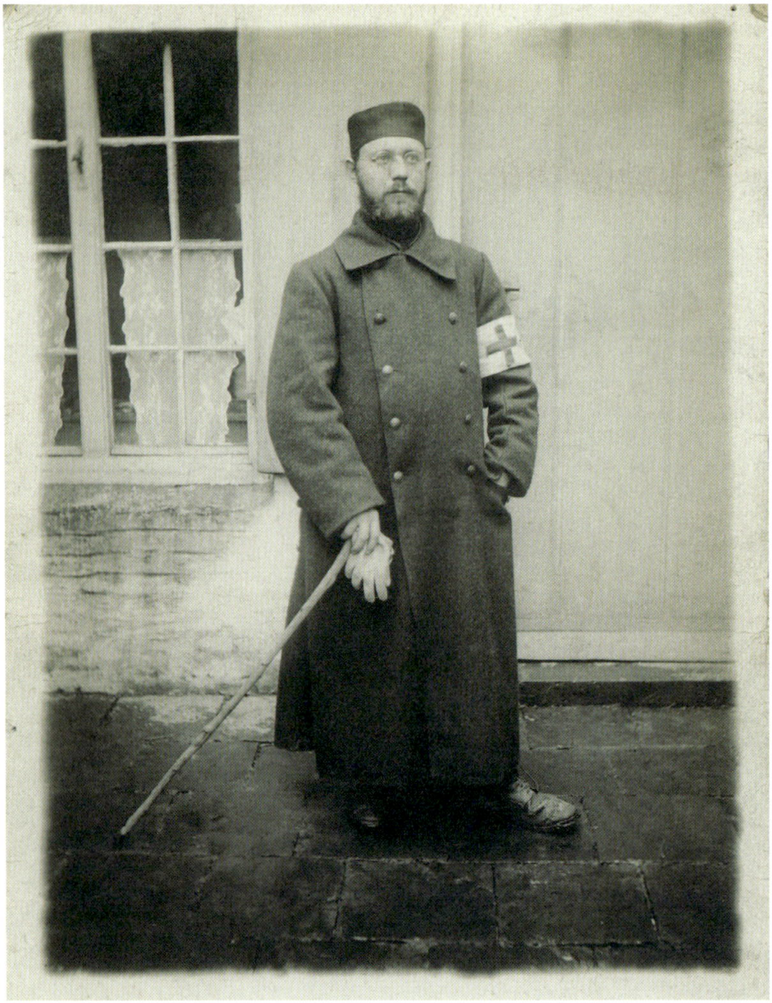

Lodewijk Van Eyck was one of the hundreds of stretcher-bearer clergymen who joined the ranks of the Belgian Army in August 1914 to help provide medical care. Photo, In Flanders Fields Museum, Ypres

constant misery. Testimonies of the medical services are therefore omnipresent and equally impressive a century later.

During the war, in Belgium alone we find, apart from Max Deauville, Mary Borden and Ellen La Motte, painter Max Beckmann (in 1915 as *Krankenpfleger* in Wervik and Kortrijk), French writer, filmmaker and artist Jean Cocteau (in 1916 as a male nurse with the French troops at the coast), Parisian salon figure and author Henri Ghéon (in 1915, Battalion Doctor in Nieuwpoort), Canadian poet and physician John McCrae (Major in the Canadian artillery in the Second Battle of Ypres, then Lieutenant Colonel in a base hospital in Wimereux) and author Philip Gosse (in 1916 and 1917 a member of the RAMC in French-Flanders and in the *Ypres Salient*). There are also some impressive testimonies of neurosurgeon Harvey Cushing, German physicians Max Mohr and Stefan Westmann, paramedics Elsie Knocker-Tserclaes and Mairi Chisholm, nurse F.A. Voigt, nurses Henriette Riemann and Jane Delaunoy, stretcher-bearer and later officer Teilhard de Chardin, nurse and author Sarah Macnaughton, journalist Winthrop-Young and illustrator Adrien Barrère. Famous outside the front in Flanders were, among others, writers Georges Duhamel, Ernest Hemingway, Georg Trakl, André Breton, painter Stanley Spencer, artist and surgeon Henry Tonks, composers Ralph Vaughan Williams and Maurice Ravel, sculptor Ossip Zadkine, British poets John Masefield and Laurence Binyon, and American authors Edith Wharton, John Dos Passos, E.E. Cummings and Edmund Wilson. Of literary importance are the testimonies of, among others, nurses Vera Brittain and Enid Bagnold. All had a share in the evacuation or care of victims at one time or another during the war.

WITNESSES – PATIENTS

And we have not even mentioned the victims themselves. Not a single artistic testimony about World War I omits the fate of the victims, but sometimes the fact itself of being injured and evacuated and cared for, were the immediate cause of work of universal value. No *Im Westen nichts Neues* without Erich Maria Remarque's serious injuries on the way to the opening day of the Third Battle of Ypres. No Wilfred Owen or Siegfried Sassoon without their stay at the mental hospital of Craiglockhart in the summer of 1917 and no trilogy of Pat Barker 80 years later. What was Apollinaire as a war poet without his head injury? Without a lost hand, Cendrars would have never written *La Main Coupée*. The most legible poem of August Van Cauwelaert remains his ode to the stretcher-bearers who evacuated him to Hoogstade. Would Paul Alverdes have been able to write *Die Pfeiferstube* without his throat injury in 1915? Or Céline his *Voyage au bout de la nuit* without his injury as *le cuirassier Louis Ferdinand Destouches* on the way to Poelkapelle on 27 October 1914? Would Joë Bousquet have ever become a writer without his total paralysis in the last year of the war? Would Richard Aldington, Gilbert Frankau or Robert Nichols still be worth reading without the shell shock that they had contracted?

GURNEY

On 12 September 1917, composer, poet and soldier Ivor Gurney became slightly contaminated by mustard gas in the Third Battle of Ypres. He had hoped for a stay in a Casualty Clearing Station, but after several weeks' stay there he was given a single ticket home: *Blighty*! He was later discharged from the army with *deferred shell shock* as a diagnosis. He had probably averted his psychological trauma by dealing with his fear so openly. In many texts he admits that he has it, or he says that those who do not admit this, are lying. But perhaps he had, unwittingly, still come to grief for the true reason: three weeks of Ypres...

Got to Blighty – as unexpectedly as never any
Of honest gas (but not much) got by a tale
Of five hours gas bombardment, which was true
(I brought that down) or keeping silence as to the
Real reason – which was three weeks at Ypres,
Without a rest (or laurel) (nor yet a cypress)
Having seen Passchendaele lit with a flare of fire
And Ypres a dawn light ruddy and golden of desire,
The stuck tanks – and shook at our guns going in
As my body would not stay still at such Hell of din;
Worse than any of theirs – and seen Gloucesters going over;
Many for the last time – by accident gone further. (...)

Ivor Gurney, *The Man* (1925, excerpt)

Gurney died in 1937, after an almost isolated 15-year stay in a mental asylum, as the victim of bipolar disorder, plagued by chronic gastritis (a consequence of the gas injury?) and due to delusions of torture through radio, electricity and wires (a consequence of electric shock treatment?). He wrote his best work here.

CIVILIAN HEALTHCARE IN THE WESTHOEK

We have barely mentioned the fate of civilians. World War I caused true mass migration out of Belgium: almost one and a half million Belgians fled. Many of them sought a safer place in unoccupied Belgium, not to be too far from home if peace were to suddenly return. Yet when the acts of war also swamped the Westhoek in October 1914, the civilian population who lived there and had fled was seriously afflicted.

During the First Battle of Ypres, the medical services had a shortage of staff and equipment. The only civil hospital in town, the *Notre Dame* hospital, and the three GPs in attendance were unable to provide sufficient medical aid for the sick and wounded citizens. Most civil physicians had already been included in the military medical framework. They could barely count on assistance from the British or French ambulances, as they themselves could not handle the influx of wounded soldiers. It was every man for himself. In Ypres, the local clergymen and the Friends' Ambulance Unit tried to organise civilian health care. Improvisation was key.

The *Notre Dame* hospital was attended to by Sisters of the Holy Family. The first civilian casualties were accommodated here, but on 3 November 1914 the first direct hit affected the hospital. The entire evacuation followed four days later, the *Friends* worked themselves to death. Father Delaere, Sister Margriet and several others decided not to leave the people of Ypres to their own devices and established the significant *Comité Provisoire*. Aid was not self-evident in an overcrowded sieged town where 20,000 civilians (estimate of Stopford) were packed together and hiding in increasingly damp cellars. The bleak autumn and the impending winter foreclosed living conditions. The water supply was affected and the water was polluted. Late November 1914, the *Friends* noticed the first cases of typhoid fever, at the same time Achiel Van Walleghem, priest in Dikkebus, also saw the first sick arrive...

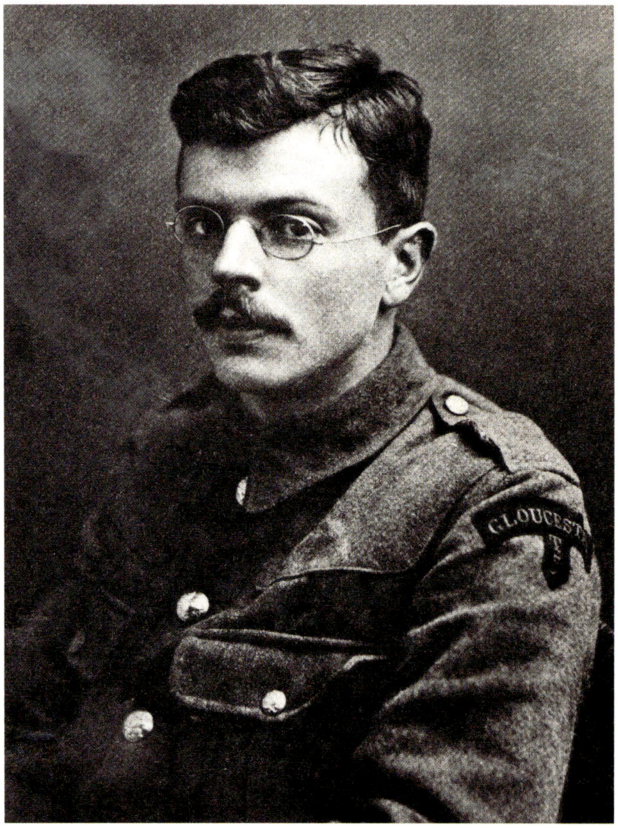

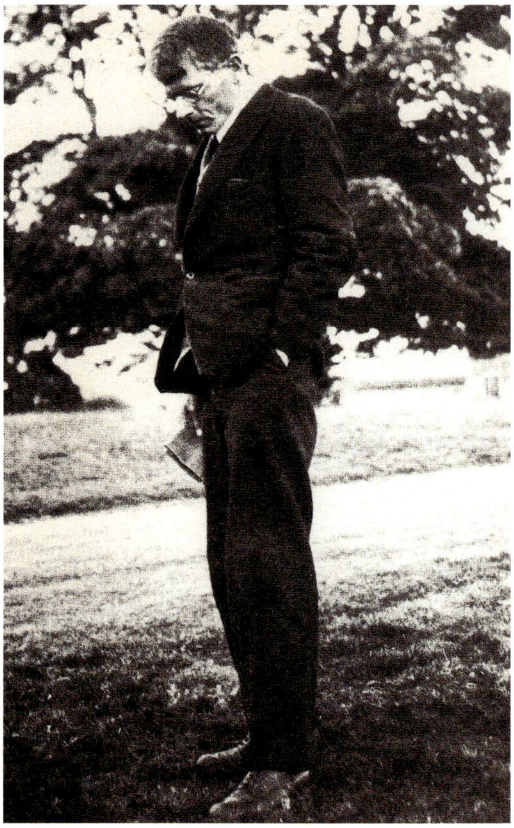

Portrait of Ivor Gurney as a bright young man in the uniform of the 2nd/5th Gloucestershire Regiment, 1915 – Later, in the early thirties, as a broken man in the City of London Mental Hospital, Dartford. Photos, Gloucester City Public Library, Gloucester City

In the former mental asylum along the road to Poperinghe the Friends' Ambulance Unit and the *Comité Provisoire* set up the *Sacré Coeur* hospital, operational from the beginning of December 1914. The greatest challenge was combatting typhoid, which took on epidemic proportions in December. The big problem was that citizens hiding in cellars were not taken in until they had been ill for two to three weeks. To take care of the cases of typhoid, the hospital was extended with several wards in January 1915 (up to 115 beds) and the Friends' Ambulance Unit set up search parties who went from house to house to track down the ill.

In January 1915 countess Marie van den Steen de Jehay opened the Elisabeth hospital with the help of a group of confidants and with the *Friends* in *Château D'Hondt*. It was the second institute in Poperinghe to dedicate itself to health care for civilians. This initiative, under the patronage of Queen Elisabeth, was financed with private funds and with about BEF 40,000 from the Belgian government, donated via Dr Rulot. In the wake of the hospital, the *Aide Civile Belge* was also founded, on the basis of a cooperation agreement between civilians and *Friends,* independent of the government with the objective of caring for the suffering population. Countess van den Steen de Jehay was the chairwoman. The hospitals in Ypres and Poperinghe were responsible for the relief of cases of typhoid. An effective treatment did not exist yet, but the utmost effort was made to gain control of the ailment: disinfection with tincture of iodine, inoculations (whether or not preventive) and properly washing and feeding the patients. It was, however, a waste of time and effort: testimonies of the FAU indicate long queue areas and, in addition, several army commanders or the Belgian government tried to steal doctors and nurses from civilian hospitals.

Major concentrations of troops in an area where typhoid raged gave various army commanders many worries. They urged an evacuation of the civilian casualties and increased pressure considerably. From February 1915, there was a gradual evacuation towards France. In Malassise (near Longuenesse) the British army made a section of the Army Hospital available, the French followed their example in Bergues. Sick civilians also ended up in Hazebrouck and Bailleul. A major factor in the choice of these evacuation regions was space, and therefore also the possibility of quarantine.

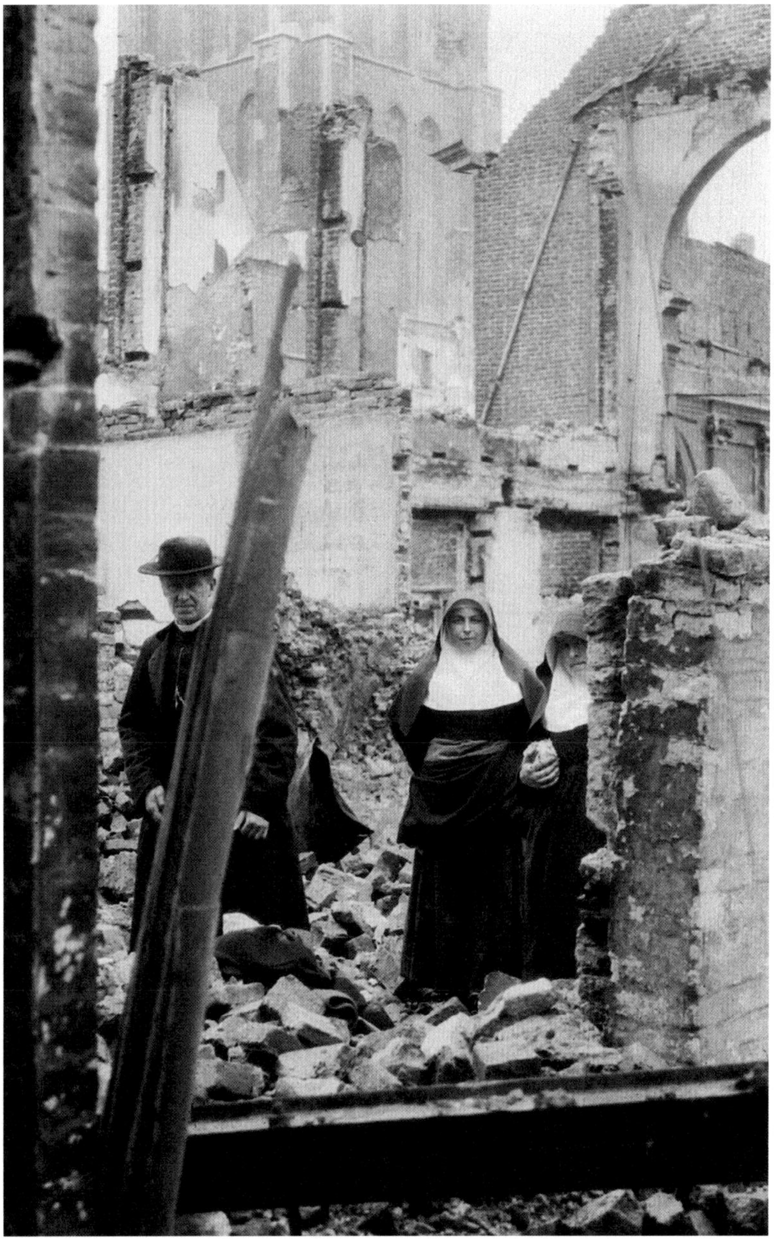

Ypres Father Delaere with several Lamotte Sisters in the rubble of Ypres, sometime at the end of 1914 or the beginning of 1915. Priest Delaere concerned himself with the civilian population that was heaped together in the sieged Ypres. As a member of the *Comité Provisoire* and the *Aide Civil Belge*, he played an important role in combatting the typhoid epidemic that had broken out in December 1914. He went from house to house with the Sisters, looking for victims.
Photo, Paul Handford, Birmingham

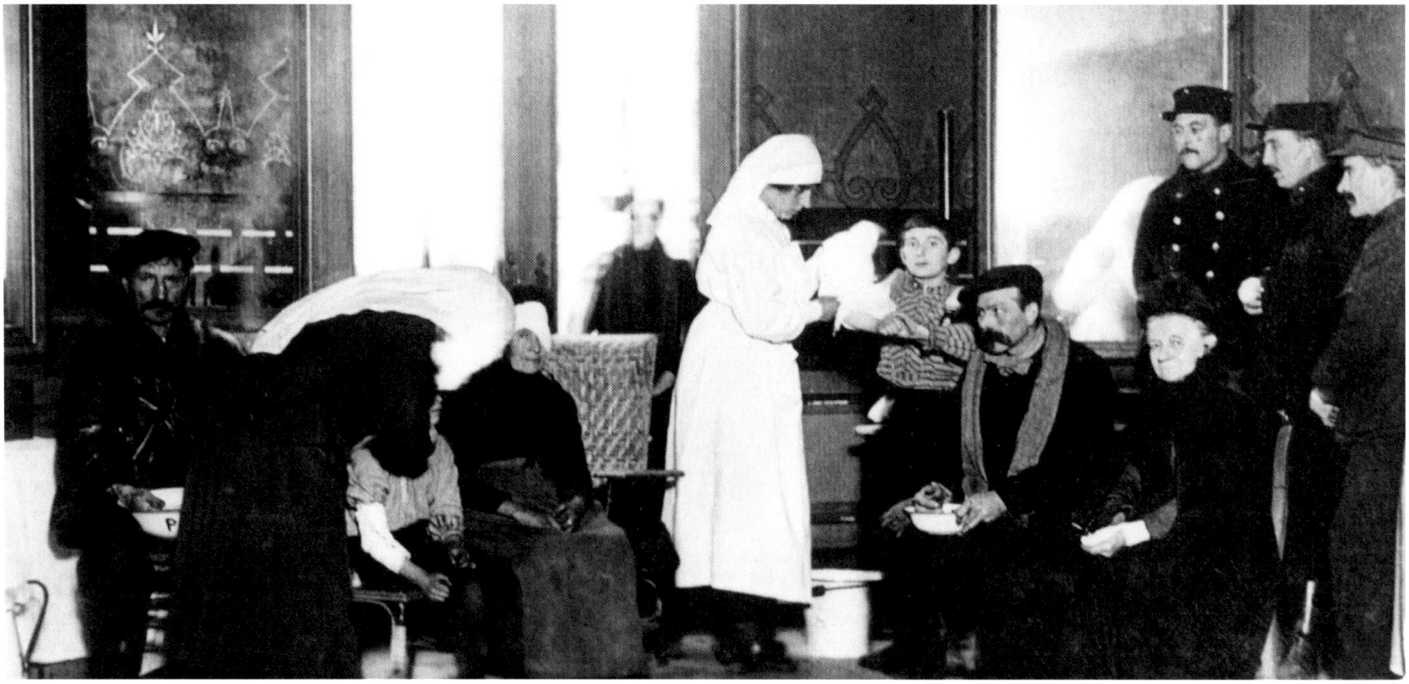

When the Second Battle of Ypres broke out, the evacuation to France gained momentum. *Sacré Coeur Ypres* was bombed heavily, in the summer of 1915 the Elisabeth Hospital suffered the same fate, resulting in a complete evacuation in August. Countess Van den Steen de Jehay tried to continue her activities in new barracks that formed a temporary small 'evacuation hospital', first with *Ferme De Rycke* in Poperinghe, later in Proven at the *Couthof*. It is unclear how long and on what scale the activities continued.

Between the First and the Second Battle of Ypres over 750 registered cases died in the said hospitals due to the typhoid epidemic. The actual amount probably is a lot higher. The disease also seriously affected the French army, which defended the Salient during this period.

Apart from those in the mentioned hospitals in Ypres and Poperinghe, part of the civilian casualties ended up in Sint-Idesbald, Coxide (contagious diseases) and in the military hospital *L'Océan* in De Panne (and later in the ward in Vinkem).

MARIE CURIE

A final figure from the first, hard year of war who should not be left unmentioned is Marie Curie, *Madame Curie*. The double Noble Prize winner for physics and chemistry realised in August 1914 how her knowledge of X-ray equipment could help find bullets or shrapnel in the body or analyse complicated fractures. She built X-ray machines in 20 cars that were mostly begged for from rich acquaintances, which she herself (and soon also her daughter Irène) drove to and from field hospitals in order to examine people. Apart from furnishing these mobile radiological vehicles, *les petites Curies*, Marie Curie started furnishing radiology rooms in hospitals of the French army. She soon also paid attention to Belgium. At the invitation of Ghent gynaecologist and meanwhile also regiment doctor Frans Daels, Marie Curie arrived at the Belgian Field Hospital in Veurne early in December 1914 with her own *voiture 'E'*. A month later, she went to French *Hôpital d'Evacuation No. 15* in Poperinghe, where she left behind the *petite*

Inside view of the Elisabeth Hospital that was situated in *Château D'Hondt* in Poperinghe. As suffering civilians were being cared for, the photo was probably taken before May 1915. The two men holding a white dish are probably disinfecting their hands in a special solution. Disinfection was one of the treatments for controlling the typhoid epidemic.
Photo, Royal Army Museum, Brussels

Curie No. 1. In total, Marie Curie would provide more than 200 radiological installations during World War I and undertake 45 trips herself, sometimes accompanied by her daughter Irène. When doing so, she visited medical installations in the front thirty times, eleven of which in the Westhoek. Between December 1914 and October 1915, these eleven expeditions took her to Veurne (for one visit), Hoogstade (three visits, where she left behind *petite Curie No. 10* and where Irène worked on her own for some time), Poperinghe (five), Adinkerke-Cabour (one) and *L'Océan* (one). Everywhere her cars and equipment offered tremendous help to the treating physicians. In Poperinghe she installed, in cooperation with the Pasteur Institute, a laboratory for examining and treating typhoid patients.

THE LAST YEAR OF THE WAR

The specialisation of top scientists like Marie Curie soon became a general tendency in medical care during World War I. After the initial shock and chaos, an increasing number of people responsible for medical services and the Red Cross made an effort to organise better evacuation and relief. Just as Frans Daels had used his pre-war contact with Marie Curie (for the treatment of cervical cancer through radium and radiation) and Curie had personally committed, Dr Depage would also attract top specialists to *L'Océan* in De Panne. Doctor William Osler, father of modern surgery, managed to convince former students such as American top neurosurgeon Harvey Cushing to offer their contribution. The professionalism and volunteering of all these specialists would eventually lead to a better organisation and bring about a true evolution in medical care.

MEDICAL EVOLUTION

The confrontation with new types of war injuries caused by modern weapons of mass destruction forced medical science and its representatives to seek creative and efficient solutions. Age-old dogmas on the medical treatments to be followed needed to be radically written off if more lives were to be saved. While doctors during the long wars of the 19th century were mainly confronted with bullet wounds, the ratios were now the other way round: artillery fire caused 80 per cent of injuries, gun fire less than 20 per cent. Other injuries caused by gas or bayonet-type weapons were proportionally minimal. Preventing infections in horrible and complex war fractures became even more important than before. A first measure concerned carefully cleaning the wound *(débridement)* by removing infiltrated shell splinters, damaged or dead tissue remnants and other sources of infection, such as clothing or earth. For the second, often essential, method, an antiseptic treatment was developed and refined. Cooperation between British biomedic Henry Drysdale Dakin and French surgeon Alexis Carrel resulted in an effective treatment that became known as the Carrel-Dakin

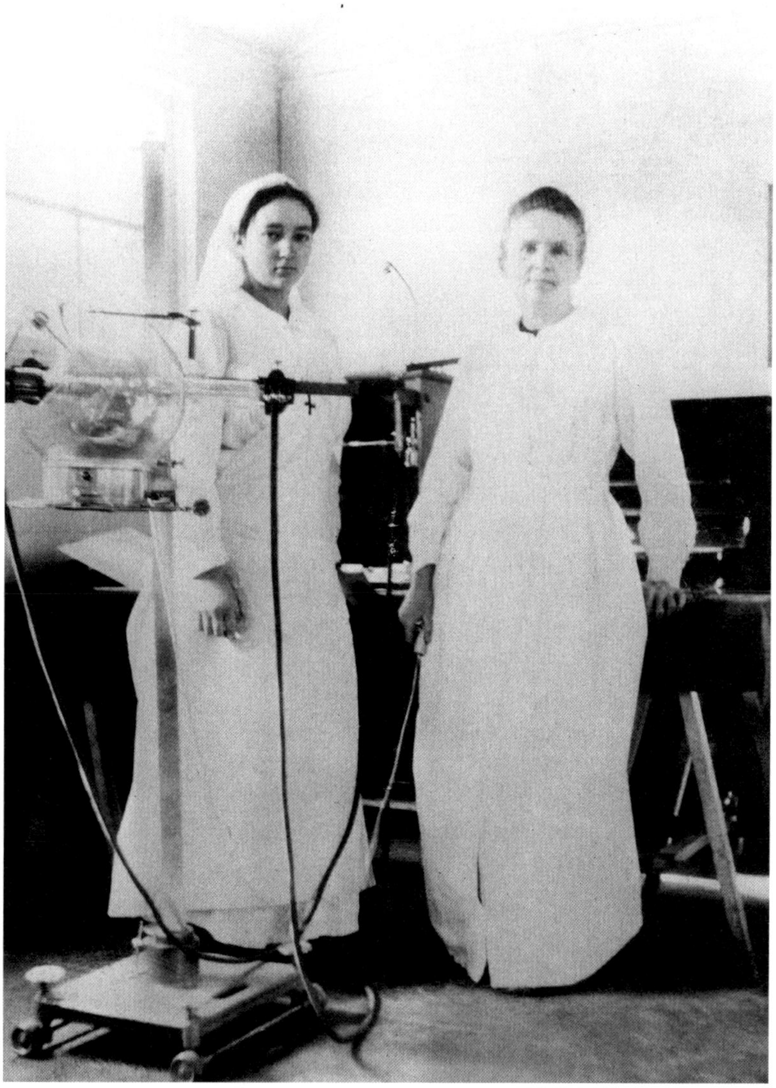

Marie Curie and her daughter Irène posing near one of the radiologic installations which they personally installed in certain French and Belgian hospitals. Photo, Institut Curie, Paris

method. The procedure consisted of long-term, thorough rinsing of the wound (after *débridement*) using a hypochlorite, the so-called Dakin's solution.

Rinsing a wound was, however, everything but a miracle solution. Some wounds could not be disinfected or limbs were crushed in such a way that only one solution was possible: amputation. Before 1914, this measure was often the ultimate surgery to save a life, only to be applied when a victim had been evacuated far from the front. After all, bullet wounds or quite light shrapnel could offer a considerable chance of survival once the projectile had been removed or the fracture splinted. However, the horrendous power of artillery destruction that was displayed during World War I created a completely new situation. It is no coincidence that the French experienced an eventful turnabout. During the first year of the war, the French army commanders thought it could compensate a lack of industrial fire power with a massive arrival of men with 'willpower', who were eventually smashed by deadly German steel. The front physicians, who saw the terrible injuries on their operating tables, were often induced to quick intervention to be able to save a life. What has become known as the *'amputation en saucisson'* – a longitudinal amputation of a long limb at the intact soft parts of heavily mutilated war fractures – broke with common traditions. After this new, 'pure' wound had healed, a second amputation could be carried out to reconstruct a stump on to which prostheses could be attached later on. Victor Pauchet and Alain Sourdat, advocates of the method, were denounced by the French military-medical authorities, but the success of the intervention technique (a major decrease of the mortality rate) proved them right. The

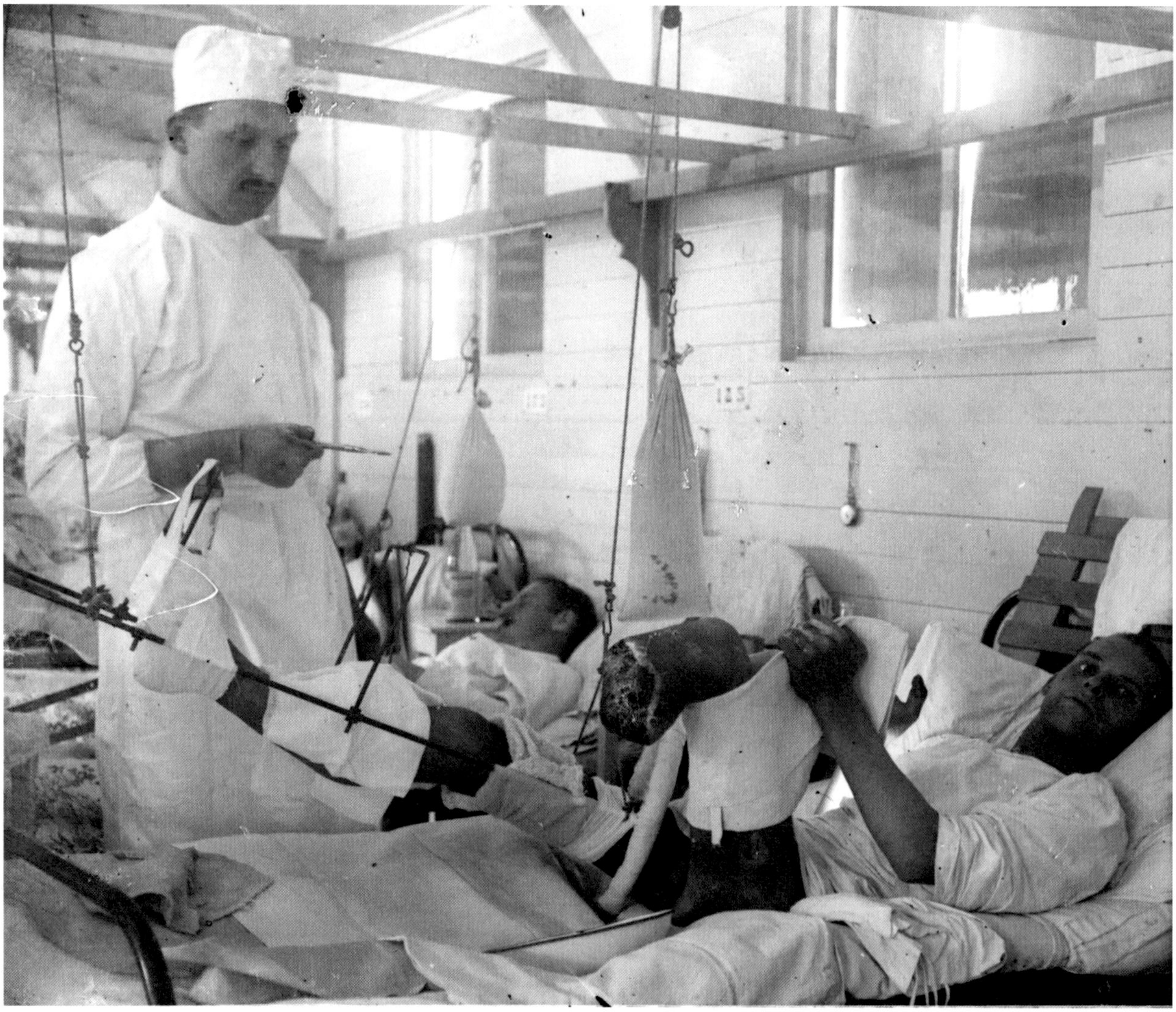

method was generally accepted; each army had its own supporters. A similar discussion characterised the treatment of stomach injuries. The 'amputation issue' as a quick approach to stomach injuries provided the integration of advanced surgical posts in the organisation of the evacuation route.

Without offering an exhaustive overview, we would like to mention that progress was also made in other areas. The treatment of complex skull and brain injuries was considerably stimulated, especially by the renowned Harvard surgeon, Harvey Cushing. In the field of peripheral nerve injuries, the Frenchman Pierre Marie made several significant contributions. Anaesthesia became something common, as did prosthesis, and under the impulse of Albert Hustin crucial steps were taken with regard to blood transfusions. The use of X-ray equipment became widespread. Contagious diseases were kept more or less under control by systematic vaccination, although there was no solution to the Spanish flu, which caused serious havoc in 1918.

Medical science, combined with the resourcefulness of engineers, ensured that the various uses were united in coherent surgical units that could act relatively near the front. This resulted in the origin of modern ambulance units, where sterilising equipment and operating rooms, radiological and bacteriological research functioned as a cohesive whole.

Inextricably bound with World War I, finally, is the development of plastic surgery, indicated in the position that the so-called *gueules cassées* concept has taken in collective memory. Early in the war, there was already a determination of the most horrendous facial injuries. In the first instance doctors limited themselves to closing 'holes' in the face, after this they would see what had to happen afterwards. This consequence generally consisted of an endless series of operations that had to ensure that the victim could eventually eat, breathe, see and 'sense' smells, according to Georges Duhamel. The discipline that first aimed to 'restore the face', became a specialisation in itself. In France, the first centres had already been established in Paris (Val-de-Grâce), Lyon and Bordeaux at the end of 1914. (In Great Britain during the war, a new centre was added in Aldershot, run by Harold Delf Gillies, a New Zealand pioneer in the field of plastic surgery. In the reconstruction of a face it

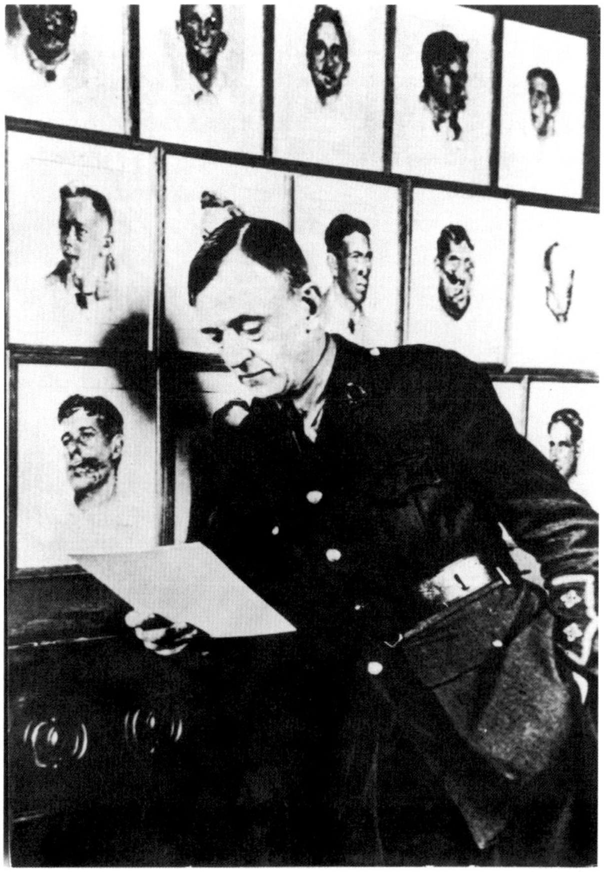

was important, also in view of passing on knowledge, to determine the various phases in the operations. Gillies himself was not a bad artist, but he met a man in Aldershot who was much better educated *and* was familiar with surgical practice: British artist Henri Tonks. Tonks had become a surgeon long before the war, but he had also developed a remarkable artistic career: he taught drawing-lessons (anatomy) at the famous Slade School of Fine Art in London. During the war, Henry Tonks had been active as a surgeon from January 1915 in the *Hôpital Temporaire* in the Château of Arc-en-Barrois in France. The British Red Cross included many artists among the medical staff: apart from Tonks, also sculptor Kathleen Scott (widow of Antarctica traveller Robert Scott), poet laureate John Masefield and poet Laurence Binyon. Tonks testified: "The wounds are horrible, and I for one will be against wars in the future: one

Weapons of mass destruction caused horrific and complex war fractures. Surgery was often required to be able to save a life. The best known intervention was the amputation of a limb. The amputation process mainly comprised a series of operations with the aim of creating a stump on which a prosthesis could later be attached.
Photo, © Dox Family, Wijnegem

British artist-surgeon Henry Tonks studying one of the pastel drawings he made of the *'gueules cassées'* who were treated by New Zealand surgeon Harold Delf Gillies at the Queen's Hospital in Sidcup.
Photo, Courtesy of Dr Andrew Bamji, Gillies Archivist, Rye

has no right to ask men to endure such suffering." In 1916, he ended up at the Cambridge Military Hospital in Aldershot, then in the Queen's Hospital in Sidcup. He assisted operations in both places. The meeting with Gillies led to close cooperation: the New Zealand surgeon asked Tonks to sketch his patients in detail, before and after their operations. Tonks took his task very seriously and apart from sketches, which were so good they could in fact serve as ready-made illustration material in a course, he also left behind a striking series of pastel portraits of *gueules cassées*, which are still iconic for the subject.

FINAL YEAR OF THE WAR – BETTER EVACUATION

In spite of the progress in medical science, the uses and success of the new techniques largely depended on another factor: the efficiency (and therefore speed) with which an injured person was taken from the battlefield to the right place for the right treatment. Not until the final year of the war was the medical organisation in theory more or less finalised, in all ranks of evacuation and care. Fully developed evacuation routes had taken shape, where each link knew what to expect: from the stretcher-bearer who evacuated to the battalion physician who bandaged up the patient to the regiment physician who assessed and triaged. On the British side, from now on each division had three fully equipped field ambulances, i.e. with a multitude of medical staff per ambulance column compared to 1914 and a strongly increased number of appropriate means of transport at each stage of the evacuation route, but also with an administration that was responsible for, among others, sufficient supplies and with other staff such as drivers and workers. Behind the 'provisions' on a divisional level, other medical units were ready who could only help the front in the field of evacuation and first aid. Similar organisations could be found in the French, German and Belgian army, albeit with several nuances.

Medical aid was brought as close to the front as possible. There were specific routes for each type of injured person: 'walking', 'sitting up' and 'lying' cases. In special advanced surgical outposts people were ready to intervene in case of serious stomach or head wounds or critical fractures. In this regard, CCS No. 44 at Brandhoek (for stomach injuries) and CCS No. 46 in Proven ('Mendinghem', led by Harvey Cushing, specialising in head and brain injuries) formed interesting centres at the Third Battle of Ypres. Further in the hinterland, some real model hospitals, such as in Etaples, were established. In these hospitals, meticulous attention was paid to equal, recognisable structures, so the medical staff also found their feet after transfer. In the meantime, even deeper into France and also in England, strongly professionalised revalidation centres existed to specifically reintegrate war victims, either in society, or in the military maelstrom. The military-medical system was a well-oiled machine working at maximum speed, continuously fed by the mass of victims who continued to rush in until the bitter end.

The Belgian medical service also qualified to take the physicians and surgeons as close to the front as possible. Apart from larger hospitals in De Panne (*L'Océan*, Belgian Red Cross), Adinkerke (Cabour, army) and Hoogstade (Belgian Field Hospital) from 1915, which was extended in 1917 to Vinkem *(Océan 2)* and Beveren (Cabour 'surgery'), three surgical outposts were set up in 1916–1917, where operations for stomach injuries or internal bleeding could be carried out. This was Abelenhof (Reninge), Croignie (Oudekapelle) and Sint-Jansmolen (Lampernisse), at three to five kilometres from the frontline. If the injured person could not be taken to the surgeon fast enough, the surgeon could always be taken to the injured person.

BIBLIOGRAPHY

Books: Harvey Cushing: *From a Surgeon's Journal*; Max Deauville: *De Modder van de Westhoek*; Jack De Moor: *Dr. Albert De Moor, spoedarts in de Eerste Wereldoorlog*; Diane Atkinson: *Elsie and Mairi go to War*; H.S. Souttar: *A Surgeon in Belgium*; Erwin Mortier (translator): Ellen N. La Motte: *Het Kielzog van de Oorlog* en Mary Borden: *Verboden Gebied*; Geoffrey Winthrop-Young: *The Grace of Forgetting*; Stephen Hurst: *Ypres, the First World War and the Re-Gilding of Memory*; Piet Chielens: 'And old Flanders went under to long ages of plough thought in my pages. De 'Ieperse' gedichten van Ivor Gurney' in: *IFFM jaarboek 2013*; Eve Curie: *Madame Curie*; Alain Larcan, Jean-Jacques Ferrandis: *Le Service de Santé aux Armées pendant la Première Guerre mondiale*; Sophie Delaporte: *Les médecins de la Grande Guerre 1914–1918*; Luc De Munck, Luc Vandeweyer: *Het hospitaal van de koningin: Rode Kruis, L'Océan en De Panne 1914–1918.*

Unpublished sources: Herman Pieter Chielens, personal file; Henri Reyns, personal file; Doctor Modeste Molhant: Oorlogsherinneringen; Armand Luchies: diary; Lode Van Eyck: letters; Charlotte Jacobs: Gezondheidszorg in de onbezette Westhoek tijdens WO1, case-study: The Elisabeth Hospital in Poperinge; Roseline Debaillie: Marie Curie in Flanders Fields.

Websites: www.nieuwsbronnen.com/tenbunderen; http://www.vlib.us/medical/; http://www.ncbi.nlm.nih.gov/pmc/articles/PMC3158130/ (Suzannah Biernoff: *Flesh Poems: Henry Tonks and the Art of Surgery*)

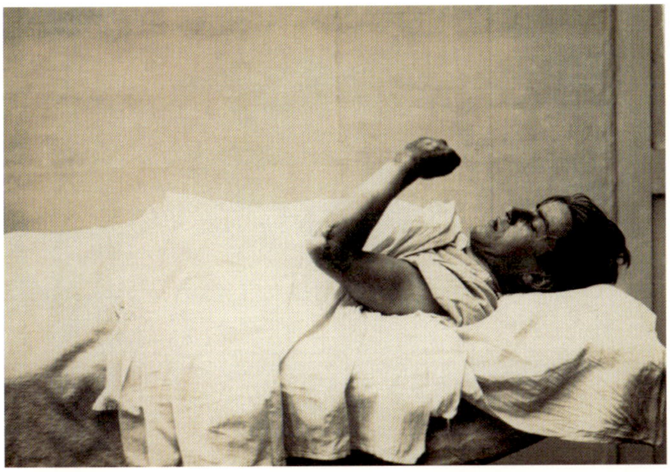
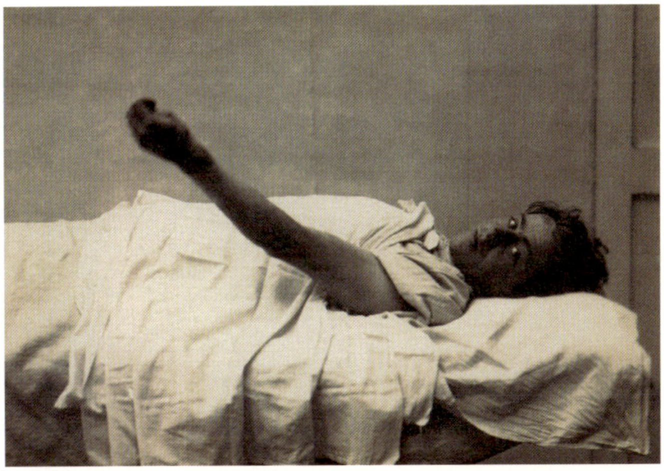
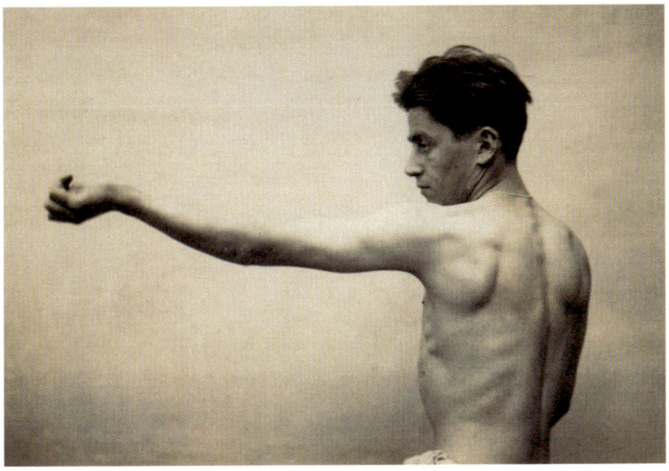
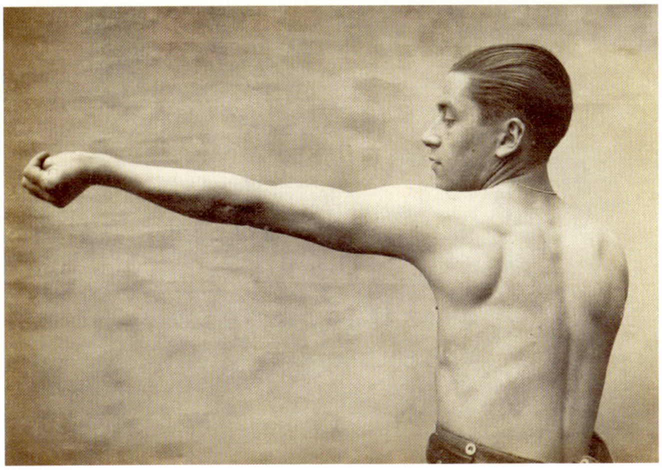

Image 1 & 2: photos of 23 Feb 1918, two days after the operation
Image 3: 10 March 1918, Image 4: 2 April 1918

Belgian soldier Hubert De Bruyker of the 22nd Line Regiment was seriously injured on 21 February 1918 near Oudekapelle. He sustained several injuries to his elbow, as well as to his left and right thighs. He was operated the same day and then went through a recovery process lasting several weeks. It is most likely that his doctor in attendance photographed his revalidation process. Hubert returned to his fighting unit and died on 28 September 1918 near Klerken (Nachtegaal) during the first day of the liberation offensive. Photos, © Family De Bruyker, Ghent-Sint-Martens-Latem

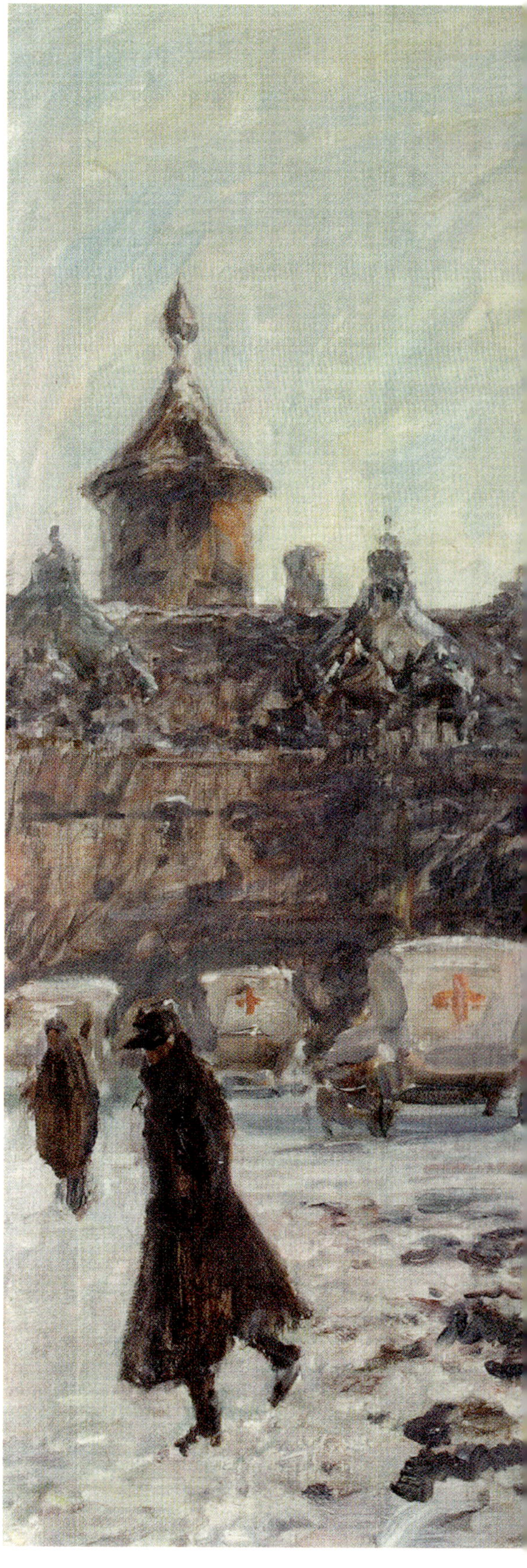

Georges Dumoulin (1882-1959): Veurne, December 1914.
Several ambulances stand in front of the town hall.
In the foreground *spahis* (North African cavalry)
are crossing the snow-covered square.

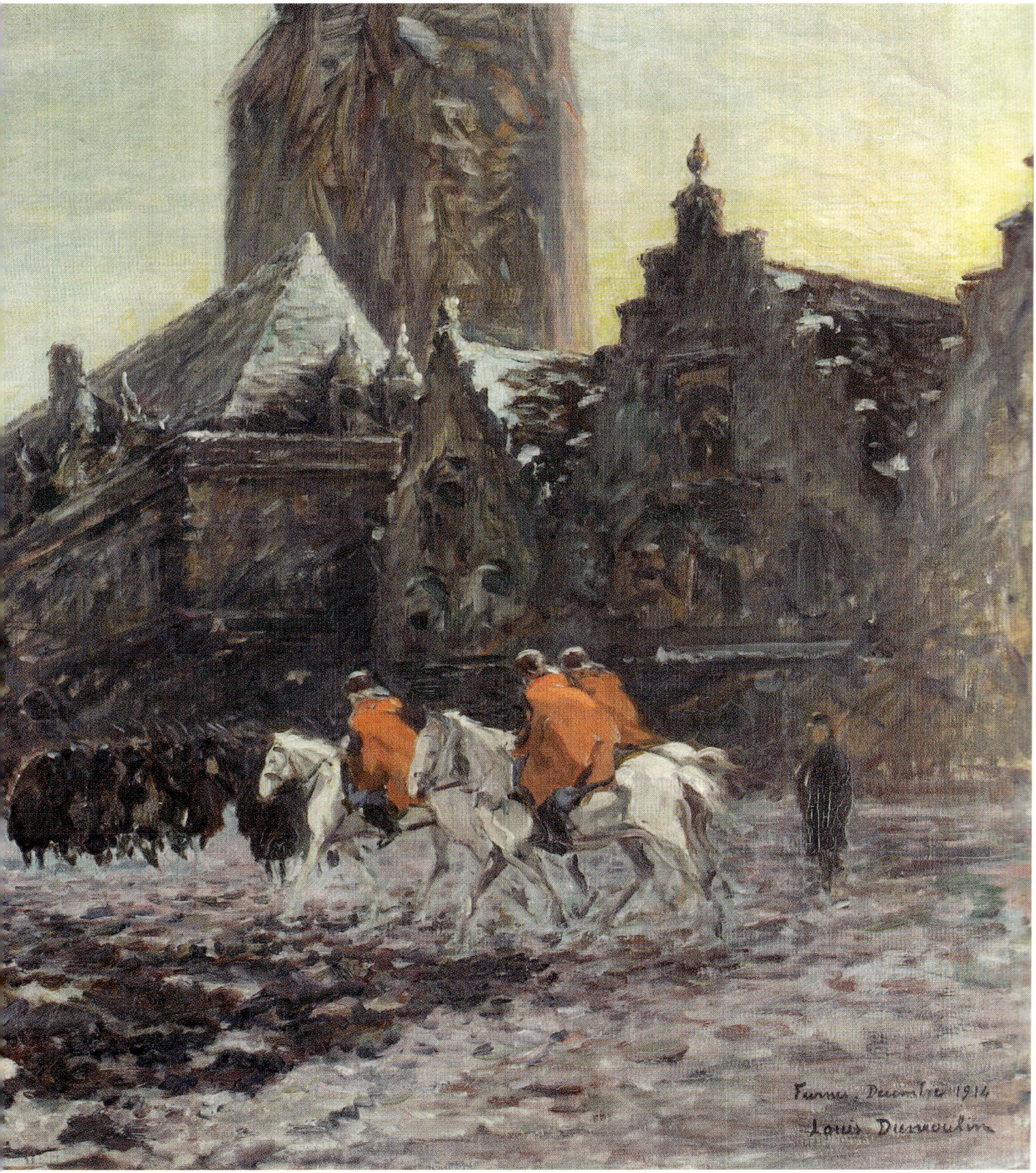
Furnes, Décembre 1914
Louis Dumoulin

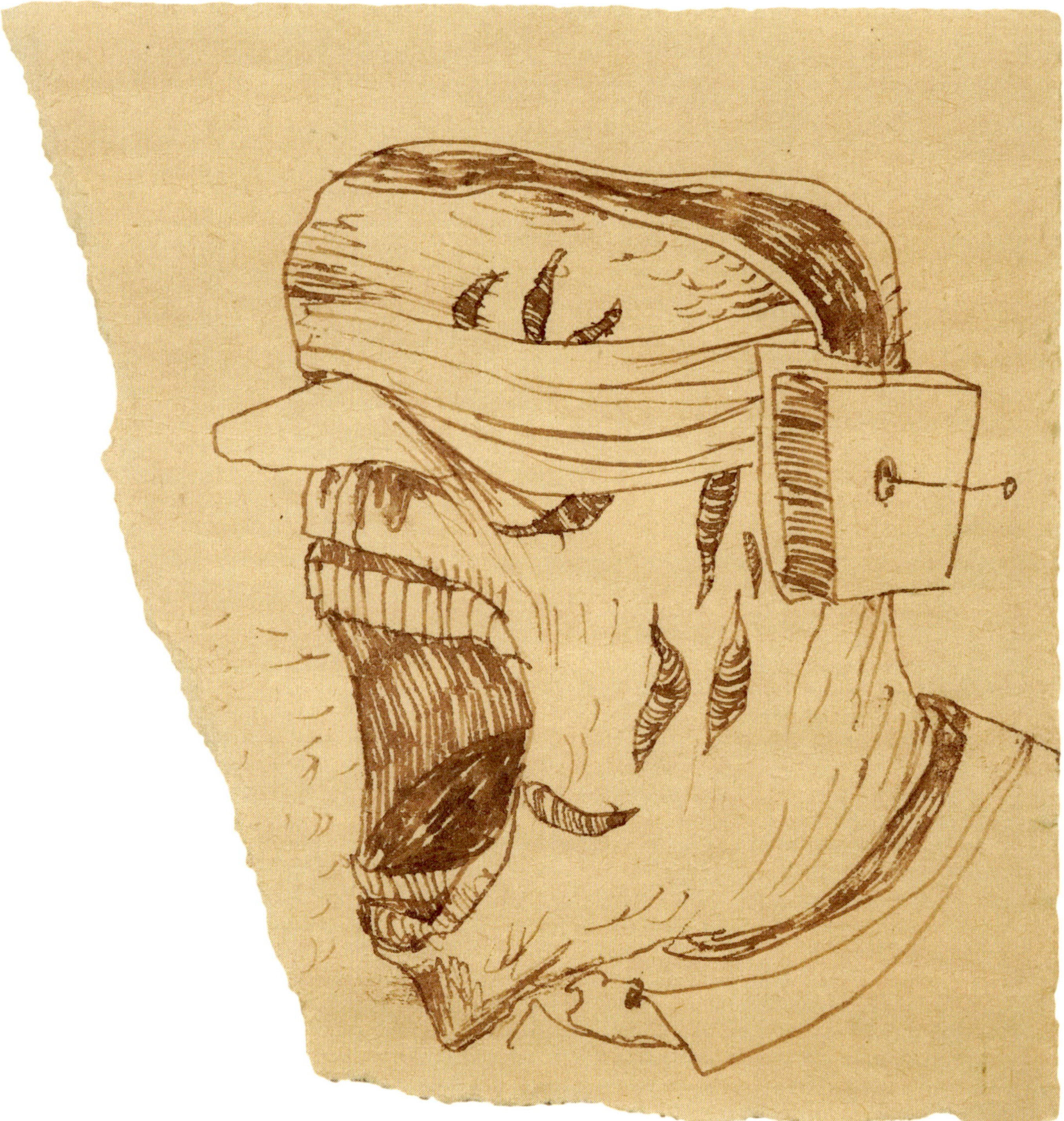

BESSEL A. VAN DER KOLK, LARS WEISAETH & ONNO VAN DER HART

Soldiers and Psychiatrists

History of Trauma in Psychiatry

All the famous moralists of yesteryear drew attention to the way in which certain events would leave indelible and distressing memories – memories to which the sufferer was continually returning, and by which he was tormented by day and by night.
Pierre Janet (1919/1925, p. 589)

Awareness of the role of psychological trauma in the genesis of various psychiatric problems has waxed and waned throughout the history of psychiatry. People have always known that exposure to overwhelming terror can lead to troubling memories, arousal, and avoidance: This has been a central theme in literature, from the time of Homer to today. In contrast, psychiatry as a profession has had a very troubled relationship with the idea that reality can profoundly and permanently alter people's psychology and biology. Psychiatry itself has periodically suffered from marked amnesia in which well-established knowledge has been abruptly forgotten, and the psychological impact of overwhelming experiences has been ascribed to constitutional or intrapsychic factors alone. Mirroring the intrusions, confusion, and disbelief of victims whose lives are suddenly shattered by traumatic experiences, the psychiatric profession has gone through periods of fascination with trauma, followed by periods of stubborn disbelief about the relevance of patients' stories.

From the earliest involvement of psychiatry with traumatised patients, there have been vehement arguments about trauma's aetiology. Is it organic or psychological? Is trauma the event itself or its subjective interpretation? Does the trauma itself cause the disorder, or do pre-existing vulnerabilities cause it? Are these patients malingering, do they suffer from moral weakness, or do they suffer from involuntary disintegration of the capacity to take charge of their lives?

TRAUMATIC STRESS: EMOTIONAL OR ORGANIC?

The question whether trauma has organic or psychological origins, or whether it represents malingering or genuine breakdown, was at the centre of the earliest scientific discussions about its effect, which focused on whiplash injuries and 'railroad spines'. In 1886, the English surgeon, John Eric Erichsen ascribed the psychological problems of severely injured patients to organic causes and warned against confusing such symptoms with those of hysteria – a condition that he and most of his contemporaries claimed only occurred in women. Not unlike their present-day counterparts, physicians in those days struggled with trying to understand body-mind relationships; physical signs of anxiety then, as now, were easily misdiagnosed as symptoms of organic illness. Erichsen's fellow surgeon, Page, disagreed, and instead proposed that the symptoms of 'railroad spine' had psychological origins. He claimed that "many errors in diagnosis have been made because fright has not been considered of itself sufficient". The German neurologist, Herman Oppenheim (1889), who was the first to use the term 'traumatic neurosis', was an organicist. He proposed that functional problems are produced by subtle molecular changes in the central nervous system. The frequent occurrence of cardiovascular symptoms in traumatised persons, particularly in combat soldiers, started a long tradition of associating posttraumatic problems with 'cardiac neuroses'. This began with such names as 'irritable heart' and 'soldier's

The Russian Foma Jaremtschuk (1907–1986) only went to school briefly and never learned to draw. Until the age of 29, little is known about him. In 1936 he became a victim of the Stalin regime and was sent to a labour camp. After his diagnosis of mental illness, he ended up in a closed mental hospital in 1947. During his stay there he made approximately 500 pen and ink drawings, populated by strange figures and animals in bizarre circumstances that often bring torture scenes to mind. In 1963 he was transferred to a different mental hospital, where he remained until 1974. No drawings were preserved of this period. He eventually died in 1986 in a third hospital for seriously ill patients.
Foma Jaremtschuk, **Without title**, s.d., ink on paper. Courtesy of Susanne Zander Gallery, Cologne / Delmes & Zander, Cologne

heart' (Myers, 1870; Da Costa, 1871) and progressed to 'disorderly action of the heart' or 'neurocirculatory asthenia' during World War I (Merskey, 1991).

Ascribing an organic origin to traumatic neuroses was particularly important in combat soldiers. Such an attribution offered an honourable solution for all parties who might be compromised by people breaking down under stress: the soldier preserved his self-respect, the doctor did not have to diagnose personal failure or desertion, and military authorities did not have to explain psychological breakdown in previously brave soldiers, or bother with such troublesome issues as cowardice, low unit morale, poor leadership, or the meaning of the war effort itself. But if trauma was an illness, how could it be defined? Charles Samuel Meyers (1915), a British military psychiatrist, was the first to use the term 'shell shock' in medical literature. However, since 'shell shock' could be found in soldiers who had never been directly exposed to gunfire, it gradually became clear that the causes were often purely emotional. Myers came to play an important role in rejecting a relationship between battle neuroses and such organic factors as 'molecular commotion in the brain', and declared emotional disturbance alone to be enough of an explanation. He, like so many after him, emphasized the close resemblance of the war neuroses to hysteria (Myers, 1940). Moran described in 1945 how, despite the acceptance of diagnosis of shell shock, doctors found it extremely difficult to distinguish it from cowardice. More than 200 British soldiers were executed for cowardice during World War II; a notable fact is that only 11% of those who were condemned to death for desertion were actually executed.

TRAUMA, SUGGESTIBILITY AND SIMULATION

An association between psychological trauma and hysteria has been noted ever since psychiatry had tried to be a scientific discipline. As early as 1859, the French psychiatrist, Briquet, started to make the first connections between the symptoms of hysteria (including somatization) and childhood histories of trauma. Of

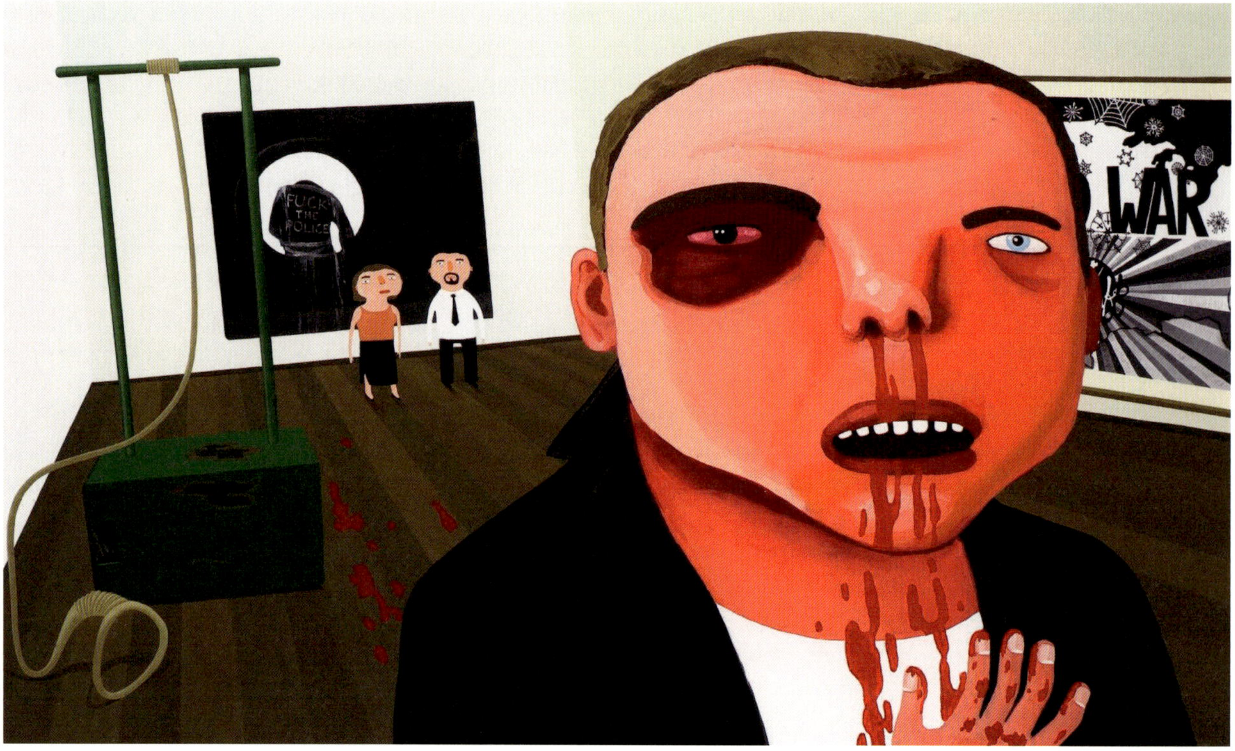

Zoya Cherkassky, **Minimalism**, 2006, acrylic paint on canvas. Gallery Adrian David Collection, Knokke

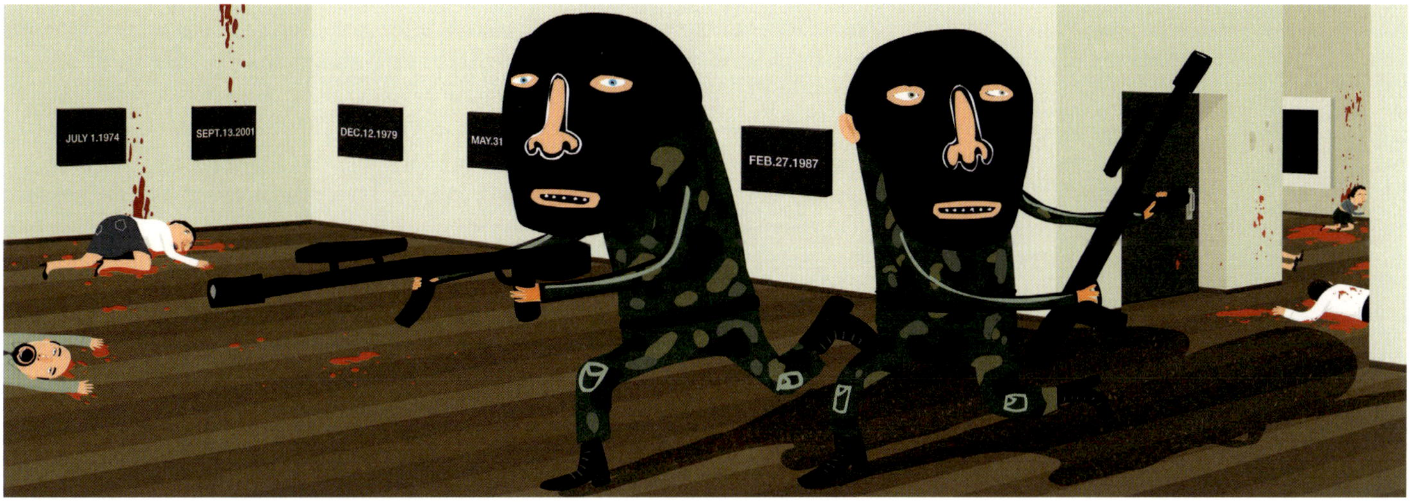

the 501 hysterical patients he described, Briquet reported specific traumatic origins as the cause of their illness in 381. Sexual abuse of children was well documented during the second half of the 19th century in France by researchers such as Tardieu (1878), a professor of forensic medicine. Almost as soon as the issue of sexual trauma in children was identified, the thorny issue of false memories was raised by people like Alfred Fournier, who described 'pseudologica phantastica' in children who were thought to have falsely accused their parents of incest.

Similar problems arose when the first systematic explorations of the relationships between trauma and psychiatric illness were conducted at the Salpêtrière. The great neurologist Jean-Martin Charcot (1887) described how traumatically induced '*choc nerveux*' could put patients into a mental state similar to that of hypnosis. This so-called 'hypnoid state', was believed to be a necessary condition of what Charcot called 'hystero-traumatic-autosuggestion'. Thus, Charcot became the first to describe both the problems of suggestibility in these patients, and the fact that hysterical attacks are dissociative problems - the result of having endured unbearable experiences.

While Charcot inspired Janet to study the nature of dissociation and traumatic memories (Janet, 1887, 1889, 1894), two of Charcot's other pupils, Gilles de la Tourette and Joseph Babinski, focused their further research on hysterical suggestibility. When Babinski took over as head of the Salpêtrière in 1905, Charcot's notions about the traumatic origins of hysteria were rejected as worthless. In their place, simulation and suggestibility became to be considered as the hallmarks of the now emphatically neurological disease entity 'hysteria' (Babinski, 1901, 1909). This development set the stage for the overriding interests during World

In the work of Kiev-born artist, Zoya Cherkassky (1976), who now lives in Israel, the grotesque is central, always in combination with a dollop of humour. Through exaggeration and satire, she tries to stir up the viewer. Her Jewish identity is also a source of inspiration. For instance, she transforms the Star of David into a golden brooch. Cherkassky made a series of paintings in which modern museums are afflicted by violence and vandalism. For example, we see masked terrorists causing a blood bath at an exhibition of On Kawara. Bodies lie all across the floor and we can see bloodstains on the walls. The works of art themselves are, however, spared. The violence manifests itself in Cherkassky's work at locations where you least expect it, making it twice as effective.
Zoya Cherkassky, **Nosebleed**, 2007, acrylic paint on canvas. Gallery Adrian David Collection, Knokke

War I, among Babinski and his French students, as well as among many German psychiatrists, in treating 'simulation' rather than in alleviating the horror of the patients' traumatic memories (Nonne, 1915; Babinski & Froment, 1918). For many French and German neurologists and psychiatrists, the treatment of war syndromes became a battle against simulation.

With the focus on simulation, the notion of 'will' became the dominant issue. 'War neurosis' ('war hysteria'), for many psychiatrists, was essentially a disease of the will, a *Willenskrankheit*. Hence, largely for political reasons, the medical diagnosis of posttraumatic stress in Germany during World War I and during subsequent decades was recast as a failure of the individual soldier's willpower (*Willenversagung, Willenshemmung, Willensperrung, Wille zur Krankheit*). As a result, treatment consisted of 'causal will therapies': the patient's 'desire for health' had to be stimulated and bolstered by physiological exercises. The treatment was so painful that many patients preferred front-line duty, and were thus considered 'cured'.

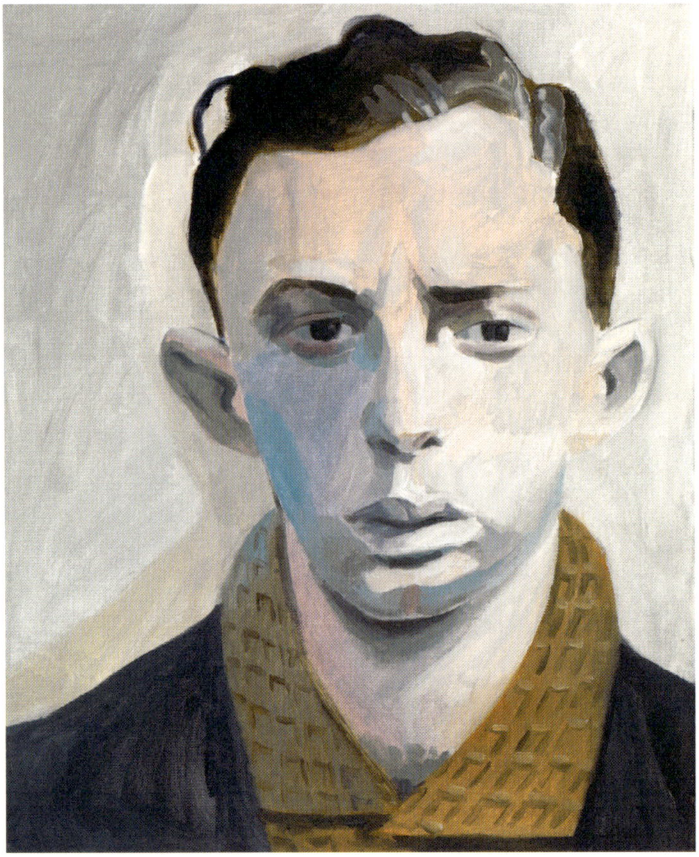

Jan Vanriet, **Moszek**, 2011,
oil on canvas. Private collection,
courtesy of Roberto Polo Gallery, Brussels

VULNERABILITY, PREDISPOSITION AND COMPENSATION

The issue of predisposition could be studied with more detachment in civilian settings, where national pride was not at stake, and compensation was less of a potentially massive economic issue. The Swiss psychiatrist, Edouard Stierlin, the first researcher in disaster psychiatry, published two works (1909,1911) based on studies of earlier calamities: an earthquake in Messina, Italy, in 1907, and a mining disaster in 1906. Stierlin was the first to study non-clinical populations, which brought him face to face with the issue of vulnerability and resiliency. He agreed with his predecessors at the Salpêtrière that violent emotions are the most important etiological factors of 'fright neurosis'. He was concerned that physicians had little awareness that emotions can cause serious long-term psychoneurotic problems, and that laypeople tended to equate posttraumatic psychological problems with simulation.

Stierlin found that a substantial proportion of victims developed long-lasting posttraumatic stress symptoms. For example, after the Messina earthquake in 1907, which killed 70,000 of the town's inhabitants, 25% of the survivors suffered from sleep disturbances and nightmares.

In the period following World War I, the leading German psychiatrist Bonhoeffer (1926) and his colleagues founded a school of thought that regarded traumatic neurosis as a social illness that could only be cured by social remedies. However, these social cures did not consist of an amelioration of social conditions. Since Bonhoeffer concluded that practically all of his 142 cases of traumatic neurosis had hereditary predispositions, dealing with these patients' inherent weakness, rather than preventing and ameliorating their misery, became the critical issue. Bonhoeffer and his colleagues believed that the real cause of traumatic neurosis among their patients was the availability of compensation (*'Das Gesetz ist die Ursache der Unfallsneuroses'* – 'The law is the cause of traumatic neuroses'). In other words, the disorder was caused by secondary gain. Traumatic neurosis was not an illness, but an artefact of the insurance system – a *Rentenneurose* (a compensation neurosis). This compensation neurosis was thought to occur primarily in predisposed individuals. Jaspers (1913) had previously proclaimed that patients with psychogenic disorders (including the traumatic neuroses) lacked premorbid personality problems and therefore had a good prognosis. This blind acceptance of psychiatric dogma meant that a poor outcome must be the result of premorbid vulnerabilities.

The *Reichversicherungs Ordnung* (RVO-The National Health Insurance Act) of 1926 cemented this position in Germany. Traumatic neurosis was not to be compensated. The philosophy behind this decision was that traumatic neurosis was incurable if and as long as patients were awarded pensions or other compensations. Only immediate shock reactions were accepted. If the victim's problem persisted, this was blamed on the interplay among predisposition, constitution, 'degenerative inclination', and compensation. The social backdrop of this discussion was a time of economic chaos and social distress in Germany. The RVO lasted through the Nazi period and beyond. It was slightly modified in 1959, but today German compensation practices continue to be much more restrictive than those of most other countries (Venzlaff, 1975).

THE PSYCHOLOGICAL PROCESSING OF TRAUMA: REALITY IMPRINT VERSUS INTRAPSYCHIC ELABORATION

In retrospect, the issue of traumatic origins of hysteria is probably the most important legacy of psychiatry in the last decades of the 19th century. As noted earlier, Charcot (1887) first proposed at the Salpêtrière that the symptoms of his hysterical patients had their origin in histories of trauma. In his first four books, Pierre Janet described a total of 591 patients and reported a traumatic origin of their psychopathology in 257. Janet noted that hysterical patients were unable to attend to their internal processes as guides for adaptive action. In line with the prevailing thinking of his day (Bergson, 1896), he considered self-awareness to be the central issue in psychological health. He believed that an individual's being in touch with his or her personal past, combined with having accurate perceptions of current situations, determines whether the person is able to respond appropriately to stress. Janet coined the word 'subconscious' to describe the collection of memories that form the mental schemes that guide a

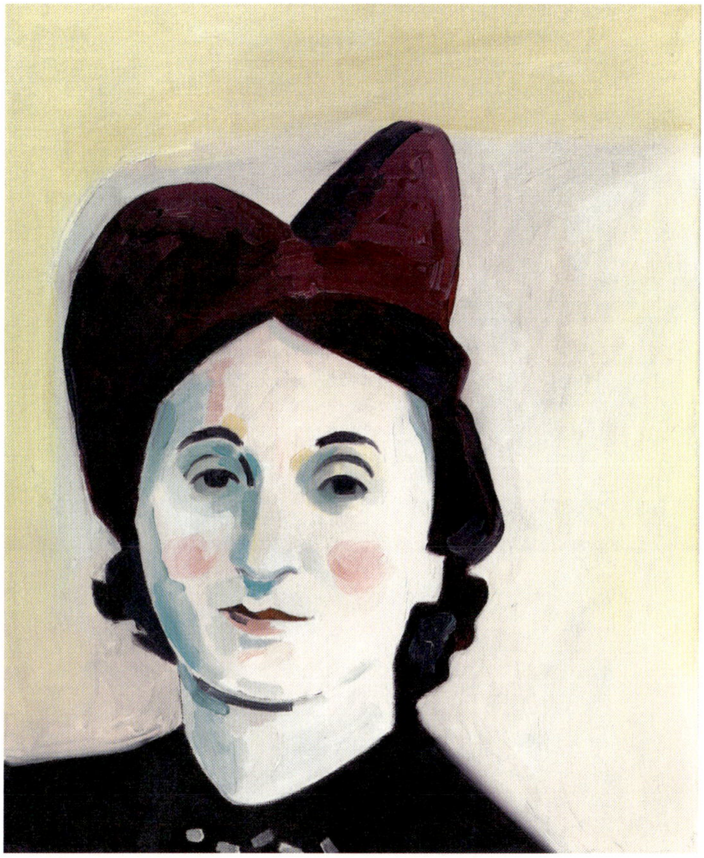

Jan Vanriet's (1948) fascination for World War II comes from his family history. Both his parents were in the Resistance and survived the concentration camps. The traumatic history of World War II is therefore a central theme in his work. Several portraits of the deported from the Kazerne Dossin form the series *Gezichtsverlies* [Loss of face]. Vanriet's work depicts human incapacity. This work centres around death, destruction, escape and fate. *Gezichtsverlies* is a series of drawings and watercolours in subdued colours. In light and pastel, Vanriet shows the faces of people awaiting a horrific fate unknown to them.
Jan Vanriet, Ida, 2010, oil on canvas. Private collection, courtesy of Roberto Polo Gallery, Brussels

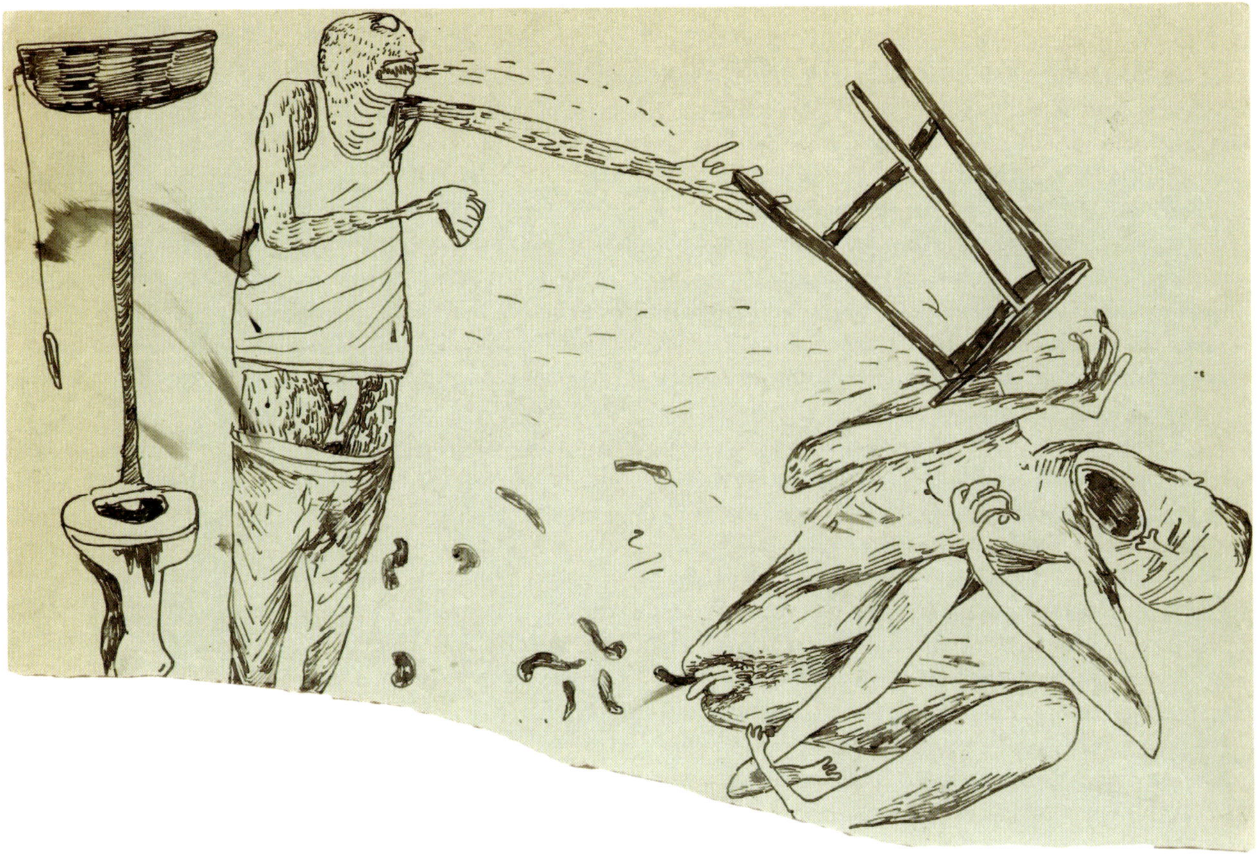

Foma Jaremtschuk, **Without title**, s.d., ink on paper. Courtesy of Susanne Zander Gallery, Cologne / Delmes & Zander, Cologne

person's interaction with the environment (1904). In his view, appropriate categorization and integration of memories of past experiences allow people to develop meaning schemes that prepare them to cope with subsequent challenges.

Janet proposed that when people experience 'vehement emotions', their minds may become incapable of matching their frightening experiences with existing cognitive schemes. As a result, the memories of the experience cannot be integrated into personal awareness; instead, they are split off (dissociated) from consciousness and from voluntary control. Thus, the first comprehensive formulation of the effects of trauma on the mind was based on the notion that extreme emotional arousal results in failure to integrate traumatic memories. Janet stated that people are "unable to make the recital which we call narrative memory, and yet they remain confronted by (the) difficult situation". This results in 'a phobia of memory', which prevents the integration ('synthesis') of traumatic events and splits these traumatic memories off from ordinary consciousness (Janet, 1909). The memory traces of the trauma linger as unconscious 'fixed ideas' that cannot be 'liquidated' as long as they have not been translated into a personal narrative; instead, they continue to intrude as terrifying perceptions, obsessional preoccupations, and somatic re-experiences such as anxiety reactions.

Until psychoanalysis – the doctrine of intrapsychic conflict and repressed infantile sexuality – crowded out competing schools of thought, Janet's clinical observations were widely accepted as the correct formulations of the effects on the mind of trauma. William James, Jean Piaget, Henry Murray, Carl Jung, Charles Meyers, Willem MacDougal, and such students of dissociation as Ernest Hilgard all acknowledged the influence of Janet's work on their understanding of mental processes. In accepting dissociation as the core pathogenic process that gives rise to posttraumatic stress, they all disagreed with the psychoanalytic notion that catharsis and abreaction are the treatments of choice. Instead, they emphasized the role of synthesis and integration. Despite Janet's large body of work and his profound influence both on his contemporaries and on the next generation of psychiatrists, his legacy was slowly forgotten. Janet's extensive work on trauma, memory, and the treatment of dissociative states was not integrated with contemporary knowledge of the PTSD until the role of dissociation in the origins of PTSD was rediscovered in the 1980s.

FREUD AND TRAUMA

When Sigmund Freud visited Charcot at the end of 1885, he adopted many of the ideas then current in the Salpêtrière, which he expressed and acknowledged in his early papers on hysteria. In much that he wrote between 1892 and 1896, Freud followed the notion that the 'subconscious' contains affectively charged events encoded in an altered state of consciousness. In *On the Psychical Mechanism of Hysterical Phenomena: A Lecture* (1893), he wrote on the nature of hysterical attacks: "We must point out that we consider it essential for the explanation of hysterical phenomena to assume the presence of a dissociation – a splitting of the content of consciousness... the regular and essential content of a (recurrent) hysterical attack is the recurrence of a psychical state which the patient has experienced earlier". When Breuer and Freud expanded this work in *Studies on Hysteria*, they acknowledged their debt to Janet and stated that "hysterics suffer mainly from reminiscences... the traumatic experience is constantly forcing itself upon the patient and this is proof of the strength of that experience: the patient is, as one might say, fixated on his trauma". Citing Janet, Breuer and Freud thought that something becomes traumatic because it is dissociated and remains outside conscious awareness. They called this state 'hypnoid hysteria'.

In *The Aetiology of Hysteria*, Freud (1896) began to develop a concept of 'defence hysteria', in which he for the first time abandoned dissociation as the central pathogenic process related to trauma, thereby beginning to make his own original contributions by claiming that repressed instinctual wishes form the foundation of the neuroses. Freud later claimed that 'I find...that there are no grounds whatever for presupposing the presence of such hypnoid states'. Although during World War I he again became interested in the nature of traumatic neuroses, the relationship between actual childhood trauma and the development of psychopathology was henceforth ignored. In Freud's view, it is

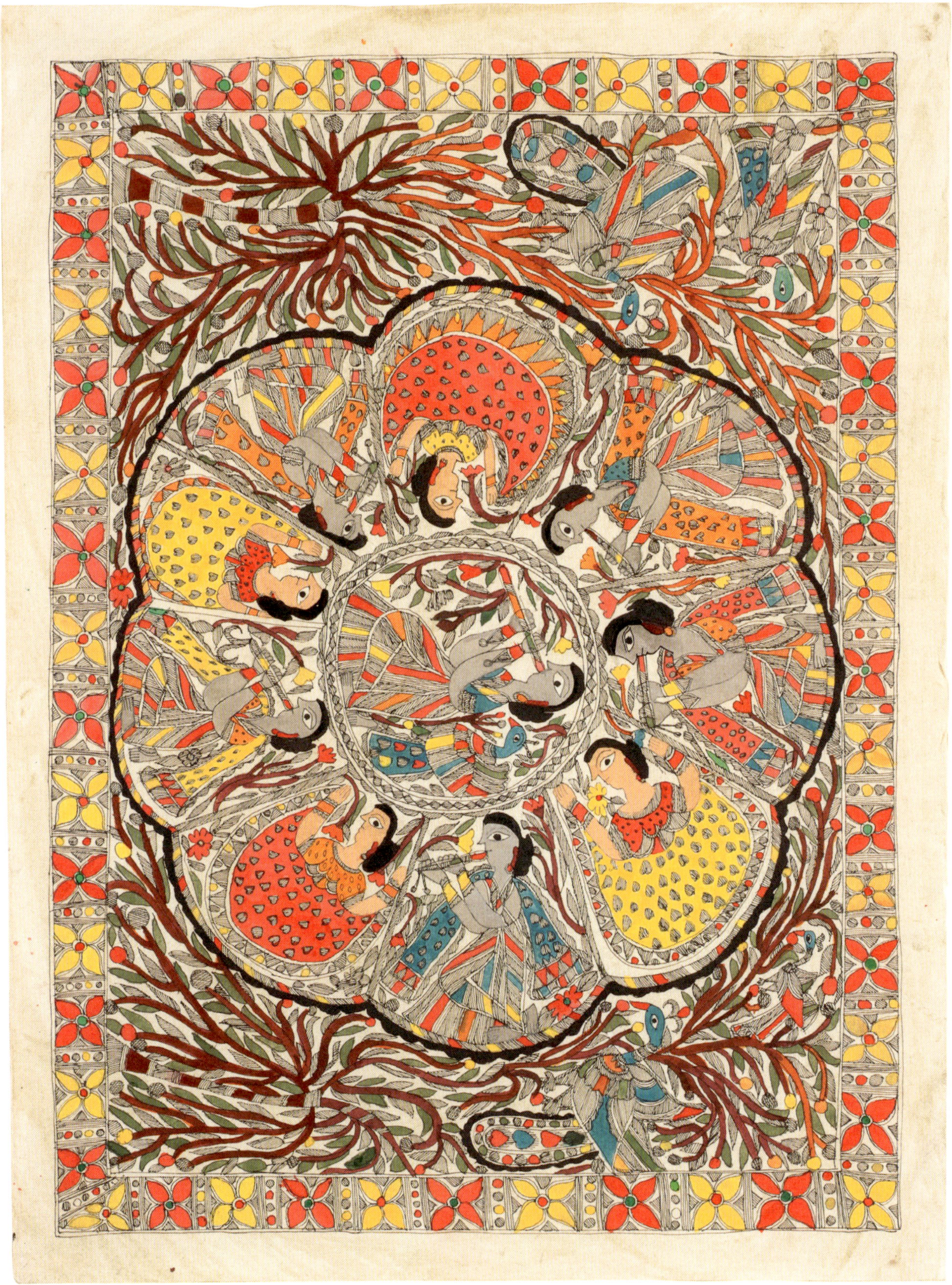

not actual the memories of childhood trauma that are split off from consciousness, but rather the unacceptable sexual and aggressive wishes of the child, which threaten the ego and motivate defences against the conscious awareness of these wishes.

Freud henceforth argued that the memory disturbances and re-enactments seen in hysteria are not the results of a failure to integrate new data into existing meaning schemes, but stem from the active repression of conflict-laden sexual and aggressive ideas and impulses, centring around the Oedipal crisis at about the age 5.

Although he tried, Freud was never able to reconcile his notions about repressed infantile sexuality with actual trauma: "Keeping up the seduction theory would mean to abandon the Oedipus complex, and with it the whole importance of fantasy life, conscious or unconscious fantasy" (Anna Freud, quoted by Mason, 1984). Focusing on intrapsychic reality and subjective experience crowded our interest in external reality. Psychiatry as a discipline came to follow Freud in his explorations of how the normal human psyche functioned: real-life trauma was ignored in favour of fantasy.

However, just as his early hysterical patients seemed incapable of getting rid of their traumatic memories, Freud kept coming back to the issue of 'fixation on the trauma.' World War I temporarily confronted the world, including Freud, with the inescapable reality of the effects of trauma on people's spirits. During this time, he revived Janet's notion of 'vehement emotions' as being at the root of traumatic neuroses: he declared that the overwhelming intensity of the stressor, the absence of abreactive verbal or motoric channels, and the unpreparedness of the individual cause a failure of the stimulus barrier (*Reitschutz*). The organism is unable to deal with the excitement, flooding the mental apparatus, resulting in mental paralyses and intense affect storms.

Rather than integrating his observations of the war neuroses with those of twenty years earlier, Freud responded by developing two separate models of 'trauma'. One was the 'unbearable situation' model; the other was the 'unacceptable impulse' model, in which symptoms may be produced through the mobilization of defence mechanisms. Freud proposed that the compulsion to repeat is a function of repression itself: "... we therefore concluded that the keeping away from consciousness is the main characteristic of hysterical repression (1920). Because the memory is repressed, the patient 'is obliged to repeat the repressed material as a contemporary experience, instead of... remembering it as something belonging to the past'". In the *Introductory Lectures on Psycho-Analysis* (1916–1917), Freud stated: "The traumatic neuroses give a clear indication that a fixation to the traumatic neuroses in their dreams, where... we find that the attack conforms to a complete transplanting of the patient into the traumatic situation. It is as if the patient has not finished with the traumatic situation".

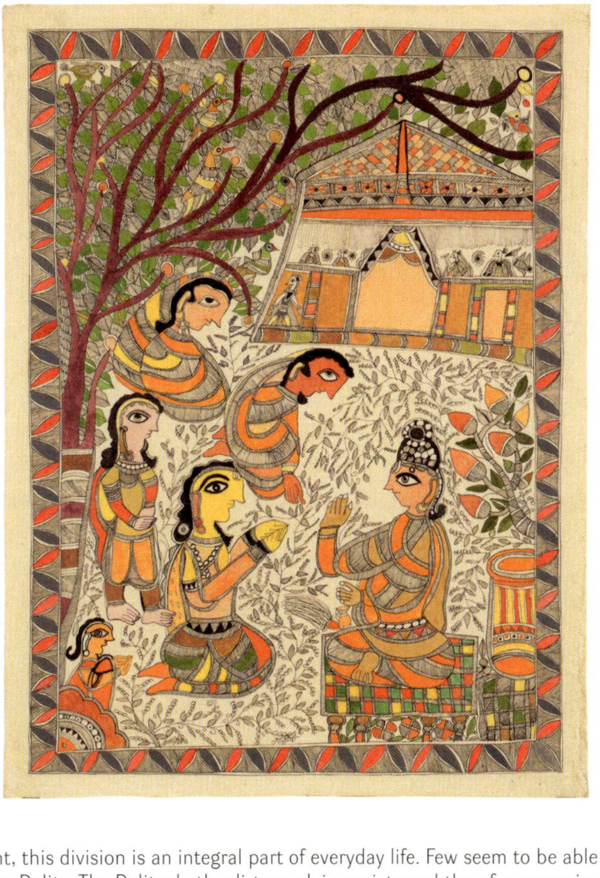

Although the caste system has been officially prohibited by the Indian Government, this division is an integral part of everyday life. Few seem to be able to withdraw from this and it is especially difficult for the so-called Untouchables or Dalits. The Dalits do the dirty work in society and therefore experience their social position as traumatising. In the Godna paintings we see part of their suffering. In bright colours, several Dalit painters have depicted their view of the world, with its own symbolism and using traditional visual language or tattoos. Their trauma, and the impurity of the Untouchables vis-à-vis the superiority of other castes, are interwoven in their work.
Dalits, **Without title**, s.d. Dr Guislain Museum, Ghent

In *Beyond the Pleasure Principle* (1920), Freud was close to reintegrating his earliest observations with his later understanding of intrapsychic reality. He was struck by the fact that patients suffering from traumatic neuroses often experienced a lack of conscious preoccupation with the memories of their accidents. He postulated that 'perhaps they are more concerned with NOT thinking of it', but he did not connect this observation with the notion of *la belle indifference* in hysterics.

The acceptance of psychoanalytic theory resulted in a total absence of research on the effects of real traumatic events on children's lives. From 1895 until very recently, no studies were conducted on the effects of childhood sexual trauma. Although psychoanalysts, including Freud, tended to acknowledge sexual trauma as tragic and harmful, the subject seems to have been too awful to be seriously considered in a civilized society.

THE BEGINNINGS OF INTEGRATION: ABRAM KARDINER

Although several psychiatrists tried to apply the lessons of World War I to prevention and early intervention in civilian settings, their influence on psychiatry was minor and did not result in institutional change. One notable exception was Abram Kardiner, who began his career treating traumatised U.S. war veterans. Starting in 1923, after finishing his analysis with Freud, he first unsuccessfully tried to create a theory of war neuroses based upon the concepts of early psychoanalytic theory. From 1939 onward, as World War II was breaking out, he reassessed the meaning of his entire body of careful clinical observations, which he published in *The Traumatic Neuroses of War* (1941). Like the previous great pioneers of psychological trauma, Kardiner was a master of detailed descriptions of the complex and unusual symptoms of his patients, and a meticulous chronicler of the plethora of previous diagnoses these patients had received before a connection between the trauma and their current symptoms was made. More than anyone else, Kardiner defined PTSD, for the remainder of the 20th century.

Kardiner noted that sufferers from 'traumatic neuroses' develop an enduring vigilance for and sensitivity to environmental threat, and stated that "the nucleus of the neurosis is a *physioneurosis*. This is present on the battlefield and during the entire process of organization; it outlives every intermediary accommodative device, and persists in the chronic forms. The traumatic syndrome is ever present and unchanged". He described extreme physiological arousal in his patients, who suffered from sensitivity to temperature, pain, and sudden tactile stimuli.

Aside from the physiological alterations, Kardiner noted that the 'pathological traumatic syndrome' consists of an altered conception of the self in relation to the world, based on being fixated on the trauma and having an atypical dream life, with chronic irritability, startle reactions, and explosive aggressive reactions. The phobic elaborations on the trauma made his patients look as if they were suffering from long-standing neuroses. However, he believed that it was the result of the fact that "the ego dedicates itself to the specific job of ensuring the security of the organism, and of trying to protect itself against recollection of the trauma". Patients became 'stuck' in the trauma, and frequently had what he called 'the Sisyphus dream', in which "whatever activity (they engage in) is greeted with a certain stereotyped futility". This sense of futility often overtook them; they became withdrawn and detached, even when they had functioned well prior to combat. Over four decades later, Tichener (1986) would rediscover this phenomenon and label it 'posttraumatic decline'.

Central in Kardiner's thinking, as it had been for Janet and Freud, was this fact: "The subject acts as if the original traumatic situation were still in existence and engages in protective devices which failed on the original occasion. This means in effect that his conception of the outer world and his conception of himself have been permanently altered". Sometimes patients' fixation on the trauma would take the form of dissociative fugue states. For example, triggered by a sensory stimulus, a patient might lash out, employing language suggestive of his trying to defend himself during a military assault. Many patients, while riding the subway and especially upon entering a tunnel had flashbacks of being in the trenches. In other cases, patients had panic attacks in response to stimuli reminiscent of the trauma, while failing to make a conscious connection between their emotional states and their prior traumatic experience.

WORLD WAR II AND ITS AFTERMATH

Although Kardiner's work was available for practical application when World War II broke out, most of the lessons of front-line psychiatry from World War I had been forgotten and needed to be rediscovered. Thus, initially, the same inadequate treatment procedures (including evacuation from the front) were practiced as during World War I, resulting in great cost to the individual soldier and in manpower loss for the military. However, the essential elements of front-line psychiatry – the principles of 'proximity, immediacy, and expectancy' – were soon practiced at the front. For the first time, there was research on protective factors such as training, group cohesion, leadership, motivation, and morale.

As a result of their war experiences, psychiatrists such as Walter Menninger in the United States, and Bion and his British colleagues at the Tavistock Clinic, discovered the use of group psychotherapy and the therapeutic community. Clearly, the group had become a focus for psychiatric interest. War, as well as disasters, made the mental health profession aware that under extreme conditions, the group rather than the individual is the basic unit of study and treatment. Given the vast experience gained during the war, the dedication of the practitioners, and the solid collection of data on the combat neuroses, it is astounding how the memory of war trauma was again completely forgotten for the subsequent quarter-century.

STUDIES OF CONCENTRATION CAMP SURVIVORS

After World War II, an independent line of investigation emerged with the study of the long-term effects of trauma in survivors of the Holocaust and other war-related traumas. Studies by Eitinger and Strøm showed that in terms of pre-war health, concentration camp survivors were a representative sample of their national populations. Their increased mortality, general somatic morbidity, and psychiatric morbidity were thoroughly documented. These investigators coined the term 'concentration camp syndrome', which included not only the symptoms currently listed under PTSD, but also enduring personality changes. Perhaps the most consistent finding from these studies, however, was the devastating effect of extreme and long-lasting stress on subsequent health. This was also shown in the so-called 'war-sailor syndrome' from the allied Convoy Service and in survivors of Japanese concentration camps. The studies of people who had undergone concentration camp experiences once again, showed that extreme trauma had severe biological, psychological, social, and existential consequences, including a diminished capacity to cope with both psychological and biological stressors later in life.

Henry Krystal, a psychoanalyst who studied the long-term outcome of massive traumatisation in concentration camp victims, suggested that the core experience of being traumatised consists of 'giving up' and accepting death and destruction as inevitable. Like Janet and Kardiner before him, but in the language of psychoanalysis, Krystal noted that the trauma response evolves from a state of hyper-alert anxiety to a progressive blocking of emotions and behavioural inhibition. He noted that trauma leads to a 'dedifferentiation of affects'. Developmentally, children learn to interpret bodily states in terms of emotions that are indicators of personal significance, and that come to serve as guides for subsequent action; in contrast, the chronic hyper-arousal of traumatised people leads to a loss of ability to grasp the personal meaning of bodily feelings. Traumatised patients come to experience emotional reactions merely as somatic states, without begin able to interpret the meaning of what they are feeling. Unable to 'know' what they feel, they become prone to undifferentiated affect storms and psychosomatic reactions, which are devoid of personal meaning and cannot lead to adaptive responses. According to Krystal, this development of 'alexithymia' is central to psychosomatic symptoms typical of chronically traumatised individuals.

Most of the studies carried out in the aftermath of World War II were conducted by investigators who could identify with the 'unbearable situation'; the majority had been participants in the war or concentration camp survivors themselves. The physician who first described the 'war sailor syndrome' had himself been a sailor on a torpedoed vessel.

THE EMERGENCE OF PTSD AS A DIAGNOSTIC CATEGORY

In recent decades, much of the impetus for the development of an integrated understanding of the effects of trauma on social, psychological, and biological functions has continued to come from the participation of individuals who themselves were exposed to trauma, such as Vietnam veterans and from people working with hitherto entirely neglected traumatised populations: women and children. Amazingly, between 1895 and 1974, the study of trauma centred almost exclusively on its effects on white males. In 1974, Ann Burgess and Linda Holstrom at Boston City Hospital first described the 'rape trauma syndrome', noting that the terrifying flashbacks and nightmares seen in these women resembled the traumatic neuroses of war. At about the same time, the Kempes (1978) started their work on battered children, and the first systematic research on trauma and family violence began to appear. Although in 1980 the leading U.S. textbook of psychiatry still claimed that incest happened to fewer than one in a million women, and that its impact was not particularly damaging, people like Judith Herman (1981) began to document the wide spread sexual abuse of children and the devastation that it causes. Sarah Haley, one of the people most directly involved in the acceptance of PTSD as a diagnostic category in the Diagnostic and Statistical Manual of Mental disorders, third edition (DSM-III), was both the daughter of a World War II veteran with severe 'combat neurosis' and an incest victim herself. She wrote the first comprehensive paper on the problems with tolerating reports of atrocities in the therapeutic setting in 1974.

In 1970, two New York psychiatrists, Chaim Shatan and Robert J. Lifton, started 'rap groups' with recently returned veterans belonging to Vietnam Veterans Against the War, in which they talked about their war experiences. These 'rap sessions' rapidly spread around the country, and formed the nucleus for an informal network of professionals concerned about the lack of recognition of the effects of the war on these men's psychological health. They started to read Kardiner, the literature on Holocaust survivors, and the existing work on burn and accident victims. Based on this, they made a list of the twenty-seven most common symptoms of 'traumatic neuroses' reported in literature. They compared these with over 700 clinical records of Vietnam veterans, from which they distilled what they thought were the most critical elements. Not by accident, since Kardiner's work had helped to guide this enterprise, the final classification system was very close to the one that Kardiner described in 1941. As the DSM-III process unfolded, there were numerous committee meetings and presentations at conventions of the American Psychiatric Association (APA), culminating in the inclusion of PTSD in the DSM-III (APA, 1980). All the different syndromes – 'the rape trauma syndrome', 'the battered woman syndrome', 'the Vietnam veterans syndrome', and 'the abused child syndrome' – were subsumed under this new diagnosis. However, all of these different syndromes originally had been described with considerable variations from the eventual definition of PTSD.

The DSM-III PTSD diagnosis was not a result of careful factor-analytic studies of the symptom picture of people suffering from 'traumatic neuroses', but a compilation of symptoms that were arrived at on the basis of literature searches, scrutiny of clinical records, and a thoughtful political process. Only later was the relevance of PTSD as a diagnostic classification subjected to closer scrutiny, and both its advantages and limitations more fully explored. Scientific field trials were not conducted until the PTSD diagnosis was reconsidered for the DSM-IV (1994) and most of the results of those trials were tabled for further exploration.

As part of the DSM-III process, another group of researchers and clinical psychiatrists created a diagnostic system for dissociative disorders, without any known communication with the PTSD work group. Initially, there simply seems to have been no awareness of the relation between dissociation and trauma, and an entirely separate classification for the dissociative disorders was set up. Once these two subcommittees came to understand that they were essentially entrusted

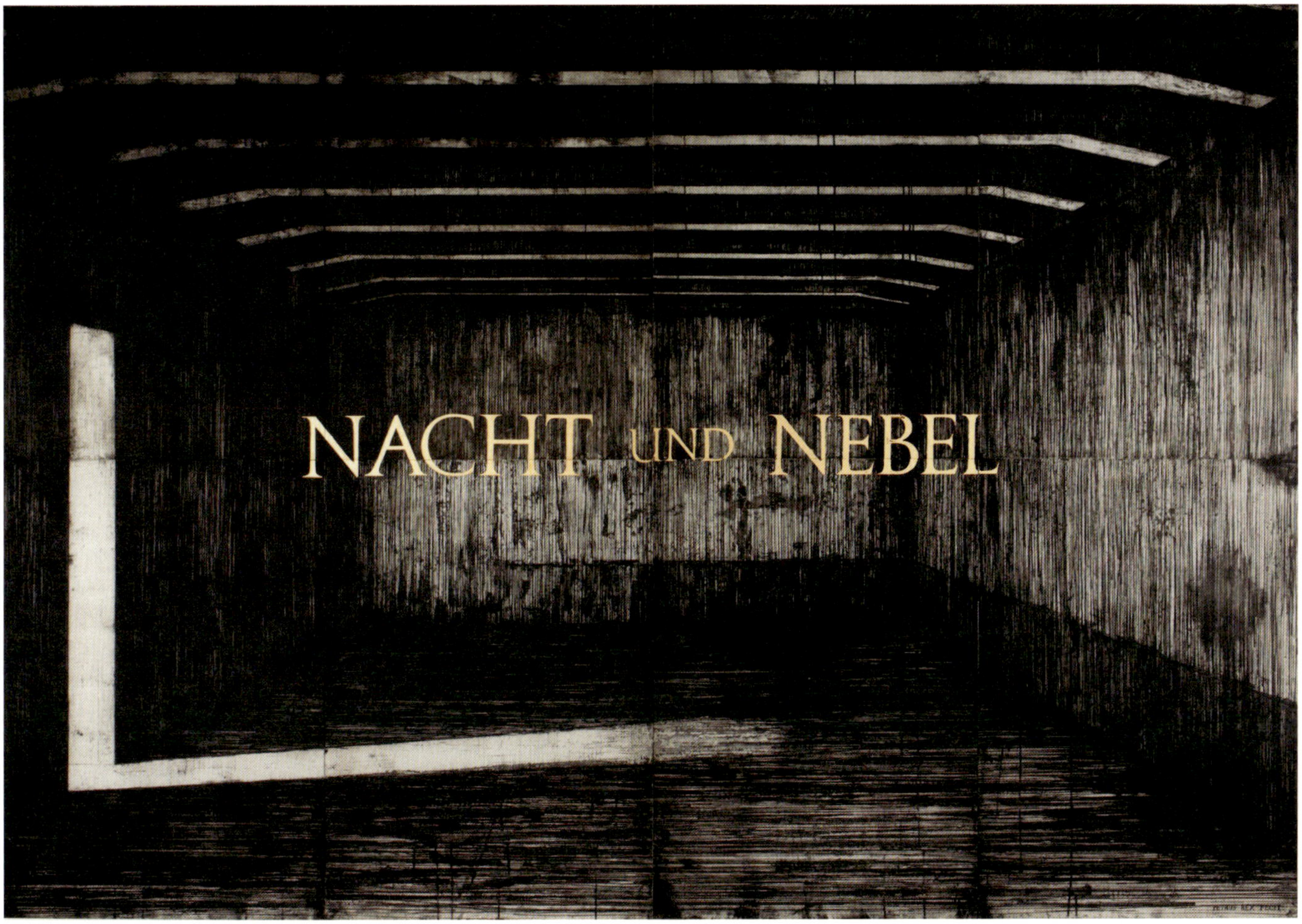

With *Eurazië* Peter De Koninck (1963) creates a series of images about the European history of the 20th century. De Koninck is always inspired by architecture. For each historic event, the artist seeks an architectural antecedent. For instance, for *Nacht und Nebel*, he ended up - via the history of transit camp Westerbork in the Netherlands - at the empty interior of the gas chamber at Auschwitz. What is remarkable about De Koninck's work is the size, bringing together several smaller etchings. Each piece is unique and etched in three layers. Unlike normal etchings, these cannot be reproduced. It is a technical task with a lengthy process that requires considerable patience and precision, but creates greater stratification and depth.
Peter De Koninck, **Nacht und Nebel**, 1993, etching, printed on Zerkall 450 gr, marouflaged on panel. Artist's collection, Antwerp

with creating diagnostic systems of overlapping phenomena, there were several attempts to merge both the subcommittees and the diagnostic categories. However, their unanimous recommendation to combine the two groups and to create a broader diagnostic system were tabled by both the DSM-III-R and the DSM-IV Task Forces.

In the United States in the mid-1970s, four authors made critical linkages between the trauma of war and the trauma's of civilian life. Mardi Horowitz's (1978) *Stress Response Syndromes* built a model for effective psychotherapy of acute life-threatening experiences. Building on Erich Lindemann's (1944) observations after the fire at the Cocoanut Grove nightclub in Boston, Horowitz defined the biphasic responses to trauma – the alternating phases of intrusion and numbing (which do not alternate, but coexist) – and presented a systematic dynamic psychotherapy for acute trauma. Lenore Terr introduced a developmental focus on the effects of trauma on psychological functioning when she started to publish her research on the children involved in a school bus kidnapping in Chowchilla, California. Henry Krystal's paper (1978) *Trauma and Affects* spelled out the effect of trauma on the capacity to verbalize inner experience, as well as the resulting somatisation and impairment of symbolic functioning. Charles Figley (1978), a Vietnam combat veteran, edited the first significant book on Vietnam war trauma. Most of these publications appeared too late for inclusion in the DSM-III definition of PTSD, but the revised DSM-III-R definition (1987) incorporated much of his work.

PROGRESS SINCE 1980

In this text, we survey the explosion of scientific research on, and clinical understanding of, many aspects of human traumatisation since 1980. This work reflects a rapidly evolving knowledge base and the discovery of often surprising new insights into the problems that vexed our predecessors. During this time, a great many basic and clinical researchers have devoted their professional lives to the study and treatment of psychological trauma. Presently there exists at least one journal exclusively devoted to the study of psychological trauma, the *Journal of Traumatic Stress*. Another, *Dissociation*, is devoted to specialized issues regarding that topic; a number of other peer-reviewed journals, including *Child Abuse* and *Developmental Psychopathology*, focus exclusively on traumatised children. Starting in 1985, professional organizations focusing on the study of the effects of trauma on children and adults were founded in Europe, Australia, the United States, South Africa, and Israel. In the United States, the National Institute of Mental Health founded a Violence and Traumatic Stress branch.

CONCLUSIONS

Perhaps the most important lesson from the history of psychological trauma is the intimate connection between cultural, social, historical, and political conditions on the one hand, and the ways that people approach traumatic stress on the other. Traumatic neurosis seems to be an 'episodic' illness, in which, for better or worse, psychiatric explanations and theories reflect the spirit of the age. History demonstrates that psychiatry is imbedded in social forces, possibly more so than any other branch of medicine. These cultural forces include the status of women and children, patriotic and financial consideration, legal processes, traditions about works' compensation, and other economic and political processes.

Psychiatry's amnesia about the importance of psychic trauma has taken the strange form of a 'repetition compulsion'. Because of periodic denials about the reality of trauma's effects on the human soma and psyche, hard-earned knowledge had been repeatedly lost and subsequently rediscovered *de nova*. In some ways the attitudes of health care personnel have closely paralleled those of the public at large, though generally they have lagged behind. Whereas compassionate lay observers have always recognized that extreme life experiences can cause psychiatric illnesses, the medical profession has been capable of maintaining decades of denial about the reality of psychic trauma. Many pioneers in the area of PTSD have been sustained in their lonely pursuits by their own firsthand experiences with psychic trauma. This is true both for those who have studied war trauma and for investigators of domestic abuse and violence.

Throughout the last century, a few professional 'outliers' have worked on lifting psychiatry's amnesia about the importance of psychic trauma. However, it has taken the massive traumas of war to break the denial temporarily. The most recent resurgence of awareness started in the 1970s. As could be expected during a period following massive denial, some enthusiasts came to inflate the concept of trauma, and found it in the overarching explanation for all psychic ills of humankind. Psychiatry is a field of fashions; dominant schools of thought, therapist ideology, and the charisma of particular clinicians have always had a powerful impact on developing untenable biases. Too often, these have led to acrimonious polarizations within the profession, at the expense of good patient care.

In psychiatry, each generation seems to have a need to formulate psychological phenomena in a new language – to find a contemporary voice, in keeping with the political tenor of the times. This may not be so serious, as long as the true nature of the phenomena is understood and communicated. However, though this continual reinvention of the psychological wheel may make for interesting careers, it does not foster a solid accumulation of knowledge or the development of an effective treatment repertoire.

Is there yet a risk that the recognition of psychic trauma and its consequences will again be denied? A hundred years of research have shown that patients often cannot remember, and instead re-enact their dramas in interpersonal misery. The professionals attending to these patients have had similar problems with remembering the past, and thrice in this century have drawn a blank over the hard-earned lessons. It is not likely that these amnesias and dissociations will be things of the past; they are likely to continue as long as we physicians and psychologists are faced with human breakdown in the face of overwhelming stress, which flies in the face of our inherent hubris of imagining ourselves as masters of our own fate, and as long as we need to hide from the intolerable reality of 'man's inhumanity to man'.

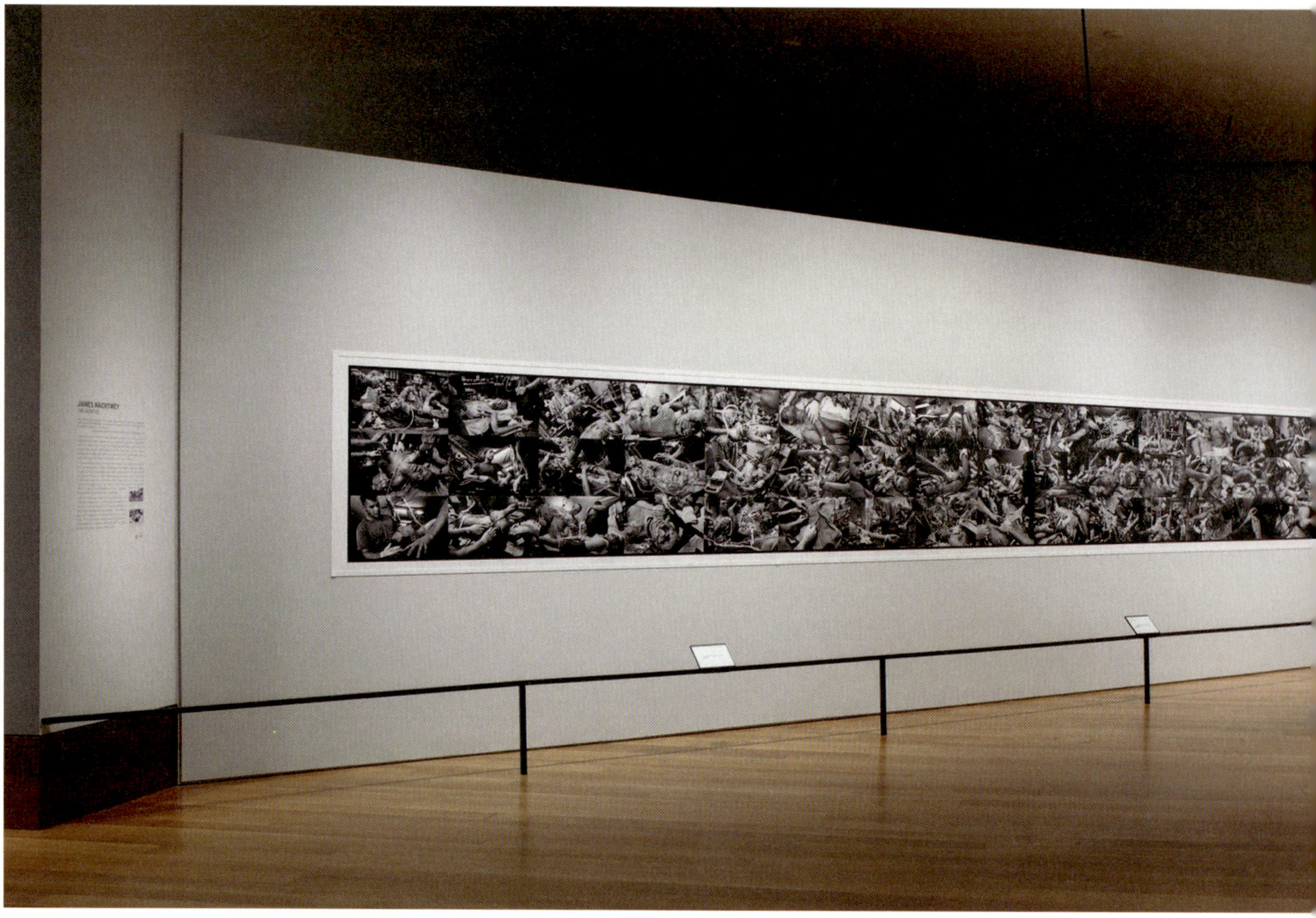

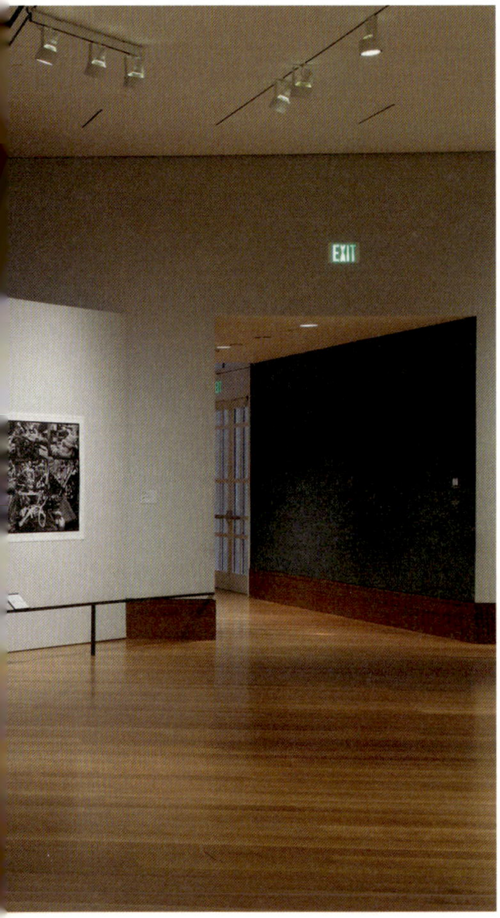

The Sacrifice was photographed in 2006 in Iraq, where I spent more than two months documenting war medicine at American combat field hospitals and trauma centers throughout the country. Single images did not convey the immediacy and intensity of the chaos and carnage I witnessed as teams of military doctors and nurses urgently attended to catastrophic wounds endured by combatants, both American and Iraqi, as well as Iraqi civilians. (Wounded enemy combatants were also given the same care in the same facilities.)

In order to give a better sense of the frantic action, as I became virtually part of the medical teams, I decided to make a large, composite installation, which viewers could experience in a non-linear, almost cinematic manner, their eyes moving from image to image, fixing on a certain moment almost at random, then shifting to another as they move, back and forth, along the length of the installation. I photographed quickly and spontaneously, placing the camera where it would take viewers directly inside the action.

The title refers to the sacrifices combatants are asked to make by their countries, and that civilians have forced upon them in wars with no front lines, where violence is purposely brought right where people live. Many of the images also suggest ancient rites of human sacrifice to appease angry gods.

At the end of 2003 I was wounded when a hand grenade exploded in the humvee in which I was accompanying a platoon of U.S. soldiers on patrol in the most hostile part of Baghdad. My colleague, Michael Weisskopf, attempted to throw the grenade out of the humvee, but it exploded as soon as he touched it, and his right hand was vaporized. He and I were medevaced by Blackhawk helicopter to the same military trauma center I would return to photograph two years later, in a kind of through-the-looking-glass experience.

James Nachtwey, **The Sacrifice**, 2006, photo installation. © James Nachtwey

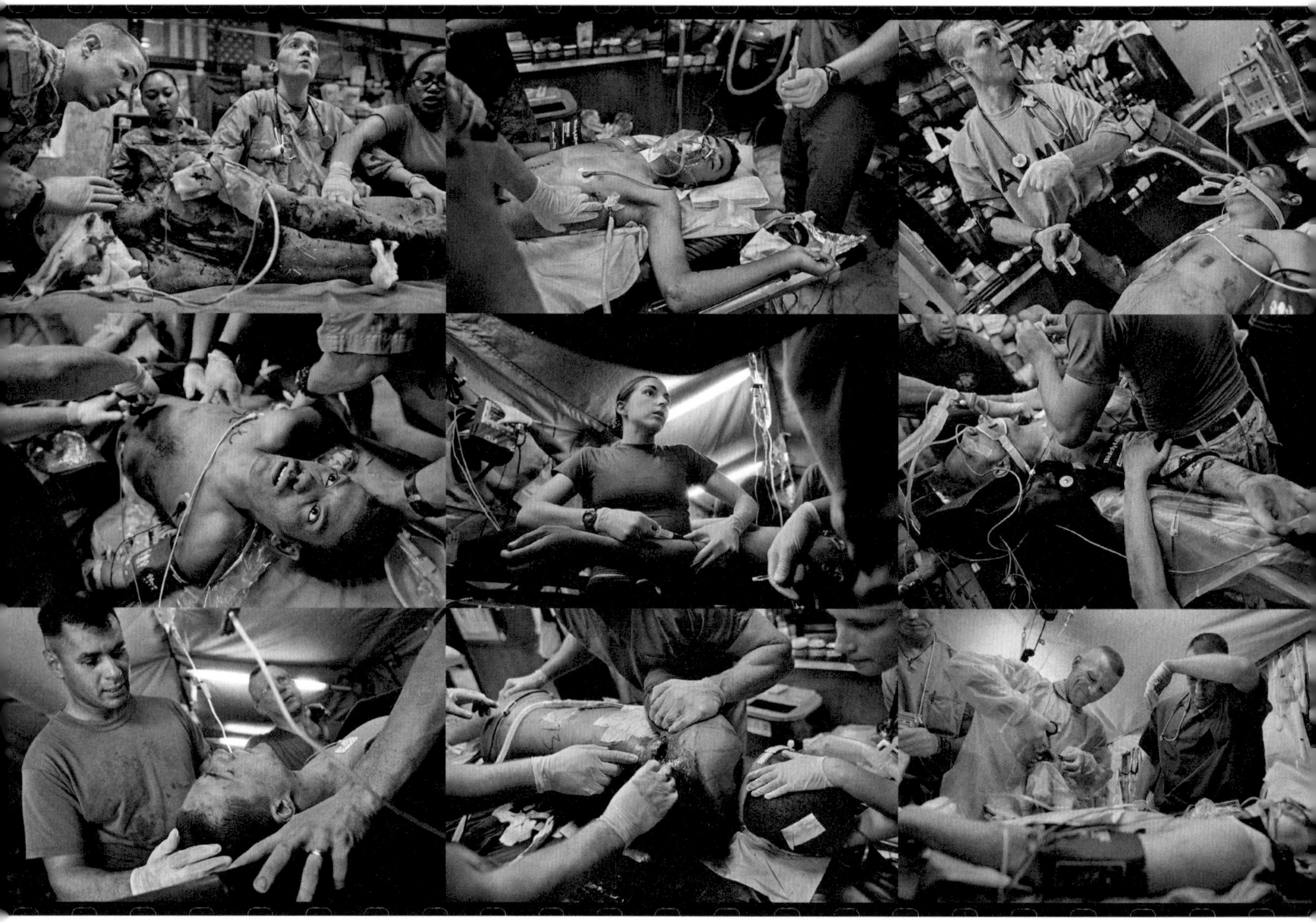

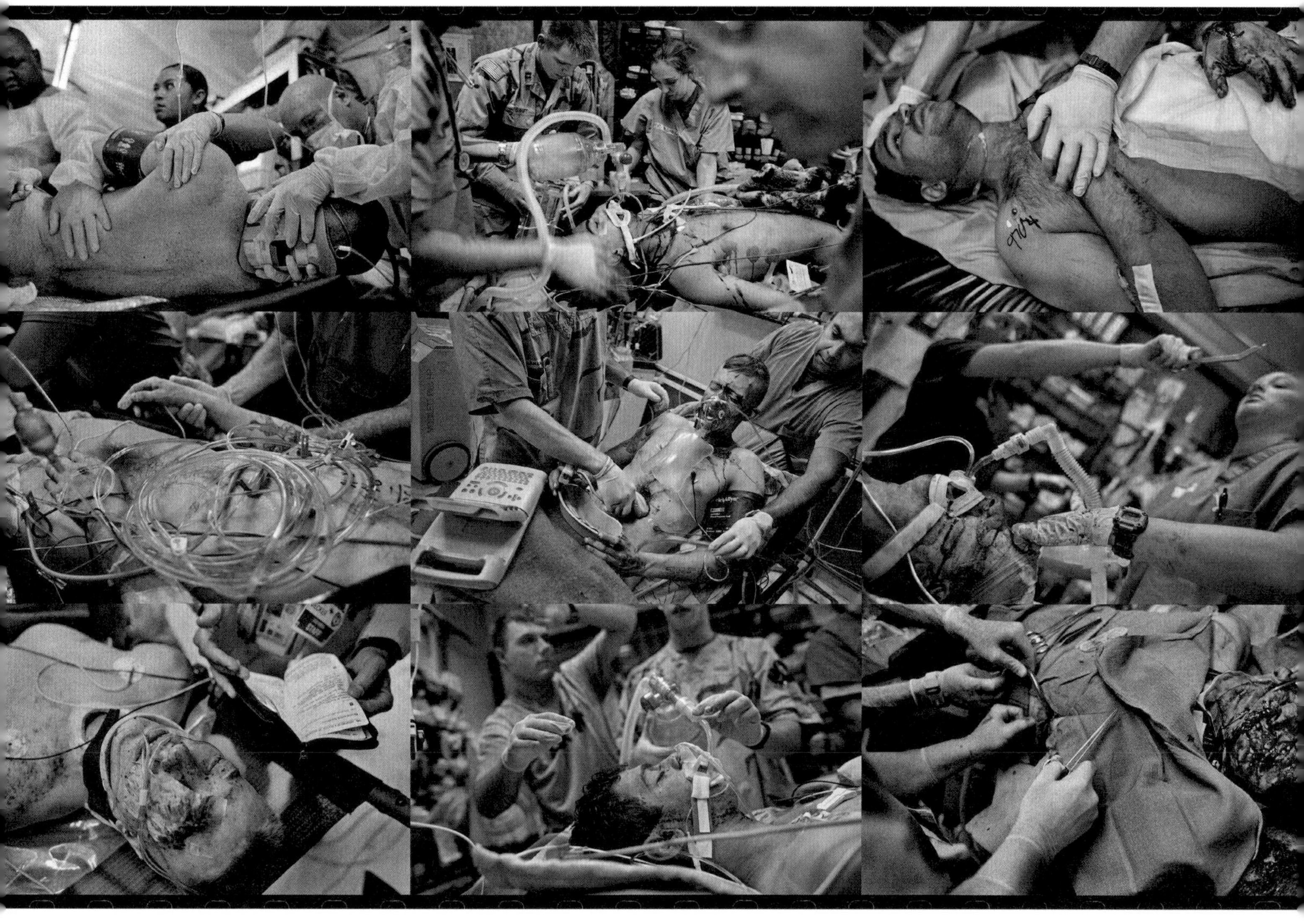

James Nachtwey, **The Sacrifice**, 2006, photo installation (detail). © James Nachtwey

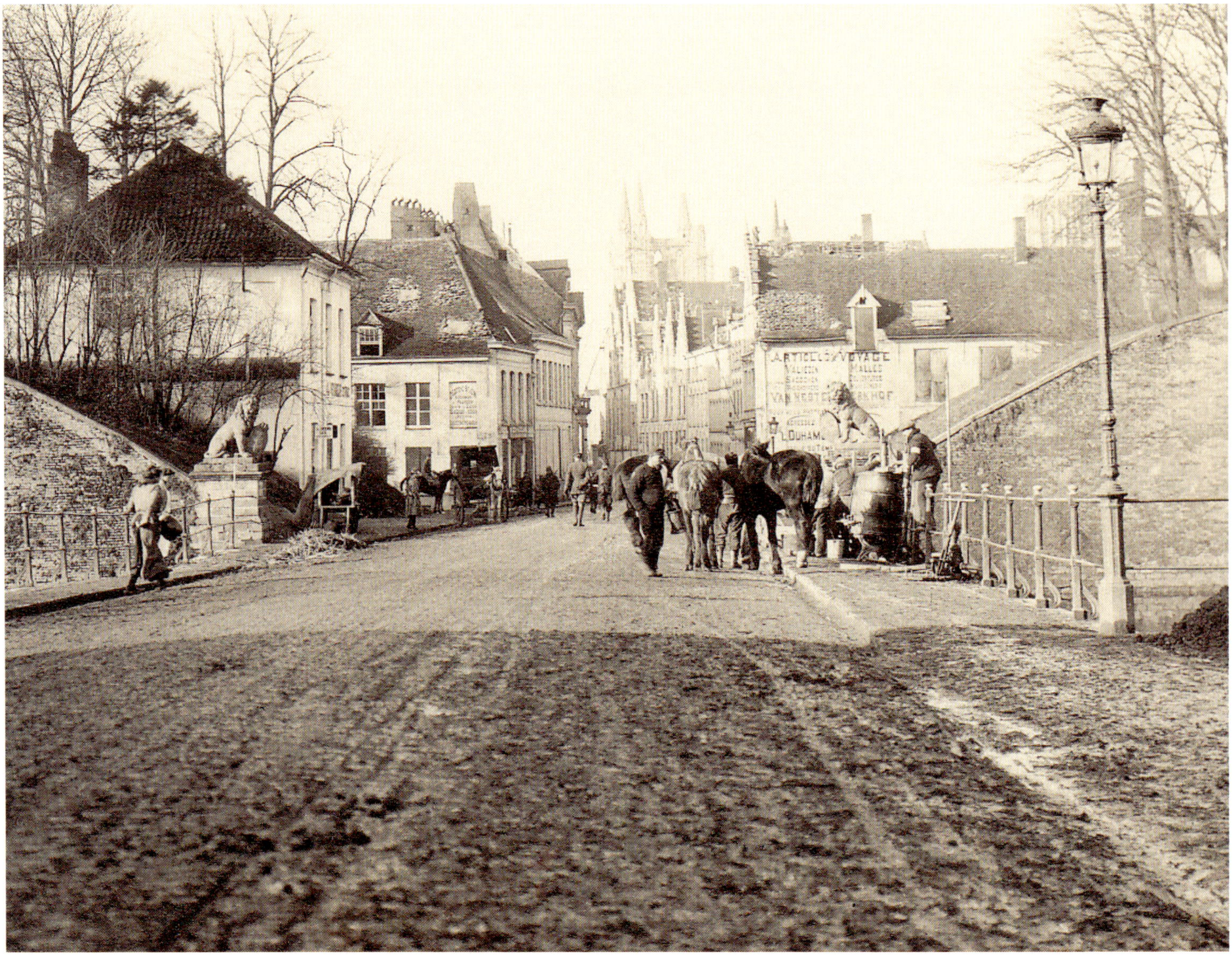
VOYAGE
MALLES
L. DUHAM

DOMINIEK DENDOOVEN

The Friends' Ambulance Unit

Medical Assistance Provided to the Civilian Population during the First World War

In the reporting of contemporary armed conflicts, the medical assistance received by the local population is afforded considerable attention; by contrast, this topic is almost entirely absent from literature about the First World War. One of the better-known aid organisations at the time was the Friends' Ambulance Unit, which operated chiefly in Ypres and its environs during the first year of the war.

This extraordinary group was born out of the British Religious Society of Friends – better known as the Quakers. Due to their beliefs, most members of this tolerant but radically pacifist Protestant religious community refused to serve in the army. However, because they wanted to make an active contribution to alleviating the suffering, and because it was believed that the existing military medical services would not be sufficient, a few young Quakers set up a medical aid unit as early as August 1914. The key protagonist was Philip John Baker (known as P.J Noel-Baker from June 1915 onwards). He was a young academic and athlete who, in 1959, after a career encompassing such roles as government minister, Labour Party chairman and diplomat, was awarded the Nobel Peace Prize for his lifelong commitment to disarmament. Money and equipment was donated to the ambulance corps by Friends from all over Great Britain, including some rich families such as the chocolate makers Cadbury and Rowntree. In the English village of Jordans – an important centre for the Quakers – a training camp was created where, in September and October 1914, around sixty young men were taught first aid, hygiene and nursing, among other subjects. On 30 October, forty of them, along with three doctors, eight ambulances and a cargo of medical supplies, left for Dunkirk. Initially they called themselves the First Anglo-Belgian Ambulance Unit, but soon rechristened themselves the Friends' Ambulance Unit. The new name was apparently suggested by Geoffrey Winthrop Young, an upper-class mountaineer and adventurer who was working in Belgium between August and October 1914 as the war correspondent for the *Daily News*. In this capacity he had seen with his own eyes how inadequate the medical services were. Young, who was not a Quaker himself, joined the Friends' Ambulance Unit and soon became one of its 'principal officers', leading its unit in Ypres. The quotation marks in the previous sentence are there for a reason: the Quakers had an aversion to hierarchies and so there were no formal ranks in an aid organisation dominated by Quakers. However, leaders were designated and the doctors exercised their natural authority. The members of the Friends' Ambulance Unit were unpaid and wore a uniform that they had to procure at their own expense. Since it had the right contacts in well-to-do circles, the unit was able to work under the flag of the British Red Cross.

On its arrival on the Continent, the Friends' Ambulance Unit made Dunkirk its base, and in November 1914 they turned a villa in Malo-les-Bains into a hospital. In the meantime, after the flooding of the IJzer plain, the Belgian Army had largely pulled back from the conflict, so they had less need for medical assistance. The British Army did not want any non-military medical services at the front, but the French welcomed the help offered by the Friends' Ambulance Unit with open arms. At first, with a medical base serving the famous 87th *Division d'Infanterie Territoriale* in Woesten, various groups within the Friends' Ambulance Unit formed an active part of the French medical evacuation chains. Under

The Menin Gate in Ypres in March 1915, photographed by Geoffrey Winthrop Young of the Friends' Ambulance Unit. Several French soldiers halt in front of the barrels that provided the population with fresh drinking water. In the background we see the already severely damaged belfry. Photo, In Flanders Fields Museum, Ypres

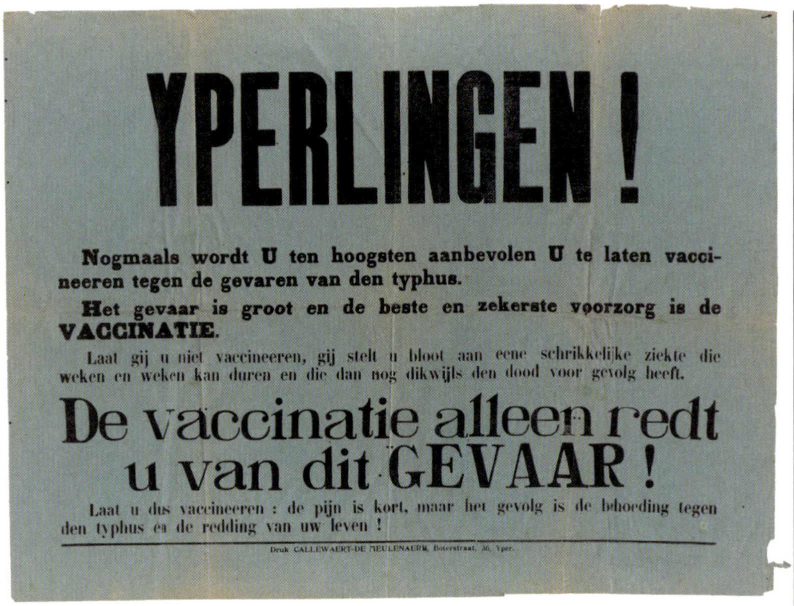
YPERLINGEN !

Nogmaals wordt U ten hoogsten aanbevolen U te laten vaccineeren tegen de gevaren van den typhus.

Het gevaar is groot en de beste en zekerste voorzorg is de VACCINATIE.

Laat gij u niet vaccineeren, gij stelt u bloot aan eene schrikkelijke ziekte die weken en weken kan duren en die dan nog dikwijls den dood voor gevolg heeft.

De vaccinatie alleen redt u van dit GEVAAR !

Laat u dus vaccineeren : de pijn is kort, maar het gevolg is de behoeding tegen den typhus en de redding van uw leven !

Druk CALLEWAERT-DE MEULENAERE, Boterstraat, 36, Yper.

Poster *'Yperlingen'*, an appeal to the population to have themselves inoculated against typhoid. Ypres, March 1915. Photo, In Flanders Fields Museum, Ypres

the name *Sections Sanitaires Anglaises*, they went on to assist the French Army for almost the entire duration of the war, particularly in Nieuwpoort and Ypres.

However, it was in another area that the Friends' Ambulance Unit would make a real difference: by providing medical assistance to the war-stricken population of Ypres and its environs. From their base in Woesten, members of the FAU had already been to Ypres numerous times and were aware of the desperate situation there, particularly after the heavy shelling of the town on 22 November 1914. It had made the hospital on the east side of the Market Square (the Onze-Lieve-Vrouwehospitaal) unusable, so the beleaguered town now had no hospital. Since the mayor, the aldermen and most of the members of the board had fled, the population had been left to fend for itself. On 1 December 1914, Camiel Delaere, the priest of St Peter's parish, asked Geoffrey Winthrop Young whether the Friends could take responsibility for setting up a new civilian hospital. The very next day an unused room in the Heilig Hart / Sacre Coeur psychiatric hospital, on the western edge of the town, was equipped for this purpose and ready to admit its first thirty patients. The most important support structure in the city itself was the Lamotte Convent in the Rijselstraat (Lille Street). This was no accident: not only was the convent centrally located and close to the home and the church of Father Delaere, but several of its nuns, including the famous diarist, Sister Marguerite (Emma Boncquet), were already actively involved in providing medical assistance together with the priest. Until the city was evacuated in early May 1915, the local care providers and the Friends' Ambulance Unit worked closely and efficiently together. Once Father Delaere and the well-known freemason Arthur Stoffel united to run the beleaguered city in harmony together as part of a *Comité Provisoire*, or Temporary Committee, the truce of God was complete: the Catholic nuns and the pious Protestant Quakers worked together closely and respectfully. There were many aspects to the work that they did in Ypres. In the Lamotte Convent medicines were given out and at certain times a doctor could be consulted, and he would do home visits afterwards as well. After every shelling, British doctors and paramedics, together with one or more local men and women from the city, would set off to care for the wounded in situ and evacuate them. The dead were recorded. The elderly, children and anyone else who asked were taken out of beleaguered Ypres to safer places. Furthermore, due to the constant shelling, the drinking water facilities had been practically eliminated. The townsfolk had to resort to the unhealthy, stagnant water in the fosses and the canal. In cooperation with a local engineer named Vanderghote, large barrels were placed in four locations in the city, including at the Menin Gate and the Lille Gate, into which the water was pumped. A combination of added chloride of lime and sedimentation made the water clean. Also, both in Ypres and the surrounding villages, powdered chloride was handed out door to door.

One major achievement of the Friends' Ambulance Unit and its Belgian partners was that the typhus epidemic was warded off. The first cases had appeared at the end of 1914, but the epidemic struck with full force from January 1915 onwards. On 5 February 1915, at the request of the British Second Army, the Friends began inoculating the civilian population in the British sector of Ypres. The programme was later extended to the French sector to the north of Ypres. In the city and the region, posters in two languages called upon citizens to come to one of the six – later eleven – inoculation centres. There, the patients were given a card on which information was written about their first injection, and also the day they had to come back for their second jab. This card, signed by the doctor, also served as proof, which was of particularly great importance after the Belgian government made the typhus inoculation compulsory in April 1915. Up to that point, it had not always been easy for the Friends' Ambulance Unit and its Belgian comrades to convince the sometimes stubborn local residents (and refugees) of the importance of being inoculated. From the last week in February 1915 the vaccination campaign was also accompanied by a large-scale "search party": house-to-house visits to see whether there were any typhus sufferers (or other seriously ill patients) living there and, if necessary, taking them to the civilian hospital. The Belgian government even gave the Friends' Ambulance Unit the power to compel any sick residents to be taken to hospital. Anyone who was not sick was urged to get inoculated. During the house-to-house visits the medics also examined the home's hygiene, food supply and drinking water situation. If a typhus sufferer was found, a yellow letter V was painted on the door. As soon as the patient had been taken to the hospital, the V was replaced by an X. Once the house had been disinfected by the division's Sanitary Section, partly with a view to making it somewhere that troops could potentially be lodged, a yellow circle was painted around the X. A record was made of every house, detailing the names of the residents, a description of the situation there, and the measures taken. After Ypres, they moved on to the neighbouring areas: by 22 April 1915 almost 6,000 houses had been inspected, 540 of which had turned out to be infected. In the summer of 1915 a second search party was dispatched, this time organised in Poperinge and led by Belgian doctor Léon Dewulf, in close cooperation with the Belgian government. This second search party conducted by the Friends' Ambulance Unit, which remained active in southern West Flanders until the end of the war under a new name – the Civilian Health and Sanitary Section – was less focused on typhus and much more on the overall health situation among the local population and the refugees.

After the start of the Second Battle of Ypres, and the German gas attack of 22 April 1915, the Sacre Coeur Hospital was evacuated, and once the last residents of Ypres had left the city, the activities of the Friends' Ambulance Unit there came to an end. The centre of their activities was now Poperinge. There, in January 1915, the spacious villa of Judge D'Hondt had been made available and renamed the *Château Elisabeth*. From the outset it was staffed mostly by Belgian nuns and nurses, under the direction of Countesses Marie van den Steen de Jehay and Louise d'Ursel. For the rest of the war, the Elisabeth Hospital remained the biggest civilian hospital behind the front in Ypres, although the Château D'Hondt was abandoned in favour of a field hospital just outside the city in August 1915. The hospital was expanded several times and several annexes were added to it, including in Chateau Couthof in Proven.

It is important to emphasise that the work of the Friends' Ambulance Unit extended far beyond medical matters: they handed out food and clothing to locals and refugees, and milk to new mothers; and they set up lacemaking and sewing workshops to give the local women the opportunity to earn a crust. The Friends also remained closely involved in the Belgian

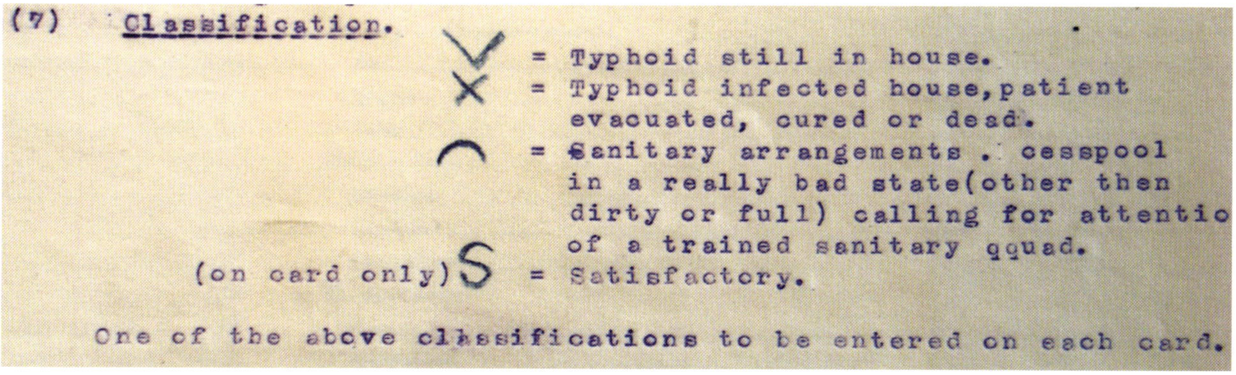
(7) Classification.
V = Typhoid still in house.
X = Typhoid infected house, patient evacuated, cured or dead.
⌒ = Sanitary arrangements . cesspool in a really bad state(other then dirty or full) calling for attentio of a trained sanitary squad.
(on card only) S = Satisfactory.

One of the above classifications to be entered on each card.

Excerpt from a document relating to the search parties who had to track down civilian typhoid sufferers in Ypres and surroundings. The document describes the guidelines to follow, including which marks had to be painted on the doors and identity cards of affected civilians. Photo, General Public Records Office, Brussels (Archives of civil hospitals at the front 1914–1918; dossier number 106)

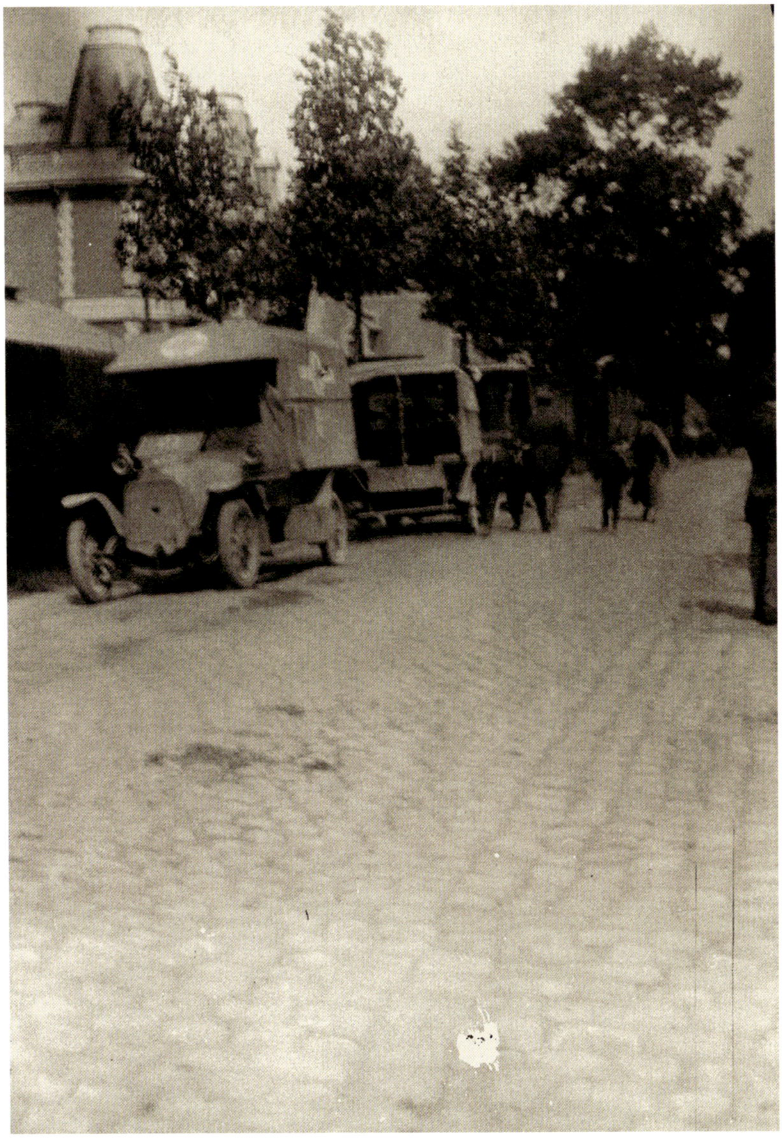

orphanages in Wisques and Wizerne. The close cooperation between the Belgians and the British members of the Friends' Ambulance Unit was formalised in May 1915 with the establishment of the *Aide Civile Belge* – an organisation led by representatives of both groups. The Belgians were gradually able to take on more and more tasks themselves, and so the Friends' Ambulance Unit regarded their work in unoccupied Belgium as complete. Apart from the Civilian Health and Sanitary Section (the second search party), whose members could now speak fluent French and the West Flemish dialect, the Friends' Ambulance Unit finally left the region in May 1916.

However, the withdrawal of medical assistance from the citizens of West Flanders was not the end of the road for the Friends' Ambulance Unit. In northern France and again in Belgium in 1918 they continued to support the local populations in the battle zones. As well as several hospitals in England, their hospitals on the French coast remained open, their ambulances

View of the Château Elisabeth Civil Hospital, which was set up in the villa of Judge D'Hondt in Poperinghe, 1915. Photo, Paul Handford, Birmingham

worked with the French Army, and they were responsible for several hospital trains and hospital ships. By the end of the war the organisation had deployed some 600 men and women overseas. Around 20 of them had perished. Moreover, in 1939 the Friends' Ambulance Unit was reformed and carried on providing medical assistance overseas until 1959. When the Quakers, also known as the Friends Service Council, were awarded the Nobel Peace Prize in 1947 for their 'compassion for others and the desire to help them', the Friends' Ambulance Unit was singled out for special mention. When Philip J. Noel-Baker was awarded the Nobel Peace Prize in 1959, there were two prizes associated with this remarkable aid organisation which did so much to help the war-stricken people in the beleaguered city of Ypres between 1914 and 1915.

LITERATURE

Diary of George Barbour (copy at knowledge centre In Flanders Fields Museum)

F.A.U. Magazine, Nr. 5, 1916

First Report of the Work of the Friends'Ambulance Unit. Oct., 1914-April, 1915. s.l., s.d., 22 p.

Soeur Marguerite (Emma Boncquet),. *Journal d'une Soeur d'Ypres. Octobre 1914 à Mai 1915*, Rouen, Imprimerie de la Vicomté, 1918, 139 p.

Stopford R., *Ypres – Then and Now 1914–1965*, London, Friends Ambulance Unit, 1965, 16 p.

Geldhof J. (ed), *Oorlogsdagboeken over Ieper (1914–1915). Eerste deel. De Dagboeken Delaere, Delahaye en Duflou*, Bruges, Genootschap voor Geschiedenis, 1974, 368 p.

Tatham M. & Miles J.E., *The Friends'Ambulance Unit 1914–1919. A Record*, London, Swathmore Press, 1919, 262 p.

Young G.W., *The Grace of Forgetting*, London, Country Life Ltd, 1953, 352 p.

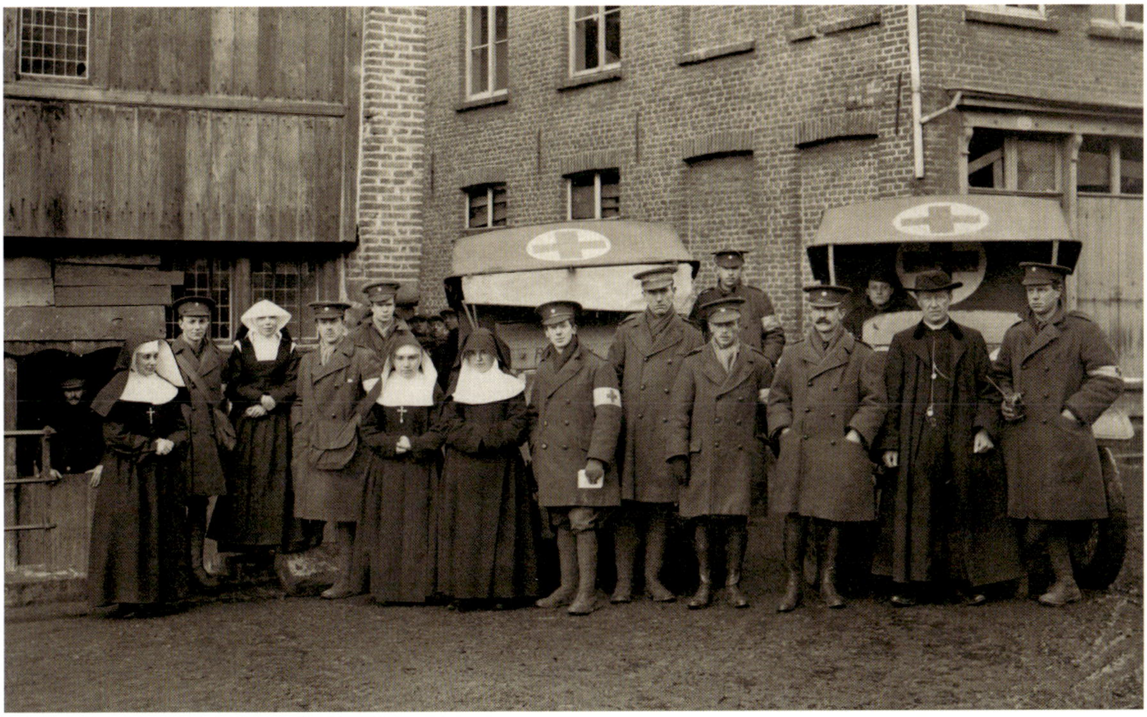

A search party posing in front of the Wooden House in Rijselstraat in Ypres (February-March 1915), with among others, Sister Margriet (far left) and Father Delaere (second from right) next to members of the Friends' Ambulance Unit. The man on the right is holding the paint and brush with which a recognition sign was painted on the doors of typhoid sufferers. Photo, Paul Handford, Birmingham

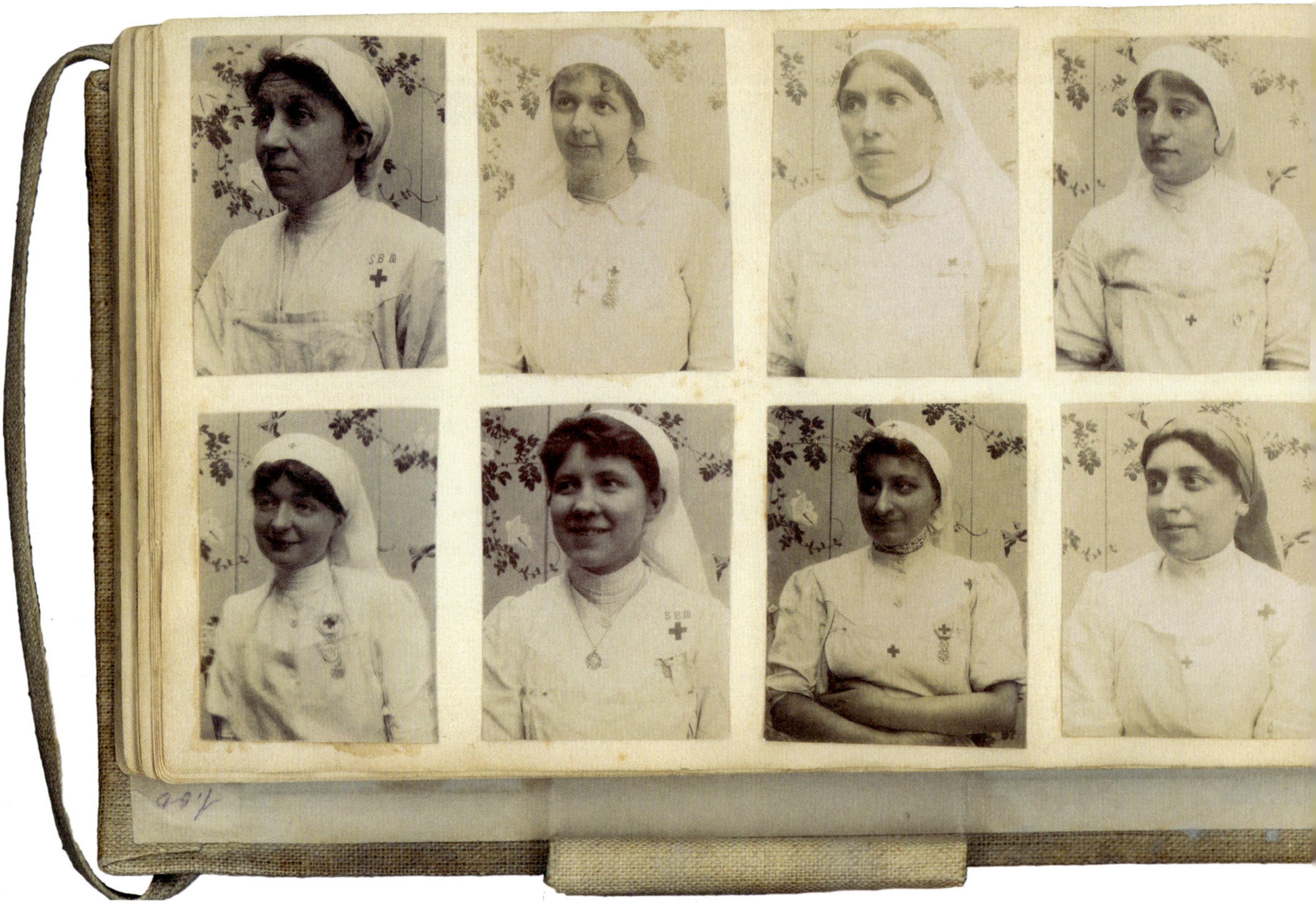

Antwerp teacher Armand Luchies experienced mobile warfare as a stretcher-bearer and then started working at the Belgian Elisabeth hospital in Calais, where he stayed until October 1915. Armand kept a diary in which he wrote about the goings on of hospital life, but also created a photo album, in which he made, among others, a collage of the hospital staff he worked with. Photo, In Flanders Fields Museum, Ypres

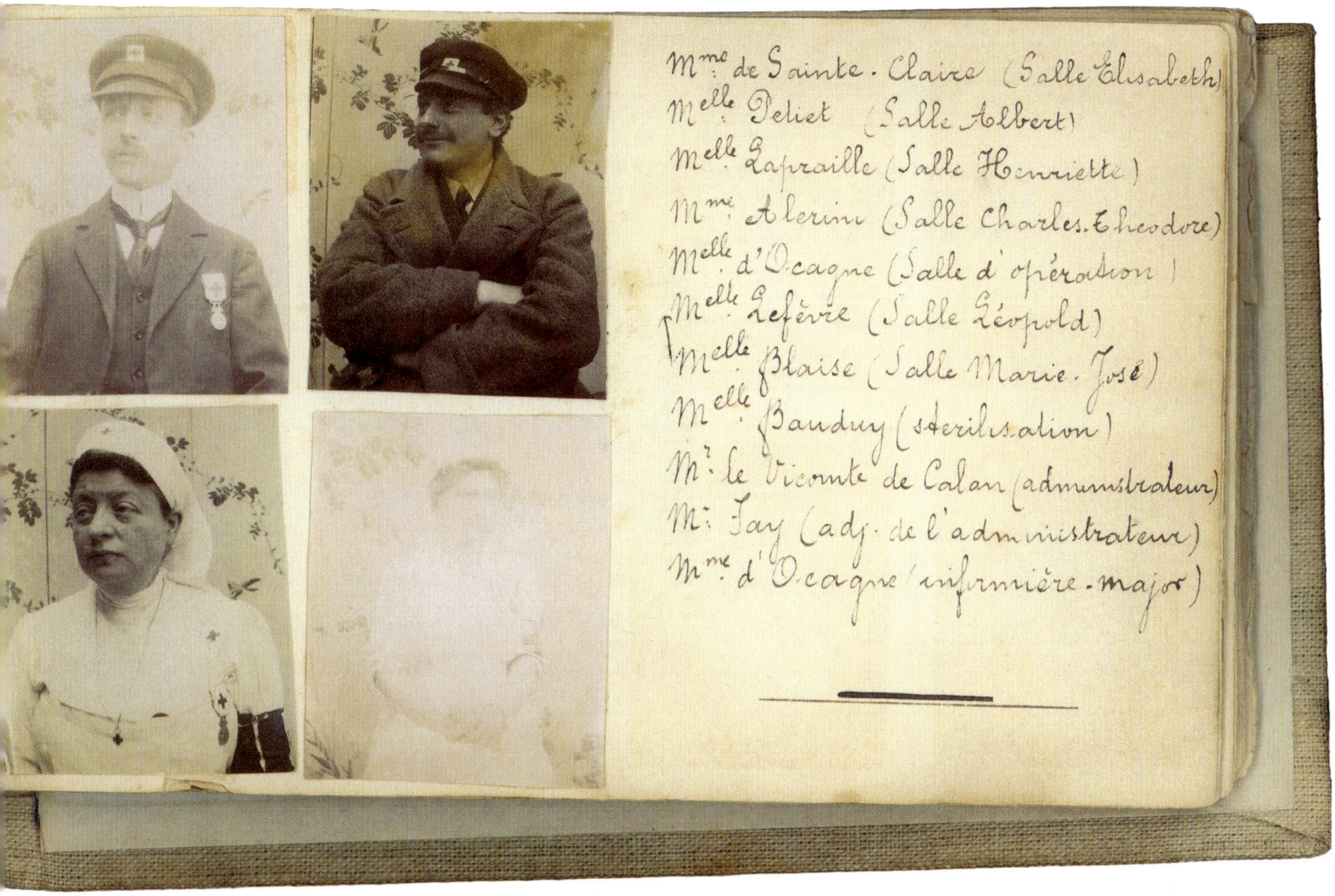
Mme. de Sainte-Claire (Salle Elisabeth)
Melle. Petiet (Salle Albert)
Melle. Lapraille (Salle Henriette)
Mme. Alerini (Salle Charles-Theodore)
Melle. d'Ocagne (Salle d'opération)
Melle. Lefèvre (Salle Léopold)
Melle. Blaise (Salle Marie-José)
Melle. Bauduy (sterilisation)
Mr. le Vicomte de Calan (administrateur)
Mr. Fay (adj. de l'administrateur)
Mme. d'Ocagne (infirmière-major)

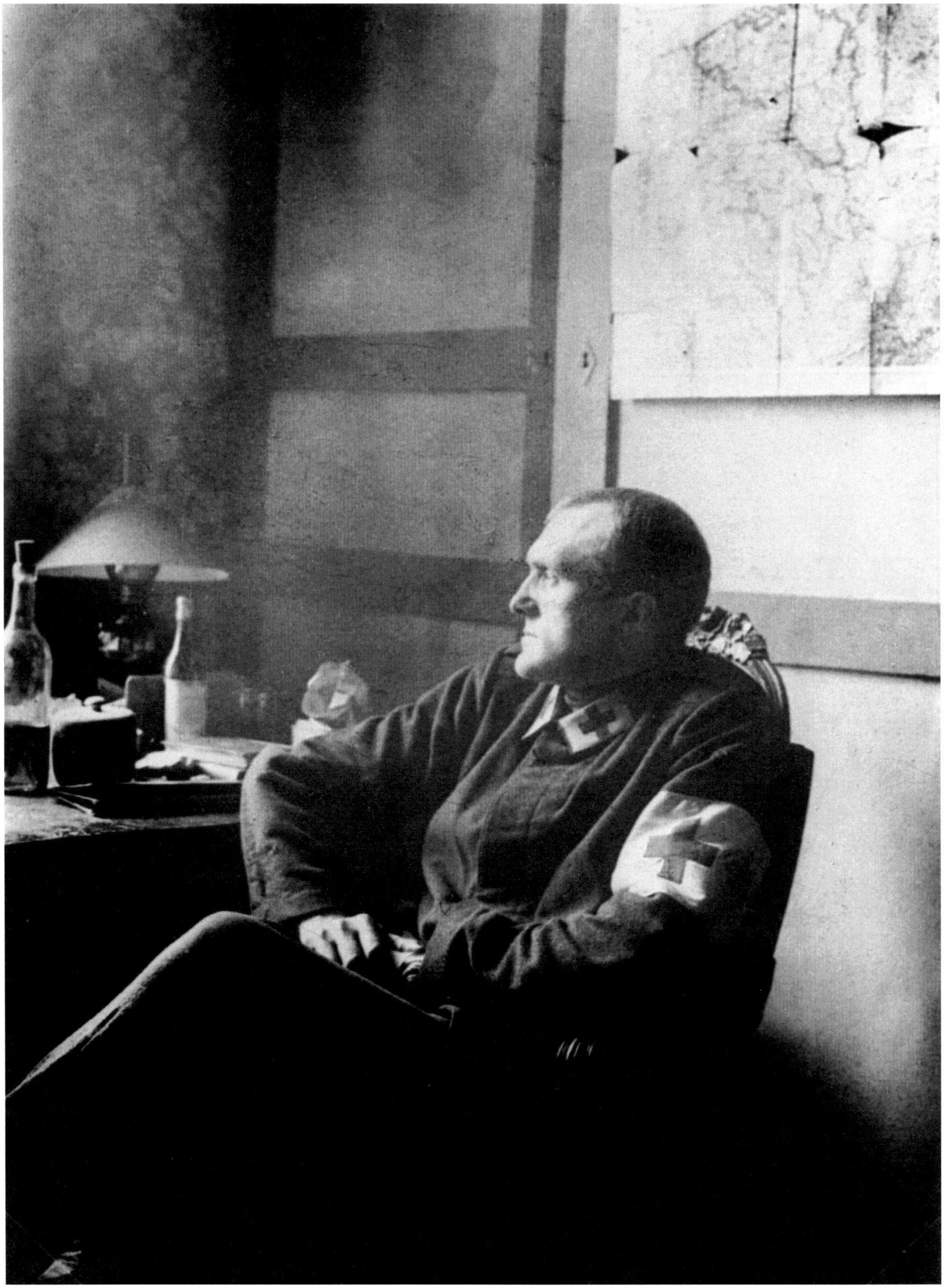

VINCENT VERBRUGGE

Max Beckmann

Or the Resistance of a Hospital Nurse *and* Artist against the Barbarity of the Second Battle of Ypres (April–May 1915)

4 MAY 1915

"There was a truly infernal racket. The air was filled with the shrill whistle of shrapnel and the fierce boom of heavy artillery. Injured people were being brought in all the time. Several poisoned soldiers twisted wildly and hawked heavily. One man had to have his mouth held open wide with a jaw clamp. I saw some incredible things. In the half-dark shelter lay semi-nude blood-smeared men, who were being bandaged up. Their facial expression was grand and heartrending at the same time. A new type of representation of the lashing of Christ."

These impressions were written in a letter by an orderly of the German Red Cross to his wife. The man had volunteered in the Germany Army at the beginning of the war and was assigned to the health services. He spent his time doing hospital work, cleaning the wounds of soldiers, assisting surgeons at the operating table in the field hospital and drawing what he observed. His name was Max Beckmann (1884–1950). Beckmann, who had previously probably been declared unfit for active military service, saw his presence at the front as a continuation of his activities before the war: aesthetic and intellectual reasons prevailed.

From the end of March 1915 Beckmann was encamped in the border town of Wervik. A small town full of German soldiers, with storage areas, depots, field hospitals and troop quarters. Beckmann acted somewhat like a 'stateless' nurse, which blended perfectly with the new quarters he described: Wervik had stopped being a border town: you could go from Wervicq-Sud (in France) to Wervik (in Belgium) and vice versa without customs control, because both Werviks then formed one administrative entity. You heard French and Flemish being spoken mixed up, and in the evening a German music band played at De Steenakker and the cafés were filled with German soldiers who ogled "the fabulous hips of the Wervik women who set them ablaze through hugely erotic fantasies". Beckmann turned out to be an active participant in these events in Wervik. He had always carried his sketchbook with him and put on paper what he saw and felt.

What did a painter aged 31 who was already known in some circles do from the end of March to August 1915 in Wervik? When he was encamped in Roeselare (February 1915) and seemingly did not have any specific function to fulfil, the Head Physician and Major Philalethes Kühn (1870–1937) of the 9th field hospital of the XV Army Corps ordered him to freshen up with frescos the delousing bath of a Wervik field hospital. Thus the bath in the annexes of ribbon weaver Dalle in Wervicq-Sud was given a monumental fresco painted by Beckmann on 1 May 1915. His letters indicate that he was also working in another field hospital and was billeted elsewhere in Wervik. He abandoned his original plan to give it an exotic theme with palm trees, desert images and oases. The moral of the new interpretation of the fresco was clear: each use of painting for relaxation and illusion was abhorrent. Beckmann could not permit any acts of fantasy in times of war. He showed what he saw in Wervik: German soldiers on horseback, infantry soldiers and other marching soldiers, with in the background the monumental gothic church of Wervik, German crosses in the garden of the White Castle of Wervicq-Sud, bombed buildings in Lille and especially portraits of people, from female Wervik

Max Beckmann as a voluntary nurse in German service at the front in Flanders, possibly Wervik, 1915.
Max Beckmann Archiv, Munich

innkeepers to Prof Dr Ferdinand Sauerbruch (1875–1951), the famous surgeon of the XV Army Corps, who operated in the Sint-Jan Hospital in Wervik. Reinhard Spieler calls his drawings from that period examples of "gruesome beauty". Beckmann almost exclusively used the drypoint technique. When the German troops left Wervik in October 1918 they destroyed the wall fresco, but thanks to a photograph in the *Kunst und Künstler* Journal, the fresco is still immortalised. Making the fresco was a challenge for Beckmann that opened up new horizons for his art: "In the afternoon, I drew frescos here for the first time in my life. One of my best experiences. It was as if it had been invented for me. A lot comes out of me when I paint these large surfaces. It's wonderful how nice the colour looks on this limestone... To me the war is a wonder, regardless of how painful it can often be. My art is fed here."

In the Second Battle of Ypres, the war and its consequences harassed Beckmann. He described war as an extreme situation that enabled crawling into the deepest of humanity and realising one's most intimate passions. In the field hospitals where he worked, he saw the misery of soldiers on operating tables; of the dead lying in their coffins, of the gazing, deserted soldiers in dark corridors. In this, Beckmann in a way recognised the true material of an artist.

When we go through Beckmann's production of drawings in Wervik (more than a hundred known drawings), we can only confirm what Helke Lauwaert writes about this: "A whimsical style and the almost disintegration of the figures drawn reveals the psychological desperation of the artist." Professor Buenger adds: "The nudes he drew from models in Wervicq were wilfully exaggerated in a drastically generalised, almost distorting mode, anticipating not only the figures in his later Resurrection but also those in most of his later wartime paintings."[1]

Beckmann's last known letter from Wervik to his wife Minna was dated 12 June 1915. What happened to Beckmann afterwards? We know of a hilly landscape dating 10 August 1915. But after that we have lost all trace of him. On 5 September 1915 he wrote to his wife: "*Für mich ist jeder Tag ein Kampf. Und zwar ein Kampf mit mir selbst und den bösen Traümen, die um*

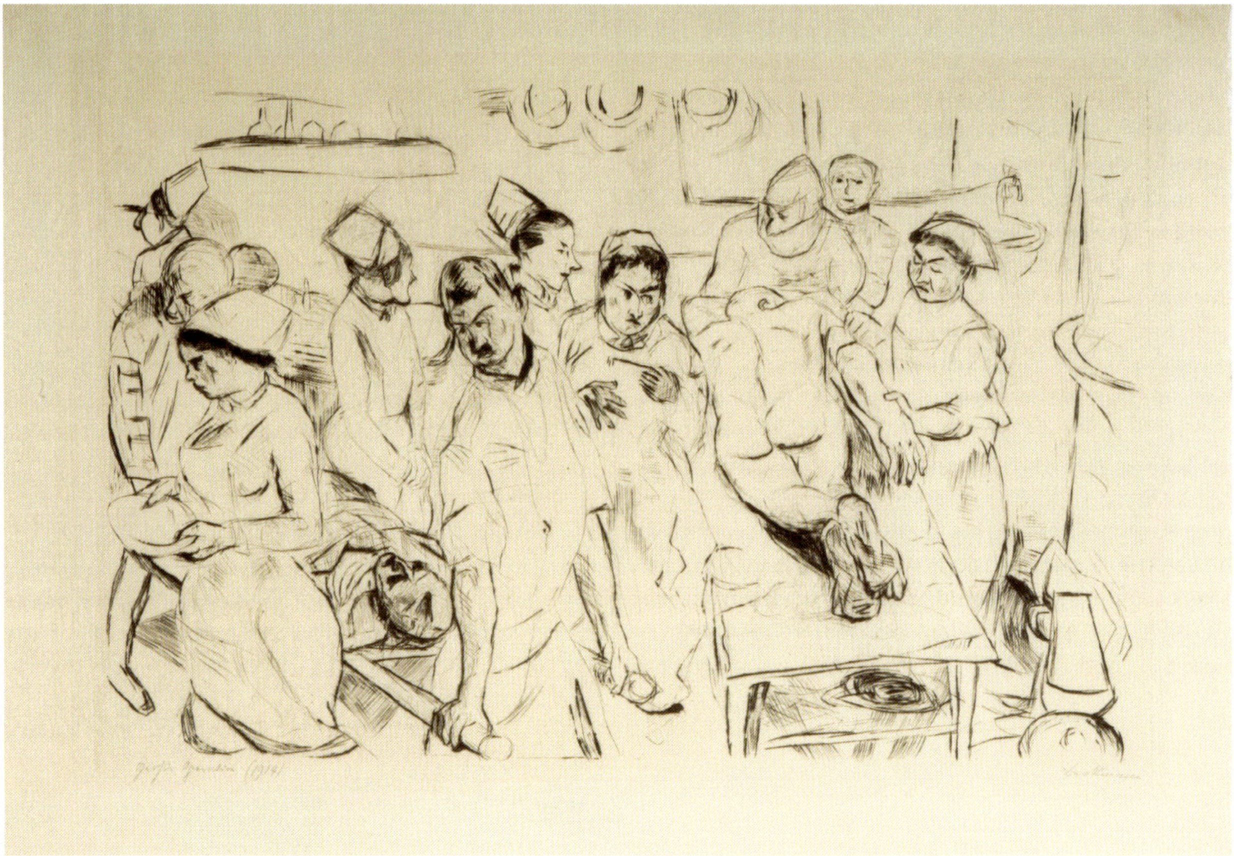

Max Beckmann, **Grosse Operation,** (Gesichter), 1914, drypoint on Japanese paper. Von der Heydt-Museum, Wuppertal

mein Haupt surren wie die Mücken." He was then in Strasburg, far from the front, which he would never see again. Perhaps it had been Doctor Kühn, who swapped Wervik for Strasburg in the summer of 1915 to hold a chair for Social Hygiene, who urged Beckmann to go to Strasburg, where he was active for some time at the Royal Hygiene Institute. In 1917, he was definitively discharged from the army, and as a consequence could no longer work as an assistant nurse.

At the end of his stay in Wervik, Beckmann had signalled that it weighed so heavily on him that he could no longer paint. In Strasburg he began to paint his well-known *Selbstbildnis als Krankenpfleger (Self-portrait as Nurse)*. It was said that Beckmann still walked around his studio in his uniform in the early 1920s. It is believed that Beckmann said the following about the painting: "*Ich habe mich sehr damit gequält.*" In this painting, Beckmann portrayed himself as an insecure man, a man without illusions, a man who endured the experiences of war deep inside him. Beckmann himself did not come back to this period of his life until later.

It is characteristic that he never spoke of a mental or physical breakdown in Wervik in the summer of 1915 or earlier. Can we derive anything from his last drawings produced in Wervik? The texture of these drawings is strongly shrunken; his portraits are incomplete and unclearly defined. His figures seem to reflect a collapsing coagulation of anatomic contours. Disorganisation and decay are key here. The man who in the beginning of his Wervik period still "followed the most refined dogfight and airplane shootings while quietly eating an orange," probably broke down mentally and physically in Ypres. In 1916, Beckmann wrote the following, in our opinion, very important words: "I drew them all, the dead, and they probably resent me for this, as they come to visit me..." With the exception of *Sturmangriff* [Assault] in 1916, the war as such was no longer part of his work, although he still sporadically drew returned soldiers in uniform. He apparently did everything to leave the front at Ypres in the summer of 1915. Had he seen enough? Were his exercise books full and could he use this material? Did he want to paint again at all costs, something he could barely do at the front? Or were his 'bad dreams' so dominating that he could even no longer give his beloved art the place he had intended during the conflict, as had he not entrusted his wife with the following: "My will to live has never been as strong as now... By drawing, I protect myself against death and danger."

1 The final part of this quote regards the war-related work Beckmann was still doing in Germany between between 1916 and 1918.

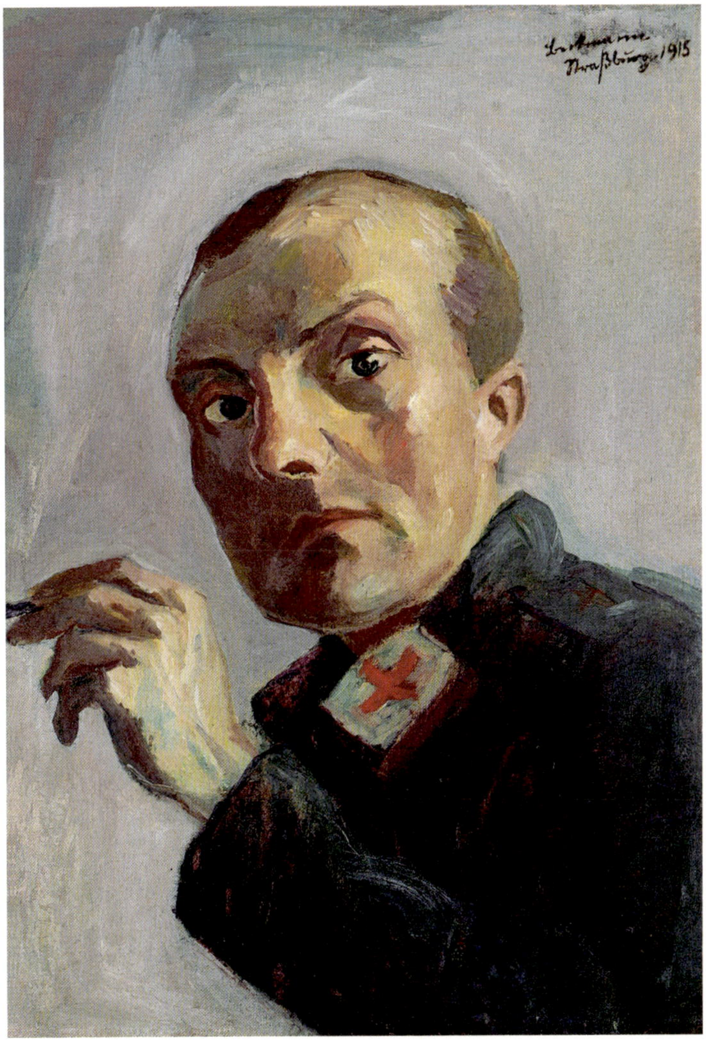

Max Beckmann, **Selbstbildnis als Krankenpfleger**, 1915, oil on canvas. Von der Heydt-Museum, Wuppertal

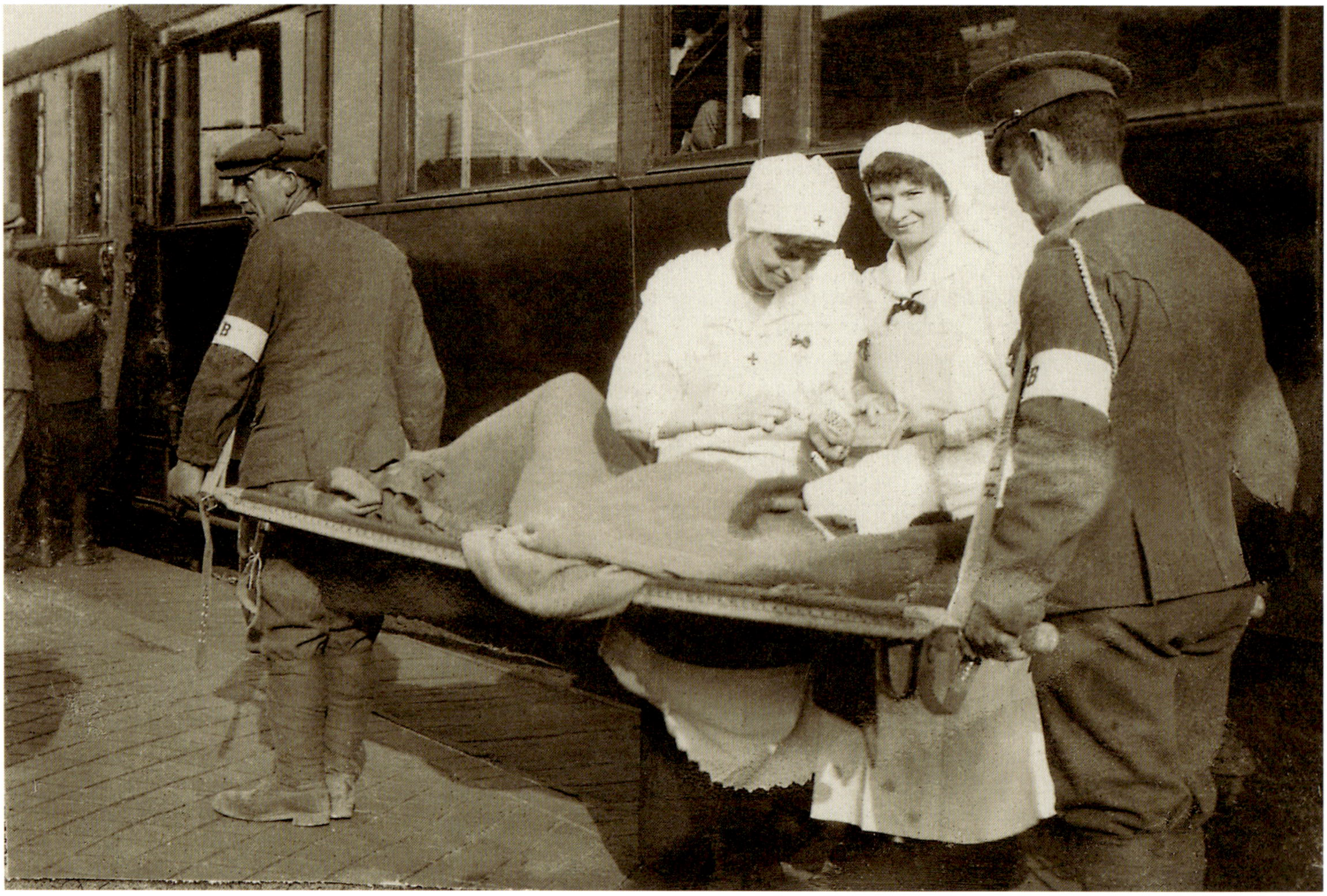

PATRICK LOODTS

Belgian Hospitals in France during 1914–1918

During the Battle of the Yser, the mass evacuation of the wounded by rail to Dunkirk and Calais was the only remedy for the Belgian Army's lack of medical facilities. Calais was quickly overwhelmed by Belgian refugees and wounded soldiers.

For the town, it was not just a question of receiving the soldiers, but of treating them as well. They would be taken off the trains after a 14-hour journey, during which they had been more or less abandoned. There were dead soldiers among them, others delirious from dehydration and fever. Once outside the carriages the wounded and exhausted soldiers found relative comfort in the station's engine house, which had been turned into a 'transit hospital'. Their dressings were changed and they were finally given something to eat and drink.

The evacuation of the wounded soldiers required a logistical effort commensurate with their huge numbers: between 1 November 1914 and 31 December 1915 76,532 wounded soldiers from 527 railway convoys arrived in Calais. The limits of the hospital ships provided by France were quickly revealed: the wounded were suffering from the lack of air and light and the layout, consisting of three stretchers one above the other, made treatment more or less impossible. The town of Calais therefore had to make numerous buildings available to the Belgians so that they could be turned into field hospitals.

Despite the transport of wounded Belgians in enormous numbers to Cherbourg and England, new field hospitals had to be opened in Calais every day. Between 18 October and 1 November, 26 of these hospitals were created in the town. These numbers will give the reader a fair idea of the atmosphere in Calais during the Battle of the Yser. Once the Battle of the Yser was over, the pace at which new field hospitals were created in Calais slowed down, but nevertheless their number continued to increase, and by early 1915 there were 42 in total. From a medical point of view, a field hospital was a place where basic care could be administered to three categories of soldiers: those with diseases, those with minor injuries, and those with serious injuries who could not be moved. All soldiers outside of these categories – more than 20,000 of them – were evacuated to England or to French hospitals, mostly situated in Normandy and Brittany.

However, in December 1914, two field hospitals in Calais were turned into proper hospitals: the Rue du Fort Louis Field Hospital (Dunkirk) and the Elisabeth Field Hospital (Calais). The Rue du Fort Louis Field Hospital was given to the Belgians by the French Medical Corps. Marie Curie equipped it with X-ray facilities, while an American patron who was an ambulance driver for the American Field Service in Paris gave the equipment for an operating theatre. A Belgian military surgeon named Dr Derache carried out 82 operations there but, because the hospital's capacity was so small (30 beds), it was soon dismantled. Another Belgian field hospital in Calais – the Elisabeth Field Hospital – was

Two nurses saying goodbye to an injured person at the platform of Calais. They are giving him some extra cigarettes before he is put on to the train for evacuation to Rennes. Photo, In Flanders Fields Museum, Ypres

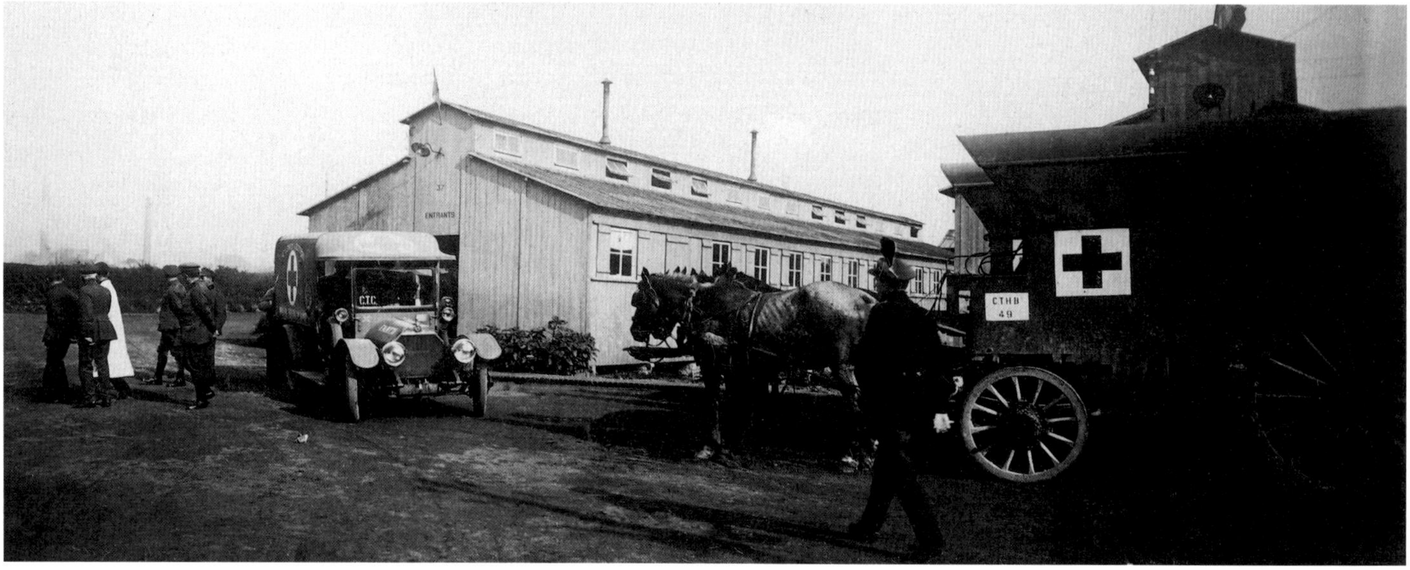

quickly turned into a small, well-equipped hospital thanks to the Duke de Vendôme, the brother-in-law of Belgium's King Albert, who gave the equipment for a laboratory, an electrotherapy and mechanotherapy department, and an X-ray room.

In April 1915, Lieutenant-General Doctor Mélis reorganised the medical service. He increased the number of field hospitals to 25 with the help of the French authorities, who authorised 32 additional hospitals to be created in Brittany where Belgian soldiers could be treated as inpatients. This welcome assistance helped to clear the field hospitals in Calais. However, it quickly became apparent that managing the Belgian wounded spread across so many different French hospitals would be incredibly difficult, if not impossible. In addition – and we might smile about this today – it was thought that French food was not suitable for Belgian soldiers. Therefore, the Belgians soon decided to create their own hospitals. These were situated mostly in Pas-de-Calais, close to the Belgian Army's rear base, and in Normandy and Brittany – regions that could be easily reached from Calais by boat, and where the French hospitals that had treated Belgian soldiers during the Battle of the Yser were located. The reader might be surprised to learn that an enormous number of Belgian hospitals was created in just a few months. This demanded an incredible amount of energy and resourcefulness on the part of the Belgian Medical Corps. This was quite a feat, as you will see from the list below.

In Pas-de-Calais, as well as the Elisabeth Field Hospital, other big hospitals were opened: the Petit-Fort-Philippe Hospital, the Virval-lez-Calais Hospital, and the Porte de Gravelines Hospital. A sister hospital to the Elisabeth Field Hospital was created further away in Cannes – the Cannes Belgian Military Hospital. In Normandy and Brittany there were military hospitals in Mortain, Cherbourg and Saint-Lô (Manche), Villiers-le-Sec and Juhaye-Mondaye (Calvados), which specialised in patients suffering from 'nerves', plus four Broqueville Foundation hospitals in Dinard: Saint-Lunaire, Saint-Jacut de la Mer (Côtes-du-Nord), and Saint-Méen and Châteaugiron (Ile et Vilaines), which specialised in patients described as 'insane'. On the banks of the Seine there was the Anglo-Belgian Hospital which later became the Bonsecours Hospital; it was non-specialist but had a cutting-edge physiotherapy department. In Ligugé (Vienne), a hospital specialising in renal complaints was opened, and in Orival a specialist venereal disease hospital, which treated more than 900 soldiers, 50% of whom had become infected in Paris! Besides all these hospitals, there were four sanatoriums especially for soldiers suffering from pulmonary tuberculosis, in

View of the entrance of a Belgian Military Hospital. A motor ambulance and a horse-drawn ambulance are waiting. Photo, In Flanders Fields Museum, Ypres

Cap Ferrat (Alpes Maritimes), Montpellier (Hérault), Chambéry (Savoie) and Faverges (Haute Savoie). Around 2000 men suffering from tuberculosis were admitted, 12% of whom died. Some of them, who were hospitalised in the Château de Faverges, were prisoners passing through Switzerland. And for incurable or invalid convalescents, specific institutions were created. Convalescents with psychiatric illnesses were sent to the Camp d'Auvours near Champegné (Sarthe), and incurables to the Camp du Ruchard (Indre et Loire) then later to Soligny-la-Trappe (Orne). For invalids, a rehabilitation centre was set up in Port-Villez, and an invalid station in Sainte-Adresse.

By way of example, below are some facts[1] about the history of these hospitals.

THE VALLOIRES HOSPITAL AND DR DETOURNAY'S INITIATIVE

Situated in the Authie Valley, this former abbey was given to the Belgians, who turned it into a convalescent hospital. Today the site in Valloires is open to the public. Dr Detournay's notebooks made for fascinating reading, and enabled me to trace the history of the Belgian hospital in Valloires: Dr Detournay was an extraordinary hospital director. He had the excellent idea of keeping his convalescents as busy as possible, to prevent them from becoming depressed. To this end he set up a small farm and vegetable gardens in the grounds of the abbey. His occupational therapy gave his wounded convalescents such a sense of well-being that he was congratulated by the Chief of Staff. Unfortunately, Dr Detournay was the victim of his own success. The Chief of Staff thought this therapy would be even more effective if applied to the 'nervous' category of patients – those soldiers with various psychiatric disorders. So the 'nervous' patients arrived in large numbers, replacing the convalescing wounded soldiers. The atmosphere in the hospital changed from day to day and the small staff of stretcher-bearers and non-commissioned officers were soon confronted with an unprecedented event in the history of the Medical Corps: a genuine mutiny among the patients! Dr Detournay was forced to seek help from a company of military police to re-establish order.

THE BONSECOURS BELGIAN MILITARY HOSPITAL, A TRAIL-BLAZING HOSPITAL BUILT BY THE BELGIANS IN 1916 WHICH STILL EXISTS TODAY, IN 2013

This hospital was built two kilometres south-east of Rouen, at the Blosseville–Bonsecours hill, and opened on 2 June 1916. It occupied an area of roughly 10 hectares. The pure and invigorating air helped in no small part to make it particularly salubrious. But the most special thing about this hospital is that it is still in operation today, in 2013. Built by the Belgians, led by Dr Deltenre, and handed over to the French authorities after the war, it was not dismantled and became a university hospital. The Belgian hospital was remarkable for its large mechanotherapy and electrotherapy department, an initiative of the Regiment doctor, Dr Waffelaert. Since it was difficult to procure the necessary equipment on the open market, this officer in the Medical Corps had the ingenious idea of getting the wounded soldiers to make it themselves, following his instructions. His work was continued and completed by two doctors – Regiment doctor Marneffe for the mechanotherapy, and Battalion doctor Stouffs for the electrotherapy. Another major innovation was a medical

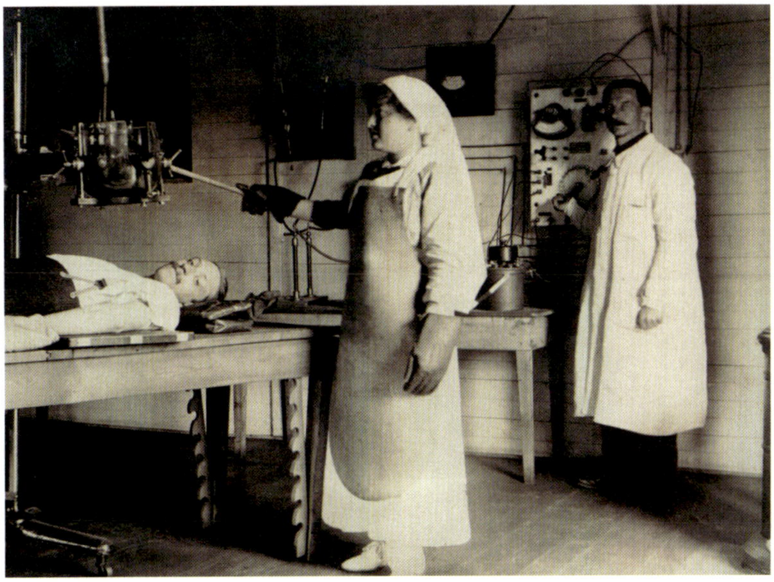

Inside view of the Belgian military hospital in Bourbourg. Nurse Maria Eskens is assisting a doctor during a radiological examination.
Photo, In Flanders Fields Museum, Ypres

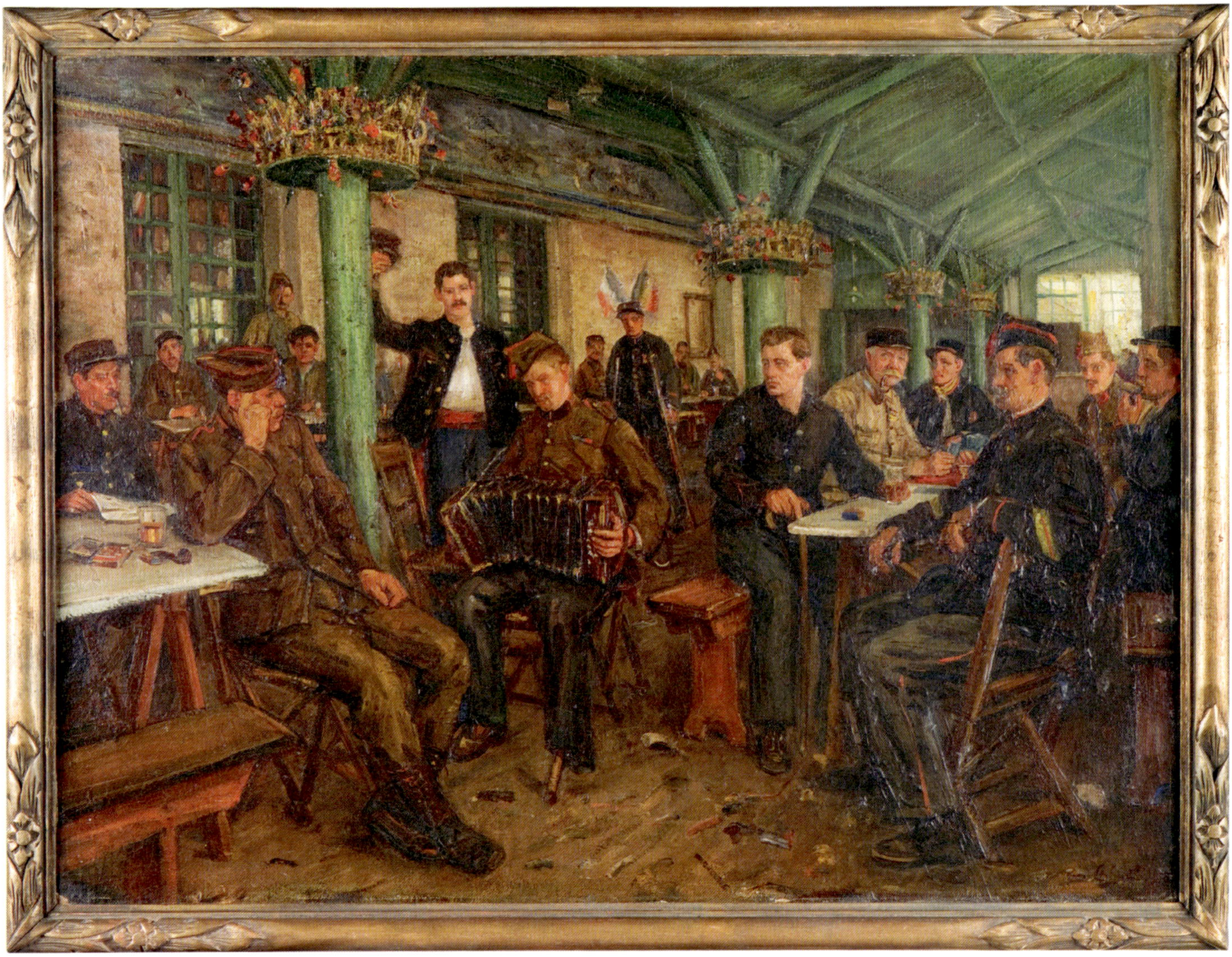

gymnastics department, which ushered in a new medical speciality: physiotherapy. At the time, physiotherapy was not taught in Belgium. This treatment was given to the invalids by 12 gymnastics doctors who had qualified at the Royal Central Institute of Gymnastics in Stockholm, under the leadership of Miss Loveday and subsequently Miss Alund. The medical gymnastics section had a well-equipped pavilion and apparatus built almost entirely in the hospital's workshops. Another uplifting aspect of this story is that doctor Marneffe ended up marrying Miss Loveday.

THE DESPOTIC RULER OF THE MORTAIN HOSPITAL

We have a particularly clear picture of what life was like for the patients at this hospital thanks to the witness account of Sergeant Gustave Groleau[2], who was among their number. The monotonous and gloomy life at this hospital was fortunately interspersed with excursions into the wonderful local countryside, which today is called the Normandie-Maine Regional Nature Park. The hospital was run with an iron fist by a doctor

Inside view of a room in the camp of Port-Villez: recovering Belgian soldiers are listening to the song of an accordion player.
M. Cassel, **Chanson Flamande au camp de mutilés Belges à Port-Villez**, Port-Villez (Yvelines), 1916, oil on canvas. In Flanders Fields Museum, Ypres

Inside view of the pharmacy in the Belgian military hospital of Porte de Gravelines in Calais.
Photo, In Flanders Fields Museum, Ypres

who was much more of a military man than a therapy man. In March 1918 the hospital, a former seminary, was brought under the aegis of the Ocean Surgical Hospital, run by Dr Depage. He was horrified by the state in which he found it. In the wards, the floors were made of straw matting and carpets that had been laid one on top of the other year after year. The sewer system and the lighting had to be completely redone. There was no sterilisation. In charge of this awful establishment was a professional doctor who assumed the dual roles of hospital director and resident commander. To ensure that discipline was maintained at the hospital he demanded that every day at least five wounded soldiers be punished. Dr Depage reacted in his characteristic fashion – very effectively but not militarily – by refusing to wait for official authorisation from the army hierarchy before taking action. At De Panne he had 200 German prisoners at his disposal. He picked 80 who were good at manual labour and had them transported in a single night in a dozen ambulances to Mortain. In less than three weeks the Mortain seminary was transformed into a proper hospital.

THE FOMGAUBAULT HOSPITAL HAD A GUARDIAN ANGEL: GEORGES BONJEAN, THE FATHER OF A FRENCH INFANTRYMAN WHO DIED IN COMBAT

In this hospital, which occupied a former abbey that had been abandoned then bought by the Bonjean family, unlike in Mortain, the wounded soldiers were treated incredibly well. It opened on 18 April 1915, a few days after the German prisoners who had been previously kept there had been removed. The monks' former guest quarters were turned into the hospital offices and the officers' quarters; the 80-metre long nave and sanctuary of the abbey church were used as a dormitory for the wounded, as were the galleries of the cloister; and the west side of the nave was set aside as a refectory. Georges Bonjean had decided that the monks' former refectory, which was fairly spacious, should serve as the wounded soldiers' 'recreation room'. Bonjean carried on living there and was like a father to the wounded Belgian soldiers. He was waiting for news of his soldier

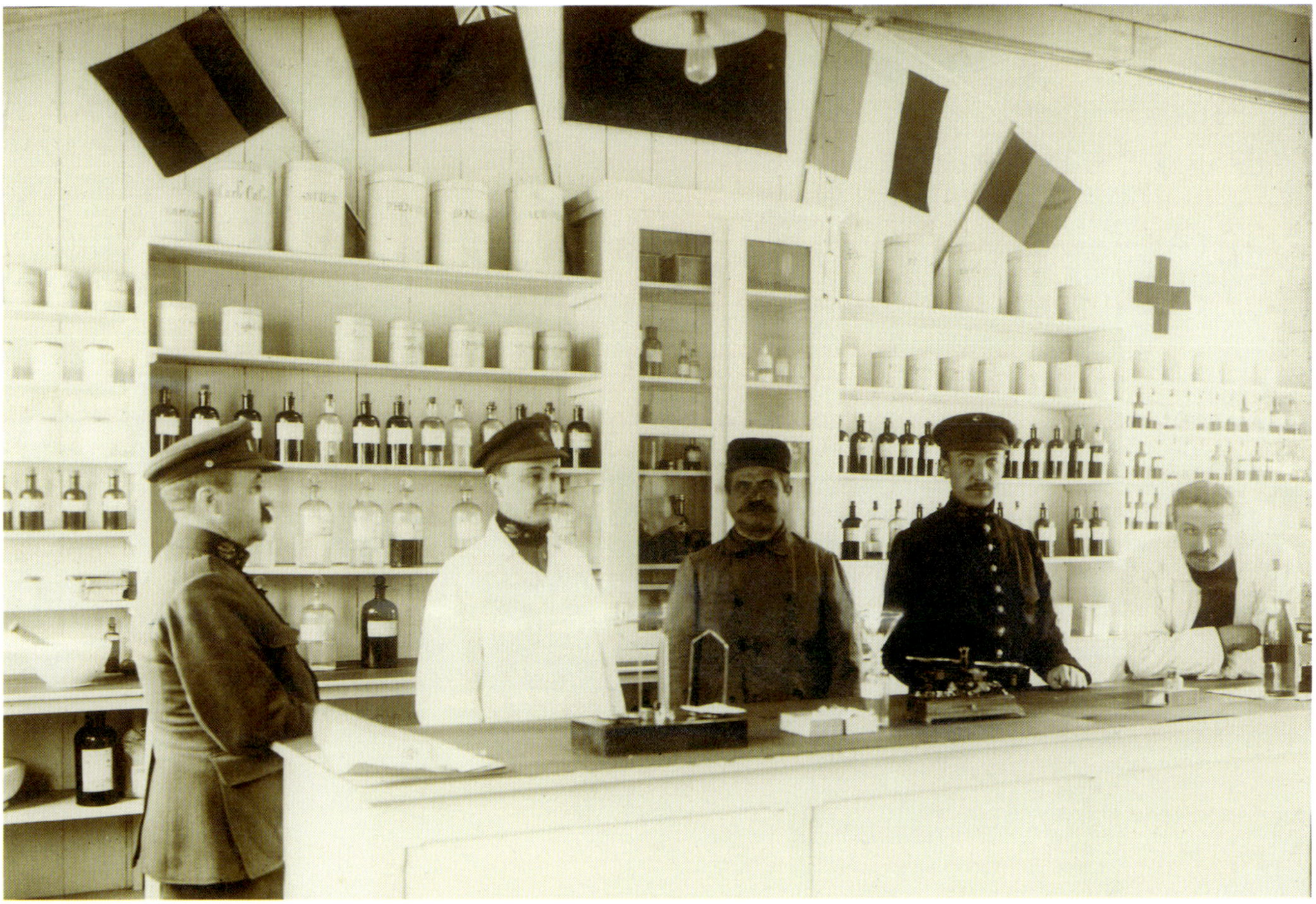

son Louis, whom he in vain hoped would return. No doubt he turned his overwhelming paternal love for his son towards the Belgian soldiers. During the four years that his home was a hospital, Georges Bonjean endeavoured to provide entertainment for his 'guests', in the form of recreational afternoons and concerts.

THE FAITHFUL, CONSOLING FIGURE AT THE MINIHIC CONVALESCENT HOME

As soon as war broke out in August 1914, in an act of patriotism, all five sons of the Count de Broqueville enlisted in the Belgian Army for the duration of the conflict. Robert, the second of the family's six children, was a captain in the artillery. During a skiing trip to Switzerland in 1912, he met Thérèse Marie Laure Bourgeois de Jessaint, born in Paris on 10 December 1886 on the slopes. They were married on 6 May 1913, and she then became the daughter-in-law of the Prime Minister of Belgium. At the very start of the war, Thérèse de Broqueville volunteered to care for the wounded, and became an ambulance driver. She had an innate business sense, and so quite naturally was promoted to assume greater responsibilities. She went on to manage the reception centres for the convalescents, including one in Minihic-sur-Rance, and there are records of the deals she struck with local shopkeepers for the purchase of bread and meat. She lived in Dinard, and came to visit the convalescents in her care every day. In the registers, it says that in June 1915 there were 48 Belgian soldiers at the additional hospital in Minihic-sur-Rance. At the end of the war, in 1918, Thérèse de Broqueville was decorated for services to her country, and made a Chevalier de l'Ordre de Léopold, an extremely high distinction, by King Albert I. Sadly she succumbed to illness in Paris on 8 November 1924, at the age of just 38.

THE GUARDIAN ANGEL OF THE SAINTE-ADRESSE INVALID STATION: FRANÇOIS SCHOLLAERT

Near Le Havre, in Sainte-Adresse, the President of the House of Representatives, Mr Schollaert, was absolutely dedicated to rehabilitating invalids and

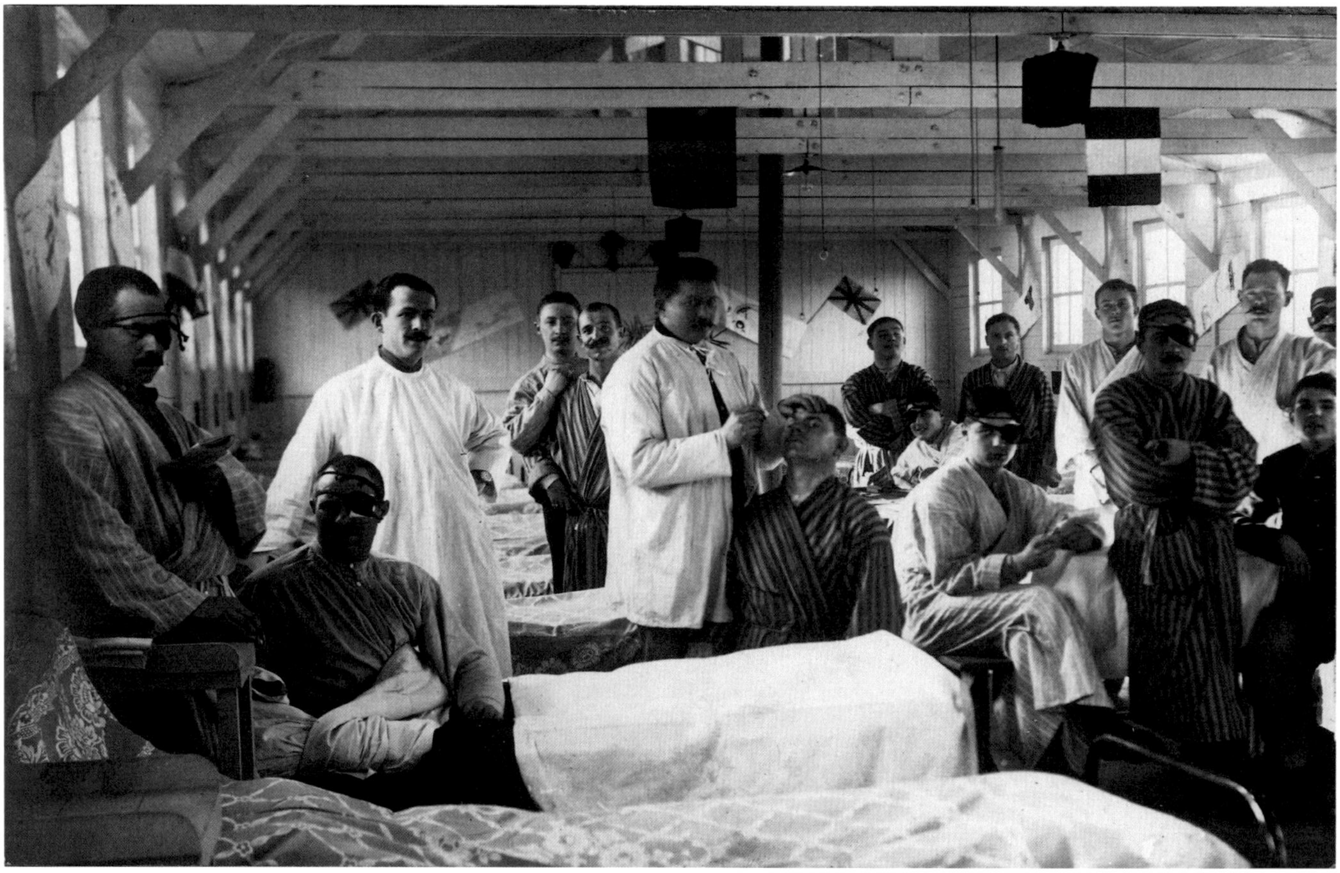

alleviating their suffering. On the day after the Battle of the Yser, some injured Belgian soldiers whose wounds had not properly healed, and had been prematurely discharged from other hospitals amid all the confusion of the melee, went knocking on Mr Schollaert's door. He was so moved by their distress that he asked the Minister of War for the authority to allow them into Sainte-Adresse, a station where they would be given shelter and medical treatment... The invalid station filled up quickly. Mr Schollaert received help from Dr Smets, a practitioner from Schaerbeek who was well known for his kind-heartedness. He quickly organised, in exemplary fashion, mechanotherapy, electrotherapy, hydrotherapy and electro-thermotherapy, and played a key role in the success of the establishment; meanwhile Mr Schollaert started workshops and courses for the soldiers' professional rehabilitation. What is remarkable is that the politician had a close relationship with the invalids, spending a lot of time with them, asking them questions, caring for their needs, taking interest in their progress and promoting improvements in their training. Mr Schollaert's unlimited devotion probably cost him his life. He was taken ill on 29 June 1917, and Mother Saint-Charles, a Belgian nun, was with him when he took his last breath in the Saint-Michel Field Hospital in Le Havre.

This brief description of these few hospitals is of course not complete enough to give us a general overview of all the Belgian military hospitals in France. Each one had its own specialities, its own patron; each had its own reputation, which may have been good or bad, and this was chiefly dependent on the doctors in charge of it. Today, even though they no longer exist, these Belgian hospitals which were spread across France have left the ultimate proof of their existence – in the Belgian military cemeteries.[3] At the rear base in Calais from October 1914 to 1 January 1918, 898 soldiers were buried, most of whom, wounded in combat, did not survive despite the treatment they were given behind the lines. The Belgian cemeteries spread throughout the region were brought together in a vast necropolis at Sainte d'Anne d'Auray in Brittany, which was inaugurated many years later, in 1984.

Inside view of the *Institut Ophtalmique* in the Belgian military hospital in Porte de Gravelines, Calais. As the war progressed, an increasing number of specialised medical institutes were established, also specifically for eye injuries.
Photo, In Flanders Fields Museum, Ypres

NOTES

1 Plenty of additional information about the Belgian hospitals in France can be found at: http://www.1914-1918.be

2 Sergeant Groleau's diary was published in 2009 by the Centre for Regional Research and Documentation, rue Sars-Longchamps, 5, 7100 La Louvière

3 See the list of Belgian military cemeteries in France at: http://1914-1918.be/france_terre_hospitalite.php

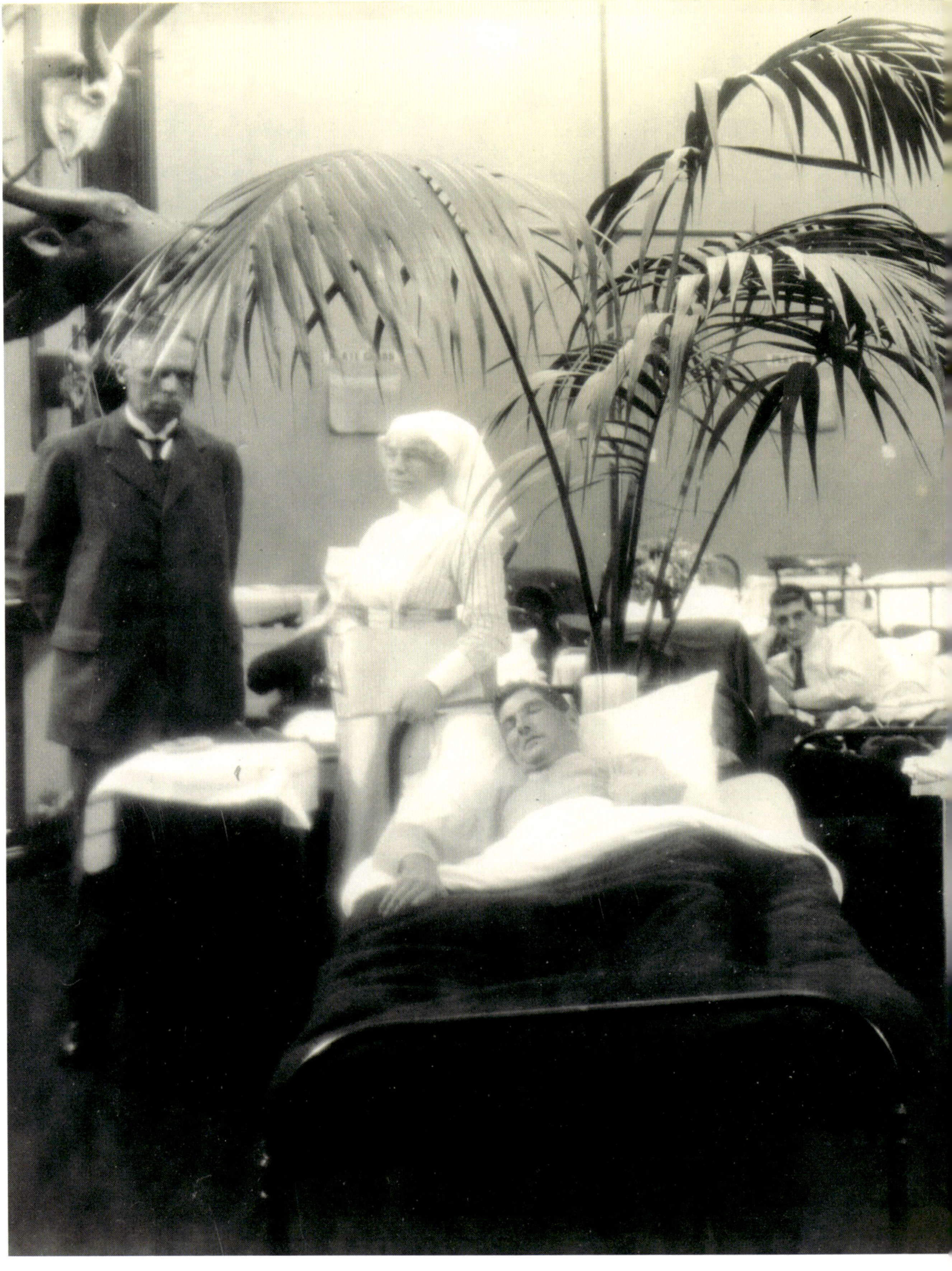

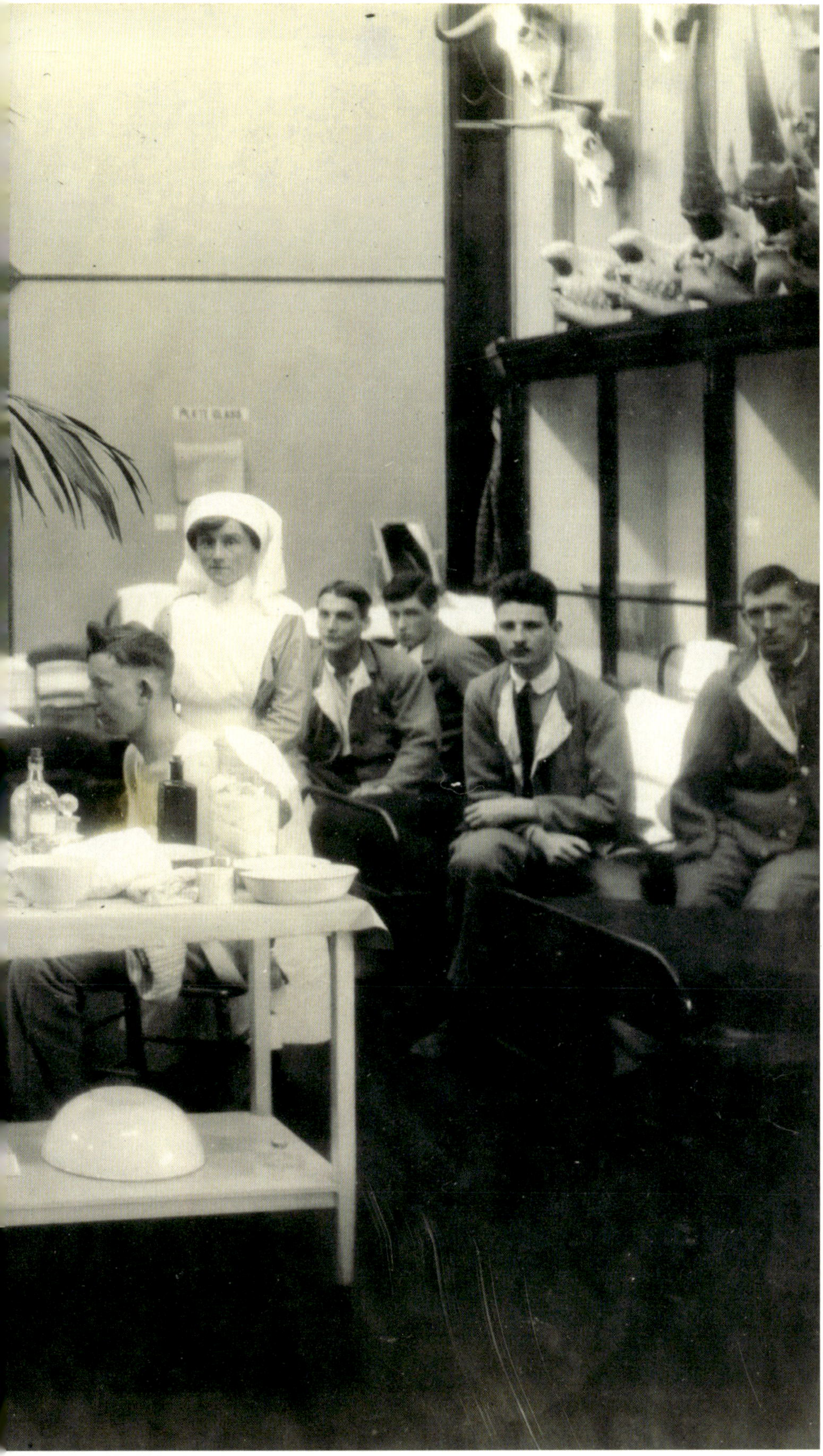

Temporary hospitals were set up all over the United Kingdom during World War I. In Birchington (Kent), Major Powell-Cotton made his mansion Quex Park with the annexed Powell-Cotton Museum available. Between 1914 and 1919, 1,241 British, Belgian, Canadian and Australian injured soldiers stayed there.
Photo, Quex Park & Powell-Cotton Museum, Birchington

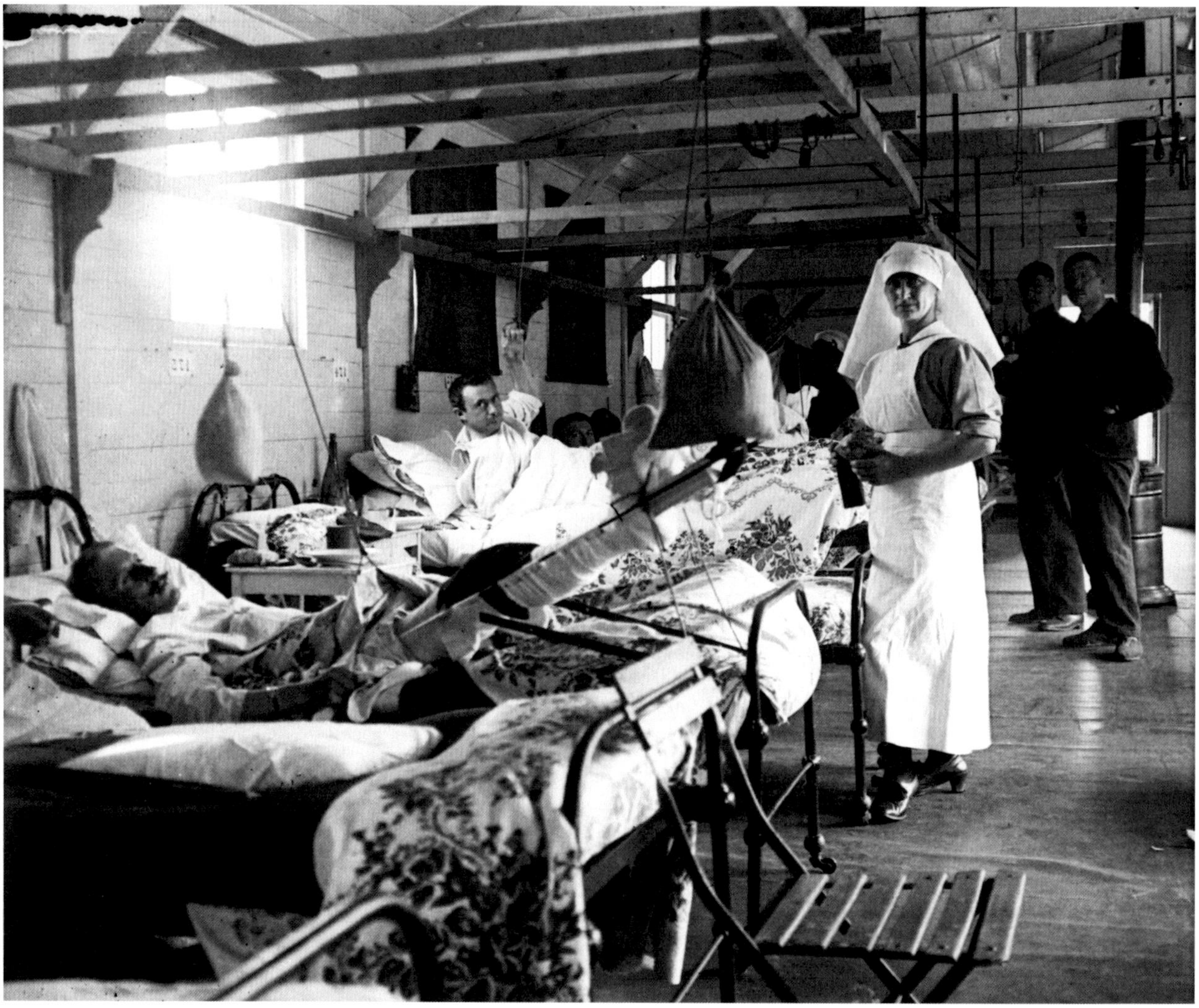

Inside view of a Belgian hospital ward. Note the nicely decorated bedspreads, which were made by charities to supplement the monotonous grey military blankets. Photo, © Dox family, Wijnegem

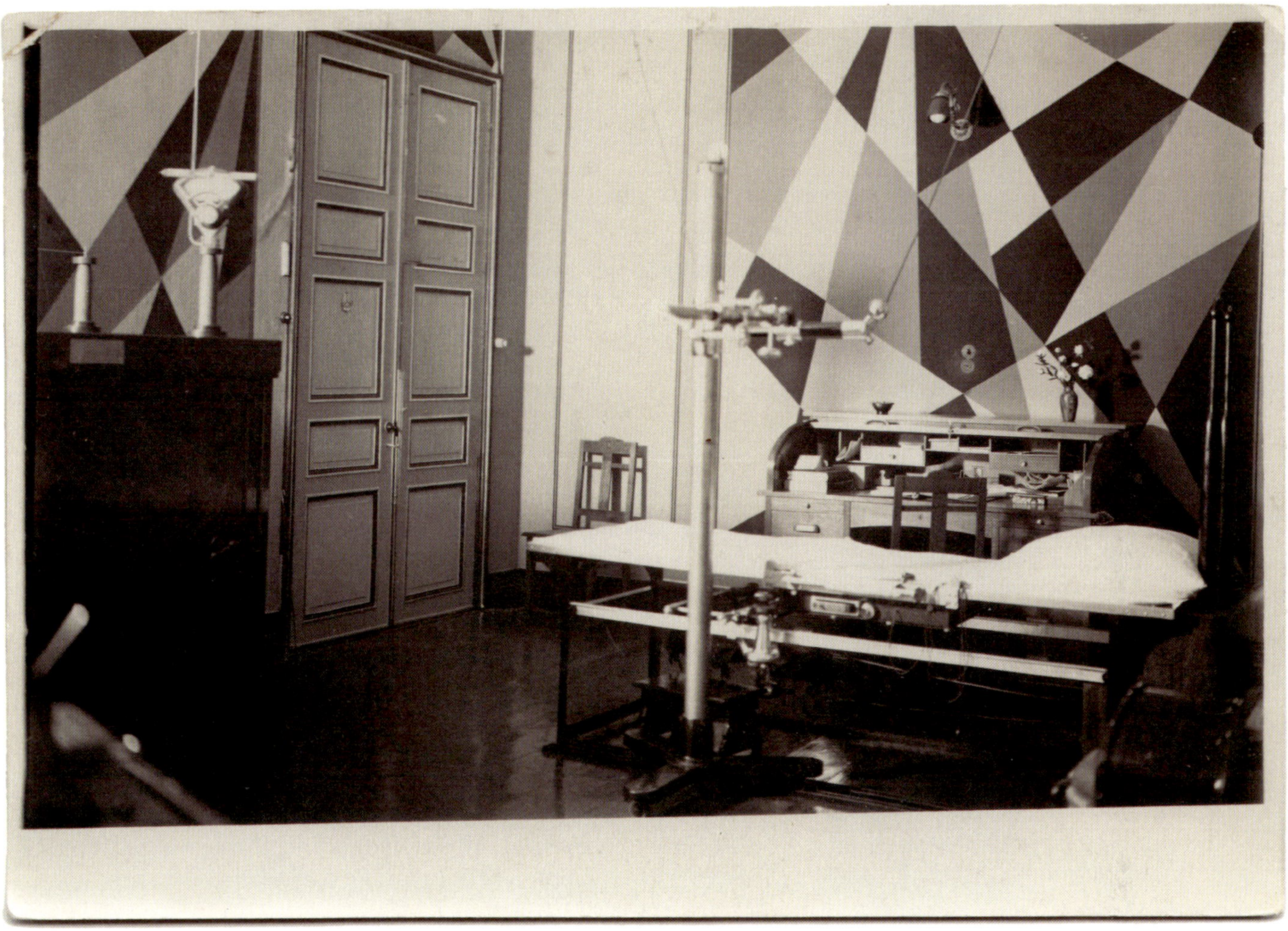

Two black-and-white photographs from 1924 are the only tangible memories of the study of the radiologist, Leon Devriendt from Kortrijk. In these photographs, we can see the abstract dispersion the medic personally applied to the walls as if visually to double the X-rays. In World War II the radiology practice, one of the very first in Belgium, was destroyed by fire. Painter Lucas Devriendt is the radiologist's grandson. Together with Hans Demeulenaere he intended a reconstruction of the office in which painting and architecture, actuality and imagination, as well as personal past and collective memory meet. During World War I radiology was used to help find bullets or shrapnel in the body or analyse complicated fractures.
Lucas Devriendt and Hans Demeulenaere, 2013, detail of installation, photo Leon Devriendt. Artist's own collection

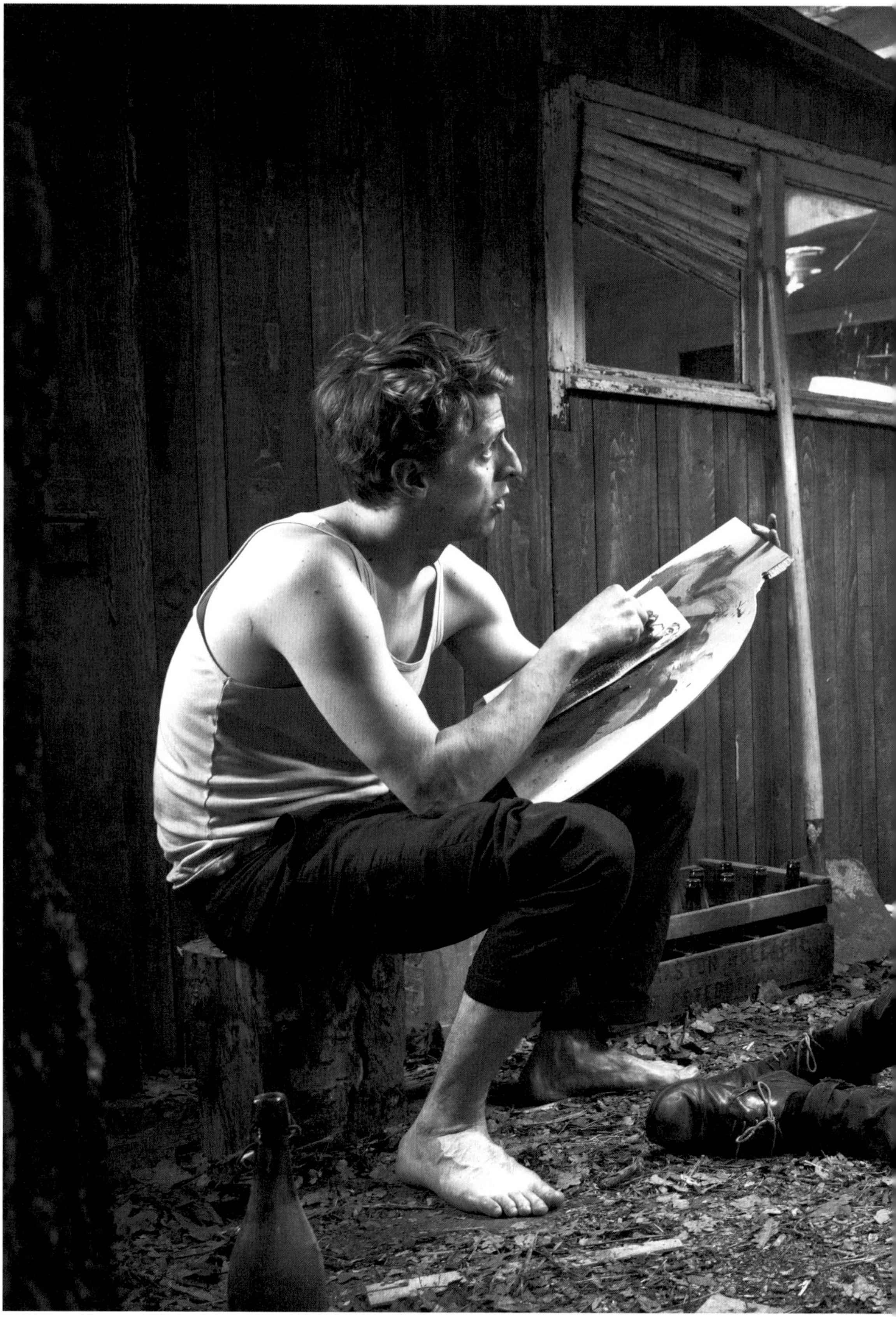

I find myself sitting on a tree trunk in a dusty, artificial scene, together with two friends of mine who are trapped in a tense pose, extremely silent, almost sculptural even, but bursting with catatonic nerves at the same time, as if they're about to explode. I am only an artist, at the service of the image and nothing else. I'm a coward. It's insane to ask myself how to draw that thousand-yard stare, through everything, at the void of complete terror. Open them up a little wider, I hear myself saying, lift your right hand just a bit more. I can see myself working in a tradition, losing myself in my distance. Just a little longer, I say, until it goes click.

Although Rinus Van de Velde (1983) cannot be called a documentary artist, his work does consist of a documentary process. His charcoal drawings show many scenes which he composed or compiled himself. Although the drawings are always the end result of his work, the photos he took or files he collected are an essential part of his art. Everything he draws, departs from photographic material. The effect of his work, however, lies in the development in charcoal. He enriches his drawings with text. He thus appropriates his found material and creates a new myth. For this exhibition the artist created an original piece. He did not use existing material, but created a photographic scene himself, resulting in a charcoal drawing.

Rinus Van de Velde, **I find myself sitting on a tree trunk in a dusty,** artificial scene..., 2013, charcoal on canvas, courtesy Tim Van Laere Gallery, Antwerp

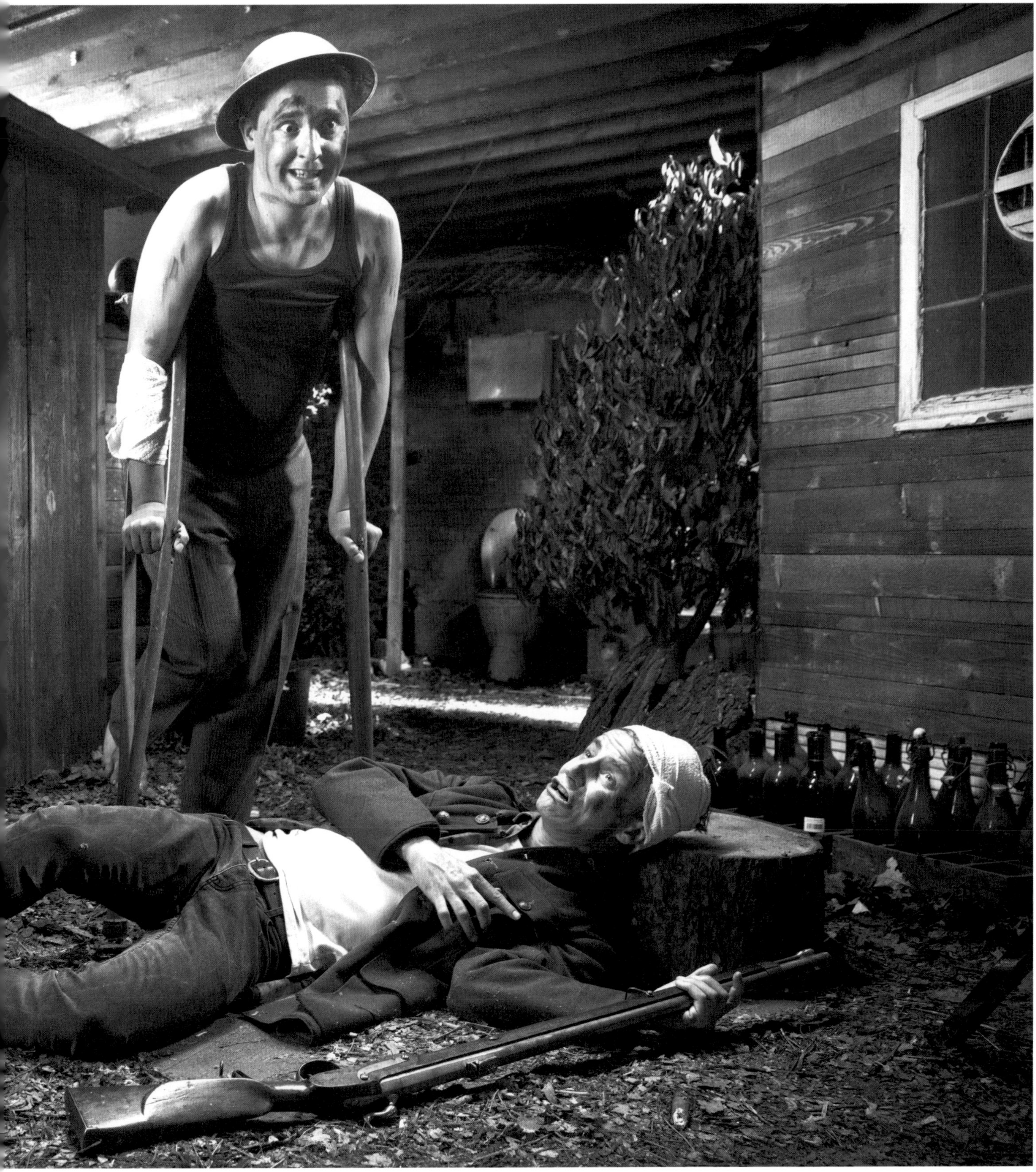

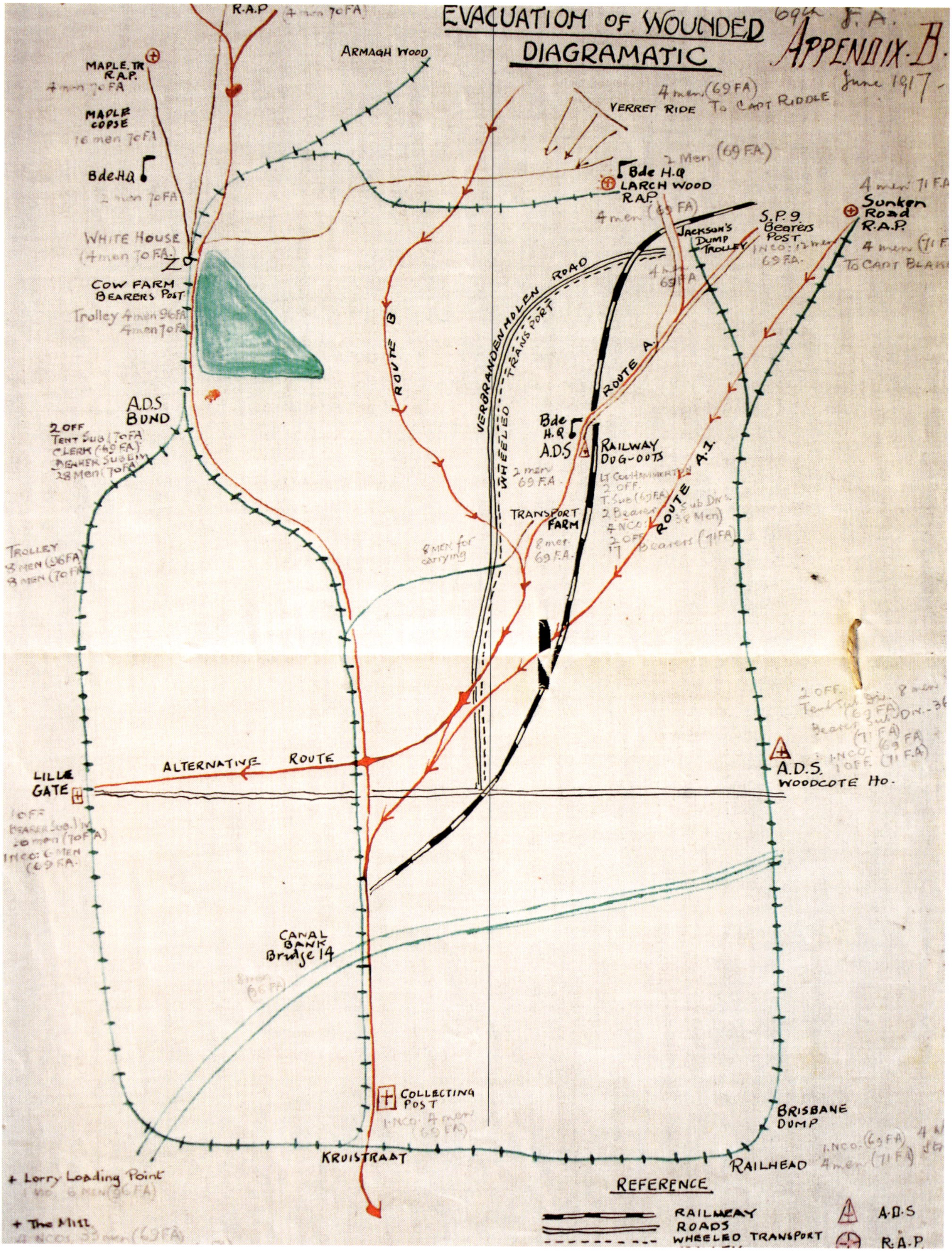
EVACUATION OF WOUNDED
DIAGRAMATIC
69th F.A.
APPENDIX B.
June 1917
R.A.P
ARMAGH WOOD
MAPLE TR R.A.P.
4 men 70 FA
MAPLE COPSE
16 men 70 FA
Bde HQ
2 men 70 FA
VERRET RIDE
To Capt Riddle
4 men (69 FA)
2 Men (69 FA)
Bde H.Q
LARCH WOOD
R.A.P.
4 men (69 FA)
4 men 71 FA
Sunken Road R.A.P.
4 men (71 F.A.)
To Capt Blake
WHITE HOUSE
(4 men 70 F.A.)
COW FARM BEARERS POST
Trolley 4 men 96 FA
4 men 70 FA
JACKSON'S DUMP TROLLEY
S.P. 9 Bearers Post
1 N.C.O. 12 men 69 FA.
VERBRANDENMOLEN ROAD
WHEELED TRANSPORT
ROUTE B
ROUTE A.
ROUTE A.1.
A.D.S BUND
2 OFF
TENT SUB (70 FA)
CLERK (69 FA)
BEARER SUB DIV
28 Men (70 FA)
Bde H.Q
A.D.S
RAILWAY DUG-OUTS
2 men 69 F.A.
TRANSPORT FARM
8 men 69 F.A.
8 MEN for carrying
TROLLEY
3 MEN (96 FA)
8 MEN (70 FA)
2 OFF.
Bearers (71 FA)
ALTERNATIVE ROUTE
LILLE GATE
1 OFF
BEARER SUB DIV
20 men (70 FA)
1 NCO: 6 MEN (69 FA)
A.D.S.
WOODCOTE HO.
CANAL BANK
Bridge 14
8 men (96 FA)
COLLECTING POST
1 NCO: 4 men (69 FA)
BRISBANE DUMP
KRUISTRAAT
RAILHEAD
1 NCO (69 FA)
4 men (71 FA)
+ Lorry Loading Point
1 NCO. 8 MEN (96 FA)
+ The Mill
REFERENCE
RAILWAY
ROADS
WHEELED TRANSPORT
A.D.S
R.A.P.

PIETER TROGH

Evacuation Routes in Flanders

The Case of the 69th Field Ambulance During the Battle of Messines (7–14 June 1917)

The first year of war was a hard lesson for the belligerent parties. Many matters needed to be contemplated, particularly the medical organisation and the care of a huge number of war victims.

After the Second Battle of Ypres (22 April – 24 May 1915) the frontline of the Ypres Salient stabilised and remained virtually the same for more than two years. During this period, the medical services tried to perfect their organisation. For instance, they learned that the medical units had to stay much closer to the frontline. The nature of injuries also required faster surgery: surgical outposts were set up. Detailed evacuation routes were gradually organised.

Those who undertake research into the system of this organisation are soon confronted with the magnitude of it all. Hundreds of evacuation routes and a multitude of stories can be found in archives and witness accounts, all equally interesting and unique, pieces of a puzzle that can be reconstructed in the landscape.

There are Belgian evacuation routes where, at an initial stage, some victims were carried away via the gateways in the inundated area – depending on the sector – to end up along surgical outposts or triage centres in several hospitals in unoccupied Belgium (such as *L'Océan* in De Panne), at the Opal Coast in France (mainly in Calais), and subsequently in revalidation centres deeper into France (for instance Port-Villez). There are evacuation routes with names such as John McCrae (the Canadian physician who is believed to have written the poem *In Flanders Fields* in his medical aid station *Essex Farm* in Boezinge), or Harvey Cushing (the well-known American neurosurgeon who was active in the *Mendinghem* field hospital in Proven), and then there is the *Lijssenthoek* story. Barely known, barely studied: the French cases that are extensively documented and illustrated in the *Journaux de Marche et d'Opérations*. These sources provide extremely detailed insight into the evacuation routes, especially for the Third Battle of Ypres (1917) and the German Spring offensive (1918). On the German side, routes are outlined from *Höhe 60 (Hill 60)* towards Wervik, from the northern Salient to the remote corners of occupied Belgium. The legibility of the German routes still shows several gaps, partly due to the reorganisation of the corresponding cemeteries.

At least two constants can be determined when researching each evacuation route: it always concerns an excursion involving extreme human suffering and it invariably results in one or several cemeteries, distressing reflections of a past medical presence in the landscape.

Within the scope of a short piece on evacuation routes, going more deeply into more than one route would be a hopeless task. This is why only one story is explored further, with a clear delineation in time and space, namely what happened to the British *69th Field Ambulance* during the Battle of Messines in 1917. The

Illustrated diagram of the evacuation routes of the British 23rd Division on the eve of the Battle of Messines, 6 June 1917. National Archives, Kew

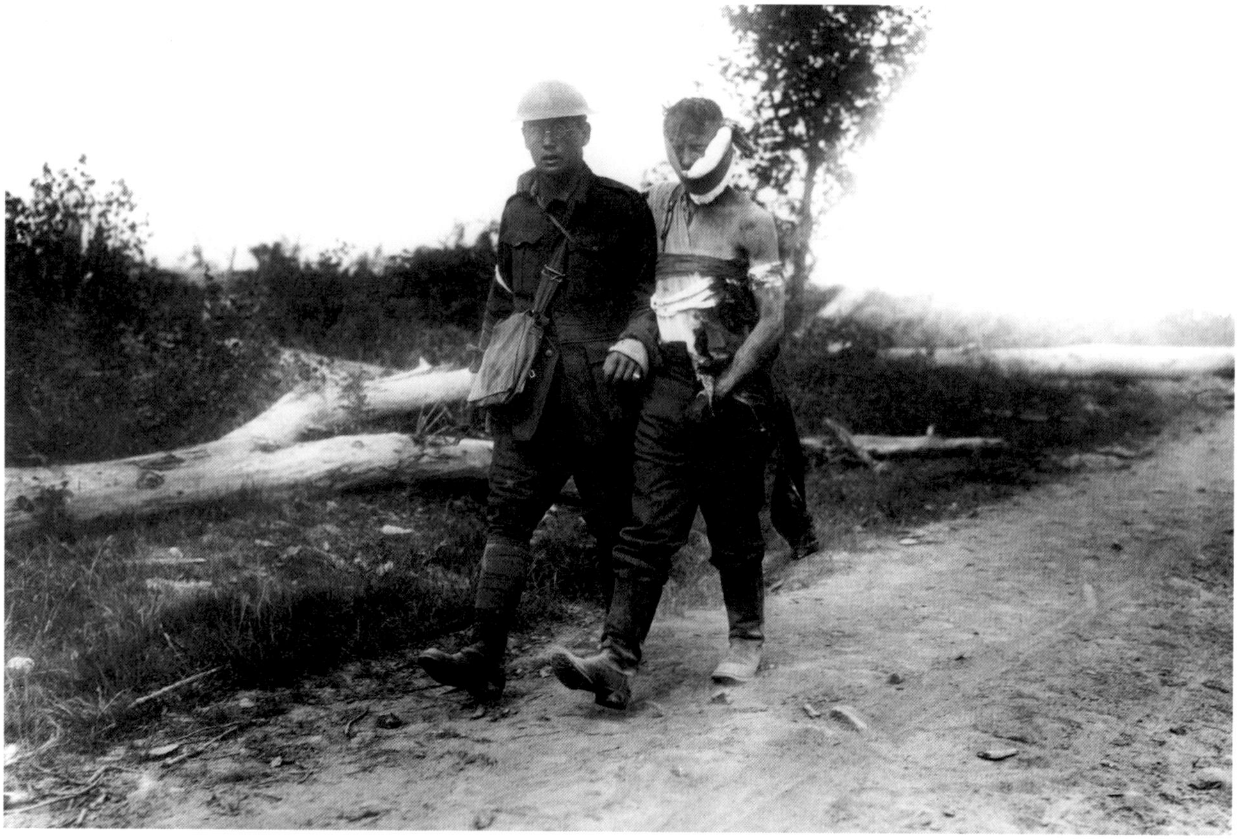

choice of this episode was on the one hand determined by the introduction to several enlightening sketches of evacuation stations in the studied zone, and on the other, because of the visibility in the landscape for a broader audience: those who take the train between Courtrai and Ypres can still notice several traces.

THE CONTEXT: THE BATTLE OF MESSINES (7–14 JUNE 1917)

What has become known as the Battle of Messines (also known as the 'Battle of the Mines'), taking place from 7 June to 14 June 1917 according to the official battlefield nomenclature, should be situated in a new Allied attempt to break the German resistance and resolve the war. After the British Battle of the Somme (1916) and the French Spring Offensive in 1917 had ended in a fiasco, British commander-in-chief Douglas Haig (again) thought the time was right to seize the opportunity for decisive action: a major offensive at the front in Ypres. Crucial for the success of this plan was conquering the West Flemish ridge. Since 1914, the Germans had occupied this higher area east and west of Ypres, which in trench warfare offers a considerable advantage.

This is why the prelude of the offensive aimed at conquering the highest parts, the crest between Zillebeke (from *Hill 60*) and Messines. The operation's architect was Sir Herbert Plumer, commander of the *2nd Army*. His plan: simultaneously exploding 20 mine shafts, buried in strategic areas under German lines. Protected by intense artillery fire, the advancing infantry would conquer a few modest targets with which the ridge would be relieved. After this the offensive in the entire Ypres Salient could begin.

In Plumer's attacking position the *23rd Division*, under which the *69th Field Ambulance* (69th FA)

Those who could still walk had to follow a separate evacuation route: walking wounded at the British front in Ypres, summer 1917.
Australian War Memorial, Canberra (E00481)

operated, formed the northern tailpiece. The railway line Ypres - Komen formed the central axis in the region that contained the mines of *Hill 60* and the *Caterpillar*.

ORGANISATION OF THE 69TH FIELD AMBULANCE

In the history of World War I, the Battle of Messines is one of the most meticulously prepared battles. The i's were dotted and the t's were crossed even with regard to the military medical organisation. In the British army the *Royal Army Medical Corps* (RAMC) was responsible for medical care. The *Corps* provided units to the various levels in the military organisation. One of these was the *Field Ambulance* (FA), not an 'ambulance' as we currently know, but a formation that took care of the evacuation between front aid stations and field hospitals. The *Field Ambulance* consisted of 10 officers and 182 other ranks and disposed of a variety of 'means of evacuation' (stretchers with and without wheels, carts on narrow-gauge railways, horse-drawn ambulances and motorised ambulances). It could also count on the help of 50 members of the *Army Service Corps*; drivers and workers responsible for transport, provisions and laying roads and connecting trenches.

During the Battle of Messines in the *23rd Division*, the 69th FA had a central role. The two other ambulance units of the division (*70th* and *71st Field Ambulance*) were used on the left- and right-side; some remained standby. The *war diary* of the 69th FA (with corresponding maps) and the sketches of A.R. Watt (one of its members who was blessed with a talent for drawing), give us an idea of how the battle had been prepared for on the eve of 7 June 1917.

Theoretically the evacuation process contained two main orders: taking care of the injured on the one hand, and transporting them on the other. In practice both were inextricably linked.

The outline anticipated the removal of two categories of wounded: 'walking wounded' (the red track) and 'lying cases' (the green track). The distinction aimed at the immediate removal from the scene of the 'less severe cases': those who could still walk did not need to be transported by the medical services. Any type of injured person had to follow the provided route as much as possible. The injured who could still walk were guided via communication trenches with duckboards: along Zillebeke Lake, route 'B' *(Fosse Way)* or routes 'A' and 'A1'. They could be cared for at every medical post they passed. All roads led to the *Kruisstraat*, the crossing of the Dikkebusseweg with the Capucienenstraat in Ypres. For walking wounded an alternative route was provided to the Lille Gate.

For the lying cases the evacuation was a lot harder. Stretcher-bearers who had been divided among the fighting units, *Regimental Stretcher Bearers*, sought victims in the battlefield and transported them to the aid stations that had advanced the furthest, the *Regimental Aid Posts* (RAP), after giving first aid. In the zone of the *23rd Division* this was *Sheba Subway, Maple Trench*, *White House*, *Verret Ride*, *Larch Wood* and finally, in the right-hand sector, *Sunken Road*. Evacuation was preferably done at night. Once an injured person ended up in a RAP, he was taken care of by battalion doctors, also called *'Regimental Medical Officers'* among the British units. These physicians were generally very close to the forces.

Near the RAPs were *Bearers Posts*: the base of operations for stretcher-bearers of the *Field Ambulance* responsible for transporting or accompanying the wounded to the nearest, advanced first aid-posts, so-called *Advanced Dressing Stations* (ADS): *(Zillebeke) Bund*, *Railway Dugouts* and *Woodcote House*. As they were often within reach of hostile artillery, they tried to fortify these posts as much as possible, for instance, by situating them below ground or digging them into railway bedding. They were always next to a road to be able to quickly send on the wounded. The aforementioned private A.R. Watt made several remarkable sketches that offer us insight into the organisation of these medical posts *and* their inclusion in the landscape. Trolleys rolling along a narrow-gauge railway were used for transport between RAP and ADS. The 69th FA had thirty trolleys that operated between the various stations. In the ADS, doctors resuscitated, stitched up injuries, splinted fractures and redressed bandages. The injured were often also given injections against tetanus. The physician gave the injured person a *tag*, an initial diagnosis of the injury in view of further treatment.

From the ADSs, the injured were transported (or accompanied if they could still walk) to the *Divisional Collecting Post* (or *'Station'*, DCS) at the Kruisstraat. Transport was done on *stretcher wheels* (stretchers on two wheels) as well as on trolleys. If the evacuation via the provided channels was problematic, horse-drawn ambulances or motorised ambulances could advance up to the zone of the ADSs. According to the map of the *23rd Division* these vehicles were mainly geared towards *Railway Dugouts*, to be reached via *Verbranden Road* (Komenseweg). The DCS formed the interchange of stretcher-bearers and ambulances, whether or not motorised. In addition, an *Advanced Store Depot* was installed here (referred to here as *'Lorry Loading Post'*), where medical material, blankets and stretchers were stocked.

It went from the Kruisstraat to the *Main Dressing Station* (MDS) in Vlamertinge (near *Vlamertinghe Mill*, known as the 'White Mill'), where the medical headquarters of the division was situated. The MDS was a big triage centre where administrative as well as nursing tasks were carried out. Victims were given food, warm blankets and waited for further transport to the hinterland. Bandages were redressed and some patients underwent a medical intervention in view of further transport. Not unimportant: the least serious cases were also removed from the circuit to not 'unnecessarily burden the evacuation route'. The MDS was also the base of operations of motorised ambulances and horse-drawn ambulances.

From *Vlamertinghe Mill,* it went on to the *Casualty Clearing Stations* (CCS), field hospitals with specialised medical units that carried out operations. Urgent injuries, such as stomach and head wounds, were treated according to the guidelines in CCS 12 (Hazebrouck) or CCS 46 *(Mendinghem,* Proven*)*. Those who were fit enough were transported to the *New Zealand Stationary Hospital* in Hazebrouck, a terminus, and in fact the first step back towards the front. The wounded that required further surgery or long-term revalidation, went to Boulogne-Sur-Mer and Etaples.

During the final year of war the military-medical organisation looked more or less similar among the various fighting parties, except for several nuances. But this was always theory, pen strokes on paper. In reality things always went differently under extreme circumstances such as during major offensives.

THE COURSE OF THE BATTLE IN THE ZONE OF THE 23RD DIVISION

On 7 June 1917 at 4:10 a.m. (Belgian time), the Battle of Messines began with the simultaneous explosion of 19 mine shafts along a front of about 16 km.

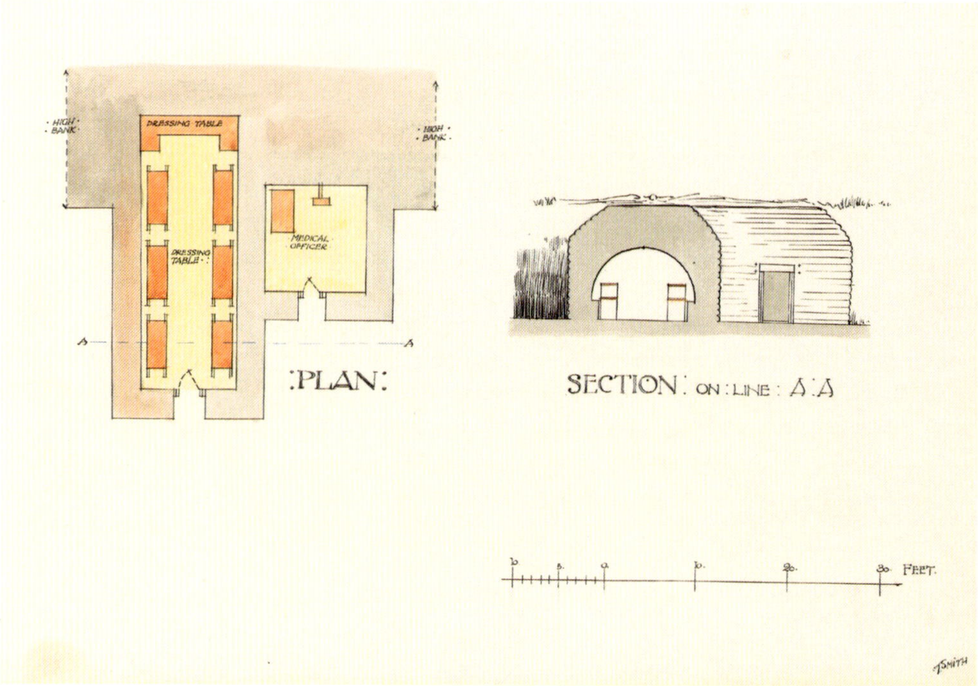

The advanced dressing station *Zillebeke Bund*, at the banks of Zillebeke River, sketched by Private A.R. Watt (69th Field Ambulance), 1917.
Army Medical Services Museum, Mytchett

The explosions of the mines at *Hill 60* and the *Caterpillar* were so severe that they were indelibly printed in the memory of both attackers and defenders as being similar to an earthquake with vicious aftershocks. On the right, the *69th Infantry Brigade* attacked and on the left, the *70th Infantry Brigade*. With great difficulty the attackers reached all targets before noon. The worst was yet to come: German counterattacks and the response of their artillery over the next few days. The battle for the conquered area was severe, yet in spite of considerable losses, the line was held until the end of the offensive. Starting from 8 June, all units were systematically removed from the line, those most severely affected first. By 13 June all troops were relieved and resting at Reninghelst or Berthen, except for a few machine gun units.

As soon as the attack troops had reached the top, the medical services also sent their people. At 4:40 a.m. on 7 June the first walking wounded had reported to *Railway Dugouts*. The groups of stretcher-bearers advanced gradually to come as close to the wounded as possible, but this was dangerous. In the sector of the 71st FA the first stretcher-bearer fell at 6 a.m. At 10 a.m. stock was taken of the amount of evacuees: *ADS Bund* counted 15 lying cases (LC) and 31 walking wounded (WW), *Railway Dugouts* 15 LC, 144 WW, *Woodcote House* 2 WW. What is remarkable is the low number of the said ADS. The reason was not that there were no wounded, but that the advance in this sector was awkward and severely under fire. *Battle Wood* (now provincial forest *Vierlingen*) was a tough obstacle. The *8/* and *9/Yorkshire Regiment* suffered serious losses who were hard to reach from *Sunken Road*.

At 11 a.m. the *Assistant Director Medical Services* (ADMS), the highest in rank in the medical service of a division, inspected the evacuation area. He believed everything had gone well, except for the problem at *Woodcote House* and the fact that several victims from the left sector had ended up in the evacuation zone of the division north of them, the *30th Division* (which is reflected in the presence in graveyards).

What befell the 70th FA indicates just how dangerous the evacuation of the wounded from the front zones was. They lost 31 men (of 182): 11 dead and 20 injured. Some of them died after a shell burst right at the entrance of *ADS Bund* (3:30 p.m.). Eight victims lie next to each other on *Railway Dugouts Burial Ground*. This type of case was not abnormal as it was common, among all belligerent parties, to isolate a front zone by attacking supply lines. The artillery that was set up kilometres further on did not distinguish a Red Cross armband.

The effect of this tactic is also indicated in the war diary of the 69th FA. An attempt to lead horse-drawn

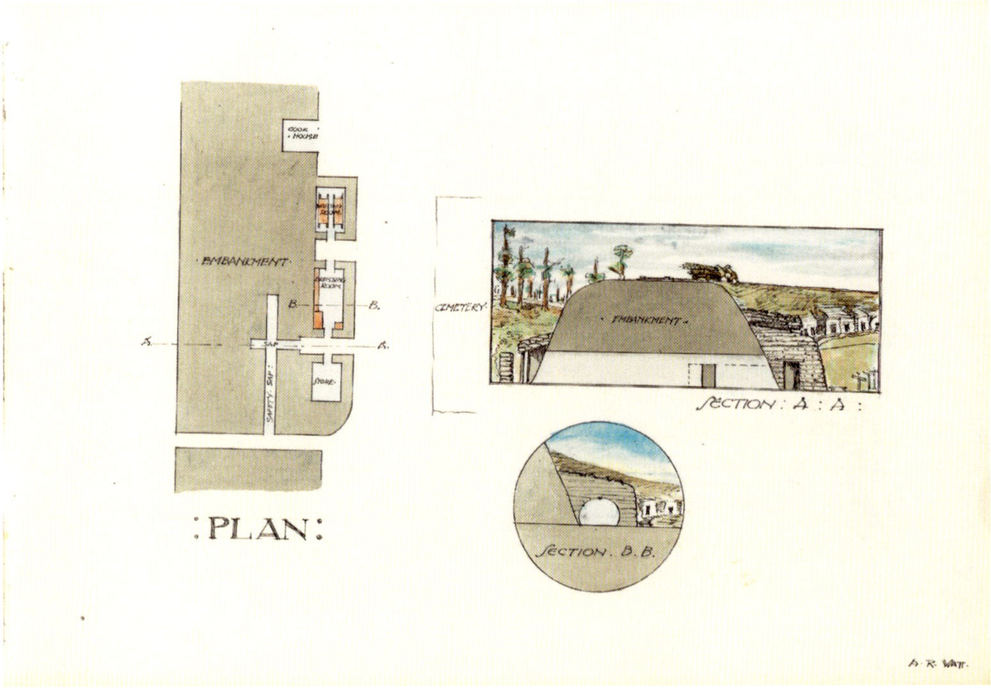

Advanced dressing station *Railway Dugouts*, entrenched in the railway bedding of the Ypres-Komen line, sketched by Private A.R. Watt (69th Field Ambulance), 1917.
Army Medical Services Museum, Mytchett

ambulances to the *Transport Farm* and *Railway Dugouts* failed because it rained (gas) grenades all evening. The evacuation line in the right-hand sector, via *Sunken Road* and *Woodcote House* was severely damaged on 7 and 8 June, the narrow-gauge railway was destroyed. Consequently, the majority of victims over the next few days were evacuated through the bottleneck *Railway Dugouts - Zillebeke Bund* OR part of them ended up in zone south (near the *47th Division*). The staff of the 71st FA was withdrawn and deployed elsewhere.

When evening fell, a new update of *'returns'* was made: at *ADS Bund* (15 LC / 31 WW), *ADS Railway Dugouts* (85 LC / 431 WW) and *ADS Woodcote House* (7 LC / 15 WW). The evacuation of wounded people sustained the next few days, but as the units of the *23rd Division* were relieved, medical staff followed. By 11 June the three Field Ambulances had withdrawn to Vlamertinghe.

THE TOLL OF WAR: 23RD DIVISION VICTIMS BETWEEN 7 AND 14 JUNE 1917

War and the exact number of victims have since human memory been incompatible. A hundred years of historiography of World War I has resulted in many statistics, but these should always be approached with the necessary caution. Parameters are oversimplified, descriptions often vague ('losses'), certain categories counted inaccurately (e.g. civilian casualties, colonial troops) or limitedly (e.g. only fighting units).

If we take a closer look at the case of the *23rd Division* during the Battle of Messines: the division's history only mentions the victims fallen among the fighting units: 390 dead, 307 missing (dead and prisoners of war?), 1,521 injured. Other units, the division deployed in the attributed zone (for instance, medical staff), are therefore not included. If we put the figures next to the counts of the *Advanced Dressing Stations* of the 69th FA, we get a total of 1,740 wounded (602 supine cases and 1,138 walking wounded).[1] Restriction of *these* figures: a) the wounded who ended up in the evacuation zones of neighbouring divisions are not included, b) those missing disappeared off the radar, c) there is no distinction between those injured who ended up further away and those who died and were buried on the spot. Drawing an overall picture is therefore not clear-cut.

The most realistic approach can be achieved by counting head per head what we are sure of: those who did not make it. Those who died in one of the stations of the evacuation route were buried on the spot, which explains the systematic increase of cemeteries. The case of the *23rd Division* teaches us that in eight days of battle 718 people died, who are commemorated in 21 different areas. This amount only applies for the period of 7 to 14 June.[2] The vast majority is remembered at Menin Gate (528). This concerns victims of whom nothing was ever found as well as those who were originally buried but whose grave was destroyed during the continuation of the war. The nearest cemetery where victims of the *23rd* ended up is *Railway Dugouts Burial Ground* (40). Although the line *Sunken Road – Woodcote House* was barely used, 16 victims still ended up at *Bedford House Cemetery*. Victims who died in the MDS were buried in Vlamertinghe (14). The wounded who reached Poperinghe were mainly treated in the *Casualty Clearing Stations* at *Remy Siding* and *Mendinghem*. Those who did not make it were buried in *Lijssenthoek Military Cemetery* (54) or *Mendinghem Military Cemetery* (16). The furthest cemeteries that connect the division to the Battle of the Mines are *Boulogne Eastern Cemetery* (6) and *Etaples Military Cemetery* (1).

What traces of this story do remain in the modern-day landscape? Those taking the train towards Ypres (departing from Courtrai) will pass Comines station, one stop before Ypres. From the moment the train starts to depart from Komen, it takes 4 min. 56 (without delays) before it crosses the railway bridge of *Hill 60* and the *Caterpillar*. The 500 – 800 metres you see passing by in 10 seconds gives you an idea of the distance stretcher-bearers sometimes had to cover. If you take the inclination of the landscape and the historic air photos into consideration, you understand that this was not in the least commonplace.

A little later (14 seconds), you can see the *Larch Wood Cemetery* to your right where a RAP was set up behind a hill at the time, neatly tucked away out of the opponent's sight. What is striking is that not a single

View of the transport of a group of 'lying cases' via trolleys over the narrow gauge railway, as was also done in the evacuation zone of the 23rd Division. Photo, In Flanders Fields Museum, Ypres

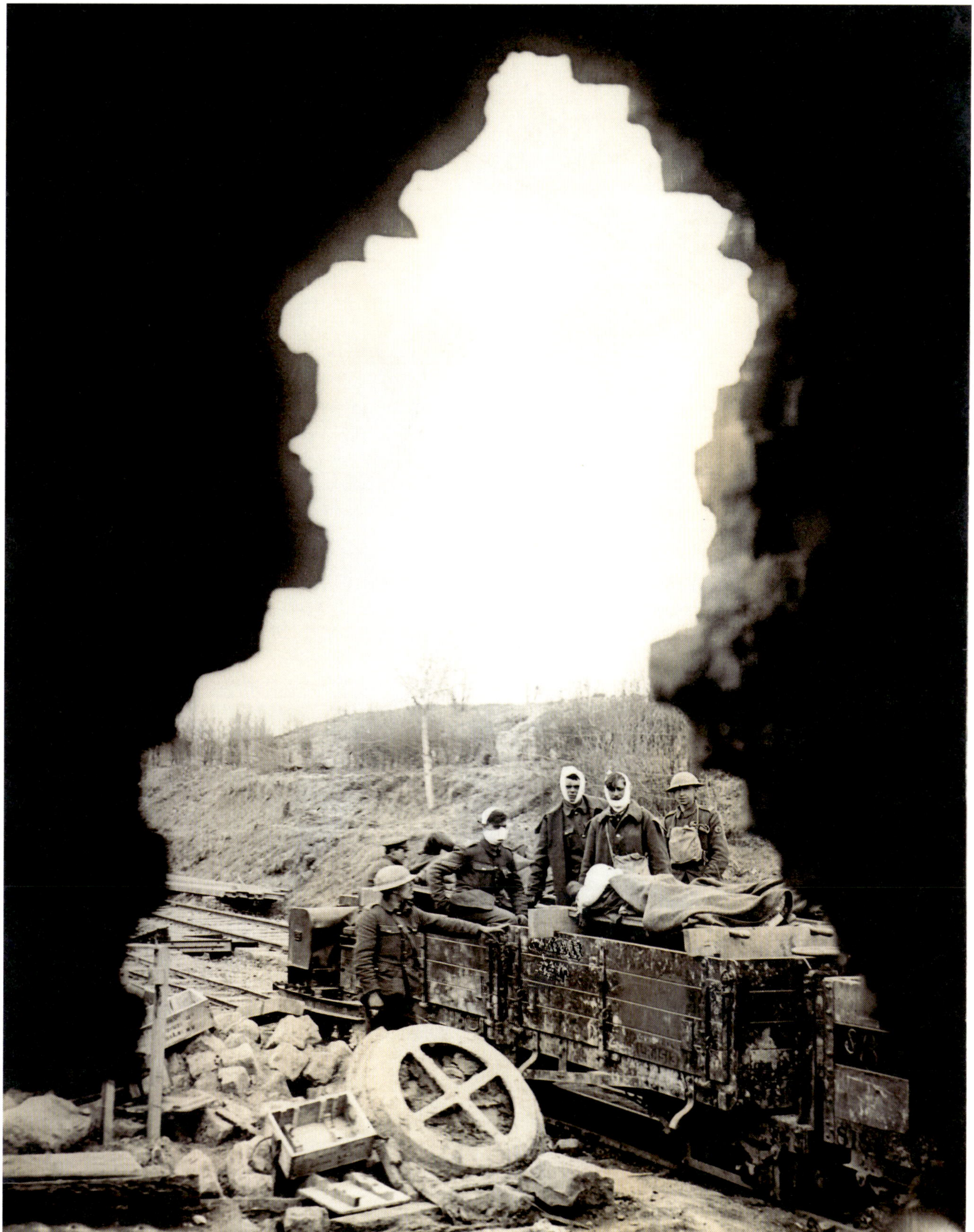

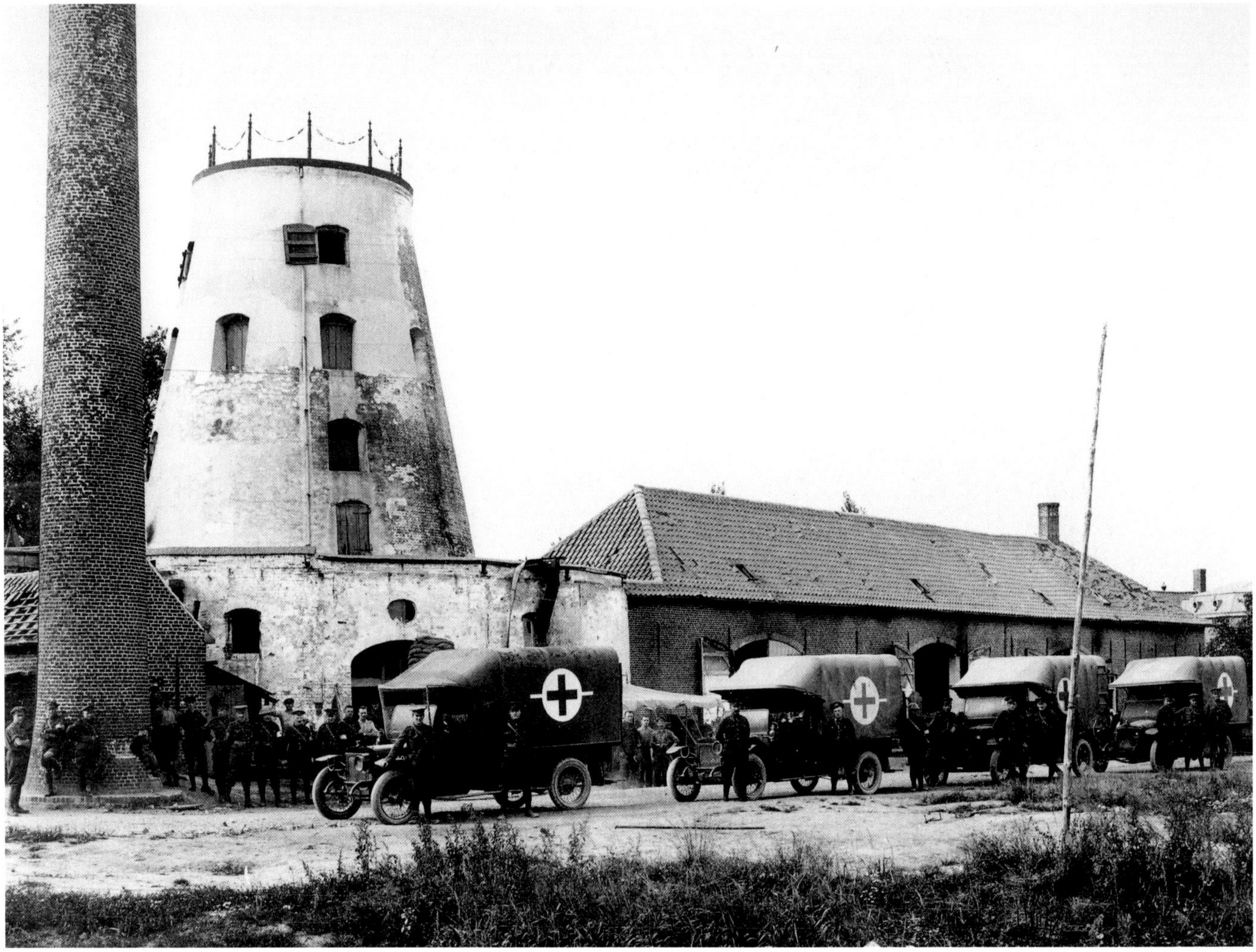

headstone at *Larch Wood (Railway Cutting) Cemetery* is reminiscent of the presence of the *23rd Division*. A possible explanation is that the cemetery was temporary unused (after all, between 19 June 1917 and the armistice, another 235 were added). Another 20 seconds later you pass *Railway Dugouts Burial Ground* and in the distance you can see, behind the row of trees, Zillebeke Lake. Hundreds of victims were evacuated through this area. Once you have passed *Railway Dugouts* immediately turn to the left and in the distance you will see *Bedford House Cemetery*. ADS *Woodcote House* was situated nearby, main supplier of the cemetery.

The zone of the 69th FA only formed part of the entire evacuation network that had developed at the front of the Battle of Messines. Along the whole front zone of this battle were a dozen similar zones, leaving their traces all over. The Battle of Messines was considered a great success. In eight days thousands of victims fell, including 6,000 dead who are commemorated in Belgium. The medical services had got a taste of what was to come during the next few months, during the Third Battle of Ypres.

Headquarters of the medical services of the 23rd Division were situated at the former 'Witte Molen' in Vlamertinge. From here, the injured were evacuated to the field hospitals in the hinterland. Photo, Imperial War Museum, London (CO2236)

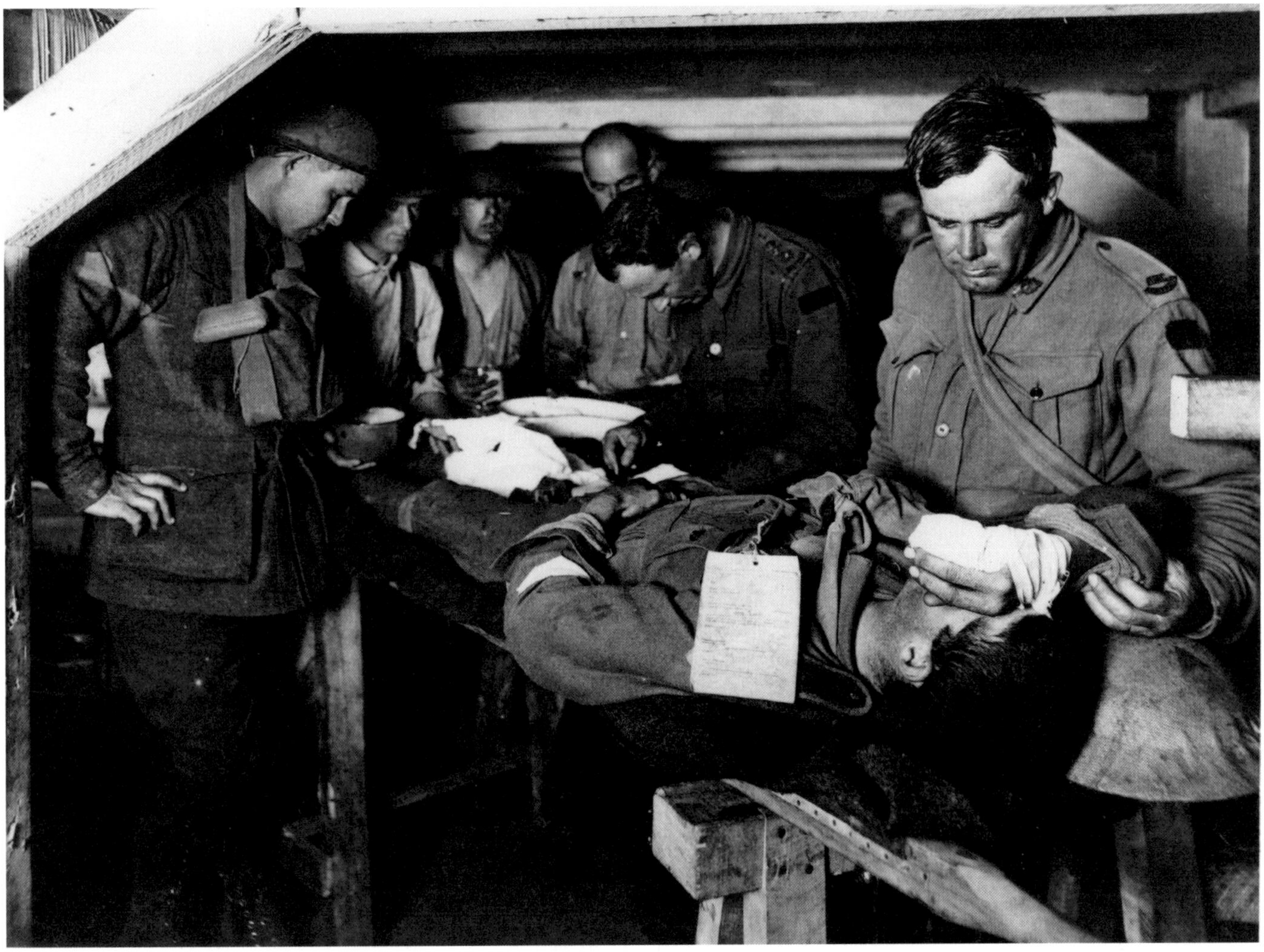

NOTES

1 The counts were made between 7 and 10 June 1917, after which the unit was relieved. The 70th FA did not have any figures. The 71st FA does provide figures of a further stage in the evacuation route: there are therefore unavoidable double counts.

2 It is probable that another part drew their final breath after 14 June as a result of participating in the battle (38, between 15 and 19 June, even more dependent on interpretation).

SOURCES AND LITERATURE

Army Medical Services Museum (Aldershot, UK), with thanks to Pete Starling.

National Archives (Kew, UK), war diaries of the 69th, 70th and 71st Field Ambulances and of the ADMS of the 23rd Division.

Chielens P., Dendooven D., et al, *De laatste getuige: het oorlogslandschap van de Westhoek*, Tielt, 2006.

Edmonds J.E., Falls C., *History of the Great War. Military operations in France and Belgium: 1917*, London, 1940.

Koch K., *De Derde Slag bij Ieper: 1917*, Antwerp, 2007.

Sandilands H.R., *The Twenty-Third Division: 1914–1919*, Edinburgh / London, 1925.

www.cwgc.org/

http://www.vlib.us/medical/

http://www.ramc-ww1.com/index.html

With thanks to the team of the IFFM Knowledge Centre, especially Dries Chaerle and Dominiek Dendooven.

Inside view of an Advanced Dressing Station, where an injured person is being treated. Note the wound tag on the victim's jacket: it includes the first diagnosis and instructions for further treatment in the next evacuation stations he will be passing.
Photo, Australian War Memorial, Canberra (E00714)

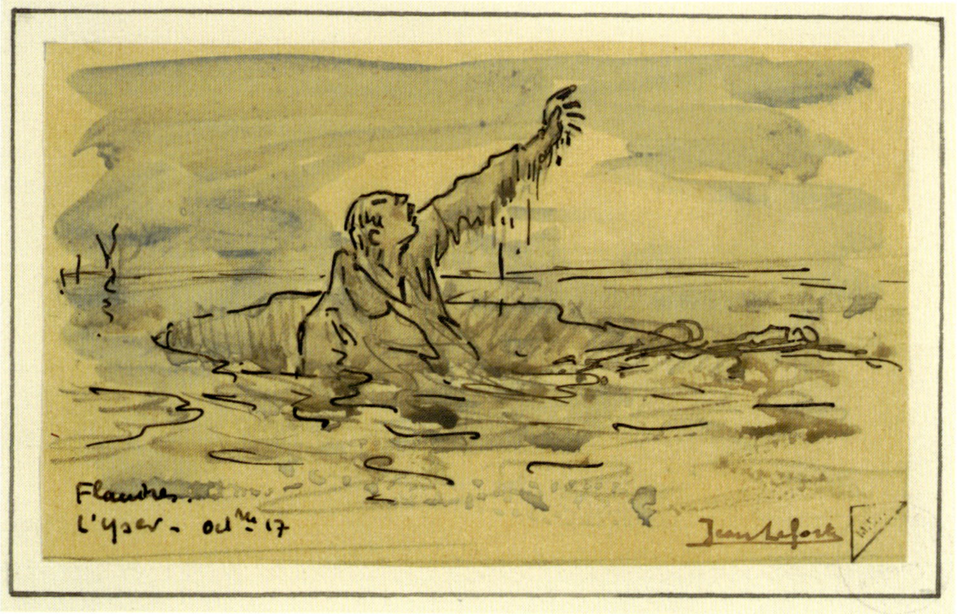

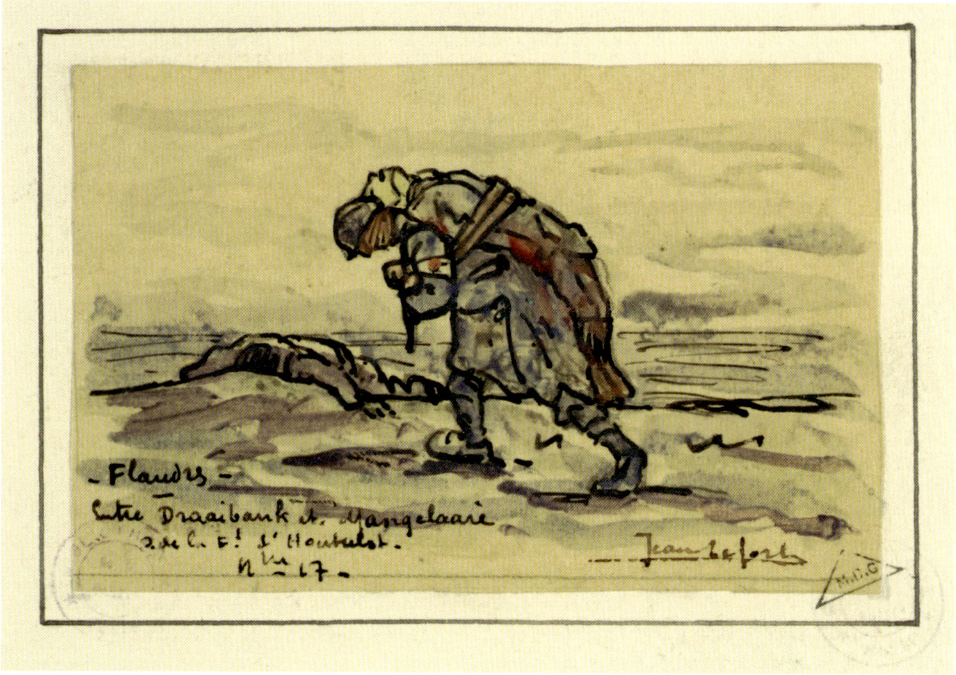

Jean Lefort (1875–1954) was an artist from Bordeaux who joined the French army shortly after the outbreak of the war. He first served in fighting units (237RI, later 360RI), but from March 1917 he was included in the topographical section of the *1re Armée française* because of his talent for drawing. In this capacity he experienced the Third Battle of Ypres. Lefort witnessed the horrors of the offensive and captured these in striking watercolours. During the war he made a total of 600 to 700 watercolours. This part of his oeuvre still forms a strong testimony of daily life in the French army.
BDIC–Musée de l'Histoire Contemporaine, Paris

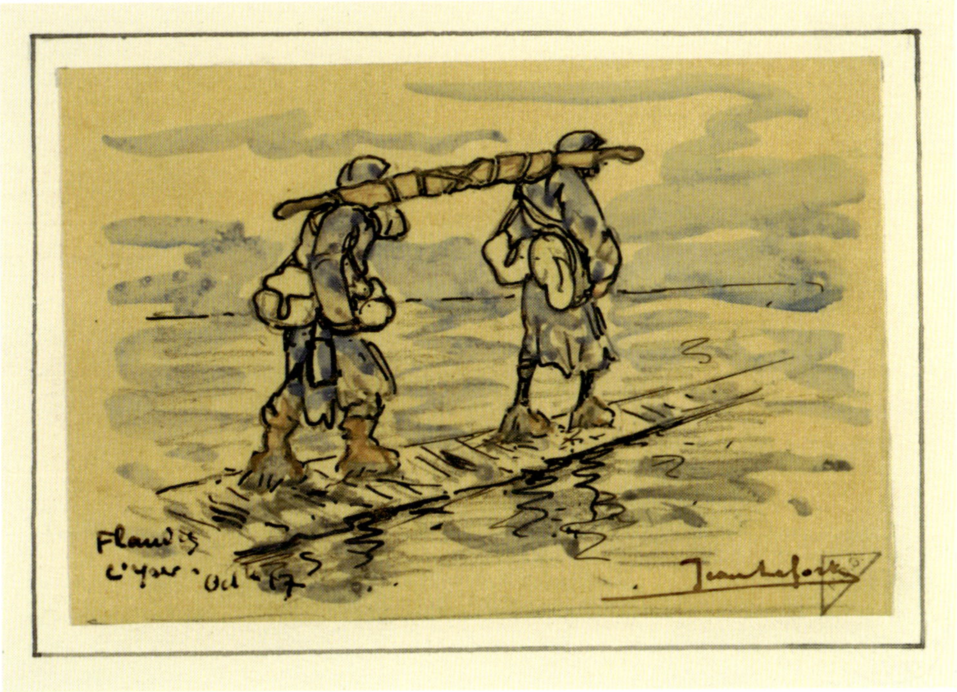

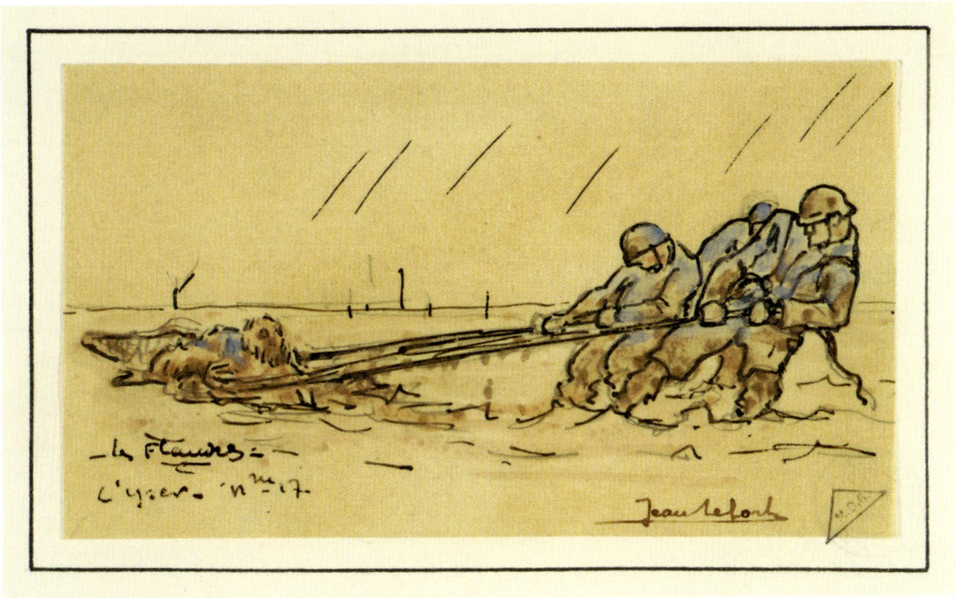

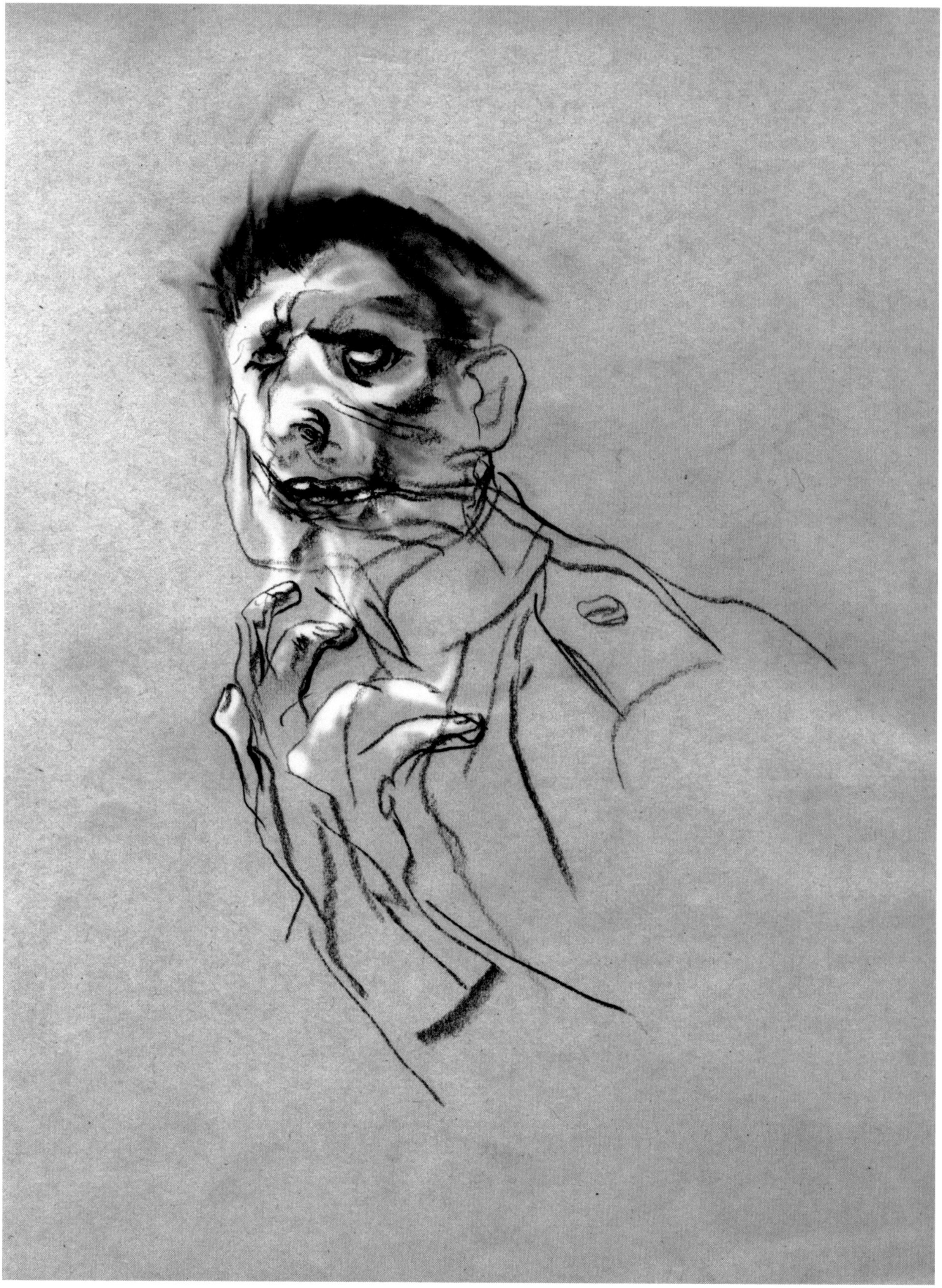

DR SUSANNE MICHL

Ethical Conflicts in Wartime Medicine

The Medical Profession between Military and Humanitarian Duty

"Medicine should first and foremost prepare for times of peace. In the midst of the horrors of war it - and in essence it alone - is obliged to be present on the battlefield as a representative of humanity and peace among peoples. Without distinguishing it should offer help to friend and foe, to heal bloody wounds, look after wounded limbs and refresh thirsty mouths. [...] Let us, as high priests of humanity, bring blessings for all in wartime."

It was Rudolf Virchow, renowned physician at the Charité clinic in Berlin, who described medicine as a neutral and humanitarian participant in the bloody battles at the beginning of the Franco-Prussian War in 1870/71[1]. Virchow believed that the representatives of world peace were doctors themselves, who helped victims of war regardless of their nationality. Equally, medical science would be solely focused on new research with the objective of improving life across international borders.

This view of the role of medicine and doctors during wartime would also be upheld in later wars - although bodies and minds were much more severely damaged in the First World War than Virchow could have ever imagined during the War of 1870/71. Thousands of mobilised physicians – whether military or civilian doctors in uniform – considered that wearing the Red Cross implied acceptance of its ideals and therefore did not experience a fundamental crisis of conscience over their actions in war. But also social values, sensitivities towards specific ethical dilemmas and conscience have a history. Doubts concerning the exclusively humanitarian role of medicine during war, as we can intuitively feel today, do not have a long history. The work of doctors during wartime was not questioned and did not lead to discussions in society and among doctors until the Cold War. Worldwide recognition took place in 1985, when the federation 'International Physicians for the Prevention of Nuclear War' won the Nobel Peace Prize.

It is thus an almost anachronistic undertaking to outline the ethical issues of World War I. What did the neutrality and humanity, so empathetically proclaimed by Virchow, mean in the context of medical care during the First World War, particularly on the Flemish battlefields? And to which extent did physicians experience such ethical dilemmas?

MEDICAL AND MILITARY LOGIC – THE QUESTION OF NEUTRALITY

Doctors were also affected by the mass mobilisation of men during the First World War. About 24,000 German doctors were called to arms or volunteered to provide health care. Among the Allies, 30,000 doctors were mobilised in the west alone[2]. Most of them were civilian doctors who undertook their military service not with weapons but with surgical scalpels and first-aid kits. How did these doctors, who no longer practised their profession in a civilian but in a military context, see their role in wartime?

In 2002 Prometheus published *Niemands Land* [No-mans-land], a collaboration between Tom Lanoye, Michiel Hendryckx and Gert Dooreman. Lanoye translated and adapted 32 poems of war poets such as Wilfred Owen and Siegfried Sassoon, Hendryckx made 26 photos and Dooreman drew seven portraits of soldiers. Dooreman (1958) is a graphic designer for leading arts centres and publishers and is Tom Lanoye's permanent designer.
Dooreman, **Kramp**, 2001, pencil on paper with digital processing, archive designer

Neutrality, as described by Virchow in 1870, became an ethical principle in medicine with the establishment of the Red Cross and applied most importantly for wartime work, which had to reduce pain rather than inflict it.[3] The basis of this principle was the idea that, under the flag of the Red Cross, each soldier, regardless of their nationality, had the right to aid – an equality of treatment that outweighed national interest and the aims of war. Physicians themselves, however, seemed less convinced that war medicine was a neutral given which was not allowed to become involved with military strategy under any circumstances, but was linked instead to its own humanitarian logic. On the contrary, the first war with modern arms technology, which was specialized on the destruction of mass armies, created a close interaction between military and medical interests and logics.

Both German and French doctors placed themselves at the service of national interest. They felt their contribution lay in passing a large part of the male population fit for military service, in making wounded soldiers ready for battle as soon as possible, in shedding light on feigned illness or problems, and - as experts and advisors - by scrupulously weighing up each injury against national, economic interests.

Apart from this commitment the war, military structures and the mass mobilisation of a large part of the male population offered unprecedented possibilities for intervention and opportunities for extending research in various medical disciplines such as public hygiene, psychiatry and neurology, surgery, bacteriology, pathology and legal medicine. In this regard the war, as medical historian Wolfgang U. Eckart aptly summarised, seemed like a "huge in vivo experiment"[4]. Many physicians thus welcomed World War I, not only because they wanted to serve for patriotic motives, but also because the war offered considerable opportunities for their own purely medical, professional, social and political interests.

SOLDIER DUTIES AND PATIENT RIGHTS?

In times of national wars and patriotic enthusiasm, the individuals' commitment for the community counts. This dedication became a normative requirement in which the individual was subordinated to the moral of the collective. Conversely, our current medical-ethical debates are strongly determined by individual moral values. The central point is the protection of the individual – the necessity of gaining their approval after they have been given detailed information, and their right to refuse any form of therapeutic intervention.

Against this backdrop it is surprising that German, and more so, French doctors still wondered whether, in wartime, a physician could simply intervene, without the consent of the soldier/patient. Both the German and the French medical profession recognize the taking of coercive measures as an undermining of the civil and trustful relationship between physician and patient[5]. Even though war sometimes made such interventions necessary, it still had to be clear that these were undertaken on orders from the military health department and that the mobilised doctor was just carrying them out. Both German and French doctors were concerned that the trust-based relationship between physician and patient which existed in civilian life would not be damaged by the temporary war situation and changing power structures. In France, a doctor's attempts to force treatment on the zouave, Baptiste Deschamp, caused widespread controversy. Deschamp suffered from camptocormia (a forward curvature of the torso) and refused electroshock therapy to make his contorted torso supple again. The incident led to intense debate in the national press and even in political circles[6].

This type of public discussion about medical ethics and the right of self-determination over one's own body during wartime was unascertainable in Germany. Against protestations that the civilian physician-patient relationship was not infringed, many doctors, especially in Germany used their position as military members for test forms of therapy. For instance, the majority of war neurotics were treated with 'verbal suggestion', a medical term that actually meant harsh military commands, which the soldier had to obey to avoid interruption of service due to illness. Many doctors used unconditional military obedience and threats of punishment in cases of non-compliance with orders to enforce their chosen treatments. It is therefore not an exaggeration to state that military discipline and procedures were introduced into medicine.

But whether of their own accord or under pressure of public opinion, French physicians seemed less at ease in a military uniform than their German colleagues.

WAR AND TRAUMA – A HUMANE MEDICINE?

Apart from preserving the role of doctors as a neutral, friend- and foe-helping authority, Virchow also referred to another ethical principle: humanity. The presence of doctors on the battlefield was in this sense a counterbalance to the bloody events of war. For Virchow it was pre-eminently medicine, as a humane science, that symbolically guaranteed humanity the development towards the good, progress and civil values.

Understanding this humanity as a basic ethical principle is not easy. It is even harder to ascertain to what extent doctors at the front, area or military hospitals were actually regarded as helpers 'offering blessings' to soldiers. Let us take a closer look at the contact with soldiers traumatised by war: physicians were indeed confronted with completely new syndromes; soldiers trembling and shaking; the war had quite literally got under their skin and into their entire body. These cases meant physicians also had to face moral challenges: what was this apparent endless war with its unprecedented accumulation of traumatic experiences doing to fighting men? Could one withstand so many traumas and should these soldiers be given the status of war invalids, by analogy with their comrades who had lost arms or legs? If we define the ethical principle of humanity, as Virchow proclaimed for doctors and medicine, as respect for the suffering individual, then one must wonder whether World War I physicians did, in fact, act humanely towards the increasing number of traumatised soldiers.

If we consider the sometimes extremely cruel forms of therapy that soldiers with shell shock had to undergo, we can hardly talk of fundamental respect for the suffering individual[7]. These forms of therapy seem more like examples of the increasing brutalisation of war - a brutalisation, hospital wards were also not protected from. German doctors in particular stigmatised soldiers with shell shock as unmanly, neurotic and morally negligible individuals who let down their comrades in the trenches. They all opposed the pity and attention these soldiers were met with in society. Max Lewandowsky, consultant neurologist of the army stated: "Contempt for neurotics should be generally accepted[8]". French physicians, however, indicated that other interpretations were also possible. Admittedly, when it came to forms of therapy they scarcely differed from their German colleagues, but the psychiatric-neurological debate was slightly different to that in Germany[9]. They mainly tried not to deprive soldiers who had reached the psychological limit of their combativeness of their heroic status. A study about "les anxieux" [the anxious] by Albert Devaux and Benjamin Logre, two pupils of the

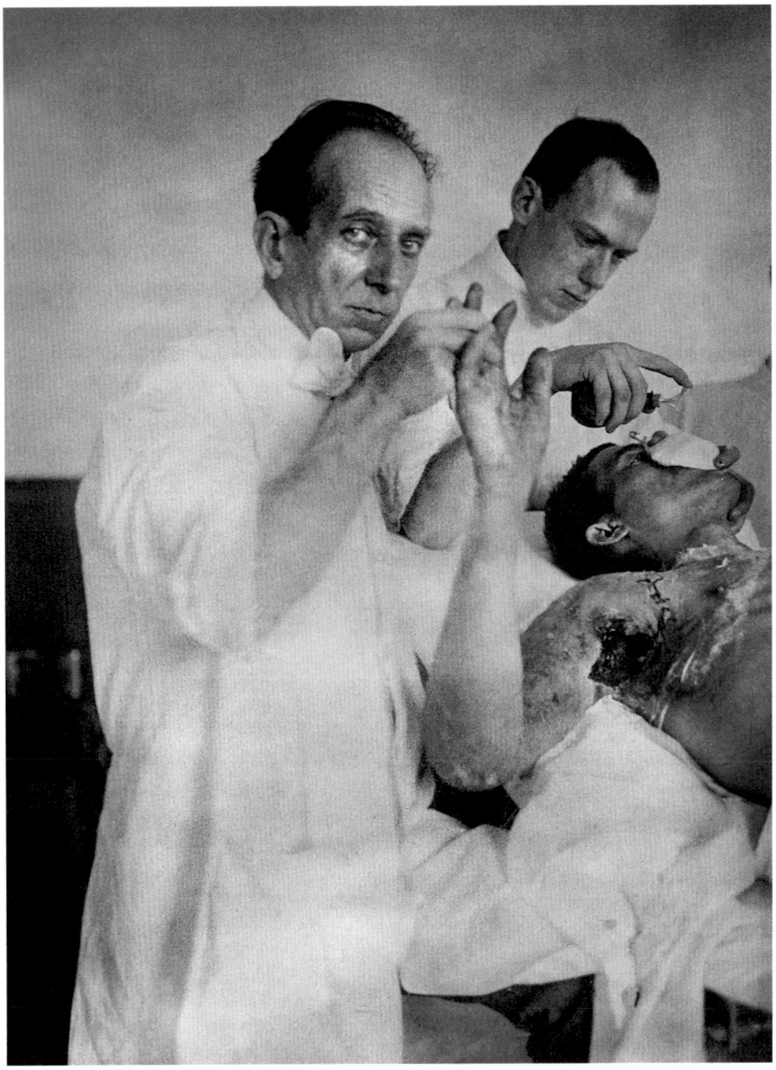

Two doctors *anaesthetising* an injured patient. Western Front, 1914–1918. Photo, In Flanders Fields Museum, Ypres

well-known neurologist Ernest Dupré states: "A major emotional shock, whether or not combined with physical shock and injury, makes a brave person a coward. His soldier's courage has dwindled [...]. This acquired cowardice is the result of trauma contracted during his war service. A soldier who has been affected physically would have a right to the respect the wounded are met with. The soldier who is injured mentally in fact has the same rights. He is, in the actual and military sense of the word, an invalid, but a mental invalid, invalid when it comes to his courage."[10]

In France the events of war were more seriously regarded and soldiers who had become ill with post-traumatic stress disorder as a result of an unprecedented accumulation of traumatic experiences were stigmatised far less.

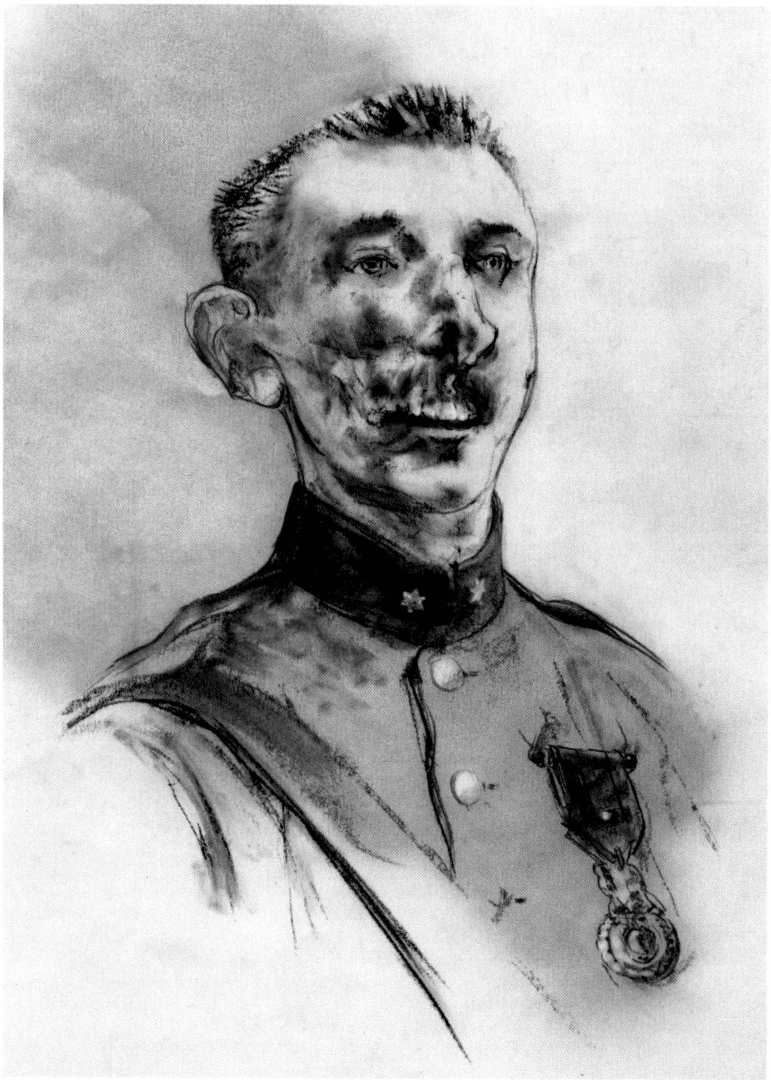

Dooreman, **Mutilé**, 2001, pencil on paper with digital processing, archive designer

The war had irrefutably brought about a collective sense of morality - or at least strengthened it. Apart from ideological reasons for approving war, the military hierarchy also provided a favourable structure for officers, doctors and other opinion formers, which made them, support the seemingly unshakable "logic of war". It is a logic that determined if the individual had to serve the greater national interest.

Yet although the moral of the collective prevailed, normative values with a focus on individuals and their protection had not completely disappeared from doctors' discourse. In their professional ethics, most doctors were quite aware of their double role: a military and a civilian one. This mainly manifested itself in the discussion of a patient's right to refuse a treatment. However, the collective's moral was also disturbed on another level - in a totally unforeseeable way and with disastrous consequences for the actual participants of the war. The length of the conflict, the horrors of trench warfare and its murderous offensives, all meant that coping with and overcoming war experiences was no longer regarded as a matter of collective victory or defeat, but as an individual responsibility. It came down to withstanding the existence of war itself while simultaneously remaining mentally fit. Each illness or injury was a battle. The scene of action was no longer collective and it became extremely personal. The fact that this completely different form of individualisation of war experience also had ethical-normative consequences became apparent in the - until then - unprecedented stigmatisation of soldiers suffering from shell shock: they had lost the battle and were therefore not heroes. Against the background of this shift in responsibility from a collective to an individual level, medicine and especially the German psychiatrists turned away from the moral principle of humanity understood as a profound respect for the suffering individual, so empathetically proclaimed by Virchow.

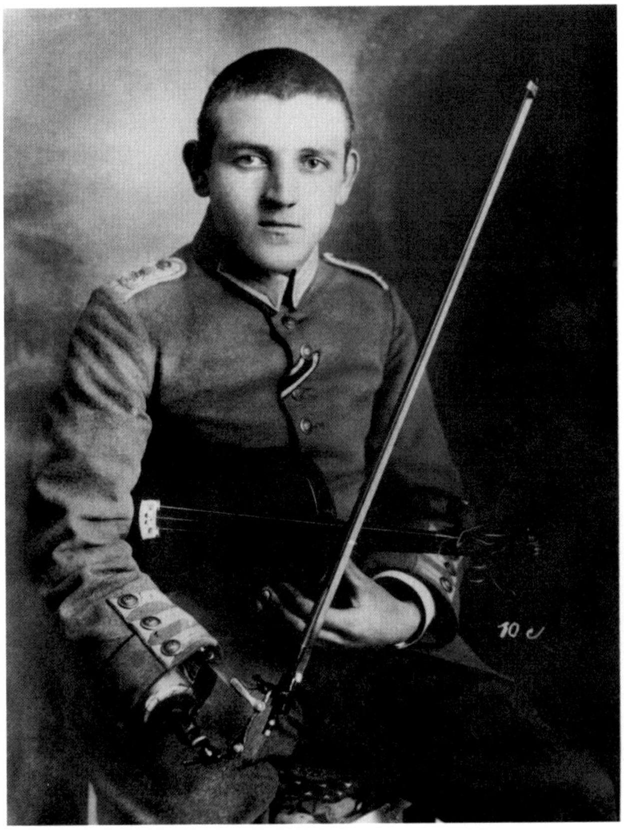

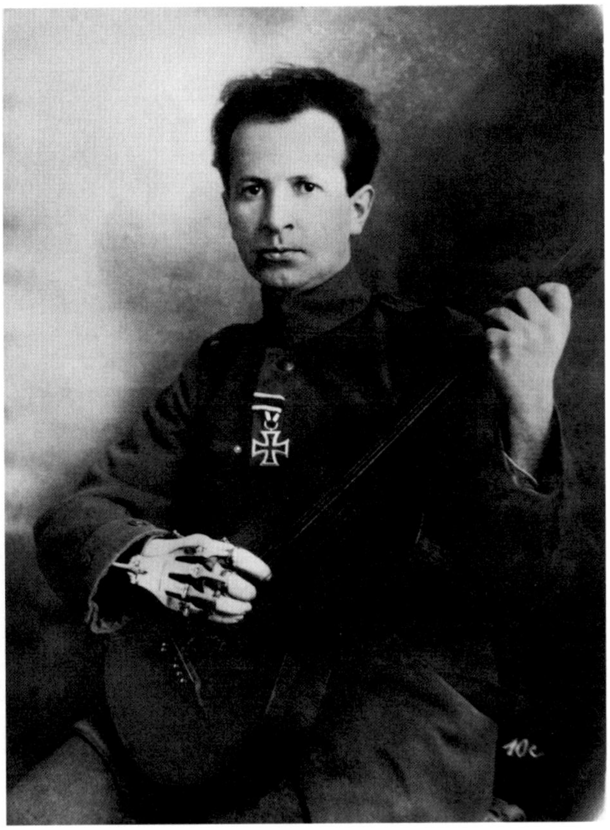

NOTES

1 In this regard, also see Bleker J., 'Medizin im Dienst des Krieges – Krieg im Dienst der Medizin. Zur Frage der Kontinuität des ärztlichen Auftrages und ärztlicher Werthaltungen im Angesicht des Kriegs', in: dies./Schmiedebach H.-P. (ed.), *Medizin und Krieg. Vom Dilemma der Heilberufe 1865 bis 1985*, Frankfurt am Main, 1987, pp. 13-25.

2 Pöhlmann, M., 'Sanitätswesen', in: Hirschfeld G., Krumeich, G., Renz, I. (eds.), *Enzyklopädie Erster Weltkrieg*, p. 812.

3 On the history of the Red cross: Riesenberger D., *Das Deutsche Rote Kreuz: eine Geschichte 1864–1990*, Paderborn, 2002; Eckart W. U., Osten P. (eds.), *Schlachtschrecken – Konventionen: das Rote Kreuz und die Erfindung der Menschlichkeit im Kriege*, Freiburg, 2011.

4 Eckart W.U., '"Der größte Versuch, den die Einbildungskraft ersinnen kann" – der Krieg als hygienisch-bakteriologisches Laboratorium und Erfahrungsfeld', in: ders./Gradmann (ed.), *Die Medizin und der Erste Weltkrieg*, Pfaffenweiler, 1999, p. 299.

5 Mandry, 'Über die Zulässigkeit ärztlicher Eingriffe an Heeresangehörigen. Militärärztlicher Vortrag vom 14. April 1917', in: *Medicinisches Correspondenzblatt des Württembergischen Ärztlichen Landesvereins*, 30. June 1917, nr. 26, p. 289f*;* Delmas P., 'Comment faut-il entendre les rapports respectifs du chirurgien et du blessé dans l'armée', in: *Paris Médical*, vol. 27, 1918, p. 50.

6 Roudeboush M., 'Un patient se défend', in: *Le choc traumatique, 14-18, Aujourd'hui, Today, Heute*, Paris, 2000, pp. 56-67; Delaporte S., *Les médecins dans la Grande Guerre*, 1914–1918, Paris, 2003, pp. 161-186.

7 Lerner P., *Hysterical Men. War, Psychiatry, and the Politics of Trauma in Germany, 1890–1930*, Ithaca, 2003, pp. 86–123.

8 Lewandowsky M., 'Was kann in der Behandlung und Beurteilung der Kriegsneurosen erreicht werden?', in: *Münchener Medizinische Wochenschrift*, 31.7.1917, p. 1031.

9 Roudebush M., *A Battle of Nerves: Hysteria and its Treatment in France during World War I*, Ann Arbor, 1996; Delaporte S., 'Les réponses thérapeutiques', in: Winter J. (ed.), 'Le choc traumatique et l'histoire culturelle de la Grande Guerre', in: *14/18. Aujourd'hui. Today. Heute*, nr. 3, 2000, pp. 37–55.

10 Devaux A., Logre B.J., *Les anxieux*, Paris, 1917, p. 297.

Portraits of German war victims with a hand prosthesis with which they could again pursue their passion, playing the violin.
Photos, In Flanders Fields Museum, Ypres

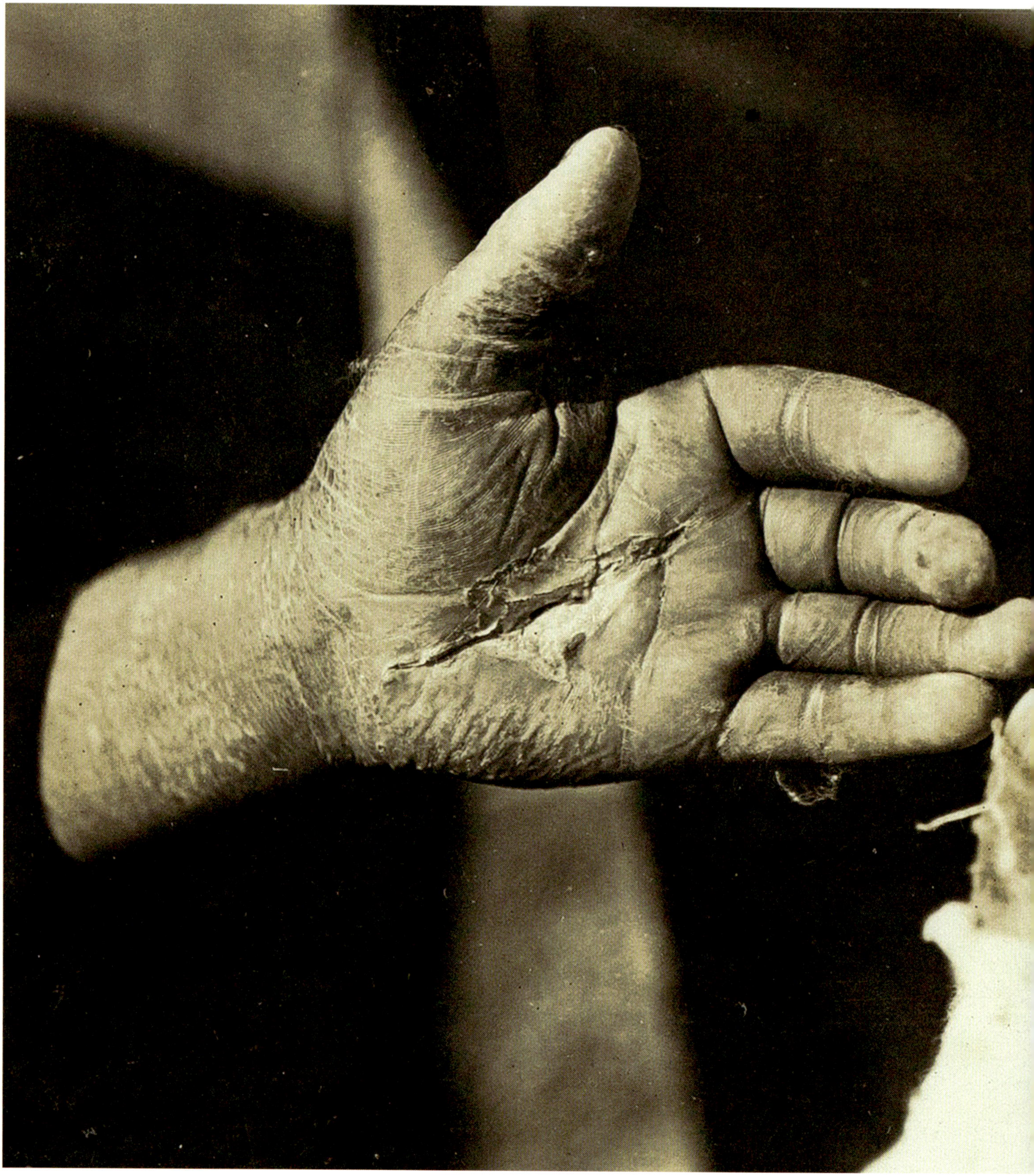

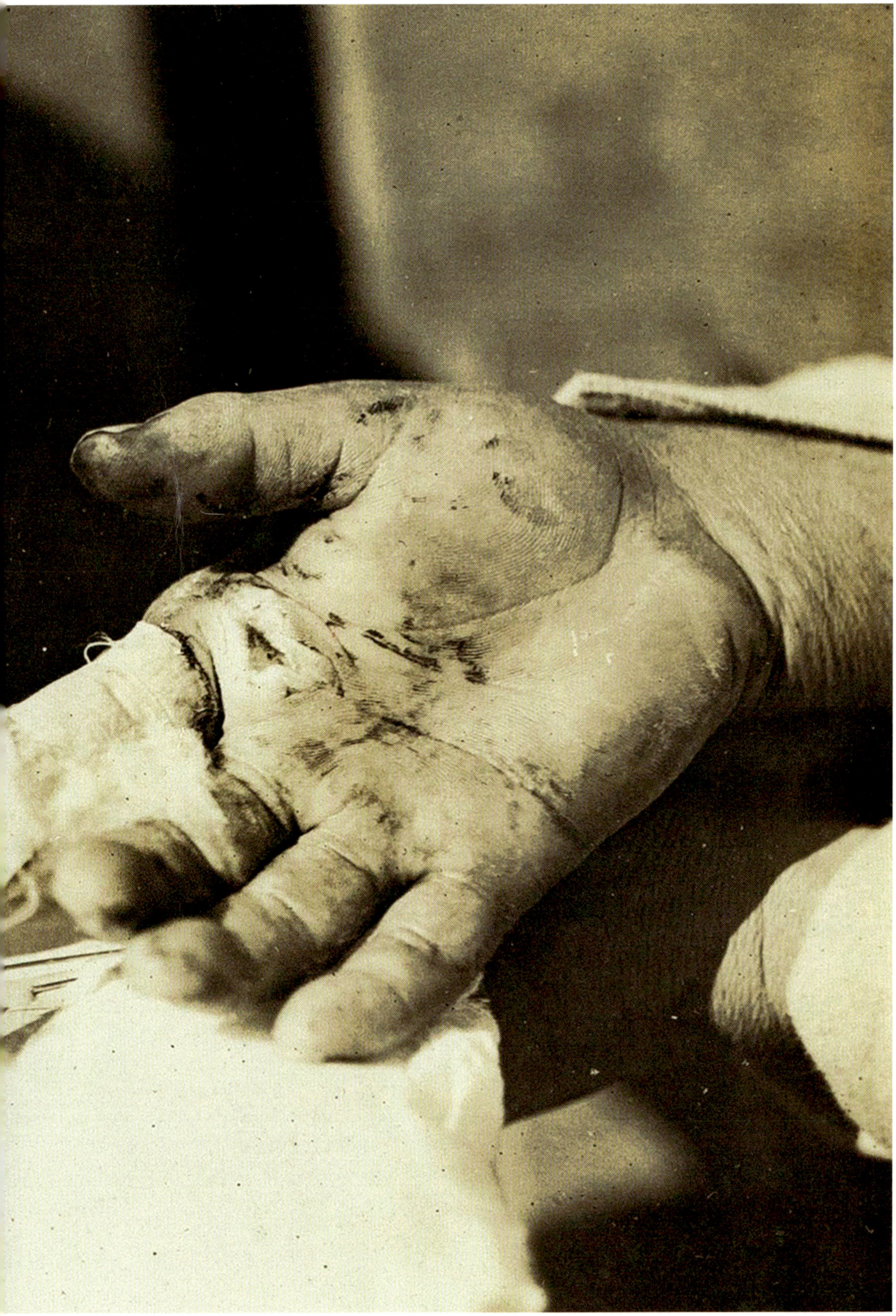

'Self-inflicted wounds', circa 1917–'18. Some soldiers hoped to escape the horrors of war by injuring themselves. If they were caught, they risked the court martial. Photo, The RAMC Muniment Collection in the care of the Wellcome Library, London

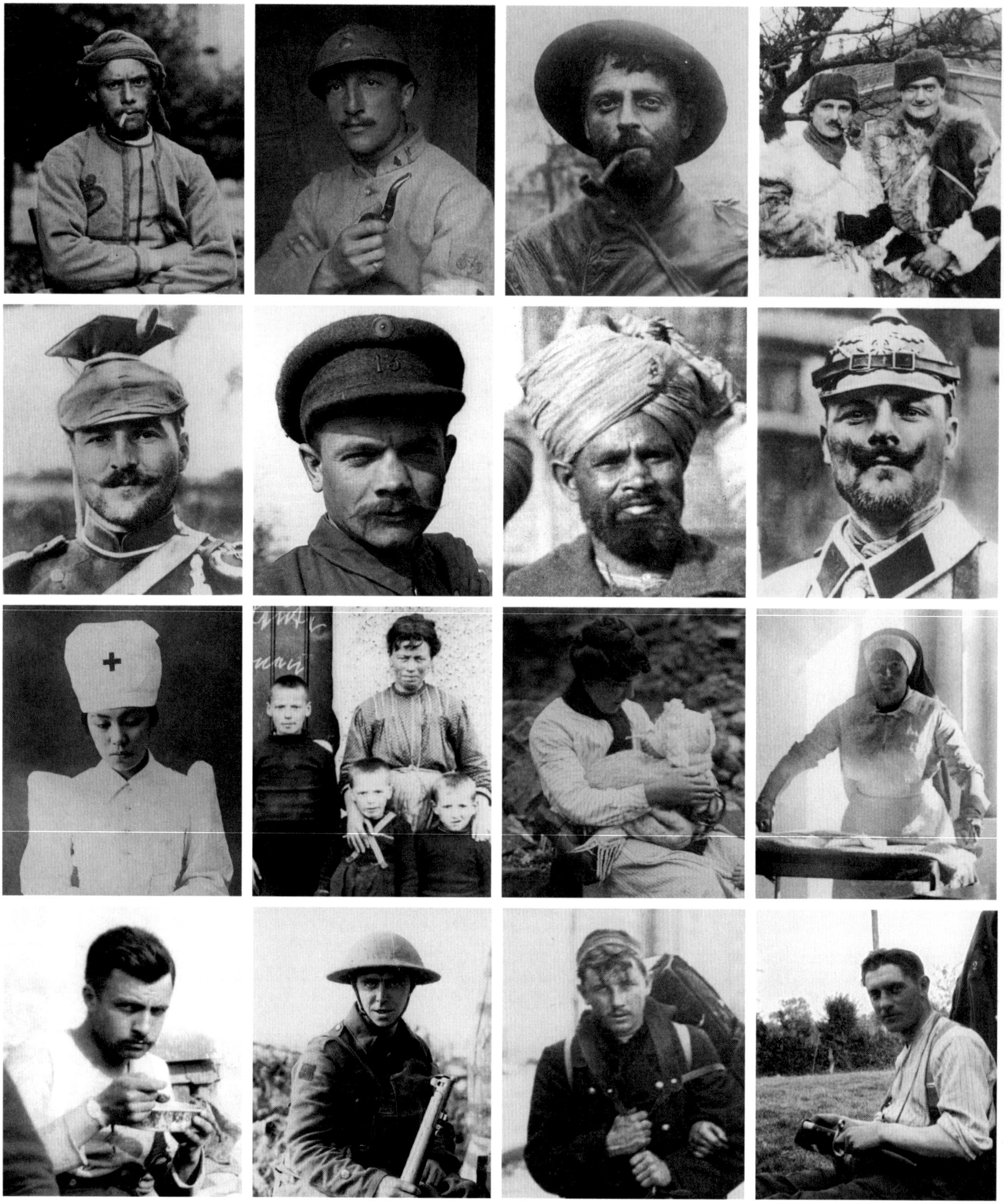

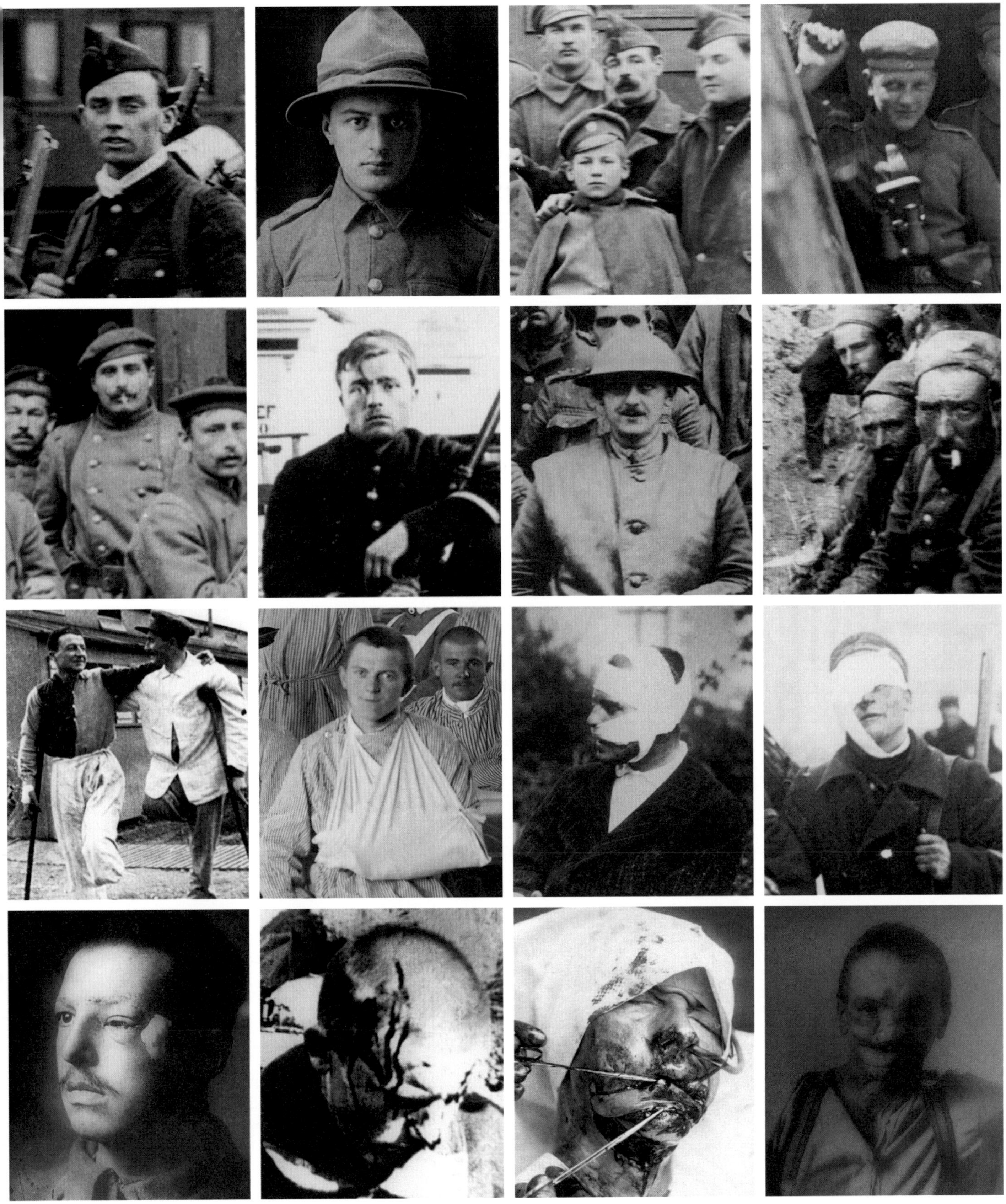

114)

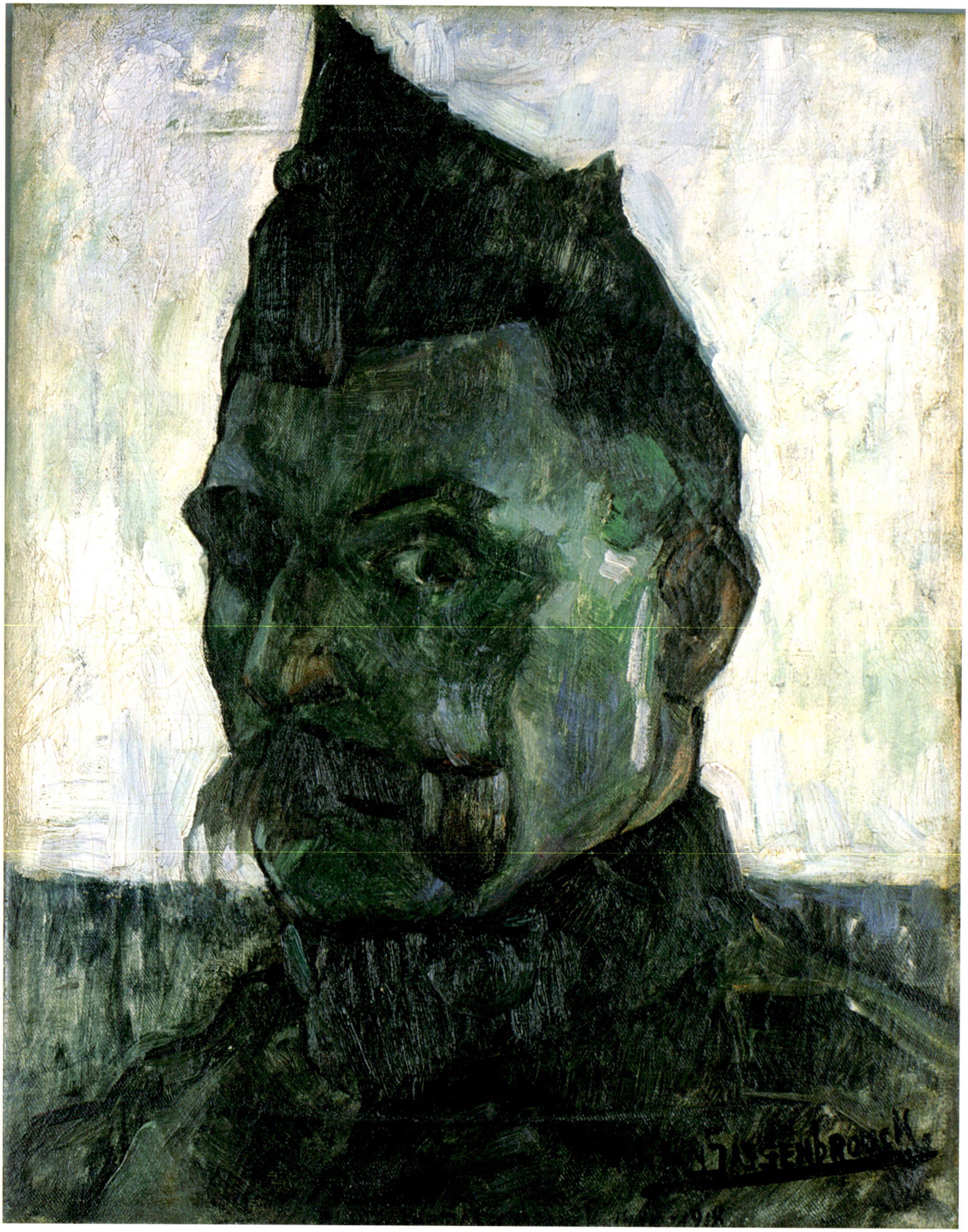

SANDRINE SMETS

Achille Van Sassenbrouck

A Wounded Body, a Healing Oeuvre

Achille Van Sassenbrouck was 29 when he was wounded, under a storm of steel, on 10 December 1915. The young lance corporal of the 1st Carabineers Regiment was on night watch in a communication trench in Caeskerke, near the De Koning farm, in the Dixmude sector. He suffered serious eye damage as well as nervous disturbances after a shell exploded very close to him.[1] It was a brutal experience that turned his life upside down and changed his work forever.

AN ARTIST IN THE MAKING BEFORE 1914

When he voluntarily enlisted on 12 August 1914, Achille Van Sassenbrouck was an artist trying to make a name for himself. His trajectory was far from linear. Soon after he turned 12, he left his family home. After a few months' wandering around, he enrolled at the Académie de Bruges, where he learned decorative painting between 1899 and 1909. His talent was quickly recognised, and earned him seven medals. But the artisan had other ambitions. Despite his financial difficulties, he enrolled at the Institut Supérieur in Antwerp. His intention to participate in the 1911 Prix de Rome was foiled by typhus.[2] Regarded as a promising artist at the time, the war years would reveal his true talent. Following the traumatic event, Van Sassenbrouck no longer painted in order to become a painter: he painted in order to find a new pictorial language.

HIS ARTISTIC PRACTICE: FROM CATHARSIS TO SELF-CONFIDENCE

After being wounded, Van Sassenbrouck was evacuated via Adinkerke to the military hospital in Calais. At the end of his convalescence, in May 1916, the artist was declared unfit for duty and was sent, in July, to the Port-Villez Institute for the Wounded, Invalids and Orphans of War, whose mission was to retrain the invalids to prepare them for their future social and professional reintegration. Seventy-three trades were taught there. Achille Van Sassenbrouck taught painting in its art workshops. The main aim of the artistic training was to give the invalids the know-how to earn a living. However, it was also undoubtedly therapeutic, both for the pupils and the teachers. The Port-Villez school offered a reassuring, safe environment[3] in which the victims of the violence of war broke their silence by sublimating their creeping anxieties, which could then gradually be changed and transformed into acceptable images.[4] Creative activity has a cathartic role, enabling pathogenic affects to be disposed of. Moreover, it gives individuals greater self-worth, allowing them to gradually leave behind their victim status and take control of their lives again. Learning or practising a trade[5] is a means of recapturing a primordial independence and self-confidence.[6] Wiser for this experience, Van Sassenbrouck left the school. On 21 September 1917, having been designated a member of the *Artistic Section of the Belgian Army,*[7] he returned to the front to document the war through drawings and paintings.

TRAUMA – SOURCE OF CREATIVE CRISES?

When he found himself under fire once again, he produced an astonishing self-portrait in an Expressionist style[8]. It is a head and shoulders, slightly three-quarter view of him in uniform. He gazes at the spectator with his left eye, which is partially obscured by the smoke rising from his pipe. He had lost the use of this eye,

Achille Van Sassenbrouck, Self-Portrait in Uniform,
Belgium, 14 February 1918, oil on canvas. Royal Army Museum, Brussels

which looks without seeing, with no timidity whatsoever. The disturbing atmosphere of the painting is reinforced by the use of sombre green tones and highly contrasting backlight. These colour surfaces, simply juxtaposed and accentuated by a black line that follows the contours of the figure, give the portrait the look of a collage. The elements of the work that could suggest depth are squashed into a single plane: the pipe in front of the face, the figure with its angular features, and the neutral background. This annihilates perspective. Everything in this self-portrait creates a sense of anxiety, as experienced by the soldier confronting war, confronting death. According to Didier Anzieu, 'anxiety, suffering, terror and the interior void can be so great that creativity appears to be the only other outlet'[9]. The author associates creativity with a state of crisis, and talks about 'creative crises'. With Van Sassenbrouck, they are expressed through a passion for painting,[10] as if for him painting represented the only means of living and inhabiting the world. To paint is to create, to give life, and in so doing, to thumb one's nose at the violence of war and its destructive power, as though proximity to death merely affirms life.

A HEALING OEUVRE

The trauma of being wounded found another outlet in his creative process: the birth of a new style or, a reinvention of his artistic language. At the beginning of the war, the artist painted small pictures in a rather bland, representational style, whereas after being wounded, he developed a highly personal style all of his own. His paintings after his convalescence are reminiscent of Fauvism, sometimes with Expressionist accents. His colour palette is enriched with bright colours and there is interplay of powerful contrasts. His brushstrokes fragment in certain places, and in others the paint is applied in wide blocks of colour. The contours become geometric, and the forms are outlined with a stroke of black. Some of the aesthetic choices he makes are evidently due to his partial blindness, which radically changed his visual perception. But beyond the physical injury, his psychological trauma also changed the way he painted. His disability ruptured his physical integrity. So the black outline is, for the artist, a way of rebuilding his body image, and also the elements that make up the space that the body occupies and interacts with. His

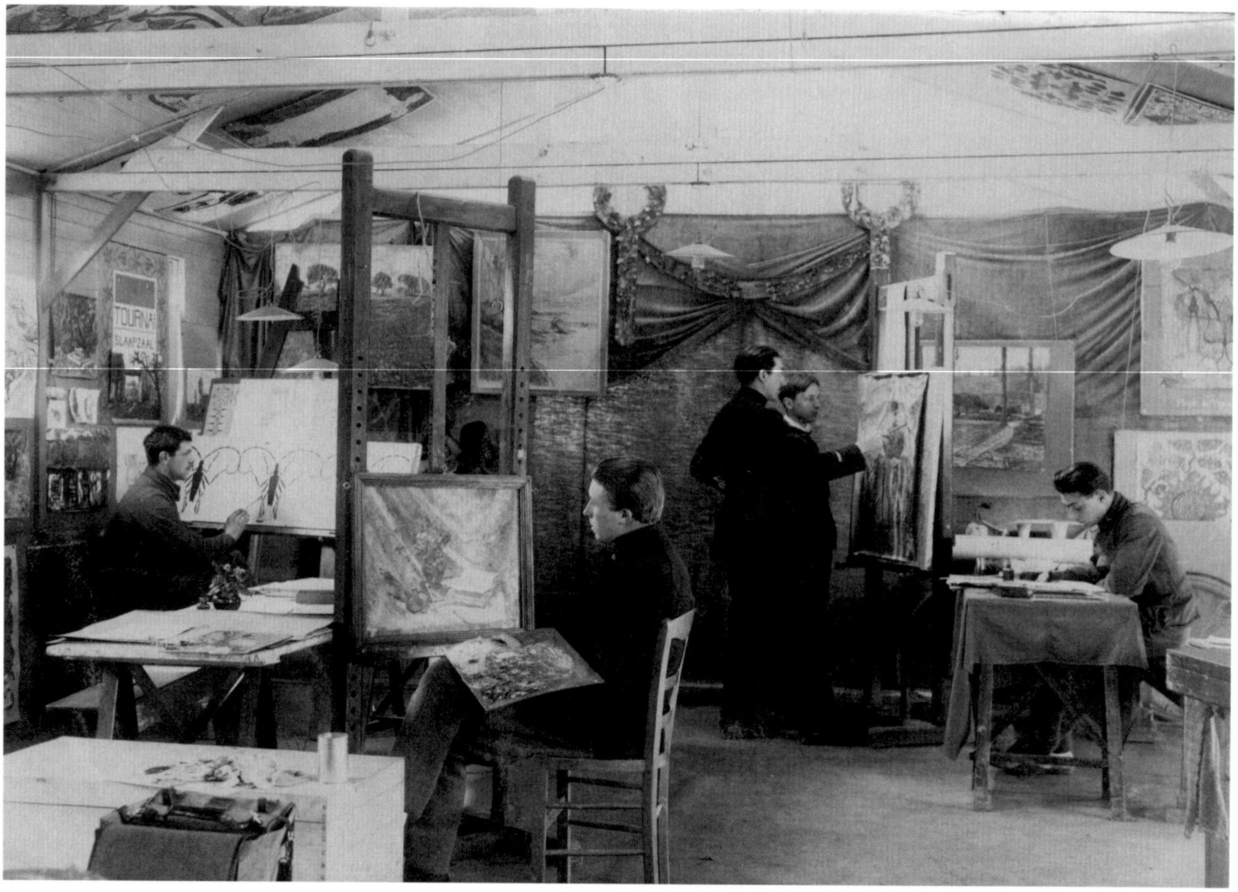

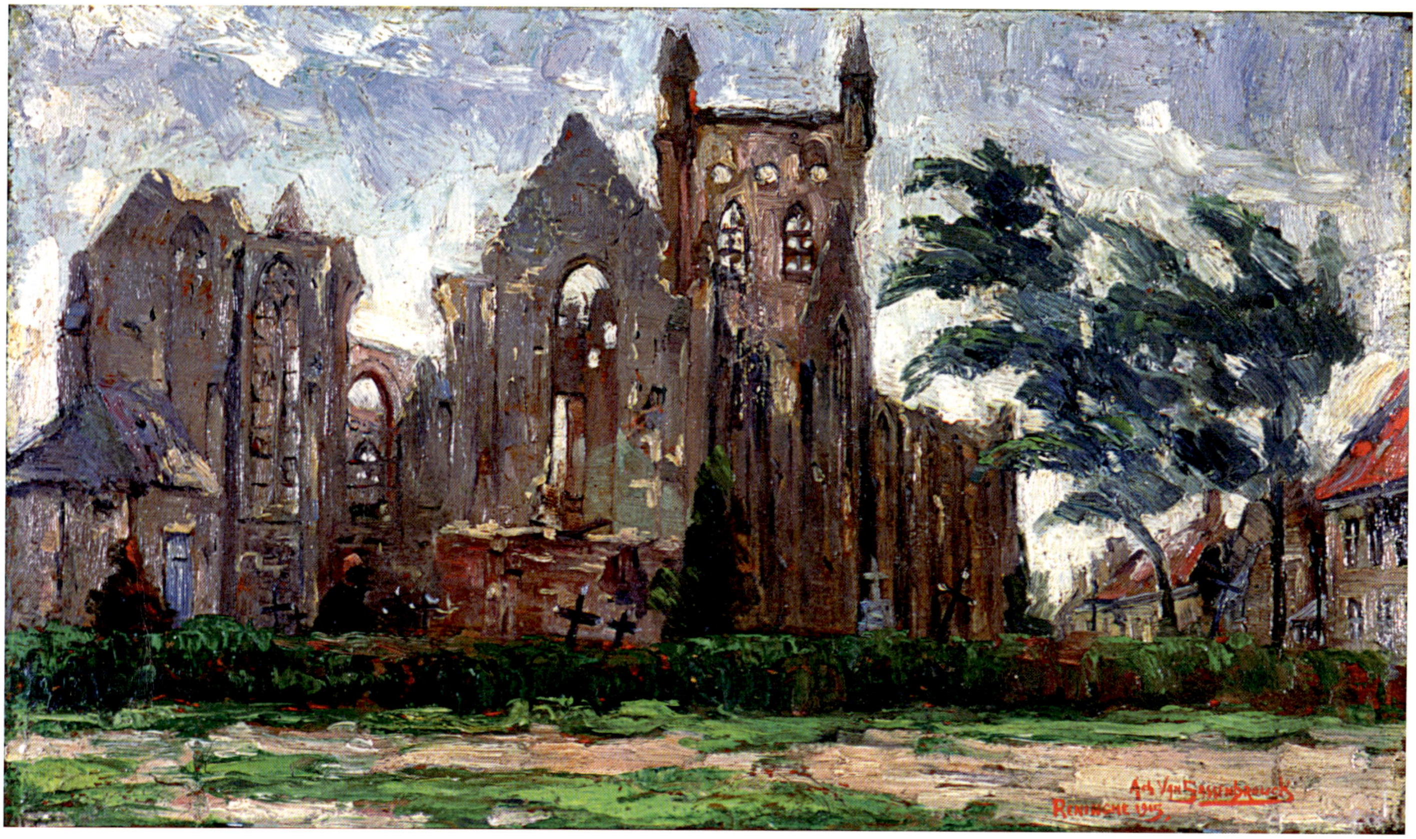

experience of war also gave rise to other stylistic metamorphoses. The explosion of colours represents the strength of emotions and expresses the devastating violence of battle. But disability and experience are not the only factors behind this change of style. During his time at Port-Villez, Van Sassenbrouck visited Claude Monet's studio in Giverny, the neighbouring village on the opposite bank of the Seine. It is likely that the two artists talked to each other about how their eye problems made it difficult to work (Monet developed cataracts in 1908). Achille Van Sassenbrouck gradually entered into a long process of symbolic appropriation of his experiences at the front by reconstructing his buried feelings through image, form, paint and colour. His relationships with his fellow teachers, pupils and Claude Monet also played an essential role in this development. These are the contributory factors to his resilience, which allowed the artist to convert his suffering, and his mourning for his wounded body, into a healing oeuvre.

AN INDELIBLE TRACE

Demobbed on 15 May 1919, Van Sassenbrouck continued to produce numerous paintings on the subject of war, from Armistice Day until about 1920. The artist was declared 'severely wounded' with 60% invalidity, which made him eligible for an annual pension and life annuity of 2,457 francs. He was decorated with several Belgian orders and medals commemorating the First World War, including the Fire Cross in 1936. However, above all, the Great War was anchored in his physical and psychological history. Van Sassenbrouck succeeded in coming to terms with the irreversible reality of his

Inside view of the painters' studio of the *'Institut militaire belge de Rééducation professionelle'* in Port-Villez. The man in the middle who is teaching the pupil is presumably Achille Van Sassenbrouck.
Photo, Royal Army Museum, Brussels

Van Sassenbrouck made this painting in 1915, before he was injured.
Achille Van Sassenbrouck, **Destroyed Church of Reninge**,
1915, oil paint on wood. Royal Army Museum, Brussels

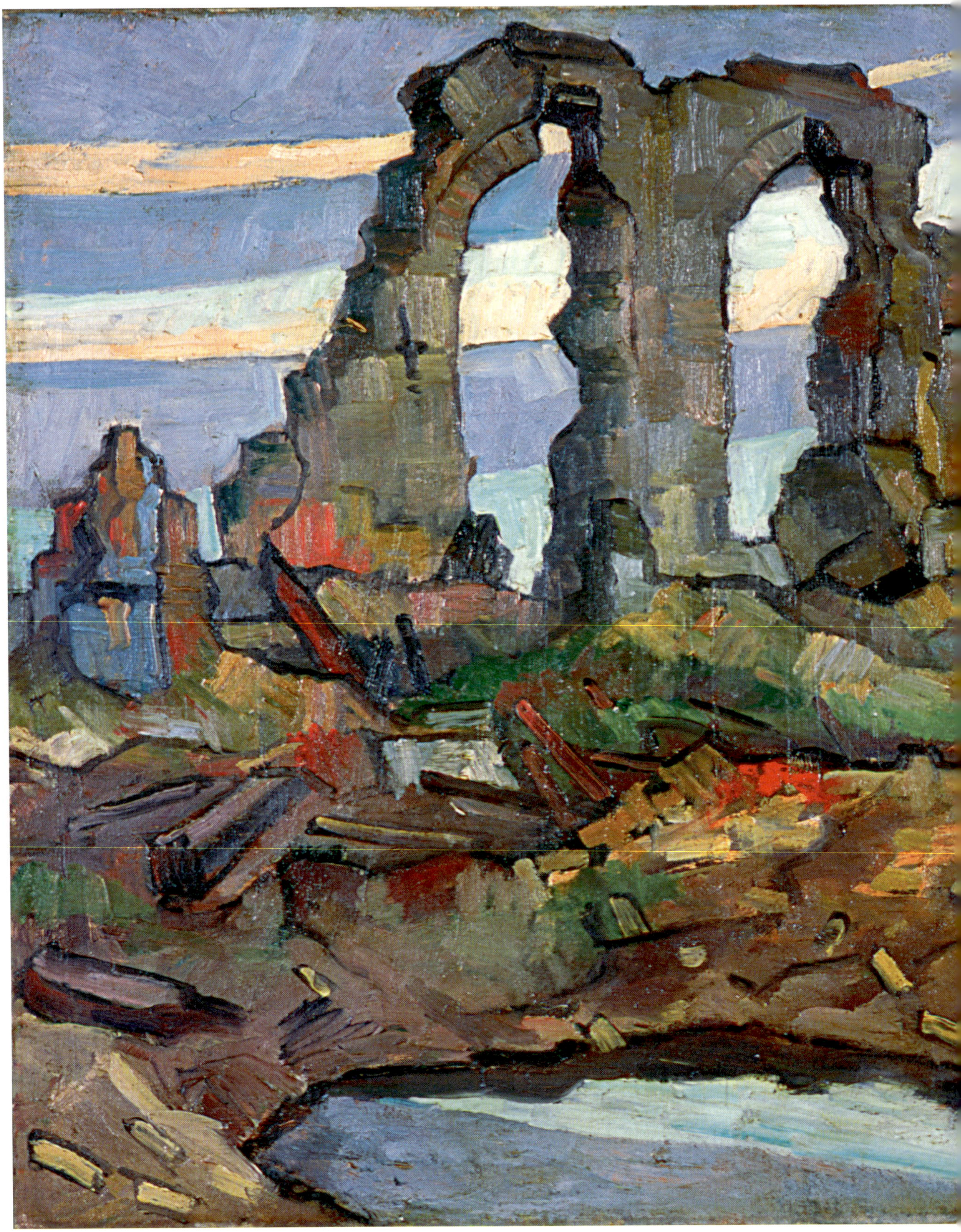

The artist completed this work after his injury, in 1919. Achille Van Sassenbrouck, **Ruins of the Beguinage Church in Diksmuide**, 1919, oil painting on wood. Royal Army Museum, Brussels

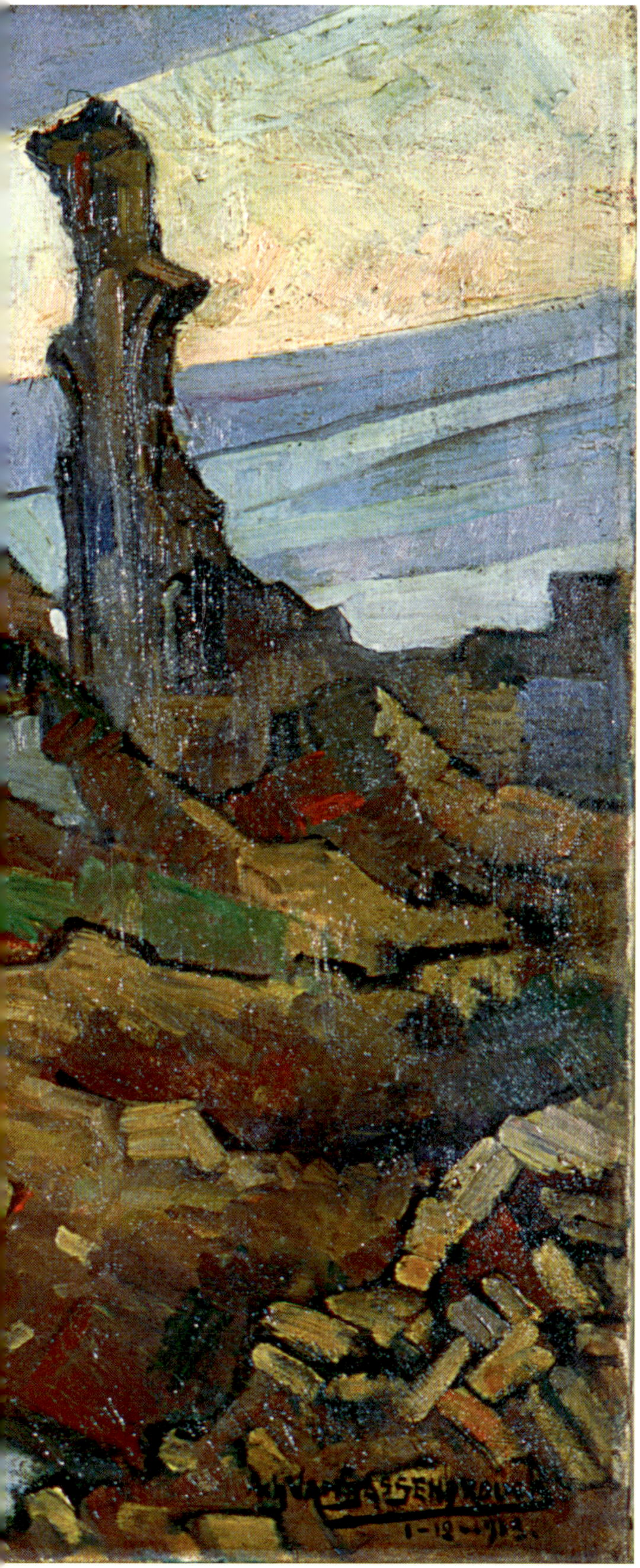

disability, in feeling at one with it, thereby neutralising the pain and coming out the other side all the richer for it. Even though his style of painting continued to evolve, the black outline remained, like an indelible trace of the trauma he suffered. Who can claim that the experience of war is inexpressible? Surely proximity to imminent death finds even more of an outlet in aesthetics and style than in iconography?

NOTES

1 Brussels, MRA, Documentation Centre, Regimental File on Achille Van Sassenbrouck, no 6033390.

2 De Vleeschouwer F., 'Achiel Van Sassenbrouck', in *Nationaal biografisch Woordenboek*, Brussels, vol. X, 1983, col. 571-579.

3 The school sits on a plateau which overlooks the Seine Valley, and is surrounded by woods. The location is quiet, without being completely isolated (trains and river traffic pass by), and the air is healthy there. All the conditions are right for rehabilitation, to give the invalids 'the strength and appetite for work'. See: de Paeuw L., *La rééducation professionnelle des grands blessés de guerre et l'Institut Militaire Belge de Rééducation Professionnelle de Port-Villez-lez-Vernon (Eure). Conférence faite le 15 janvier 1916 à l'Ambulance de l'Océan à La Panne*, Port-Villez, s.d., p. 15.

4 It is difficult to determine how much creativity it was possible to bring into these artistic training courses, particularly the decorative painting sections (imitation wood and marble; painting of letters, labels and signs; ceramic and porcelain painting; glass painting). The *artistic painting* section was no doubt the one that allowed the most freedom. It gave rise to 'original forms and colour combinations that were both bold and cheerful' (see: de Paeuw L., *La rééducation professionnelle des soldats mutilés et estropiés*, Paris-Nancy, 1917, p. 120).

5 Van Sassenbrouck was extremely proud of his status as a teacher at Port-Villez. In a letter to Mademoiselle Belpaire dated 20 December 1916, the artist writes beneath his signature 'Teacher / Port-Villez par Vernon (Eure)'. See: Antwerp, Het Letterenhuis, Letter from Achille Van Sassenbrouck to Marie-Elisabeth Belpaire, dd. 20 December 1916.

6 A pioneering, if incomplete, form of art therapy. See: Klein J.-P., *L'art-thérapie*, Paris, 2010 ; Hamel J. & Labrèche J. (dir.), *Découvrir l'art-thérapie. Des mots sur les maux. Des couleurs sur les douleurs*, Paris, 2010.

7 Smets S., 'La section artistique de l'armée belge', in *1917*, Centre Pompidou-Metz, 2012, p. 264.

8 Brussels, Royal Army Museum, inv. 200400367, Achille Van Sassenbrouck (1886–1979), *Autoportrait en uniforme des carabiniers*, 4 February 1918, Oil on canvas, 42,5 x 33 cm.

9 The first outlet being dreams. See: Anzieu D., *Le corps de l'œuvre. Essais psychanalytiques sur le travail créateur*, Paris, 1981, p. 20.

10 In September 1918 the artist exhibited 62 works in a solo exhibition at De Panne, which shows the intensity of his production during barely one year.

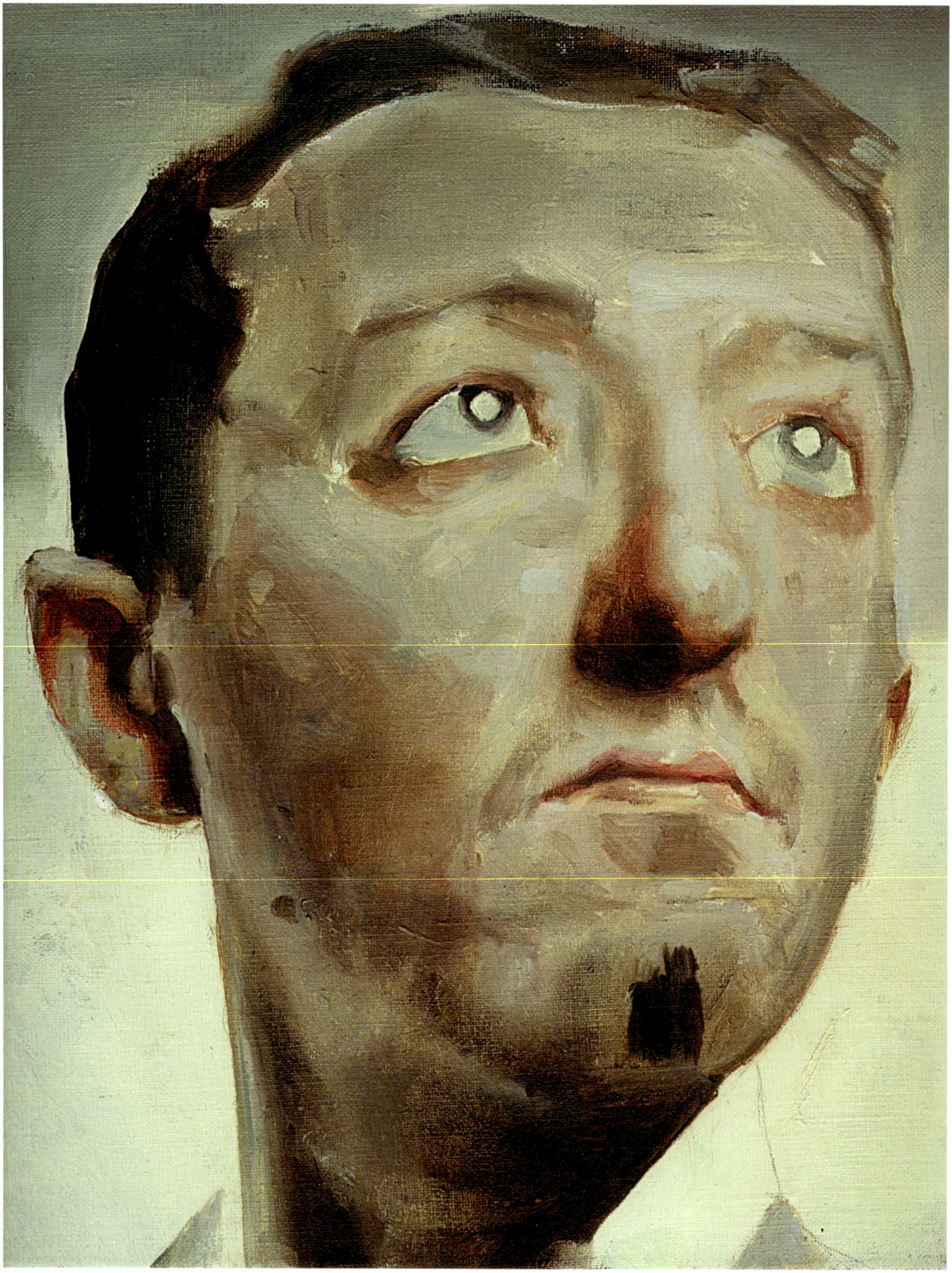

CHRISTINE VAN EVERBROECK

Three Life Stories about War and Psychiatry

Albert G[1]

ST GILLES 5/12/1886 – ?

This 1st class battalion doctor, who was married with two children, was 38 when the war broke out. He worked alternately at the front and in the hospitals behind the lines, mostly in Calais. But in April 1918, he was hospitalised himself: first at the Bonsecours Hospital near Rouen, then at the Dinard Military Hospital. His colleagues diagnosed drug addiction following a bout of nervous asthenia (depression), which he developed while serving at De Panne.

He was put on a drug withdrawal programme, and given tonics and sleep medication, combined with isolation – all under close observation.

In June 1918, he was sent to a hospital for military personnel suffering from nervous disorders housed in the former Abbey of Juaye-Mondaye, in Normandy, for a month. He then returned to duty in Calais, but by the end of the war he was back in hospital again. His health problems – a consequence of his drug addiction – continued after the war. He was described as "(...) suffering from physical depression and nerves following morphine abuse, for which he has already received treatment for several months (Calais and Brussels). (...) As a result, this Health Service officer seems disinclined to break free from his gloomy disposition which, taken thus far, suggests that battalion doctor G. has experienced a mental decline, or at the very least a cognitive weakness, incompatible with the responsibilities he must assume as a military doctor."[2]

His psychiatric problems forced him to give up work in May 1920 and, a year later, led him to be committed to the asylum in Strop, Ghent, for the first time. There Dr Maere confirmed that he was addicted to heroin and compared his body to a sieve, since he had injected himself so many times. The patient alternated between passivity and agitation, depending on whether or not he had taken the drug. After three months, Albert G left the hospital, despite the fact that his addiction had not been cured. The chief physician of the Malines Military Hospital, where the army's psychiatric patients were treated, also did not believe he had been cured, and was proved right, because in November of the same year, Albert G was committed to Strop again.

Dr Maere observed that the patient had indeed left too soon. The time was too short for him to be rehabilitated, and he fell more deeply into drug addiction than ever before. His symptoms – despondency, congestion, lethargy and inactivity – returned, along with the craving to procure the narcotic by any means possible. Before he was committed, Albert G would go to numerous different pharmacists to procure a relatively moderate dose of the drug for himself each time. It was his father, in desperation after seeing his son go through rehabilitation without success six times in various institutions and from which he had run away, who had him committed. Dr Maere at Strop considered him to be a danger to himself and others.

The paintings of Jan De Maesschalck (1958) bathe in an atmosphere of melancholy, abandonment and silence. Young women reading books, sitting and staring in loneliness. Empty interiors or nightly scenes that occur when everyone is sleeping and the streets seem empty. The glance of the man and woman in the two paintings is mysterious and raises questions. What are they looking at? Apparently something up high. Are they looking at the same thing? Perhaps at something awful, as is suggested by the look in their eyes. But they simultaneously also exude resignation, a sense of impotence and forced acceptance.
Jan De Maesschalck, **Untitled (the builing)**, 2010, oil on canvas. Courtesy Zeno X Gallery, Antwerp

A few months later, on 3 July 1922, Albert G left Strop for the last time. His condition had evidently improved this time because he turns up in records a few years later as head of the State Lunatic Asylum in Tournai.

1 Military medical archives (HM Bxl): Bonsecours register 6/4/18-30/5/18 MRA, file DO 7928. Strop medical records 1918–1939

2 4/12/19: consultation certificate of Dr Léotard of the Arlon Military Hospital

Dr Léon Spaas[1]

HAMONT 18/8/1880–14/12/1946

Léon Spaas was born in Hamont (Limburg) on 18 August 1880. He completed his medical studies in 1905[2]. During those studies, he was called up for military service. In October 1900, he joined, like many of his fellow students, the army's medical service.

Two years after obtaining his degree, he was appointed Chief Physician at the mental institute in Munsterbilzen (Limburg) at the age of 27.

At the onset of World War I, Léon Spaas was conscripted. He became Assistant Reserve Physician with the rank of captain in the second line regiment in Antwerp (Beveren-Waas). Spaas was imprisoned at the fall of Antwerp. He was briefly confined but was soon released under the stipulations of the Geneva Convention, which protects medical staff. As of 19 October 1914, he was affiliated with the base in Calais where the medical department of the Belgian army, which had retreated behind the Yser, was situated from then on.

General Practitioner Roland, director of nursing at the base in Calais, recognised Spaas' specialisation in psychiatry and entrusted him with the supervision of the medical department for nervous and mental disorders in the Belgian army from 6 December 1914. On 17 January of the following year, Spaas established himself in the acclaimed rooms of the Saint-Emile school in Calais, the military neuro-psychiatric centre where almost all servicemen who were admitted for observation for mental problems were sent. He became the medical-legal expert for mental-medical assessment for the military tribunals and courts. He was also "responsible for the medical service for neurotic or insane officers who are treated in the various hospitals of the base [of Calais][3]".

From the start of the conflict, Léon Spaas was aware of the responsibility of the war for the occurrence of nervous disorders and psychological problems: "The war, with its internal and external emotions, especially the effect of heavy artillery, has largely contributed, in many soldiers, to the rise of nervous and psychological disorders, and especially to the resurgence of latent disorders. Hereditariness and personal precedents were examined in each individual case. Of all mental disorders, mental confusion was the most prevalent. The longer the battle, the more and the more quickly

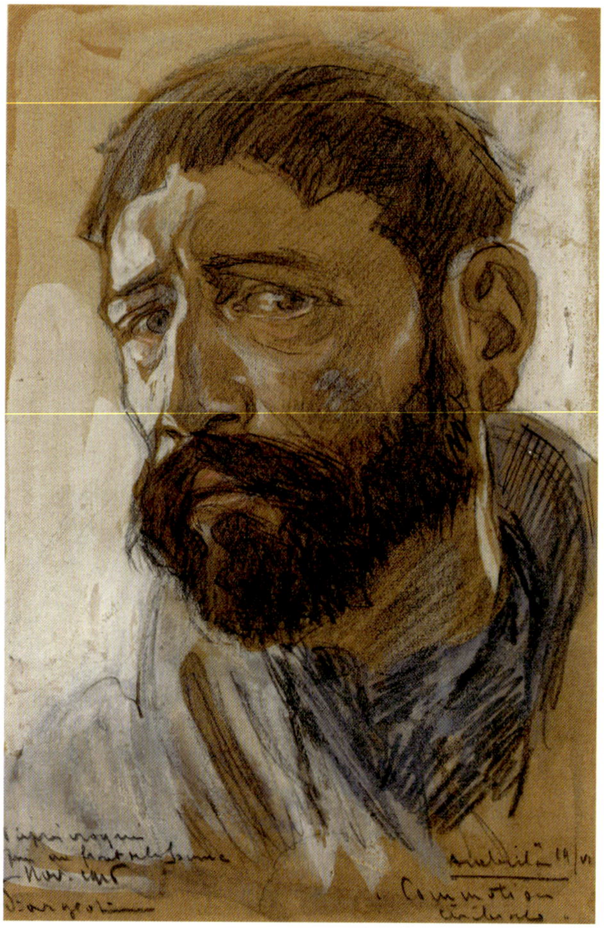

Ferdinand Fargeot, **Sketch of a Soldier in Shock**, s.d., gouache. Musée du Service de santé des armées, Val-de-Grâce

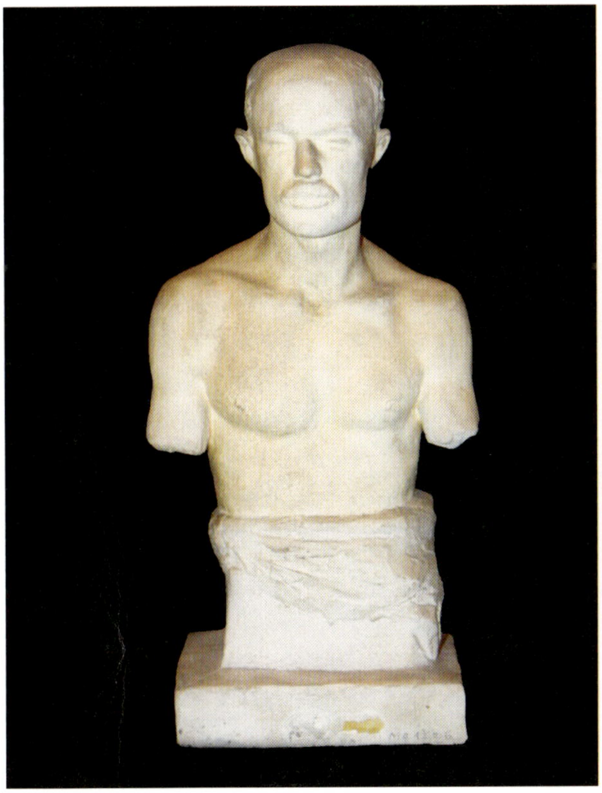

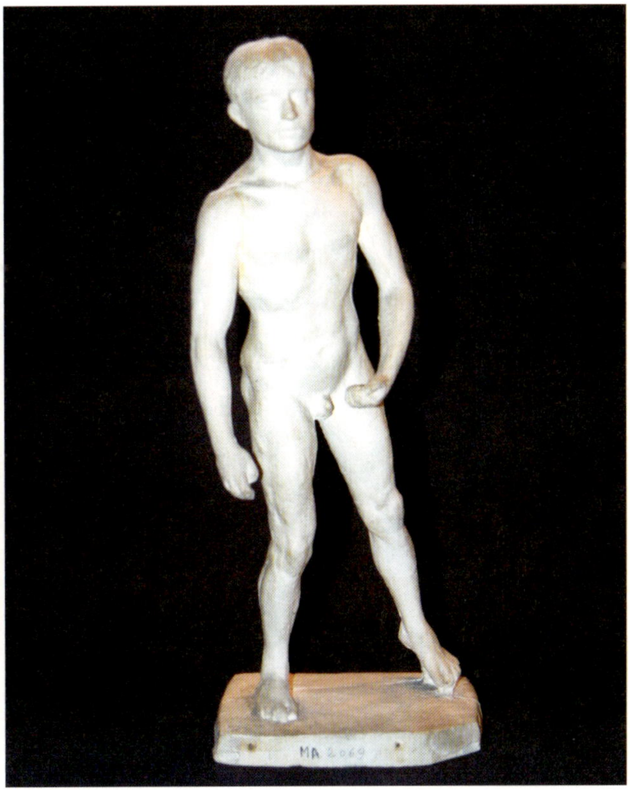

the number of servicemen with mental disorders, neurasthenia, nervous breakdowns and so on increases[4]".

Dr Spaas's task, as psychiatrist but also as legal expert, was extremely delicate. The destiny of the charged soldiers depended on his expertise and assessment of the clarity and the simplicity with which he could convey his opinion to the officers in charge. His medical reports indicate an attentive and understanding personality, a man who never forgot the circumstances in which his patients were having to live. Yet he still, as did his Belgian colleagues and European specialists, set great store by predisposition and hereditariness. For him, the war often simply brought problems that were latently present to the surface. He regretted that recruitment did not take account of selection on the basis of the mental condition and that for this reason, soldiers were drafted who had no place in the army.

Spaas's lieutenant-colonels were aware of his qualities. "Physician-assistant Spaas is a very diligent and extremely dedicated officer who always practised his difficult and delicate profession to my greatest satisfaction[5]". Until the end of the war, he remained in service in Calais. However, as soon as the truce had been signed, the institution in Munsterbilzen reclaimed him[6]. Spaas himself requested unpaid leave as of 11 December 1918. After acceptance of his request, he left Calais on 20 January 1919 to rejoin his patients in Munsterbilzen.

After the war Spaas had a dual career: medical and political.

Apart from his responsibilities in the institution, he was appointed inspector of health care in schools[7] in May 1922. He was also a member of the Belgian Mental Healthcare Association.

However, he was mainly a committed Fleming. As a member of the association of Flemish war veterans, VOS, he was the Honorary Chairman of the *Vlaamsche Jonge Wachten* [young Flemish sentries] in Bilzen and campaigned for the *Flemification* of Ghent University. He also took part in the intellectual and scientific

The images in the collection of military hospital Val-de-Grâce in Paris were made shortly after World War I. They show soldiers who became the victim of shell shock.
Marc Leriche, **Pseudoparalysis of the Back**, s.d., plaster. Musée du Service de santé des armées, Val-de-Grâce
Marc Leriche, **Post-Shock Hemiplegia of Chest and Limbs**, s.d., plaster. Musée du Service de santé des armées, Val-de-Grâce

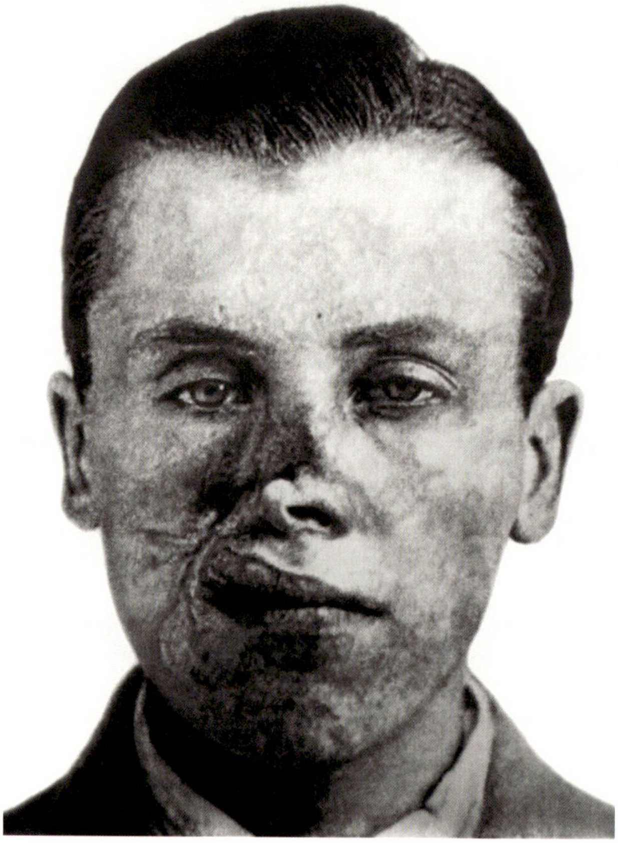

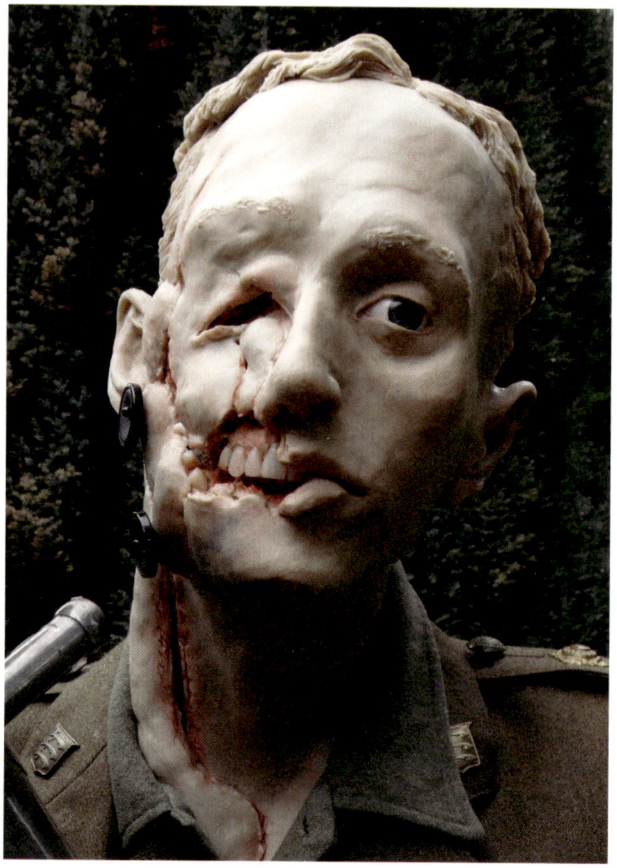

debate during the *Wetenschappelijke Vlaamsche Kongressen* [Flemish scientific conferences]. He was part of the Flemish wing of the Catholic party and became a member of the provincial council of Limburg[8] in 1926.

He married Maria-Josepha-Angelica Bijvoet. The couple had five children. She died in 1927 at the age of 53. Léon Spaas died in Munsterbilzen on 14 December 1946.

1 Military dossier MRA DO 02778
2 Annuaire médical belge, 1925
3 Letter of Spaas to the Ministry of War, 20 December 1918
4 Royal Army Museum: Ex-CDH, Cdt supérieur de la base de Calais (CSBC), farde 6, Rapport sur l'organisation du service sanitaire de la base de Calais. Handwritten text of 9 March 1916, méd. Gal du ss de la base, 10p., Rapport du Dr Spaas, 1/3/1916
5 Description of 23 February 1918 by the Superintendent
6 Report of the institution during the 1914–1918 war, handwritten notes, s.d., archives of Medical Centre Sint-Jozef Munsterbilzen, letter of 23/4/2012
7 *Het Laatste Nieuws*, 15/5/1922
8 *De Standaard*, 2/10/1919, 24/7/1919, 15/12/1920, 12/7/1926. *Het Laatste Nieuws*, 11/7/1922, 28/5/1921, 20/6/1921, 16/11/1921. *De Volksgazet* 10/8/1923

French artist Eric Manigaud (1971) is known for his large hyper-realist pencil drawings, for which he is inspired by existing historic images. For instance, the murder scenes based on photos of Alphonse Bertillon (1853–1914), who developed a method for documenting and studying corpses, but also wanted to identify criminals on the basis of anthropometry. For the portraits of 19th century psychiatric patients he was inspired by photos of the Salpêtrière in Paris.
War is also a recurring theme: signs of death and destruction from World War I and bombed out towns during World War II. The many photos of *gueules cassées* also appeal to his imagination.
Eric Manigaud, **Gueule Cassée**, 2006, pencil and graphite on paper.
Private collection Antwerp, Courtesy Fifty One Fine Art Photography, Antwerp

Inspired by images of so-called 'Gueules Cassées' from World War I, British artist Eleanor Crook created a group of sculptured soldiers. The wounds in their faces bear the marks of war and show the interventions of plastic surgery. The soldiers come from various wars, including World War I and II. Together with its technological developments, each war has its own type of injuries, which can be seen in this work of art. The set-up as a military band shows the bond between the soldiers, but simultaneously ridicules the marching music that should encourage them. They are united in misery. For many soldiers their facial injuries resulted in a serious psychological trauma.
Eleanor Crook, **'And the band played on', a military band of historic plastic surgery patients from the Crimean War until now** (detail), 2013, life-size, in wax and mixed material. Collection artist

Arthur C[1]

LEKE 18/4/1892 – ZELZATE 5/8/1965

Arthur C, a navvy from Leke, north of Dixmude, left his region before the German advance. He was 23 when he was called to arms under the 1915 special conscription order, which required all Belgian men between the ages of 18 and 25 not already in military service and residing in non-occupied Belgium, France or Great Britain to enlist.[2] He served in the infantry (6th heavy regiment) and was wounded in Boesinghe, on the Yser Canal, north of Ypres, in June 1916, during one of the incessant artillery battles between the Germans and the Belgians. He was hit in the face by shrapnel. After spending about four months in hospital, he trained as a machine gunner at the dedicated instruction centre in Criel-sur-mer, Upper Normandy. With his new skills, he joined the 11th heavy infantry regiment in October 1916, to which a company of machine gunners was attached. However, his injuries evidently affected his mental state and, a year later, he was sent to the military neuropsychiatric centre in the St Emile Field Hospital in Calais for observation. He was suffering from mental lethargy, and seemed inert and indifferent. After two months Dr Spaas, the centre's chief physician, sent him

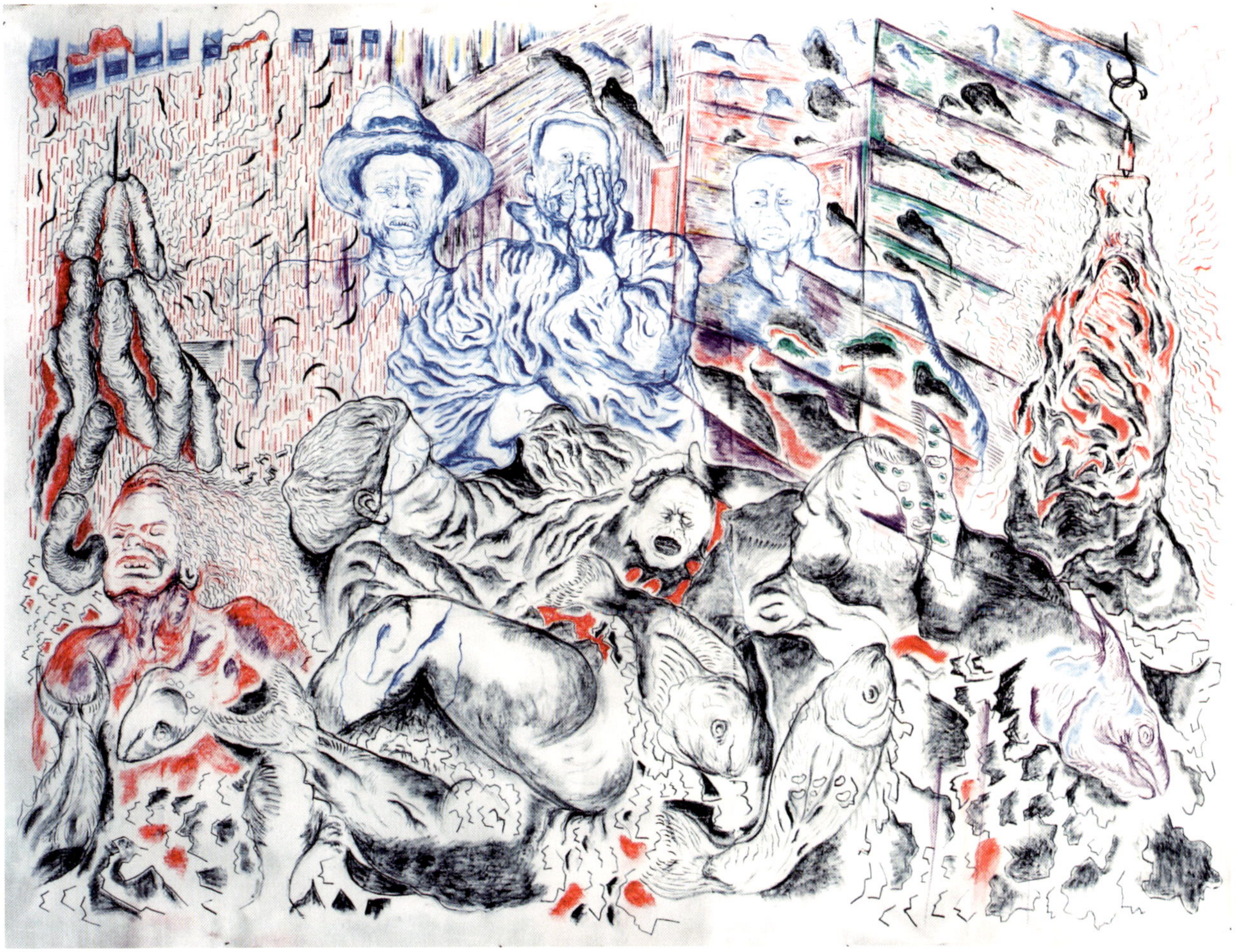

The work of Israeli artists Noam Omer (1982) is based on his family history. His grandmother became seriously traumatised during World War II, when she lost both parents and six brothers and sisters in just one day. By painting the family trauma the whole family managed to cope better with the memories of the Holocaust. He, for instance, made a series in which he depicts the experiences of two families during World War II: that of his own family and that of a German friend of his father. For this, Omer was inspired by recordings of family stories, which he listened to again and again. For the series he painted the figures as they are now, old and wrestling with disease and death.
Noam Omer, **My Father's Birth**, 2008, pastel on canvas. Collection artist

to convalesce at the special hospital for soldiers with psychiatric problems in Châteaugiron, Brittany. The establishment occupied the outbuildings of a medieval château. The Belgian mental health specialists in charge of the hospital, Doctors Van Hirtum and Hoven, tried to apply the Geel method, by sending some patients to live with local families, with varying degrees of success. Arthur C remained in Châteaugiron until all the hospital's patients were repatriated to Belgium, after the end of the war, in March 1919. They were moved to the military neuropsychiatric centre which was re-established temporarily within the Zelzate Psychiatric Institution on the Dutch border, north of Ghent.

In October 1919, still a committed patient, he was demobbed and sent to the civilian asylum of St Jean-Baptiste de Zelzate, which was run by the Brothers of Charity. The chief physician, Dr Mabilde, observed that, as well as being indifferent to the outside world (as had already been diagnosed during the war), he was now also suffering from a delusion of persecution complicated by hallucinations. Arthur C presented as either downcast or agitated, depending on the delusions that haunted him. The Father Superior of the asylum wrote to the burgomaster of Arthur C's home commune, asking him to tell his parents that their son had been committed. Like most Belgian families, it is very likely that they did not know what had happened to their son. They had returned to their devastated village and were living in a makeshift shack built by the King Albert Fund. Despite their precarious living conditions,

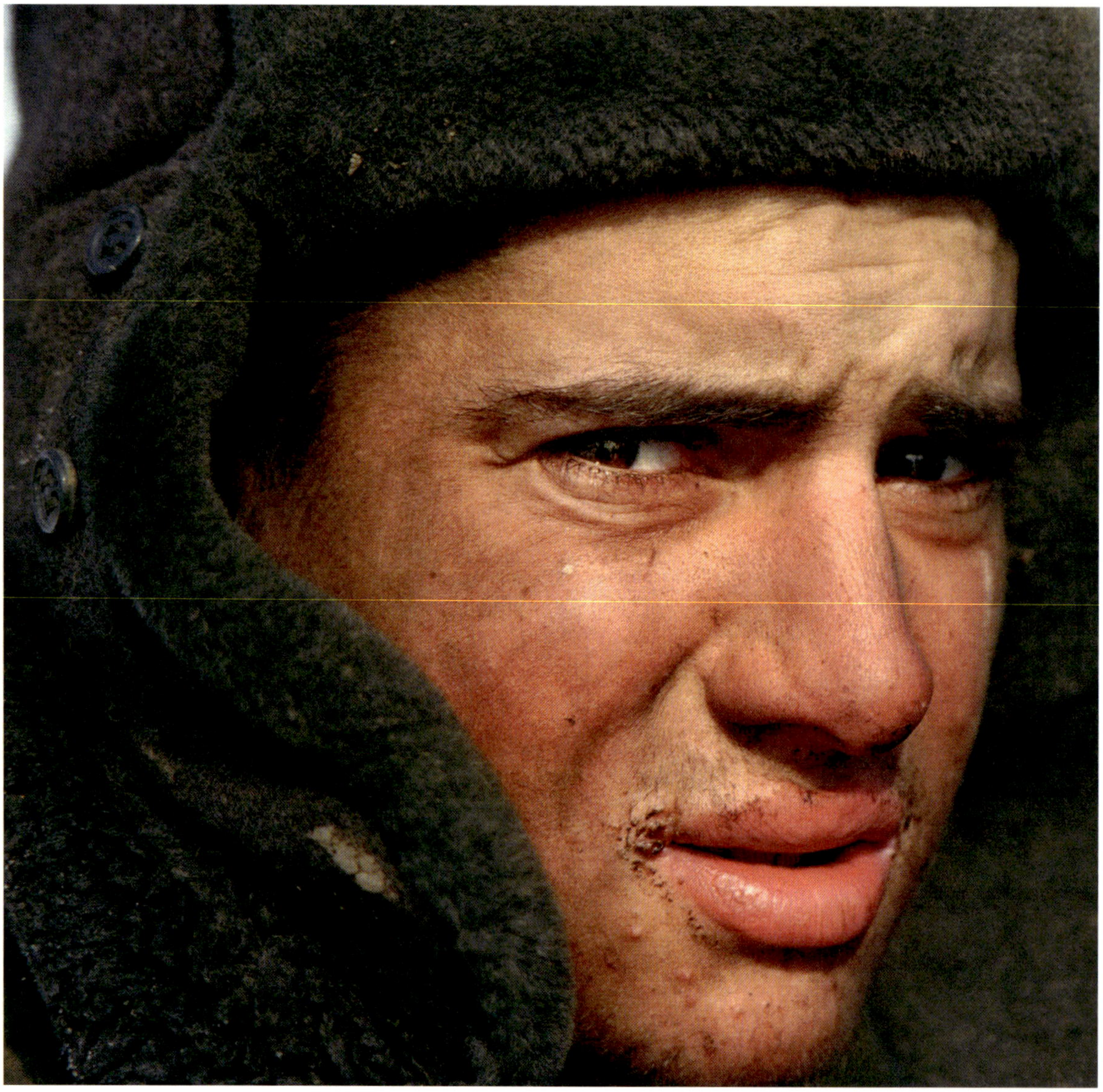

Sergey Maximishin,
A Soldier in Alchan-Kala,
Chechnya, 2000, photo.
Courtesy of RTR Gallery, Paris

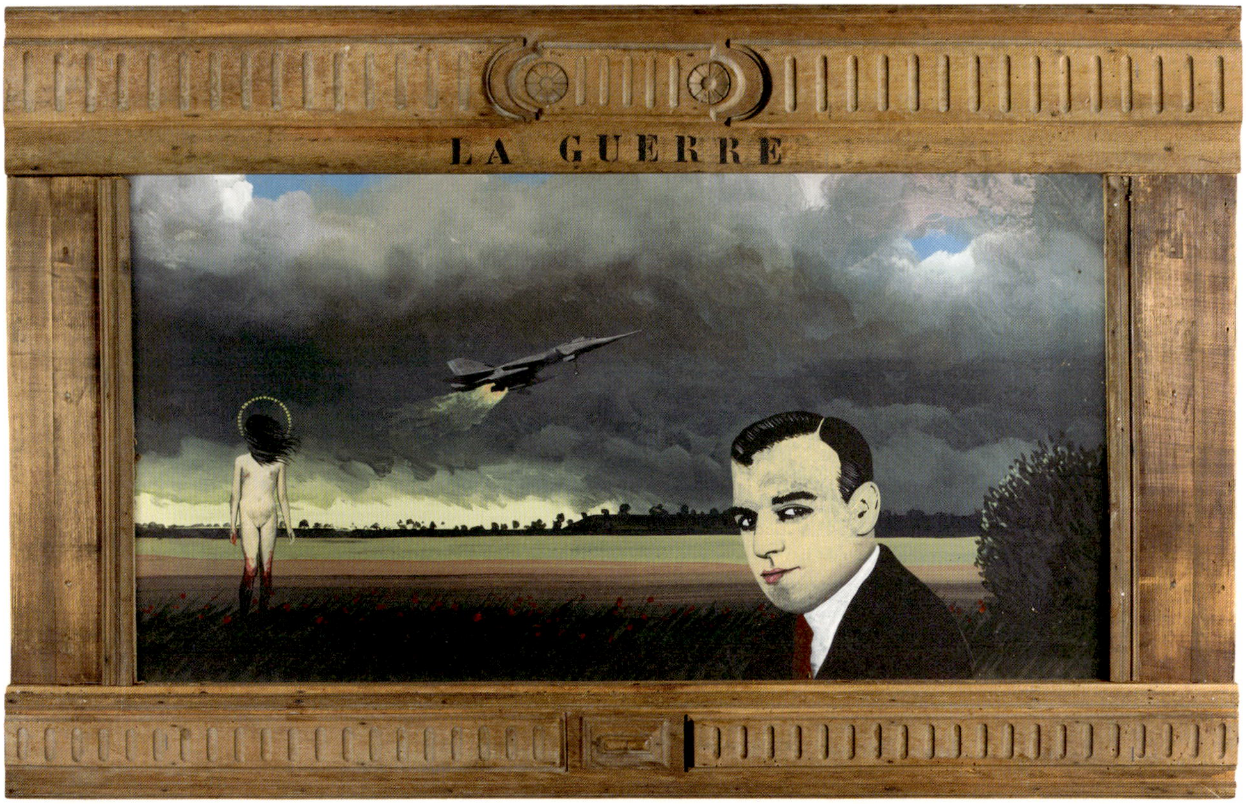

a few months later the father wrote a moving letter to Dr Mabilde asking him to send his son home. He and his wife longed to see him again after so many years and were convinced that he would not present a danger. Like so many other parents, they hoped that their love would lift their son out of his depression. But their plea was refused. The asylum's governors were convinced that the patient was not suitable for home care and that his impulsive nature could make him a danger to others. The Father Superior emphasised that in Zelzate, Arthur C was surrounded by his military comrades and that a change of environment might not be appropriate. His parents would never see their son again – he was too far away for them to visit. They had to make do with news of him from the Father Superior.

Arthur C survived his parents and a second world war. He died in the asylum in 1965, at the age of 73.

1 Registers of admission and observation, Zelzate medical file, Military file at Evere (HGR/A-n)

2 Royal decree on the contingent of the army, 1/03/1915, Documentation on Recruitment Commissions, Rouen, A. Baine, s.d.

The work of French artist Francis Marshall (1946) partly consists of stuffed puppets, made of objects found on the banks of the Seine. On the other hand, he makes paintings that almost always depict the same figures: a girl in a type of school uniform and a neat man in a suit, his hair combed perfectly. Marshall paints the landscapes on location, and adds the figures in his studio. He does not wish to clarify who the figures are. In *La Guerre* we see a nude, black-haired girl on the left with an aureole and her hair in front of her face. Her lower legs seem to be covered in blood. A jet fighter flies through the air, while on the right a man looks at us penetratingly. Marschall's paintings always have a surprising and threatening atmosphere that is hard to grasp but always exude a certain 'guilt'. The blood-covered girl seems to be a symbol of all innocent victims of war.
Francis Marshall, **La Guerre**, oil on panel. Private collection, Dr Guislain Museum, Ghent

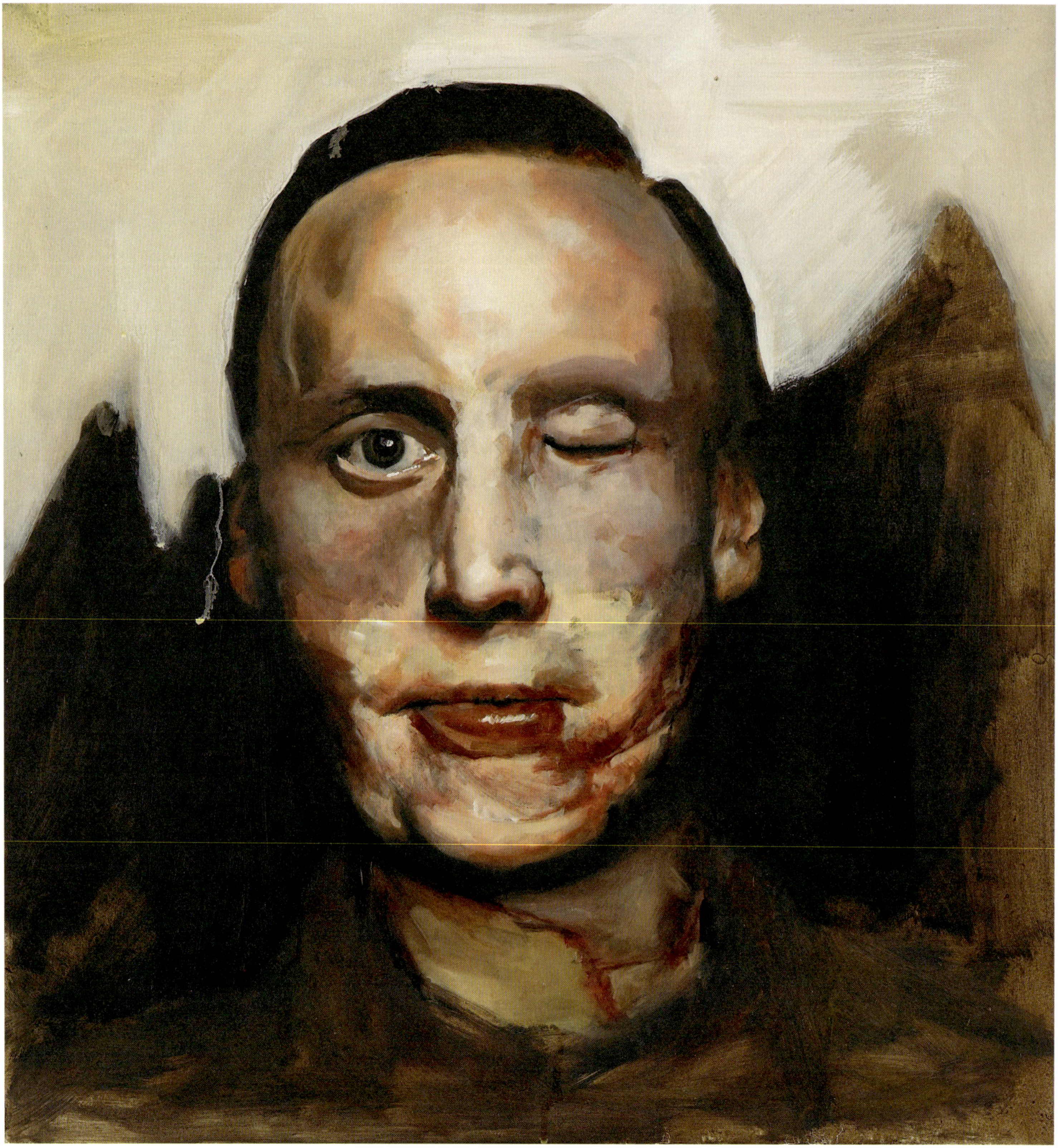

MARIA HERMES

Between Medical Discourse and Psychiatric Practice

How German Psychiatry Dealt With Psychological War Traumas in 1914–1918

"But after a few months [of World War I, M.H.] we were confronted by something we had rarely seen before: symptoms of 'hysteria virilis' or 'male hysteria'. Charcot had already described this clinical picture in Paris, to which we had at the time replied: 'Things like this only occur among the French; there are no hysterical men in Germany'. However, we now saw the same hysteria occur increasingly in all possible forms".[1] This was written by Max Nonne, neurologist and psychiatrist at the university hospital of Hamburg-Eppendorf, in 1972. He looked back on a specific form of mental illness, which German psychiatrists increasingly noted in men since the beginning of the war. Before 1914 propaganda had always boasted about the 'strong nerves' of the German people: the German Reich would win the next war thanks to its strong nerves and strong will. In the discourse during the war the 'crucial properties of the modern fighter'[2] were summarised under the concept 'immunity to stress'.

German psychiatrists were therefore very surprised when a large number of soldiers had become ill 'on the nerves' shortly after the beginning of the war. Some of their symptoms that were described in military-psychiatric journals were striking: the men trembled, constantly threw up, suffered from psychogenic deaf- and dumbness, had contractures or symptoms of paralysis, all this without recognisable physical causes.[3] This is why they were described at the 'home front' as 'Kriegszitterer' (people who were *scared of* the war).

World War I is known as the first industrialised mass war. In these specific circumstances over 600,000 soldiers of the field and occupying forces began to suffer from nervous disorders.[4] For years a lively debate arose in the public military-psychiatric discourse of the war about how to deal with war disorders. On the one hand, the question was whether it actually concerned diseases and not feigned disorders. There was only talk about the latter in secret, but at the time there were concerns that such behaviour could put ideas in the minds of other soldiers. On the other hand, there were different ideas about the origins of genuine diseases: were these a direct consequence of the war or were they mostly caused by the soldiers themselves?

Apart from the medical aspect, this issue also had a political dimension: if one assumed that the disorders had been caused by the war, and that the soldiers had thus suffered during their military service, the military treasury faced many requests for war victims' benefit.

At the so-called war conference of the 'German Psychiatry Association' and the 'Society of German Neurologists' in September 1916, 'neurologists' discussed how the diseases should be diagnosed from then on. Reverting to the '*Simulationsstreit*' of the 1890s, two camps arose[5]: referring to this illness as 'traumatic

According to Scotsman Philip Gurrey (1984), the past is never far behind, we always take it with us. World War I is known for its photos and stories. Gurrey processes these photos, mixes them with images from another time and thus creates a new, modern depiction. We still, however, associate this processed image with the Great War and with the sadness that this traumatic event has caused. During World War I, plastic surgery was first used to give mutilated soldiers a normal face again. By cutting and reassembling various images, Philip Gurrey refers to the vanity and uselessness of modern plastic surgery. While these types of operations were originally carried out to give mutilated people a new socially acceptable appearance, plastic surgery today mainly serves the beauty ideal.
Philip Gurrey, **Eye**, 2007, oil on panel. Fondation Francès, Senlis © SABAM Belgium 2013

neurosis', as was wanted by the group of physicians around Hermann Oppenheim, meant that they were recognised as being caused by events of war. By contrast, psychiatrists such as Robert Gaupp, Max Nonne or Fritz Kaufmann (to name but a few) had a preference for the – specifically German – diagnosis of 'Hysteria', which may not simply be translated into the English term 'shell shock'. Just *one*, albeit very important for the individual, consequence of the diagnosis 'Hysteria' was based on the implication that those who became ill during the war must have been ill before the war. In other words, they had to have a psychopathological personality, be a victim of heredity or show signs of degeneration. The physicians harked back on the social-Darwinist interpretation patterns of long before 1914. Yet with the diagnosis of hysteria[6], which for a long time was regarded as a specifically female diagnosis, it was also insinuated that the soldiers affected had in a sense become effeminate. This is also why Max Nonne was so surprised when a considerable number of soldiers seemed to suffer from hysterical behaviour after 1914 – German soldiers, who had not previously been considered as effeminate by the German army.

If these soldiers were to be dismissed as being *unsuitable* for battle, their mental disorders would also decimate the strength of the army, which was far from a desired consequence in view of the mass war. The resulting demand for a faster and more effective treatment was met with the therapeutic pessimism of German psychiatry from before the war. Although considerable knowledge had been gathered about mental disorders with pathologists such as Wilhelm Griesinger and Emil Kraepelin and although the *'Reichsirrenstatistik'* of 1901 applied as the pathological system of the discipline of psychiatry[7], which was not even a hundred years old at the time, there were barely any effective methods for treating the mentally ill. Long-lasting baths, bed treatments, the occasional wet compresses and work therapy were long-term treatments, but their effect was not specific and they barely seemed suitable in the circumstance of war.

As of spring 1915 a specific discourse arose in military-psychiatric journals about the treatment of soldiers suffering from mental disorders. So-called 'active methods' were developed.[8] According to Paul Lerner this consisted of two principles: on the one hand they had to force the patient out of his illness; on the other hand they had to make it clear to the patient that he was not really ill.[9] These methods include feigned operations, but also hypnosis or special use of psychotherapy, which was, however, only practiced during the last months of the war.[10] In turn, psychiatrist Fritz Kaufmann developed a method for treating soldiers with an electric current, which was named after him. Especially soldiers with psychogenic motion disorders had to be treated in a suggestive atmosphere with electric current on random parts of the body. This was followed by forced military movement exercises during the break. This was the best known method of treatment at the time in order to get soldiers back to the front.

For a long time historical research assumed that these active methods of treatment were a common practice in German army psychiatry. Only recently did Paul Lerner indicate that soldiers in field hospitals at the front were mainly treated with work therapy.[11] We can assume that things were similar in the many originally civic hospitals of the German Reich, where additional field hospitals were furnished in 1914. This is also apparent in the example of Bremen.

Just like in so many other originally civic hospitals, psychiatric hospital St. Jürgen, in the North-German city of Bremen, provided psychiatric care to soldiers from the beginning of the war alongside male and female citizens. Its own reserve field hospital was furnished in October 1916. Much can be learned from a comparison between the treatment of soldiers and civilians.[12] Electric current therapy was only applied as an 'active' method of treatment here, albeit on only four of the almost 2,000 patients who were hospitalised here during the war (two soldiers and two male civilians). There was no difference between the treatment of soldiers and civilians.[13]

The explanation speaks for itself: the 'active' methods of treatment described in military psychiatric journals required too much of an effort from staff, which in view of the war circumstances was barely feasible. Soon after the beginning of the war, doctors were included in the army in all psychiatric institutions of the German Reich. After some time, there was only one doctor for 150 patients at the St. Jürgen hospital.

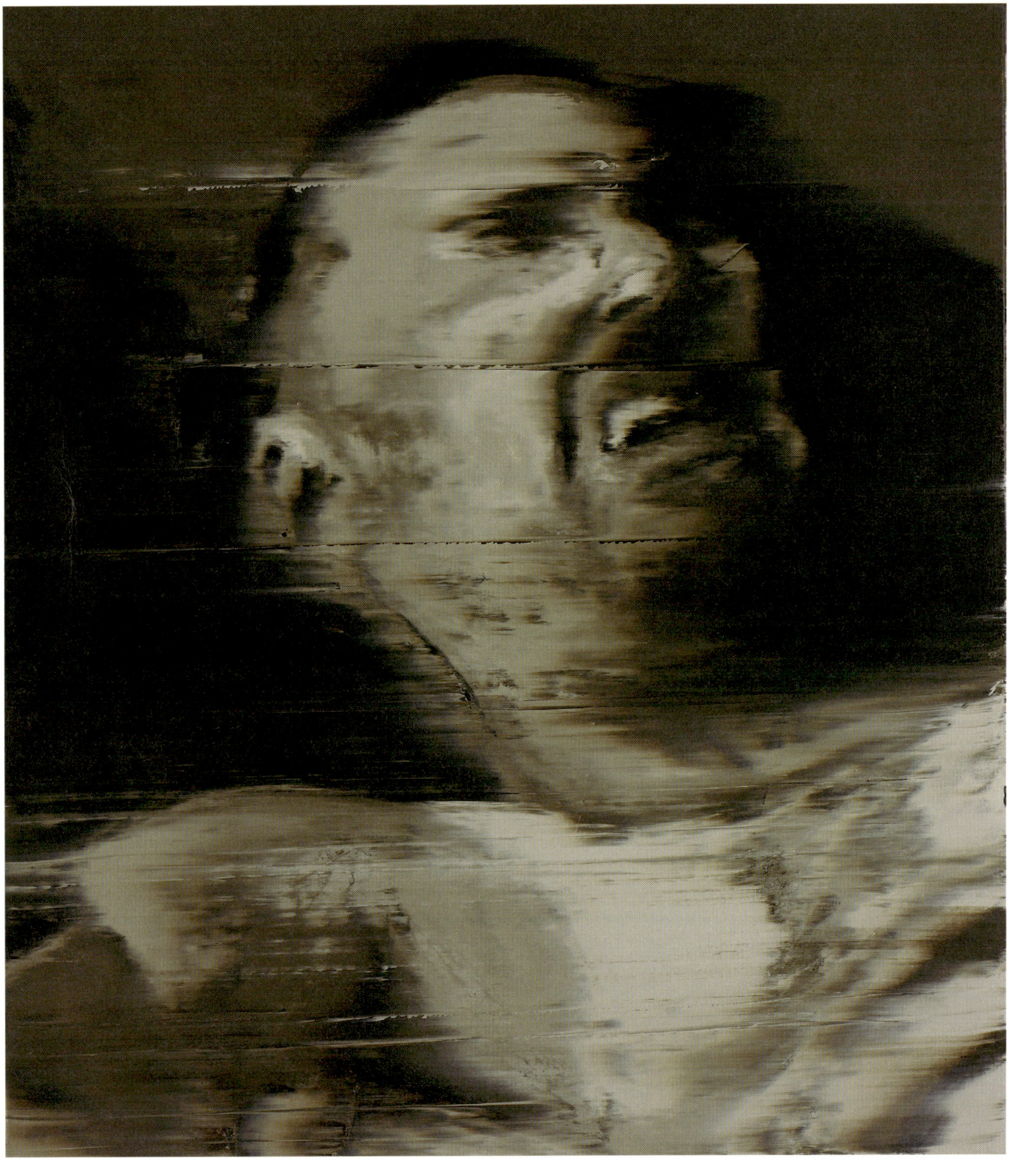

The paintings of Swiss Andy Denzler (1965) look like still, paused video images. He creates emotions through atmosphere, by abstracting the figures and the background. In this painting of an unknown soldier, the trauma and horror of war can be felt. Especially during World War I, many soldiers were never found. Those who did return were often unrecognisable due to the damage of the war. With this painting, Andy Denzler indicates the unprecedented sadness of the unknown soldier.
Andy Denzler, **Unknown Soldier**, 2005, oil on canvas. Fondation Francès, Senlis

Individual care was impossible under these circumstances. After 1914, mainly long-term bed treatment[14] and work treatment[15] were applied and, in exceptional cases, long-term bathing[16]. The aim was a long-term form of therapy for patients. Dealing with the experiences of war, as is now part of each psychiatric and psychotherapeutic treatment of soldiers returning from war, did not occur, corresponding with the physical view of the concept of illness that applied at the time; we refer to the famous statement of Wilhelm Griesinger that mental disease should be seen as a physical disease of the brain. The experiences of war therefore did not play a part in the practice of mental healing, neither with regard to the therapy, nor the diagnosis.

But how, during the war, were the causes of mental disorders estimated in the patient files of the originally civic psychiatric institution in Bremen? Here the doctors also based themselves on social-Darwinist interpretation patterns regarding the heredity of mental illness, patterns coming from long before 1914, as indicated in examination reports. If someone became ill because of the war, this always had to be linked to a special event, usually to a physical injury. 'Normal' war experiences were not – neither in daily life nor at the front and definitely not the 'home front' – included in events that could lead to a disease. Soldiers had the best chance that their illness would be seen as a result of war. This type of causal connection was rarely assumed in civilians. This mainly had an impact on benefit requests: after discharge, most patients of the institution in Bremen did not get an allowance based on their experiences of war; the relation between mental illness and war-related experiences was simply ignored. Yet this should not just be regarded as blind obedience of the doctors: it is more a matter of social-Darwinist ideas that were the norm in medicine at the time, accidentally 'fitting' the requirements of military affairs.

These estimates in psychiatric practice show that the doctors were not only making statements about individual disorders in their diagnoses, they were also saying something about the war. The war as such was not included in the list of disorder-causing events. Not being able to deal with war was seen as a symptom of 'mental illness'. World War I at the front and the 'home front' became the normal situation here. Male and female civilians were rarely believed to have become ill because of the war: the war was male and took place at the front.

The medical evaluations in the patient files therefore met the at that time assumed dichotomy between front and home environment. But psychiatry in the German Reich between 1914 and 1918 was always psychiatry in wartime, which was inextricably linked to a stand vis-à-vis the war. Psychiatric practice in Bremen confirms this, especially because of the fact that the doctors involved were unable to see this for themselves.

NOTES

1 Nonne, Max (1971): *Anfang und Ziel meines Lebens. Erinnerungen*, Hamburg: Hans Christians Verlag. Here 177 ff.

2 Hofer, Hans-Georg (2000): "Nervöse Zitterer". Psychiatrie und Krieg, in: Konrad, Helmut (ed., 2000): *Krieg, Medizin und Politik. Der Erste Weltkrieg und die österreichische Moderne*, Vienna: Passagen Verlag. p. 15 – 134. It was believed that modern war suitability was defined by character, will, endurance and immunity to stress. cf idem p. 59. According to Aribert Reimann the language used in army field post and army newspapers had to be of a "defined soundness catalogue of the steadfast will" (Reimann, Aribert (2000): *Der große Krieg der Sprachen. Untersuchungen zur historischen Semantik in Deutschland und England zur Zeit des Ersten Weltkriegs*, Fulda: Klartext Verlag. Here p. 39) in the German Reich in support of the trench warfare that typified World War I. This catalogue of soundness translated "the tactical data of this type of war waging into a collective psychological outline [...]. The semantic internalisation of the trench war grouped itself around the depiction of an emotional indomitability, which was expressed in concepts such as this 'calm', 'resolve and 'the topos of 'stronger nerves' (idem).

3 See also Hofer, Hans-Georg (2006): Was waren "Kriegsneurosen"? Zur Kulturgeschichte psychischer Erkrankungen im Ersten Weltkrieg, in: Kuprian, Hermann J. W. / Oswald Überegger (ed., 2006): *Der Erste Weltkrieg im Alpenraum. Erfahrung, Deutung, Erinnerung. La Grande Guerra nell'arco alpino. Esperienze e memoria*, Innsbruck: Universitätsverlag Wagner. p. 309 – 322. Here 309 ff., et al.

4 See also Anonymous: *Sanitätsbericht über das Deutsche Heer (Deutsches Feld- und Besatzungsheer) im Weltkriege 1914/1918 (Deutscher Kriegssanitätsbericht 1914/18)*, 3. Band: Die Krankenbewegung bei dem Deutschen Feld- und Besatzungsheer im Weltkriege 1914/1918, Berlin 1934, here 145 ff.

5 According to many company doctors, by the end of the 19th century there were a comparably high number of diseased in the context of Bismarck's social legislation and the legal hospitalization as a result of accidents. (Cf Fischer-Homberger, Esther (2004): *Die traumatische Neurose. Vom somatischen zum sozialen Leiden*, Gießen: Psychosozial-Verlag. Here p. 171 – 196 et al).

6 The concept of 'hysteria" is derived from the Greek 'hystera', which means 'womb'.

7 See also Dörries, Andrea (1999a): Der "Würzburger Schlüssel" von 1933 – Diskussionen um die Entwicklung einer Klassifikation psychischer Störungen, in: Beddies, Thomas / Dies. (re-ed., 1999): *Die Patienten der Wittenauer Heilstätten in Berlin 1919 – 1960*, Husum : Matthiesen Verlag. p. 188 – 205. Here 202.

8 See also Lange, Fritz (1924): Die Behandlung der Kriegsneurosen. In: Bumke, Oswald / Otto Foerster (ed., 1924): *Handbuch der Neurologie. Ergänzungsband, Erster Teil.* Berlijn: Julius Springer. p. 259 – 406. According to psychiatrist Fritz, as of 1915 it originally concerned "active" therapy methods developed especially for "war neurotics": "It is concerned [...] all similar methods such as active therapy and this includes those methods of the treatment of neurosis, which with the use of all available medical energy, try to fundamentally remedy the symptoms in the shortest possible space of time, in one 'session' if possible". (idem p. 273 ff, quoted in the original).

9 cf With regard to this distinction Lerner, Paul (1997): Rationalizing the Therapeutic Arsenal: German Neuropsychiatry in World War I, in: Berg, Manfred / Geoffrey Cocks (Hrsg., 1997): *Medicine and Modernity. Public Health and Medical Care in Nineteenth- and Twentieth-Century Germany*, Washington : Cambridge University Press. p. 121 – 148, here p. 131 ff.

10 The psychoanalytic treatment of military psychiatric patients was thus intended to affect their "illness", so the soldiers again showed willingness for military service at the front. In order to deal with the massive phenomenon of sick soldiers, Ernst Simmel for instance developed a "psychoanalytic fast method" with this objective. (See also Roth, Karl Heinz (1987): Die Modernisierung der Folter in den beiden Weltkriegen: Der Konflikt der Psychotherapeuten und Schulpsychiater um die deutschen "Kriegsneurotiker" 1915 – 1945, in: 1999. *Zeitschrift für Sozialgeschichte des 20. und 21. Jahrhunderts*, 1987, Nr. 3, p. 8 – 75. Here p. 17 ff.).

11 See also Lerner 1997: 129.

12 As the first total war, the war of 1914/18 also had an impact on the mental health of the German population, whose disorders were, however, not regarded by the psychiatry of this time as suffering related to the war.

13 The following statements about the St. Jürgen hospital during World War I are based on my thesis, in which the disorders of 396 female patients of the St. Jürgen hospital were evaluated quantitatively and those of 16 female patients were evaluated qualitatively. (cf Hermes, Maria: *Krankheit: Krieg. Psychiatrische Deutungen des Ersten Weltkrieges*, Essen 2012).

14 Objective of bed treatment was therapy for a mental patient in a sickbed, mainly through rest, calming the brain as an organ and gaining insight into the illness.

15 In the Bremen St. Jürgen hospital, as an economically autonomous complex with agricultural infrastructure, industry, the cultivation of vegetables, even providing its own energy, patients worked at the centre's own setups. This form of therapy, which was very modern around 1900, aimed to promote the personal activity and responsibility of a patient, increase the sense of community and foster the feeling that one was doing something useful.

16 The objective of long-term baths was calming patients who were considered anxious. They lay in a heated bath for up to eight days.

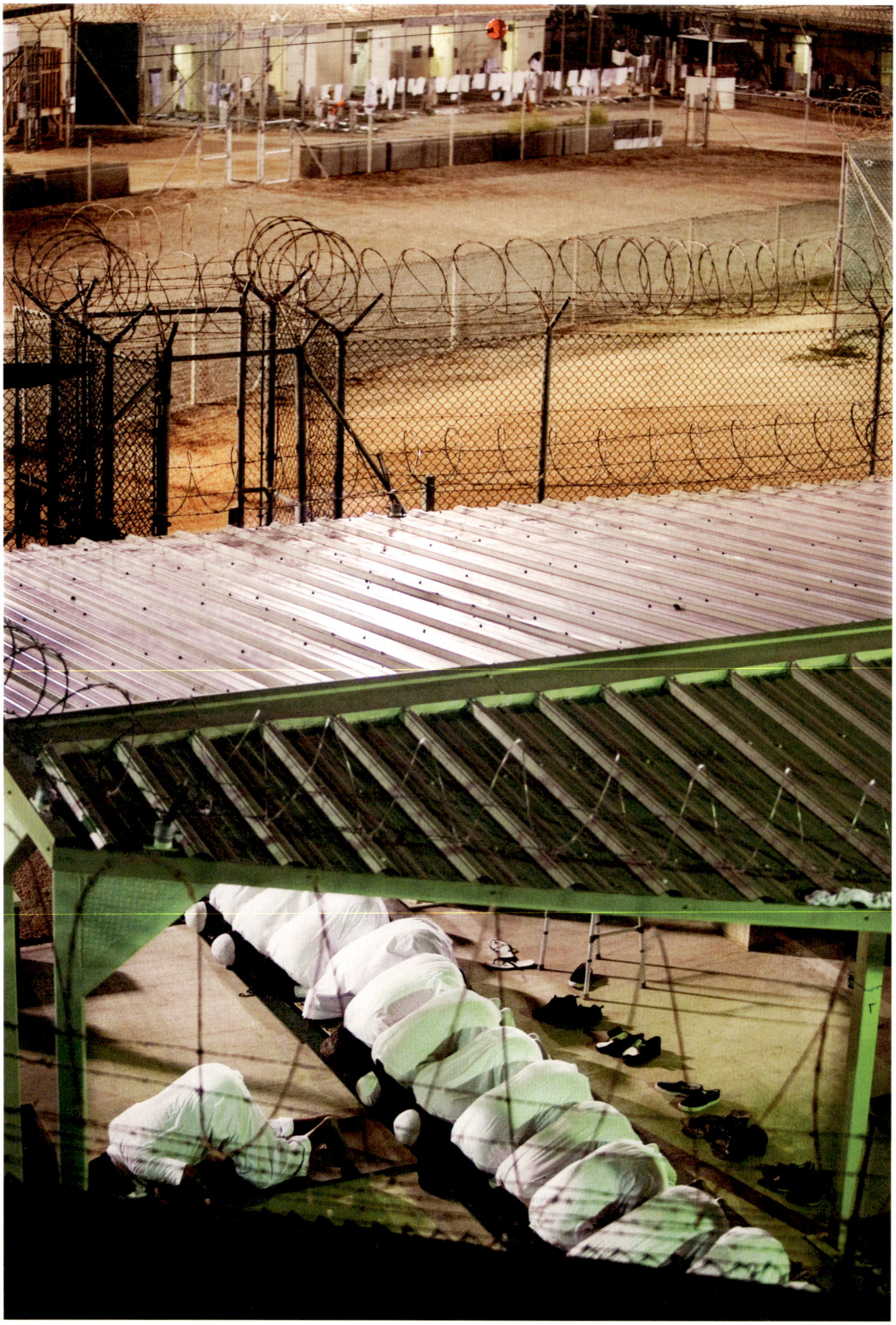

BESSEL A. VAN DER KOLK

Posttraumatic Stress Disorder

The outbreak of the First World War in 1914 once again confronted medicine and psychology with hundreds of thousands of men with bizarre psychological symptoms, unexplained medical diseases and memory loss. Early in the war, the British invented the diagnosis of 'shell shock', which entitled combat veterans to treatment and to a disability pension. An alternative diagnosis that was often used, was 'neurasthenia' for which they received neither treatment nor a pension. It was up to the attending physician to decide which diagnosis a soldier received[1].

On any given moment more than a million British soldiers served on the Western Front. In the first few hours of 1 July 1916 alone, in the Battle of the Somme, the British Army suffered 57,470 casualties, including 19,240 dead, the bloodiest day in its history. Captain Leeham wrote the following about his experience that first day: "The trench was a horrible sight. The dead were stretched out on one side, one on top of the other six feet high. I thought at the time that I would never get the disgusting smell of the vapour of warm human blood heated by the sun out of my nostrils. I would rather have smelt gas a hundred times. I can never describe that faint sickening, horrible smell which several times knocked me out altogether"[2]. As the slaughter continued for three more months, almost half a million soldiers of the British Army were injured or died on the Somme. The historian John Keegan says of the British commander, Marshall Douglas Haig, whose statue today is the most prominent feature in the Mall in London, once the centre of the British Empire: "In his public manner and private diaries, no concern for human suffering was or is discernible.' At the Somme, 'he had sent the flower of British youth to death or mutilation"[3].

As the war progressed, shell shock increasingly interfered with the efficiency of the fighting forces. Caught between taking the suffering of their soldiers seriously and pursuing victory over the Germans, the British General Staff chose to issue General Routine Order Number 2384 in June of 1917 that stated: "in no circumstances whatever will the expression 'shell shock' be used verbally or be recorded in any regimental or other casualty report, or any hospital or other medical document". All soldiers with psychiatric problems were to be given a single diagnosis of 'NYDN' (Not Yet Diagnosed, Nervous)[4],[5]. In November 1917, the General Staff denied Charles Samuel Myers, who ran four field hospitals for wounded soldiers, permission to submit a paper on shell shock to the British Medical Journal[6]. The Germans were even more punitive and treated shell shock as a character defect, which they managed with a variety of painful treatments, including electroshock 'therapy'.

By 1921, more than 65,000 British veterans received war pensions for mental problems, and as late as 1940 27 of 90 veteran hospitals in the US were primarily devoted to psychiatric disorders resulting from the First World War, but little attention was paid to the actual treatment of these shell-shocked men[7]. After 1920 there was more discussion in England, France, Germany, and the US about how war-related disabilities were the result of malingering than about devising treatments for the astronomical rates of alcoholism and suicide in these veterans.

How quickly society's attitude can turn from awe to contempt is illustrated by the so-called Bonus March on Washington in 1932. Back in 1918, when the US World War I soldiers returned from the battlefields of France and Flanders, they had been welcomed home

In March 2010, Belgian photographer Tim Dirven (1968) had an opportunity to photograph the building and the prisoners of the Guantánamo Bay prison camp. This controversial prison, which was established in 2002, was a crucial step in George W. Bush's 'War on Terror'. As foreign terrorists were kept there without trial, the US broke the Geneva Conventions and the establishment caused huge criticism from human rights organisations. Dirven's photos do not show the torture practices for which Guantánamo Bay is famous, but they depict the prison's cold infrastructure. The clinical aspect of the establishment goes against the viewer's expectations and preconceptions. Simultaneously, the coldness of the establishment dehumanises the prisoners and the images thus evoke the trauma of long-term imprisonment.
Tim Dirven, **Lost in Guantánamo**, 2010, photo. © Tim Dirven

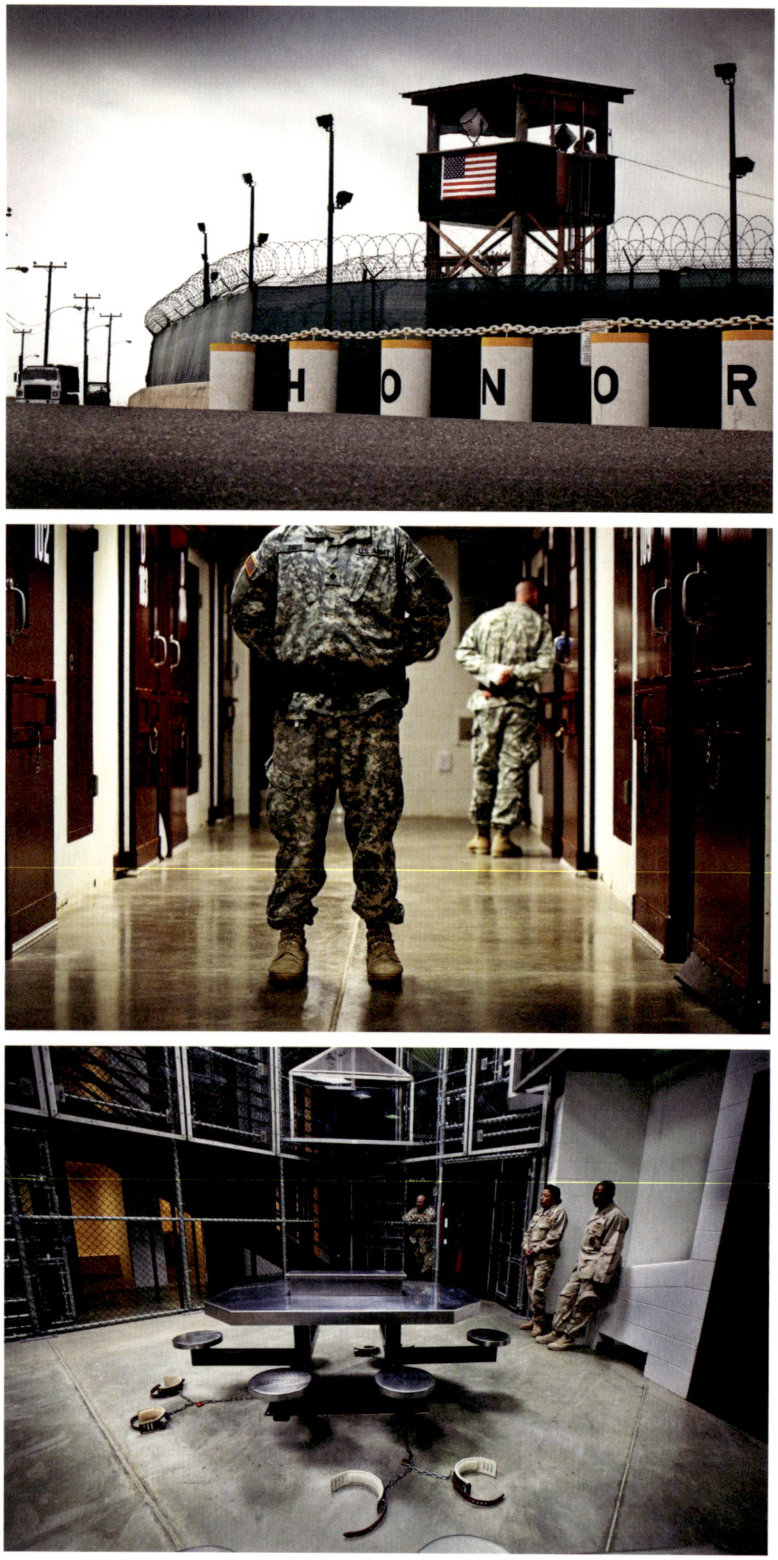

Tim Dirven, **Lost in Guantánamo**, 2010, photos. © Tim Dirven

as national heroes, just as the soldiers returning from Iraq and Afghanistan today. In 1924, Congress voted to award them a bonus of $1.25 for each day they had served overseas, but they conveniently postponed disbursement till 1945. However, by 1932 the nation was in the middle of the Great Depression. In May of that year, about 15,000 unemployed and penniless veterans converged on the Mall in Washington, D.C. to beg for immediate payment of their bonuses. They lived in shelters built from materials dragged out of junk piles from around the city – old lumber, packing boxes and scrap tin covered with roofs of thatched straw. Their leader, Walter Waters, stated, "We're going to keep ourselves a simon-pure veteran's organization. If the Bonus is paid it will relieve to a large extent our deplorable economic conditions."

On 17 June, the Senate defeated the bill for an immediate pay-out by a vote of 62 to 18. The veterans stayed in their tents until 28 July, when President Hoover gave orders to the army to clear them out. Army Chief of Staff General Douglas MacArthur commanded the infantry and cavalry troops, supported by six tanks. Major Dwight D. Eisenhower was the liaison with the Washington police and Major George Patton was in charge of the cavalry. In the late afternoon the troops massed on Pennsylvania Avenue. The veterans, assuming that it was a military display in their honour, cheered. Suddenly soldiers with fixed bayonets turned and charged, hurling tear gas into the crowd. The next morning the Mall was deserted and the camp was in flames.[8] The veterans never received their pensions.

When old soldiers are forgotten the knowledge gained in previous generations also disappears. A few months ago, a colleague in charge of a branch of the US Department of Defence's office of psychological services called me in the evening telling me that she was scheduled to testify before Congress about the treatment of PTSD the next day. She told me that she was asked to talk about the potential use of hypnosis for treating PTSD and she just wanted to check with me if I knew anything about hypnosis as a potentially effective treatment. I did: hypnosis was the primary treatment of combat stress during the Second World War, and my reading of the old journals made me think that they did as well with hypnosis back then as we do with most of the treatments that are currently available. I urged her to become familiar with that literature before giving an opinion that would have a major impact on the treatment combat soldiers with PTSD would receive. Of course, there was not enough time and she testified that there was no contemporary evidence that hypnosis worked.

NOTES

1 Mott F.W., 'Special discussion on shell shock without visible signs of injury', in: *Proc R Soc Med*, 1916, 9, pp. i–xxiv.
Mott F.W., 'The microscopic examination of the brains of two men dead of commotion cerebri (shell shock) without visible external injury', in: *BMJ*, 1917, 2, pp. 612–615.
Myers C.S., 'A contribution to the study of shell shock', in: *Lancet*, 1915, 1, pp. 316–320.
Salmon T.W., 'The care and treatment of mental diseases and war neuroses ('shell shock') in the British army', in: *Ment Hyg*, 1917, 1, pp. 509–547.
Rhein J.H.W., 'Neuropsychiatric problems at the front during combat', in: *J Abnorm Psychol*, 1919, 14, pp. 9–14.
Turner W.A., 'Cases of nervous and mental shock observed in the base hospitals in France', in: *J R Army Med Corps*, 1915, 24, pp. 343–352.
Southard E.E., 'Shell shock and after', in: *Boston Med Surg J*, 1918, 179, pp. 73–93.
Jones E., Wessely S., *Shell Shock to PTSD: Military Psychiatry From 1900 to the Gulf*, Hove, UK, Psychology Press, 2005.

2 Brown M., *Tommy goes to war*, History Press, 1978.

3 Keegan J., *The First World War*, New York.

4 Ecksteins M., *Rites of Spring: the Great War and the Birth of the Modern Age*, Boston, Houghton Mifflin, 1989.

5 Rossy K.M., *Shellshock, Suicide and Septimus: Illness as a Metaphor in Virginia Woolf's Mrs. Dalloway*.

6 Macleod A.D. FRANZCP FAChPM, 'Shell shock, Gordon Holmes and the Great War', in: *J R Soc Med*, 2004, 97, pp. 86–89.

7 See Pat Barker's trilogy about W.H.R. Rivers.

8 Bartlett, J.H., *The Bonus March and the New Deal*, New York, M.A. Donohue & Co., 1937; Daniels, R., *The Bonus March; an Episode of the Great Depression*, Westport, CT: Greenwood Publishing Corp., 1971.

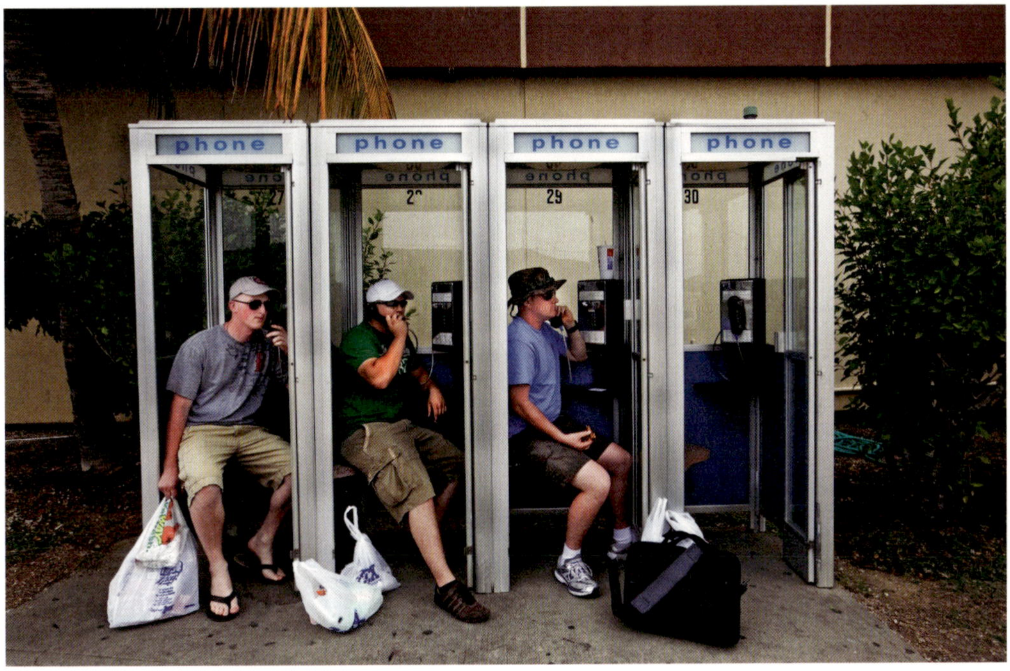

Tim Dirven, **Guards making phone calls home near the shopping mall at the American naval base at Guantánamo Bay**, 2010, photo. © Tim Dirven

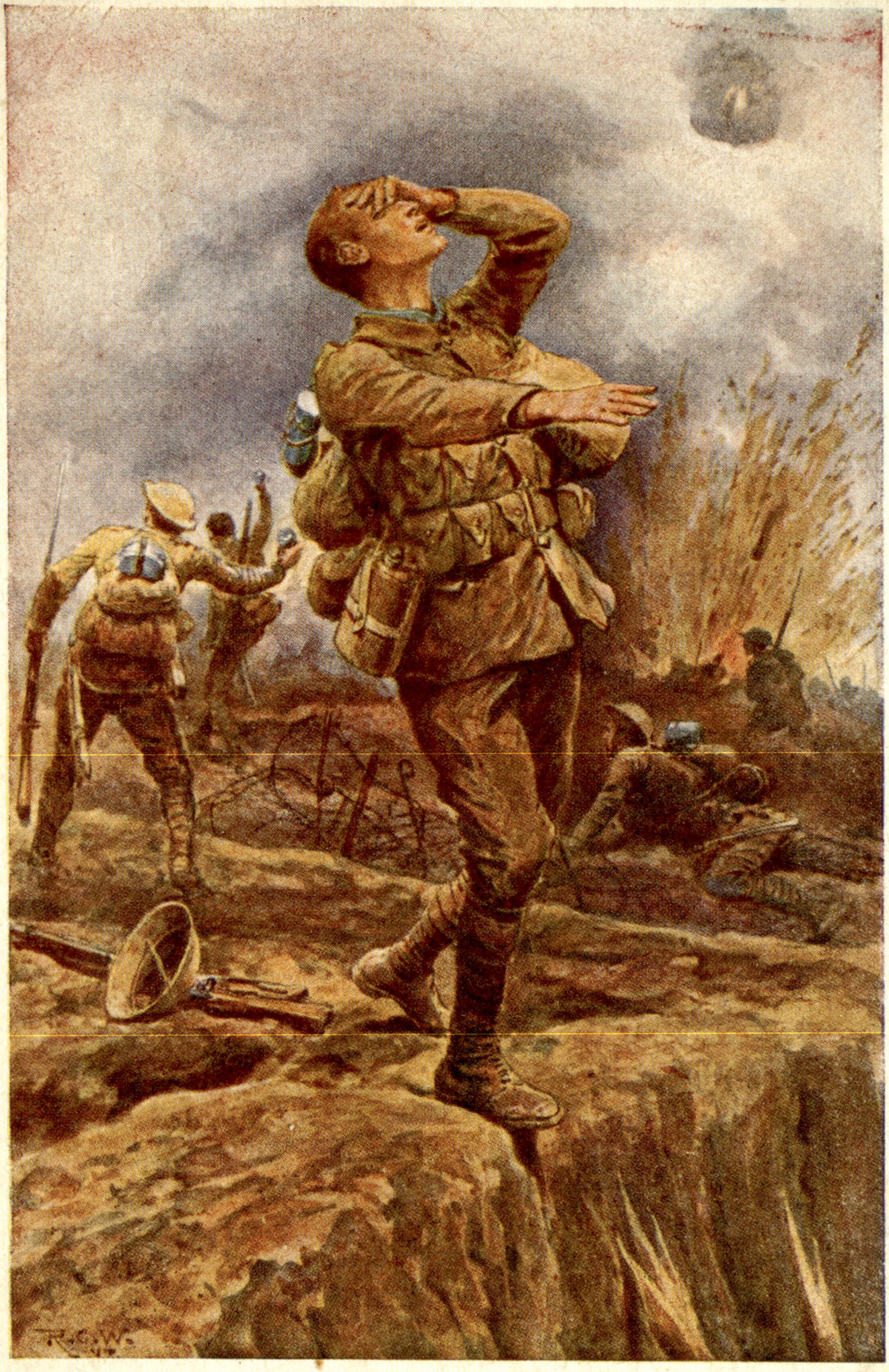

"BLINDED FOR YOU!"
From the painting by R. Caton Woodville

PIETER VERSTRAETE

Saving Private Energy

The Re-education of Disabled Belgian Soldiers during World War I[1]

In 1924, the Brussels journalist Cypriaan Verhavert compiled a series of essays that he wrote during World War I. The book *Zij die gingen ... en zij die blijven [Those Who Went... And Those Who Stayed]*, was published under the expressive synonym *I. Eenzame [I. Lonesome]* and was about, among others, the sad fate of the many men who became physically or mentally disabled during World War I. The author named one of them Achiel. Before the outbreak of war, Achiel had been an able, thinking, obedient, modest and self-effacing man who could have become a promising smith: "Had the war not broken out, he probably would have become an artist; an artist in his trade"[2]. The outbreak of war, however, tore this dream apart. Achiel was injured "and now his arms hang useless alongside his body, emaciated and exhausted by moral and physical misery, the right arm mutilated, fleshless. With a steel device, he can still carry out strictly necessary movements yet he screams in pain or due to friction[3]".

THE PROBLEM OF HUMAN WRECKS

Achiel was not the only man during the war confronted with a changed body, and who had to continue to live with a permanent disability. In total, after the signing of the Armistice, about ten million disabled soldiers returned home[4]. They were lucky enough to have survived the war, but had to adapt to the fact that one or several limbs had been amputated, their face was mutilated, their eyes could no longer see or their common sense showed indelible traces of major anxiety. Their changed physical and mental state not only forced the disabled soldiers to carry out a new task, the army command of the various forces could only stand by and watch the ever increasing contingent of disabled soldiers. After a few months – when it became clear that the war would last a lot longer than originally planned – there were considerable discussions about what had to be done to resolve this 'urgent matter'. The problem of disabled soldiers was especially pressing with regard to the Belgian forces.

After the fall of Antwerp and the withdrawal of the Belgian army behind the lines of the Yser, military lieutenant-colonels were confronted by a huge deficit of forces. Of the 130,000 soldiers available in August 1914, only 70,000 remained after withdrawal behind the flooded Yser plains[5]. A large number of soldiers had been evacuated to England or were locked up in Dutch internment camps. If one wanted to keep one's head above water, it was necessary to make use of all remaining sources of energy. These sources of energy soon also included the group of soldiers who had become disabled during the first few months. Just like the other armed forces, the Belgian army had not been spared of mutilated and injured soldiers. In a retrospective overview of activities of the medical service in 1914–1918, Léopold Mélis realised after the signing of the Armistice that the Belgian army had 6,000 disabled soldiers in its ranks[6]. Soldiers who, because of a bullet wound, illness or explosion were no longer capable of being sent to the front. Whether this figure is the exact reflection of reality is far from certain. What is certain is that the Belgian army command was already aware of the problems involving so-called 'human wrecks' during the first months of war.

In 1915, Sir Arthur Pearson founded St Dunstan's, an organisation for blind soldiers. Pearson was a newspaper magnate who had lost his sight in 1913. He visited blind soldiers in English hospitals and was concerned with their fate after discharge from the hospital. The St Dunstan's Hostel was established especially for them to "teach them to be blind" and to "give them a more valuable life than they had ever had before the moment they went blind". In order to raise money, postcards were issued during World War I with images of blind soldiers.
Blinded For You, postcard after the painting of R. Caton Woodville. Private collection

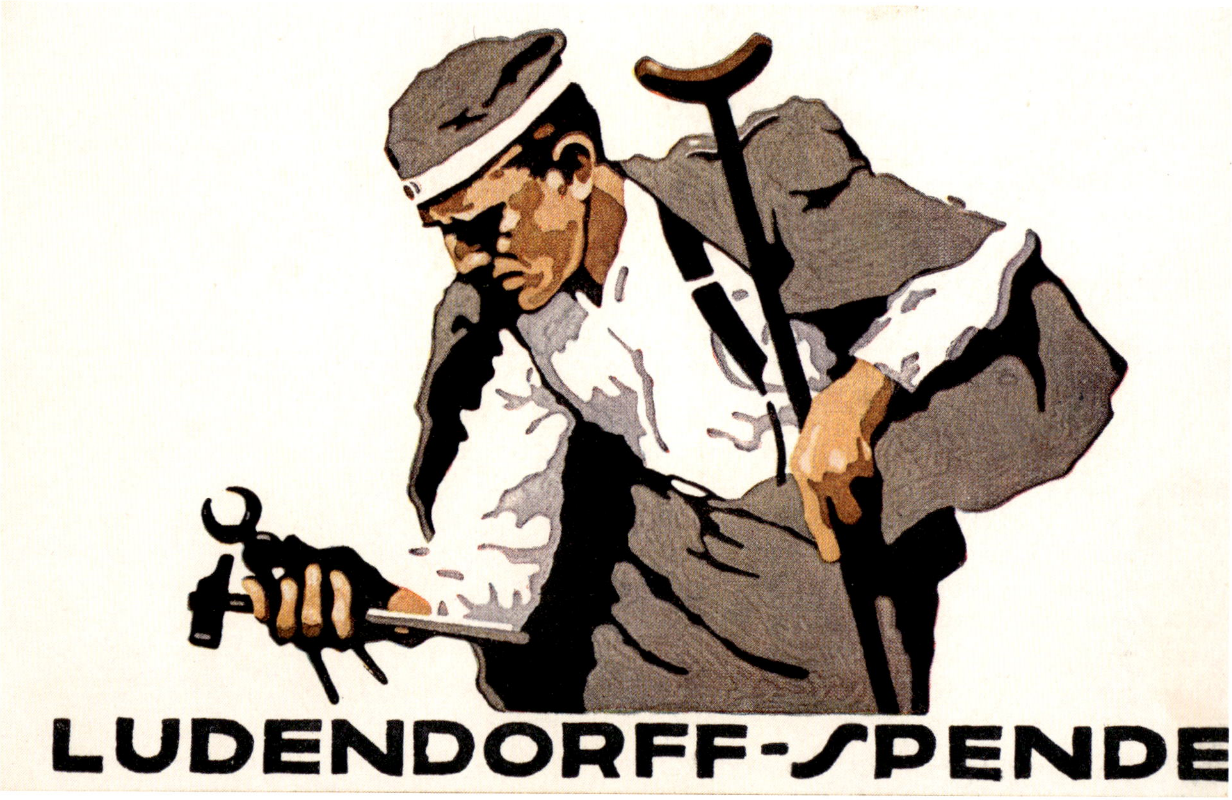

A first problem that was referred to was the realisation that Belgian army forces had lost a large number of soldiers during the field trip to the Yser[7]. The serious shortage of male soldiers ensured, among others, that ways were sought for disabled soldiers to contribute their share to the German defeat and to the liberation of the homeland. Following what had been done for the disabled miners of the Charleroi mines, the remaining energy of these soldiers was also used for military operations. Someone may have lost a leg in the turmoil of the battle or had perhaps become blind due to a bomb explosion, the remaining energy had to be reactivated and made useful. But the problem of the 'human wrecks' did not only involve the fact that they reduced the army's impact. The fact that they were free to roam the streets also had a baleful influence on the combative moral of the French population[8]. This was because Belgian disabled soldiers were publically ridiculed in the North as well as the South of France. And what could the effect of this kind of sight be? Was there no risk that a confrontation with a mutilated soldier would result in the French population no longer voluntarily reporting for military service? Confronted by the horrors of war, many citizens would not be keen on voluntarily being taken to the slaughterhouse. This baleful influence of seeing mutilated soldiers was also regarded as a major problem by the Belgian and French military authorities at the time. Finally, the post-war situation was also often referred to in order to highlight the significance of the problem of disability[9]. Once the Germans would be driven away and the homeland would be liberated, this would be followed by the confrontation with the task of getting Belgium to rise from its ashes. The homeland would have to be built up from scratch, so to speak. Here too, the number of dead, fled or mutilated male workers would be experienced strongly and one could not permit to neglect the remaining energy. On the contrary, the smallest remnant of energy had to be used for the redevelopment of Belgium after the Liberation.

During and after World War I, numerous collections were organised for victims of the war. Schools were also actively involved. In 1918, the *Ludendorff Spende* collection was created to help invalid soldiers who could not sufficiently be supported by the state. The series of cards, sold by children, depict invalid soldiers learning a new trade or learning how to practise their former occupation once again. We see for instance a wounded soldier with tools in one hand and a crutch in the other. This series was very successful and raised a lot of money.
Ludendorff–Spende, s.d., postcard. Private collection

RE-EDUCATION AS AN ANSWER

The above mentioned problems ensured that the Belgian Military authorities soon became aware of the fact that the initial guidelines would have to be adapted. At the time when people were still convinced that the war would be settled before Christmas 1914, the physicians in military service sent the disabled soldiers on leave without pay. In practice, this came down to the fact that they were no longer considered as serving soldiers. The great disadvantage of this was, however, that military authority could no longer be exerted over these soldiers. Several months after the outbreak of the war, a circular letter was sent stating that from that moment on, soldiers who were considered unsuitable for further service had to be regarded as *'Candidats de réforme'*. This meant that, in spite of their disability, they were still considered as serving soldiers and that the army thus still had certain authority over them. One of the stipulations that was linked to this is that disabled soldiers were obliged to re-educate themselves. Compared to the other allied and central powers, Belgium took a rather unique stance. But the military lieutenant-colonels – among others the Minister of War Charles de Broqueville – were convinced that this re-education of disabled soldiers provided the perfect solution to the aforesaid problems.

The first important element was of course that the re-education of mutilated Belgian soldiers would also lead to their continued contribution to the turmoil of battle. Behind the lines, these disabled soldiers were taught how to master the profession they practised before the war or a new profession in spite of their changing physical constitution. It is clear that a man who was a farmer before the war and who had lost both arms had to relearn how to till the land, or learn another profession. The re-education of the soldier was eventually only the final phase of a long-term process of rehabilitation that already started the moment the soldier was carried off the battlefield. Before the actual start of the professional re-education, the disabled soldier had to go through a fundamental process of medical surgery and rehabilitation in order to restore his body back to its normal condition as much as possible. The new profession could not be learned until the scars had healed and the muscles were more or less activated, so the soldier could be re-involved in the scene of action. The soldiers at the front needed clogs, wooden beams were required where necessary to reinforce parapets, there was a need for socks, etc. Disabled soldiers could be involved in the production of all these matters – once they had learned to regard themselves as active workers.

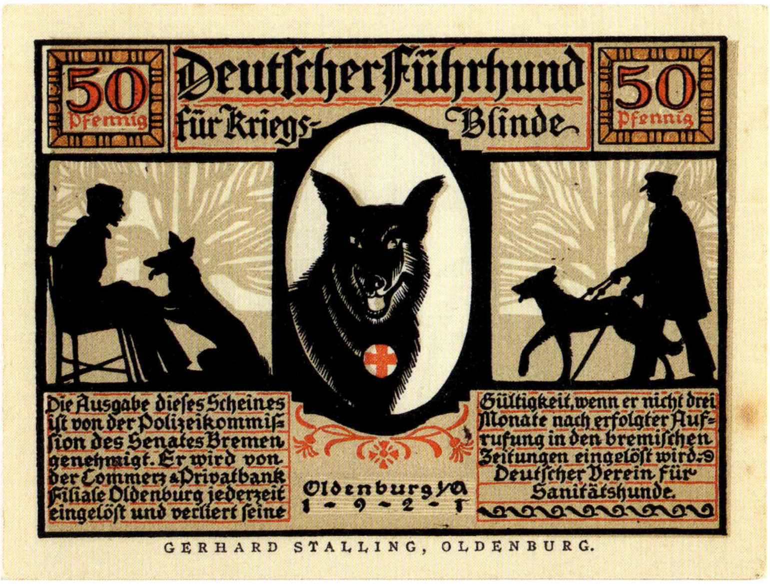

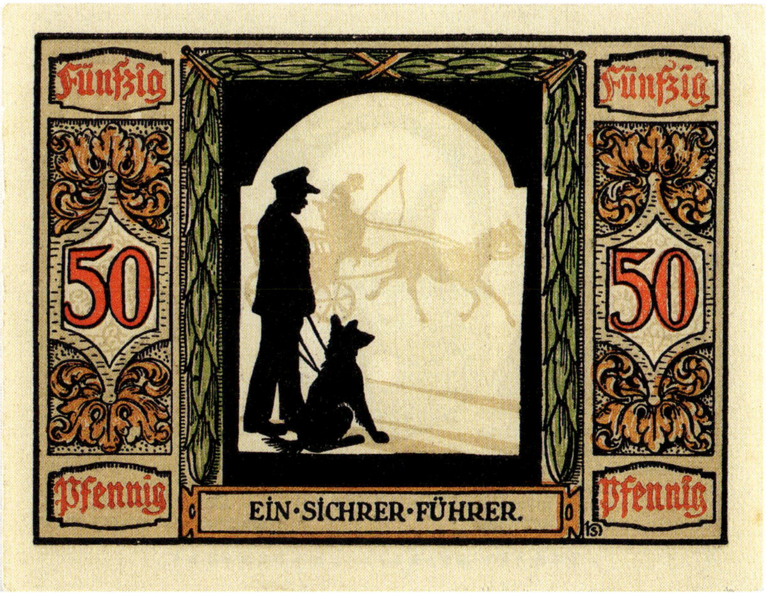

During and just after World War I, there was a major shortage in Germany of coins and paper money, on the one hand due to the great need for metal and paper for the war industry and, on the other, because people preferred cash. This is why the central bank allowed villages, municipalities and cooperation agreements to put their own money into circulation, so-called *Notgeld*. These notes from Oldenburg show blind soldiers with their guide dog.
German Emergency Money, s.d., paper. Private collection

However, this was not the only advantage of re-education. With regard to the Belgian context, the decision had been made to establish two re-education centres in the north of France. One was founded at the initiative of Senator Schollaert. The second and largest initiative was established by the Ministry of War and would eventually lead to the construction of a huge re-education institute in Port-Villez: *Belgian Military Vocational School for the Re-education of the Severely Wounded of the War*. The main advantage of this decentralised approach was that a lot of control could still be exerted over the disabled soldiers. Control that, in the light of the sparing use of remaining energy, was considered crucial. At least this is what can be gleaned from a quotation from one of the people responsible for this institute, Léon de Paeuw: "Si nous ne nous occupons pas sans retard et d'une manière énergique de leur rééducation professionnelle, ces pauvres gens ne suffiront plus à leurs propres besoins; ils deviendront des non-valeurs, peut-être des nuisances sociales. Or après la guerre, nous aurons besoin de toutes les énergies. Renflouons ces épaves. C'est un devoir d'équite que nous rendons à leurs sacrifices et c'est en même temps une excellente initiative au point de vue économique." [10]

The preceding quote clearly indicates that the establishment of the re-education institute cannot merely be accounted for from the idea that the state owed the disabled soldiers something. The idea of national duty certainly also played a part in the argument used to re-educate disabled soldiers. The state had to give something back to those who had risked their body and mind to liberate the homeland. The state owed them something. However, alongside this national duty towards national heroes – which can also be found in the discussions about these disabled soldiers – account should be taken of a number of economic interests. These economic interests were not only related to the fact that one wanted to boost energy levels during the war. It also had to do with the desire to keep pension expenses after the war as low as possible. It was said that those who would not learn a new profession, would cost the Belgian treasury a lot more than those who had taken on the challenge of re-education.

NOTES

1 This contribution is largely based on the book *Verminkte stilte: De Belgische invalide soldaten van de Groote Oorlog* which will be published in 2013 at the Naamse Universitaire Pers and was written by Christine Van Everbroeck and Pieter Verstraete.

2 Eenzame I., *Zij die gingen ... en zij die blijven*, Brussels, 't Spaeverke, 1924.

3 Ibid.

4 Cohen D., *When the war comes home. Disabled veterans in Britain and Germany, 1914–1939*, Berkeley, University of California Press, 2001.

5 De Schaepdrijver S., *De Groote Oorlog: het Koninkrijk België tijdens de Eerste Wereldoorlog*, Amsterdam, Atlas, 1997.

6 Mélis L., *Contribution à l'histoire du Service de Santé pendant la guerre 1914–1918*, Brussels, Institut Cartographique Militaire, *1932*, pp. 532-533.

7 Harris G., *Redemption of the disabled. A study of programmes of rehabilitation for the disabled of war and injury*, New York, D. Appleton & Company, 1919.

8 Ibid.

9 De Paeuw L., *La rééducation professionnelle des soldats mutilés et estropiés*, Port-Villez, Imprimerie de l'Ecole Nationale Belge des Mutilés de la Guerre, 1917, Préface.

10 De Paeuw L., *Conférence à l'Océan*, s.d., p. 13.

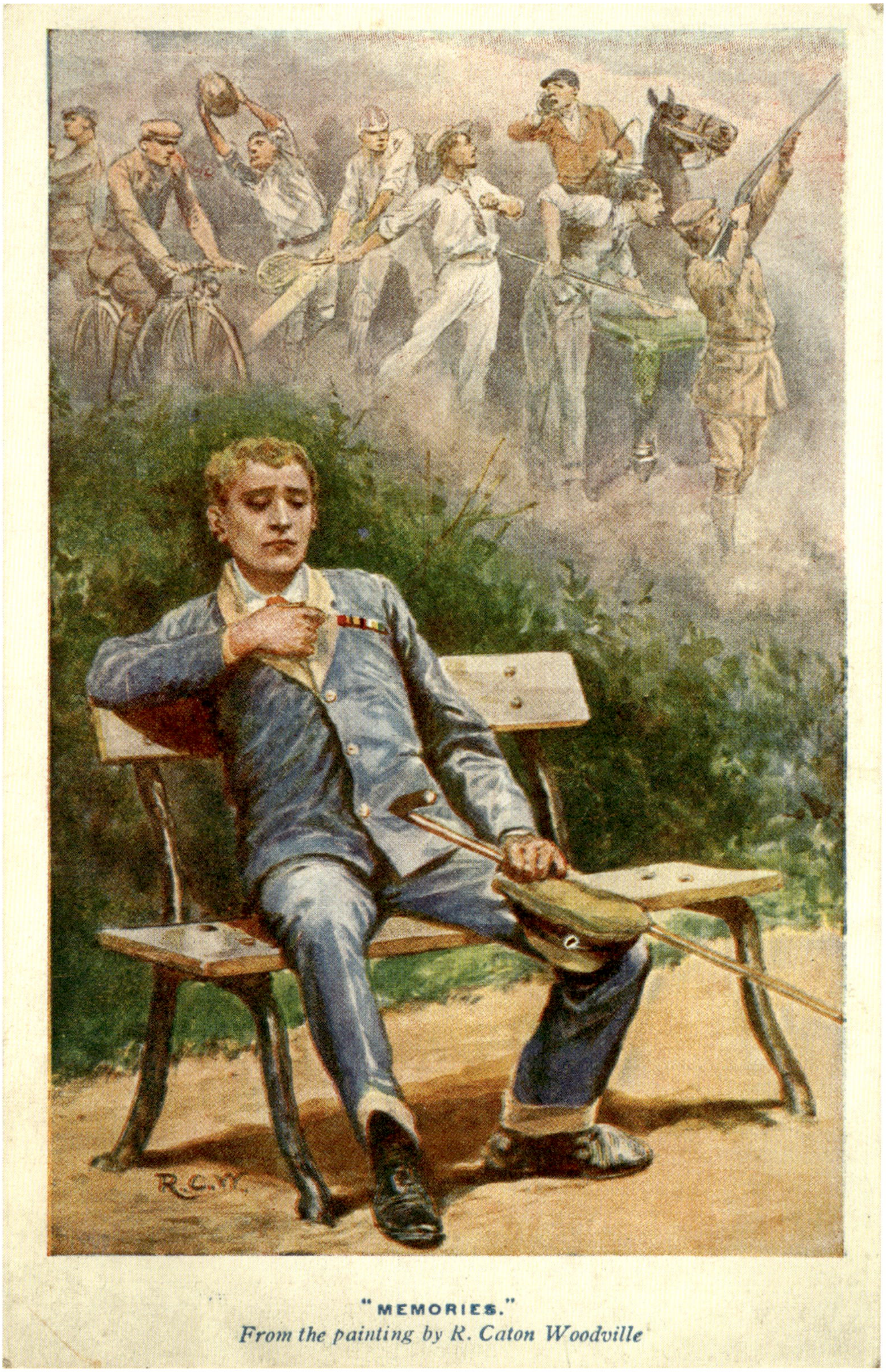

Memories, postcard after a painting of R. Caton Woodville. Private collection

Scissor Cut, 1980

For punishment the Kwong sisters were forced to cut the front lawn with scissors.

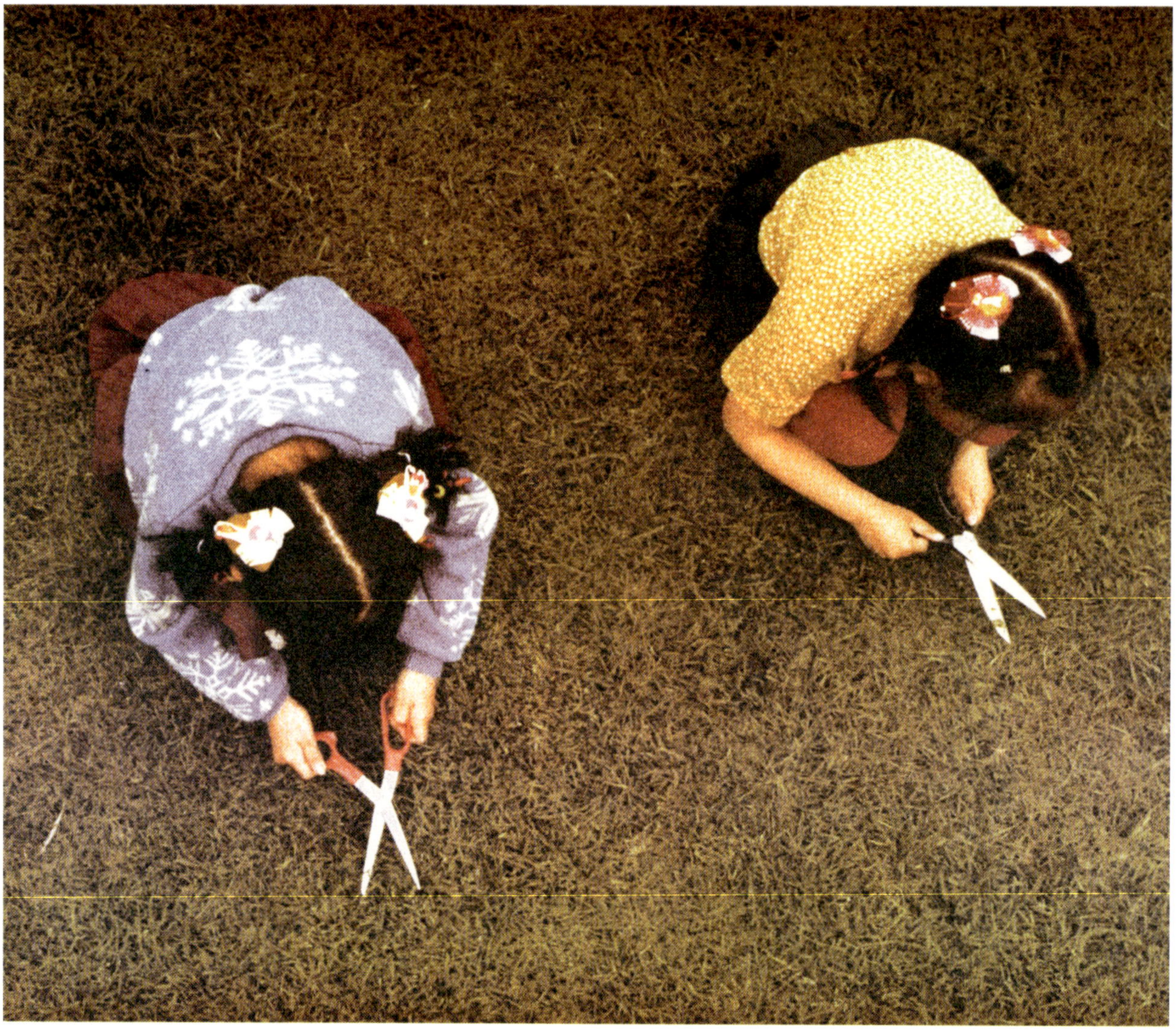

Tracey Moffatt

Tracey Moffatt (1960) is an Australian photographer and filmmaker. She began her career in experimental video and as a director and producer of video clips. In her work, conflicts of power and inequality are the main focus. As an Aboriginal of the 'Stolen Generations', she was taken away from her mother and forced to live with a white family. The series *Scarred for Life I* and *II* are about relationships of power. Photos of children in a variety of situations refer to the layout of *Life* magazine in the 1960s. While the photo reports of *Life* reported about world affairs, Moffatt focuses on the small but traumatic humiliations of everyday life, which mark us forever. The artist was inspired for the series by the true stories of her friends and by her own memories.
Tracey Moffatt, **Scissor Cut, 1980**, series Scarred for Life II, 1999, offset print. © Tracey Moffat, courtesy of L.A. Galerie-Lothar Albrecht, Frankfurt

Homemade Hand-knit, 1958

He knew his team mates were chuckling over his mother's hand-knitted rugby uniform.

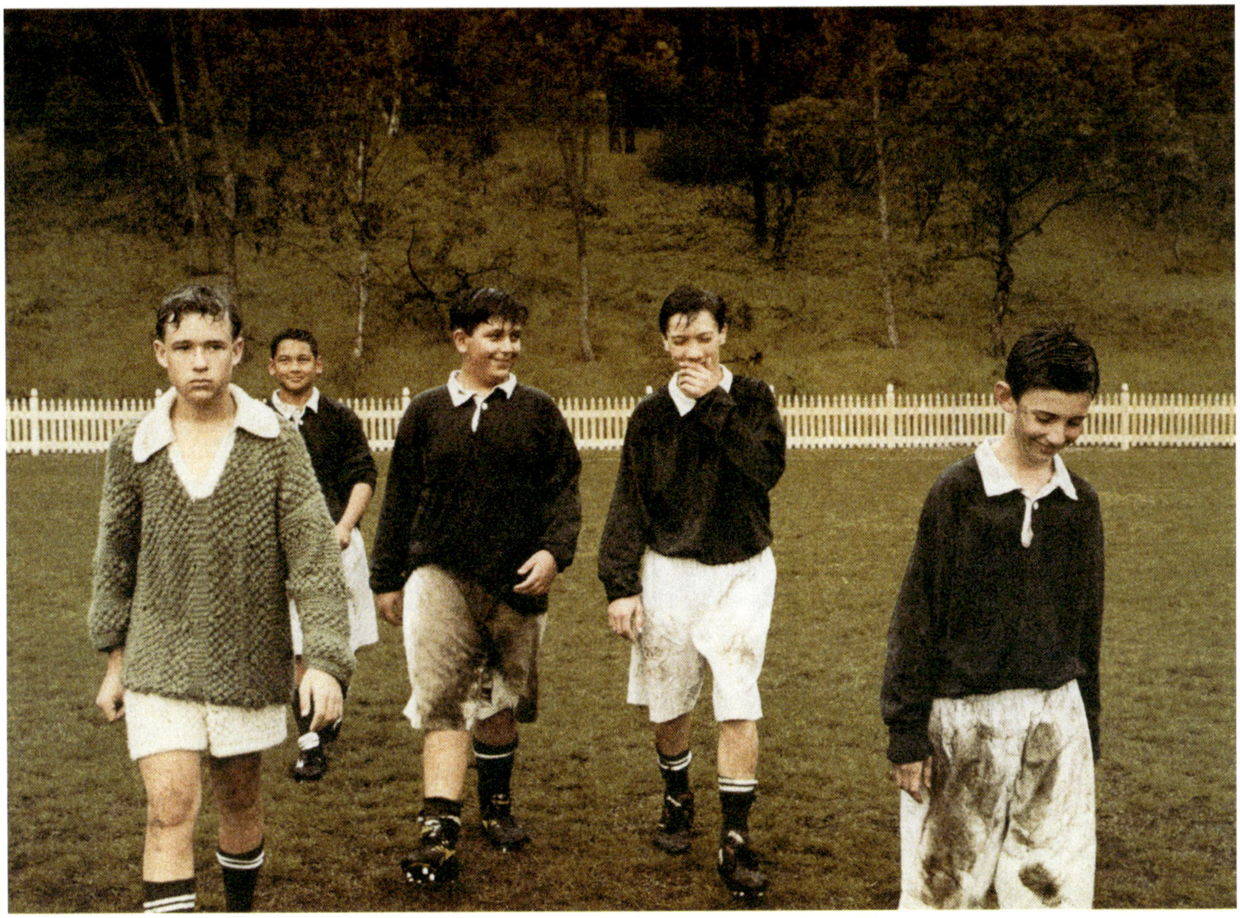

Tracey Moffatt

Tracey Moffatt, **Homemade Hand-knit, 1958**, series Scarred for Life II, 1999, offset print. © Tracey Moffat, courtesy of L.A. Galerie-Lothar Albrecht, Frankfurt

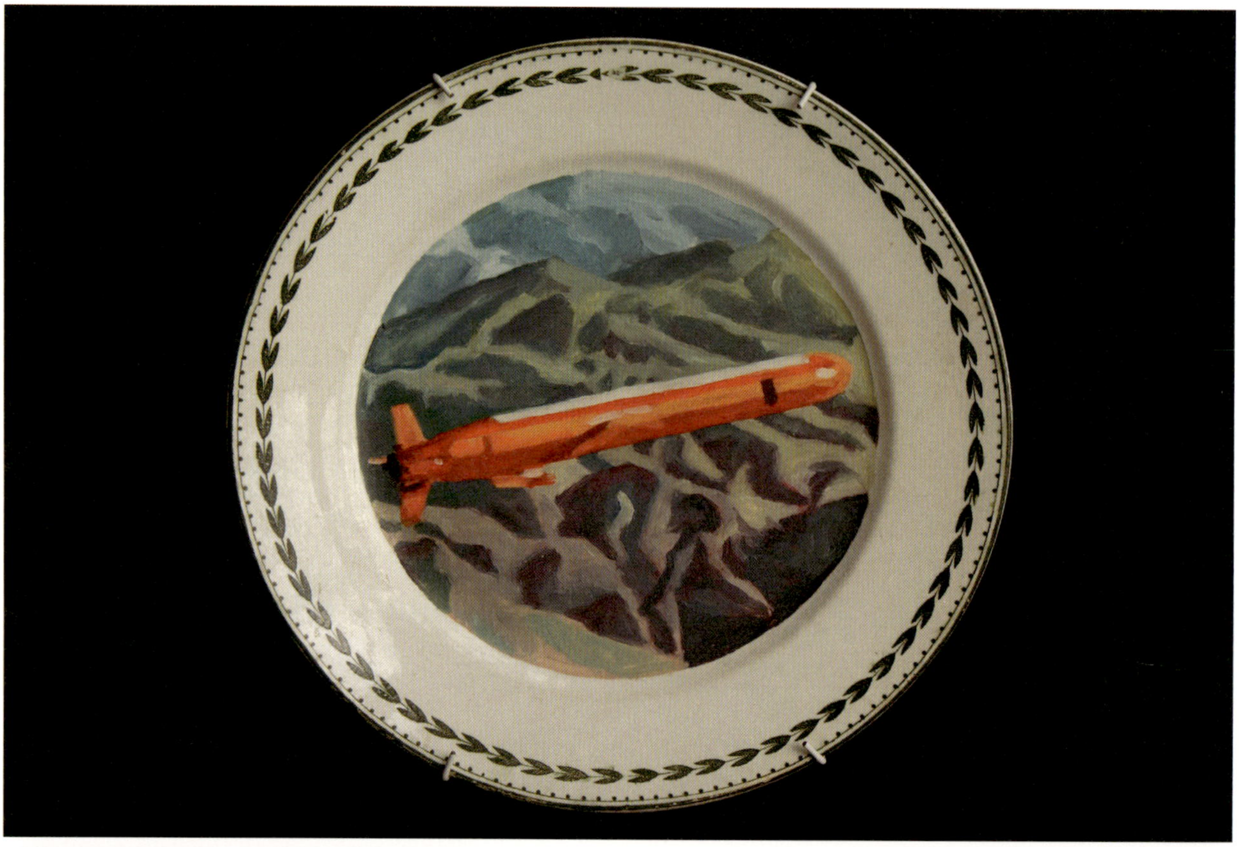

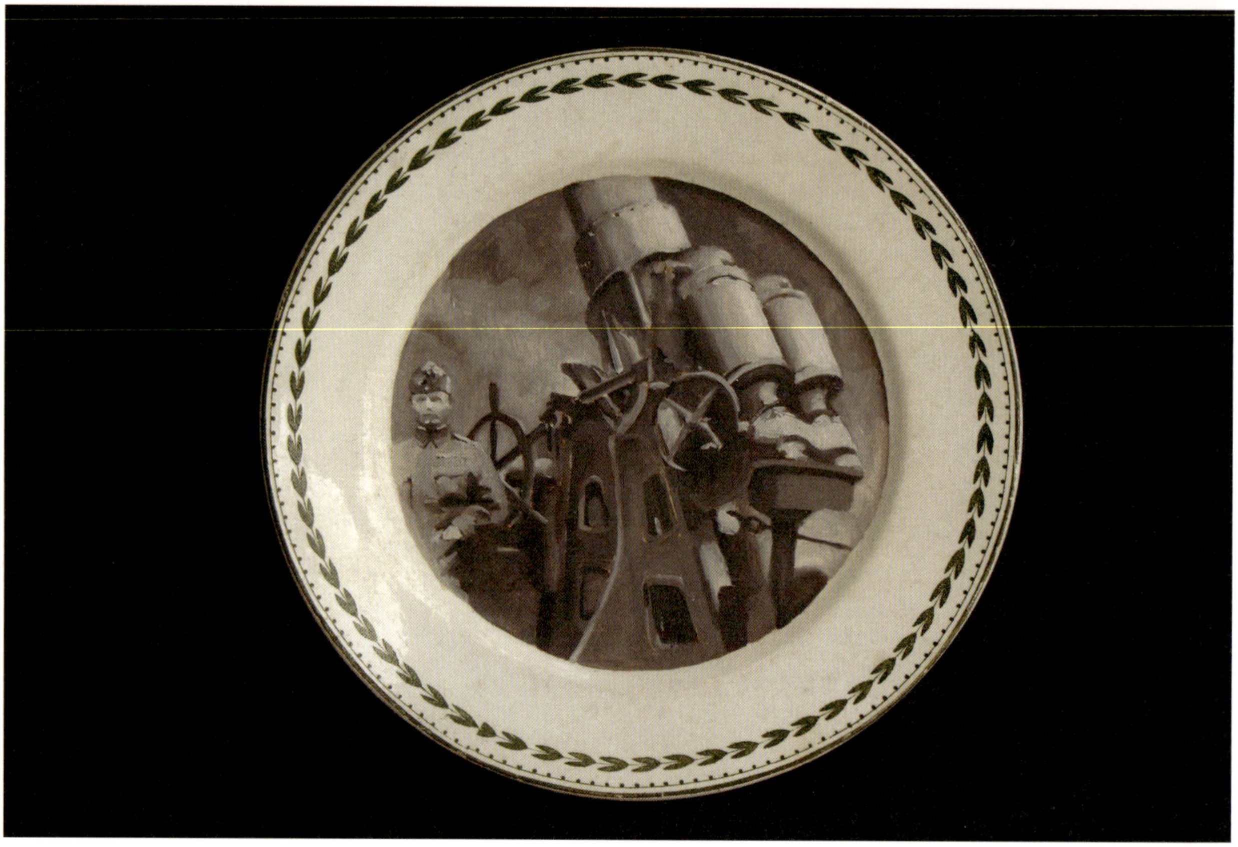

DIRK VAN PEER

I Contain Multitudes[1]

The Volcanic Work of Koen Broucke

A few days ago, I was invited by Dr Hahneman to report to Dr Guislain. This must be a group practice, I thought. But who is ill? Why does the doctor want to speak to me? Does he need my advice? Confused, I entered his office. The artist asked me what I thought of his work. He asked me to add some notes or thoughts. But this was an impossible question. How could I grasp this polyphony? Immediately the words of the wise Rilke came to mind. He told a young poet that "works of art are of an infinite loneliness and nothing can reach them as little as criticism. Only love can grasp them and keep hold of them and be just to them". But because the artist insisted, I tried to say something kind about the work of Koen Broucke.

Dr Hahneman is a creation by Koen Broucke, a fictitious psychiatrist who treats sick artists or art lovers, his alter ego. Koen Broucke needs this figure to bring order in his creative mind, to create oneness in the diversity of his creations. But it also stems from his own urge for order, science and seriousness. It enables the artist to be freed from these feelings in his creations. Hahneman is the father of all the fictitious figures Koen Broucke had to bring to life. It can be said that Koen Broucke is not only the doctor, but also the patient of Dr Hahneman. He is a duplicate, a complexity. Various worlds inhabit this artist. He "withstands everything better than his own versatility". Koen Broucke "is grand". Dr Hahneman channels this grandness.

What is striking in the oeuvre of Koen Broucke is the early and continuous interest in war as a subject in his art. He processes the theme of war in series of paintings such as *Bagdad*, *Unsterbliche Soldaten* and especially in the *Moeder aller Oorlogen [Mother of all Wars]* series.

There is, for instance, the thematic connection with war. His paintings include tanks, volcanoes, soldiers, fighter jets, guns, shell bursts, horses and riders – in short: objects of eruption and destruction – alongside flowers, pianos and dancers. What is the artist trying to tell us? Possibly, that beauty and horror are inextricably linked. Possibly, the at first sight incoherent elements may refer to the thought that only art can give solace during times of horror. Survivors of concentration camps such as Alice Herz-Sommer bear witness to the power art gave them in their battle. It kept her and her fellow prisoners alive. However, Koen Broucke may be saying that life always contains elements of struggle and of beauty and that, independent of your view, you perceive one or the other. This interpretation becomes more credible when we focus attentively on the *Mother of all Wars* series. Due to the use of various techniques the objects depicted are only visible under a certain incidence of light. Depending on how you position yourself vis-à-vis this universe you see tanks or dancers, you are struck by guns or awaited by a pianist. Is this a hint of the artist? Does the artist want to tell us that we should still try to preserve the love of beauty even in the most horrific circumstances of war? Art as therapy?

Apart from the thematic relationship of the paintings and drawings it is - and perhaps especially - the

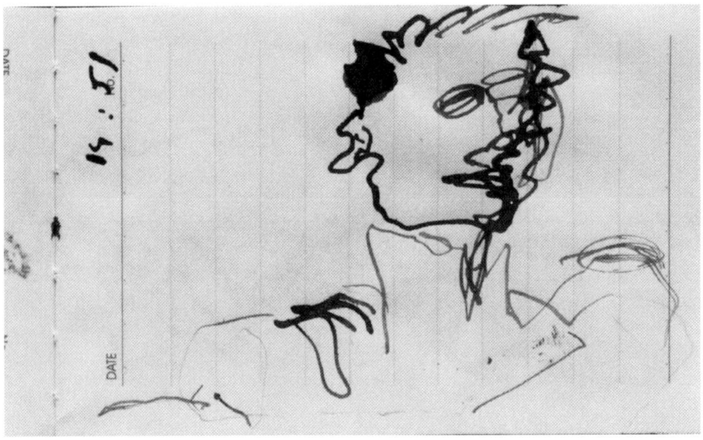

Koen Broucke, **Galerie des batailles**, 2005, paint on porcelain. Artist's collection

Koen Broucke, **The Armed Man**, 2009, ink on paper. Artist's collection

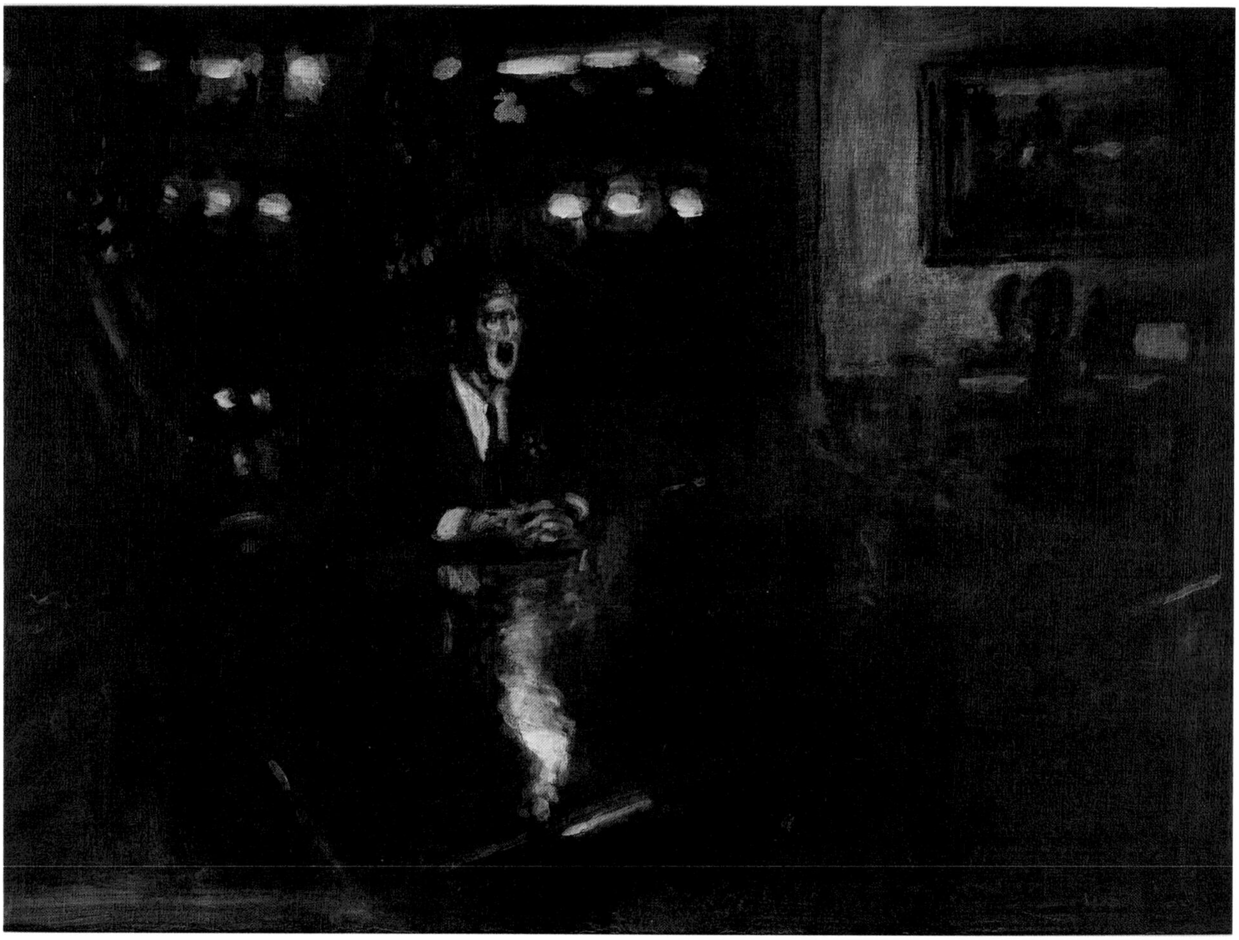

style that makes this work war art. By using painted backgrounds – which Koen Broucke inherited from the renaissance artists – the painter creates a threatening and nightly atmosphere. For instance, his work seems like "a great shadow. A sum of connected shadows moving in the night". In the paintings we hear "the roar far away and nearby of this European war. We hear the boom of a universe of disaster. Which terrors and which death and which new types of beauty strew the darkness" of these works of art? The *Mother of all War* looks like "sulphurous craters" and "streams of puss", like a hallucination after a gas attack. But his paintings do not only look like war scenes. All our senses are addressed. His canvases taste of mud, smell like gunpowder and sound like the rattling of war. A lot more can be said about the musicality of Koen Broucke's visual art. I will only point out the stroke in the paintings and drawings that clearly show the act of painting. Koen Broucke does not try to hide the movement of his hand on the canvas or paper. We could call his work figurative improvisations. The fluidity of the stroke is reminiscent of a musical experience. In his visual work the artist aims for the same musical immateriality.

Why does an artist choose a theme such as war even though he never experienced it himself? Undoubtedly, Koen Broucke the historian has something to do with this. The man who has developed a natural interest in this phenomenon through his studies. Perhaps he has an eye for the aestheticism of war? The badges, the uniforms, the posters and flags or even the heroism of the scenes? The underlying causes are probably deeper. Creations by artists do not originate from nowhere. Works

Koen Broucke, **Declaration of War**, 2003, acrylic paint on canvas. Private collection of art are conscious or subconscious indications of the ground they spring from. "Forgotten, war lives on in all things". In the stories of our grandparents, in annual commemorations, in village squares and perhaps most of all in the media that makes each war our war. Koen Broucke updates the memory of the demented insanity of war in each of us.

In conclusion, a brief description of the lives of several patients of Dr Hahneman, who are included in the *War & Trauma* exhibition.

Francis Lennox (Orsmaal, 12 January 1958) is a historical painter of the Great War, the trenches, fighter planes and pilots and the bombings on Bagdad. He suffers from paranoia and posttraumatic stress disorder (DSM IV).

Geoffrey Hougoumont (Sint-Amandsberg, 18 June 1961) is a visitor and painter of battlefields, mainly the battlefield around Ieper (Ypres). He is the author of *Mother of all Wars* and collects maps, reference books on battlefields and miniature soldiers, *Paris Match* and the like. He suffers from posttraumatic stress disorder (DSM IV).

Marcel Quineau (The Hague, 3 December 1921 – 1 December 1944) was a painter of quasi monochrome small canvases painted in a darkened room at the Hofvijver in The Hague and Liège during WW II. His oeuvre is incomplete: his final piece dates from his return trip from Bruges when he was hit by a lost American bullet. He suffered from pyromania, agoraphobia and social phobia.

Tariq Al Malouf (Bagdad, 29 April 1937) is a curator of the first museum of weapons of mass destruction. His collection contains the scale model of the gallery with painted signs (the so-called La Galerie de Batailles), paintings of death masks of German generals from WW I (the so-called *Unsterbliche Soldaten* of Max Simoneit), sketchbooks with pen drawings of, among others, bodies and also work of the knife maker, the gun painter and the re-inventor of the 'Dazzle Painting'. Tariq has a paranoid personality disorder and posttraumatic stress disorder (DSM IV).

Johannes Rodrigo Schwarz (Brussels, 6 April 1979) is the author of a filled to the brim exercise book with historical data on every movement of artists during WW I. His syndrome is characterised by horro vacui, nosophobia and obsessive compulsive disorder.

1 The quotes are extracts from war poems of various poets, compiled in the book *Het lijf in slijk geplant, Gedichten uit de Eerste Wereldoorlog*, compiled and introduced by Geert Buelens, Ambo, Manteau, 2008. The excerpts are by Fernando Pessoa, Gabriele D'Annunzio, Emile Verhaeren, Johannes R. Becher and Guillaume Apollinaire. The article begins with several references to Walt Whitman's *Leaves of Grass*.

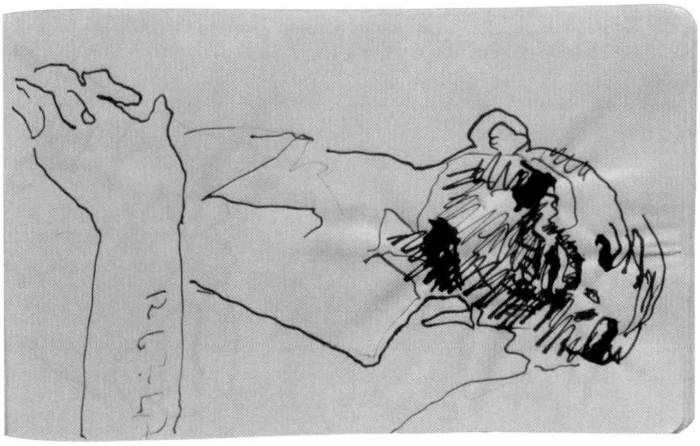

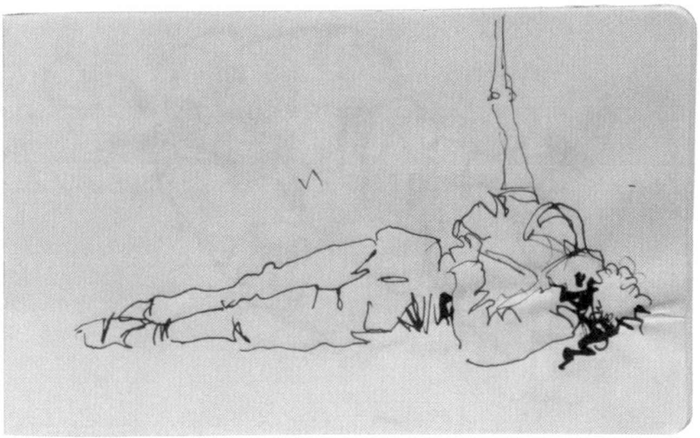

Koen Broucke, **The Armed Man**, 2009, ink on paper. Artist's collection

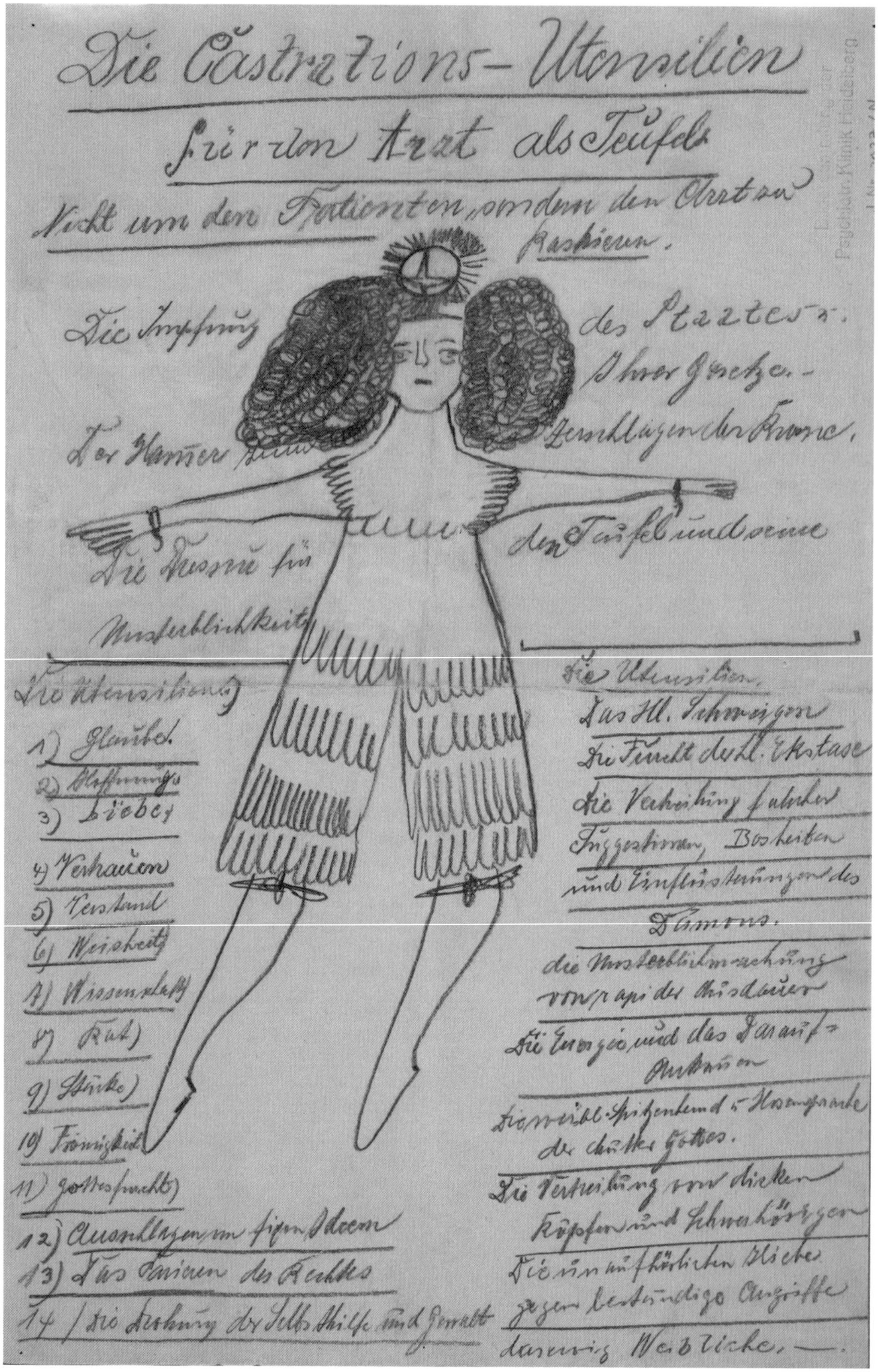

Alois Dallmayr's (1883–1940) drawings have sharp taut pencil lines. They are full of religious symbols, but also full of scientific references and personal stories. His work is not limited to drawings, but is completed by parts of pamphlet text, medical terms, names and references. Although he was voluntarily hospitalised in a psychiatric institution, he demanded his release in his work. He often signed his drawings with 'God' or 'Genius' and called himself 'the Spirit of Truth', but was met with a lack of understanding by the doctors, who viewed his strength as an illness. Dementia praecox was the official diagnosis of Dallmayr's condition. His thoughts were increasingly predominated by death. He also glorified his death in drawings. Dallmayr was probably killed in the Hartheim/Linz euthanasia centre.

Alois Dallmayr, **Die Castrations-Utensilien für den Arzt als Teufel**, s.d., pencil on paper. Sammlung Prinzhorn, Heidelberg

PETRA FUCHS

The National-Socialist 'Euthanasia' Programme

The Murder of the Mentally Ill, Disabled, 'Parasite Races' and Politically or Socially 'Undesired' People in Europe between 1939 and 1945

In the national-socialist era, the word 'euthanasia' was used as a veiled term for the first systematic mass murder by the naziregime.

The main victims of these crimes were children, women and men in psychiatric institutions, educational and care institutions and homes for the elderly or people with a disability. As the war continued, the 'euthanasia' programme extended to convicts, prisoners in concentration camps, political dissidents, Jews, Sinti and Roma, 'anti-socials', prisoners of war, traumatised soldiers, civilians and patients in the occupied countries.

According to the current state of research, at least 300,000 people were the victims of this murder programme in Germany and occupied European countries.

Actively killing seriously ill and disabled people was not an idea of the national socialists. All over the world academics had debated terminal care for the incurably ill since the mid-19th century, under the heading of 'euthanasia' (Greek: good death).

The discussion on killing upon request was soon intertwined with the question whether society should have the right to kill the 'incurable mentally or physically ill'. Racial hygiene and economic points of view were also significant here.

These discussions reached a peak against the backdrop of the social and economic consequences of World War I. In 1920 lawyer Karl Binding and psychiatrist

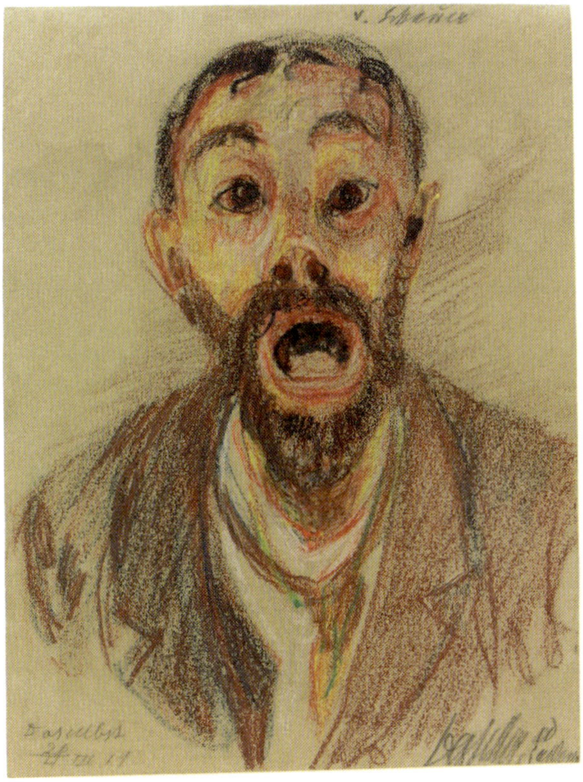

The work of Franz Karl Bühler ranges from portraits in pen and ink to colourful, imaginative scenes in pastel crayon. Although his psychiatrists saw the development in his oeuvre as slipping into insanity, art collector Prinzhorn praised his creations and saw no deterioration in them. Bühler began his career as an ornamental metal worker, but after a failed education and afflicted by paranoia, he went from one psychiatric institution to the next. He spent 42 years of his life in such institutions and here too he remained tormented by, successively, paranoia and a fear of being poisoned. Apart from imaginative scenes, he also made self-portraits and pen drawings of fellow patients, which he considered valuable for their treatment. This outsider artist also became a victim of the Nazi regime's euthanasia programme, although the official cause of death was a cardiac muscle disease. Proof of Bühler's annihilation disappeared with his cremation.
Franz Karl Bühler, **Das Selbst**, 1919, pastel crayon on watercolour paper. Sammlung Prinzhorn, Heidelberg

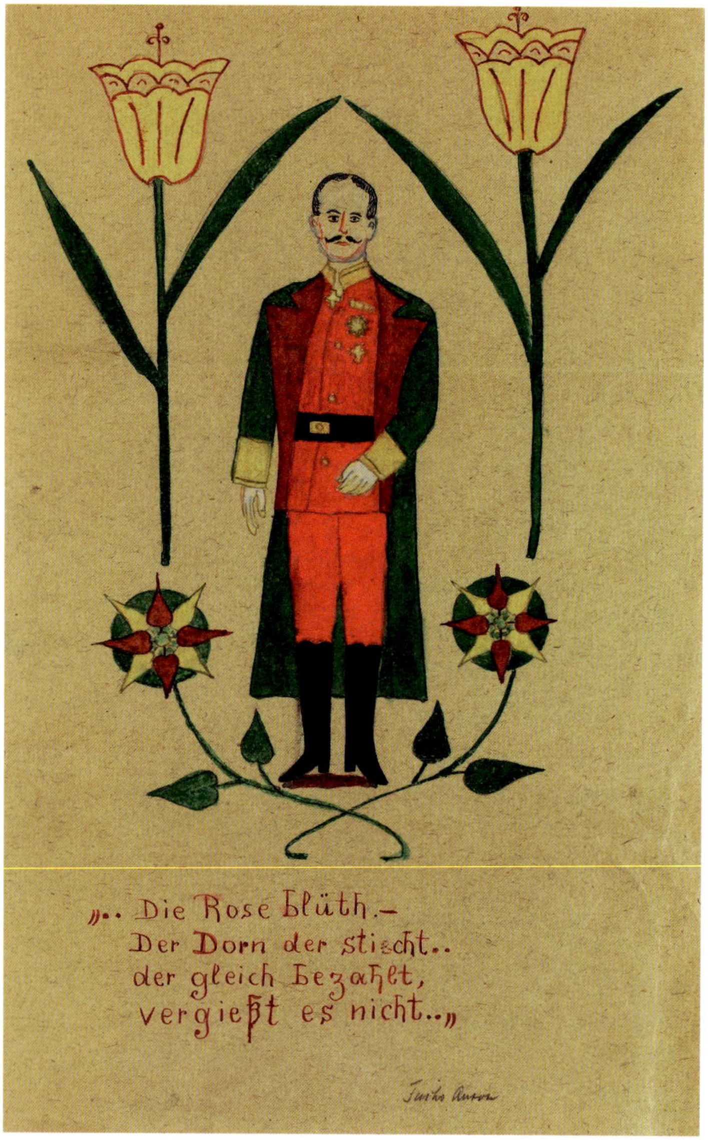

A lack of understanding and conflict dominated the life of German artist Anton Fuchs (1896–1941). He was hospitalised in psychiatric institutions at the age of 19 after a turbulent life path. At school or in the army he did not interact well with others. Due to conflicts during his military service, they decided to make him retire as a war invalid. He also caused arguments and conflicts during his hospitalisation in several psychiatric institutions. Even doctors could not be empathetic towards him. People generally assumed that he could have made more of an effort to behave better and be a better person. Shortly before his death, a doctor described him as a "deficient storyteller. A parasite by nature". Fuchs focused on painting and wood cutting until he was killed in a euthanasia centre.
Anton Fuchs, **Untitled**, s.d., ink, paint and pencil on paper. Sammlung Prinzhorn, Heidelberg

Alfred Hoche laid the theoretical foundation for national-socialist 'euthanasia' with their publication *Die Freigabe der Vernichtung lebensunwerten Lebens.*

They motivated killing 'incurable imbeciles' and comatose patients by labelling them 'empty shells of people', 'mentally dead people' and 'deadwood beings' to society.

The vision of Binding and Hoche was still controversial in the Weimar republic and there was a lot of discussion on the matter. Only at the start of World War II and in new political circumstances, the national-socialist regime put their ideas into practice.

BEGINNING OF METHODICAL NATIONAL-SOCIALIST 'EUTHANASIA': 1 SEPTEMBER 1939

The beginning of the war was also the start of the killing of the ill, called 'euthanasia'. In an informal letter on private stationary Hitler ordered his personal physician Dr Karl Brandt (1904–1948) and the leader of his chancery, Philipp Bouhler (1899–1945), to appoint physicians whose task would consist of "granting the incurably ill mercy killing". This 'authorisation' remained the only basis for the systematic extermination of mentally ill people and people with a mental disability in Germany and in the occupied European territories. This was also murder according to the penal code during the time of national-socialism. Until 1945 not a single bill for the legalisation of 'euthanasia' applied. Killing psychiatric patients was thus done in secret.

DESTROYING THE USELESS – THE CENTRALLY GUIDED NATIONAL-SOCIALIST 'EUTHANASIE-AKTION T4': 1940/41

The best known national-socialist 'euthanasia' crime is the centrally guided *Aktion T4*, named after the address of the administrative centre of the killing of the ill, Tiergartenstraße 4 in Berlin. Over 70,000 male and female patients from psychiatric and care institutions, among whom 4,200 children, became the victims of this centrally operated phase of the killing of the ill.

The 'central office T4' was divided into four

departments with several authorities: the *Reichsarbeitsgemeinschaft Heil- und Pflegeanstalten* (RAG) (Reich Work Group of Sanatoria and Nursing Homes) was responsible for the registration of the victims, i.e. sending and assessing the registration forms. The *Gemeinnützige Kranken-Transport-GmbH* (Gekrat) (Society of Public Utility for Transport of the Sick) arranged everything related to the deportation of patients to the death institutes. The *Gemeinnützige Stiftung für Anstaltspflege* (Society of Public Utility for Institutional Care) acted as employer of the approximately 400 employees, concluded leases and concentrated on all economic issues and the *Zentralverrechnungsstelle Heil- und Pflegeanstalten* (ZVST) (Compensation Office for Sanatoria and Nursing Homes) arranged all financial matters and took care of the correspondence with the cost bearers.

Officially this special semi-government administration came under the 'chancery of the Führer' but, for reasons of secrecy, they were not allowed to go public as being responsible for 'euthanasia'.

In autumn 1939, the ministry of the interior sent forms for the registration of all male and female patients in psychiatric and care institutions of the German Reich.

The heads of the institutions returned the completed forms to the administrative centre in Berlin. Here 41 medical 'experts' and three 'top experts' decided about the life and death of each registered patient with a blue stripe or a red cross.

On the basis of selection the central agency of *T4* drew up transport lists with the names of the patients of the institutions in question who had to be deported with 'grey buses' or by train. From the summer of 1940, due to increased confidentiality and a more flexible and efficient organisation, the ill were accommodated in 'temporary institutions' for several days or months until their deportation to the gas chambers.

Traveling physician committees were deployed on the spot –in the psychiatric and care institutions – to check the data mentioned in the registration form, but also to pursue a selection in the institutes themselves.

The decisive criterion with regard to living or dying was employability, or 'learning suitability' of children and youngsters. But 'disturbing behaviour', the need for assistance and the 'incurability' of the disease were arguments for the selection. Women had a greater risk of becoming victims of 'euthanasia', because their work achievements and their behaviour in the institutions were often regarded as more negative than that of male patients.

MURDER IN SIX DEATH INSTITUTES

The organisation of *Aktion T4* chose six psychiatric institutions where gas chambers were installed: Grafeneck/Württemberg, Brandenburg/Havel (gas chamber in the house of correction), Hartheim near Linz/Upper Austria, Pirna-Sonnenstein near Dresden/Saxony, Bernburg a.d. Saale/Anhalt and Hadamar in Hessen-Nassau.

Here, the patients were killed with carbon monoxide. Only the physician was allowed to open the gas cylinders.

In the summer of 1940, merely on the basis of the 'race' criterion, more than 1,000 Jewish men and women were registered at the central agency in Berlin,

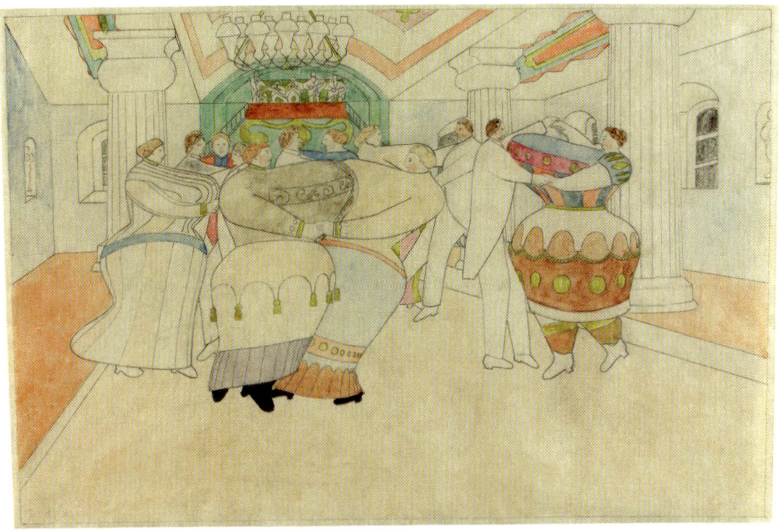

Jail sentences and hospitalisations in psychiatric institutions characterised the life of artist Gustav Sievers. He was arrested for acts of violence, begging and child abuse. He was a convinced atheist and social-democrat who did not hide his ideals and revolted and rebelled throughout his life. He converted anxieties and powerlessness into aggression and violence. He managed to escape on several occasions, but was caught each time. During his stay in institutions, he drew comics. His stories are often humoristic parables that ridicule the church and Wilhelminic chauvinism. A recurring theme in his work is the Amazon, a strong and self-aware woman who always achieves her goal. He made his drawings in pencil. They also contained text and were regularly painted in bright colours. At a later age Sievers' rebellion seemed to disappear and he became indifferent and impassive. Marked as 'uncured', he was taken to the Hadamar extermination camp in 1941 and killed.
Gustav Sievers, **Dance**, s.d., pencil, watercolour on carbon paper. Sammlung Prinzhorn, Heidelberg

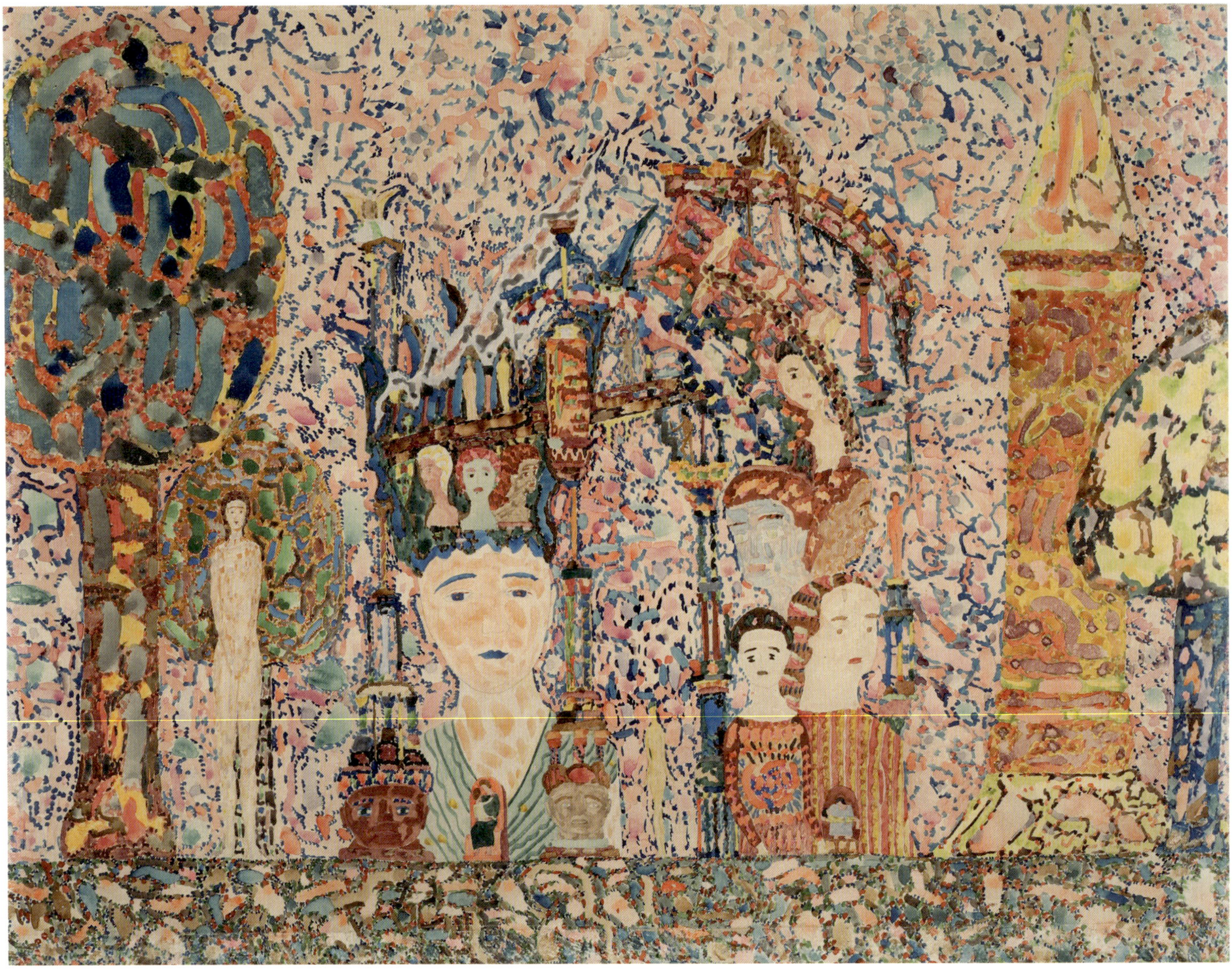

Artist and architect Paul Goesch (1885–1940) was surrounded by artists in his youth. It therefore comes as no great surprise that he concentrated on art and architecture. He dwelled in expressionist circles and was part of the November Group, which devoted itself to the involvement of artists in politics and believed in the social relevance of art. However, Goesch suffered from so-called 'nervousness' and was described as highly sensitive. Part of his work consists of a series of Madonnas which he started creating after a vision. He also made imaginative architectural designs, built pyramids with stacked boxes and created sculptures from a variety of remnants. His life was plagued by mental illness and, after several brief hospitalisations, he spent his life in mental hospitals. After a fight with a fellow patient, he was severely injured, because of which he was classified as unworthy of life and killed.

Paul Goesch, **Wall Painting (Fantastische Triomfator)**,
s.d., pencil, watercolour on paper. Sammlung Prinzhorn, Heidelberg

assembled in regional institutions and deported to the *T4*-killing centres. In June 1942 the last Jewish patients from the only psychiatric institution that still allowed them, Bendorf-Sayn near Neuwied, were deported to the East European extermination camps.

The murder of Jewish patients as part of the centrally operated 'euthanasia-Aktion T4' was the actual beginning of the genocide of European Jews.

In spite of all measures to keep everything secret as much as possible, there was unrest among the population about the killing of the ill. Many state and municipal bodies and individual people were aware of the systematic murders. However, people rarely protested in public. Only a few individuals had the guts to do this. There was no collective, organised opposition. The only resistance against the killing of the ill that is worthmentioning came from the church. Their protest, including the well-known sermon of the Bishop of Münster, cardinal Clemens August Graf von Galen (1878–1946), party-internal rejections and opposition from legal circles prompted Hitler to announce an 'end' to the gassing on 24 August 1941. According to the internal statistics of the central office 70,273 patients had been murdered in the six death institutes by this time.

After the termination of *Aktion T4*, in which leading German psychiatrists had cooperated to a major extent, the 'euthanasia' continued from 1 August 1941 to 1945 in a non-centralised manner: the selections took place in the separate institutions, ordered by the head of the institution. Part of the nursing staff who had voluntarily declared to cooperate in this 'euthanasia,' directly took part in these killings by administering overdoses of medicine and by consciously starving the patients to death.

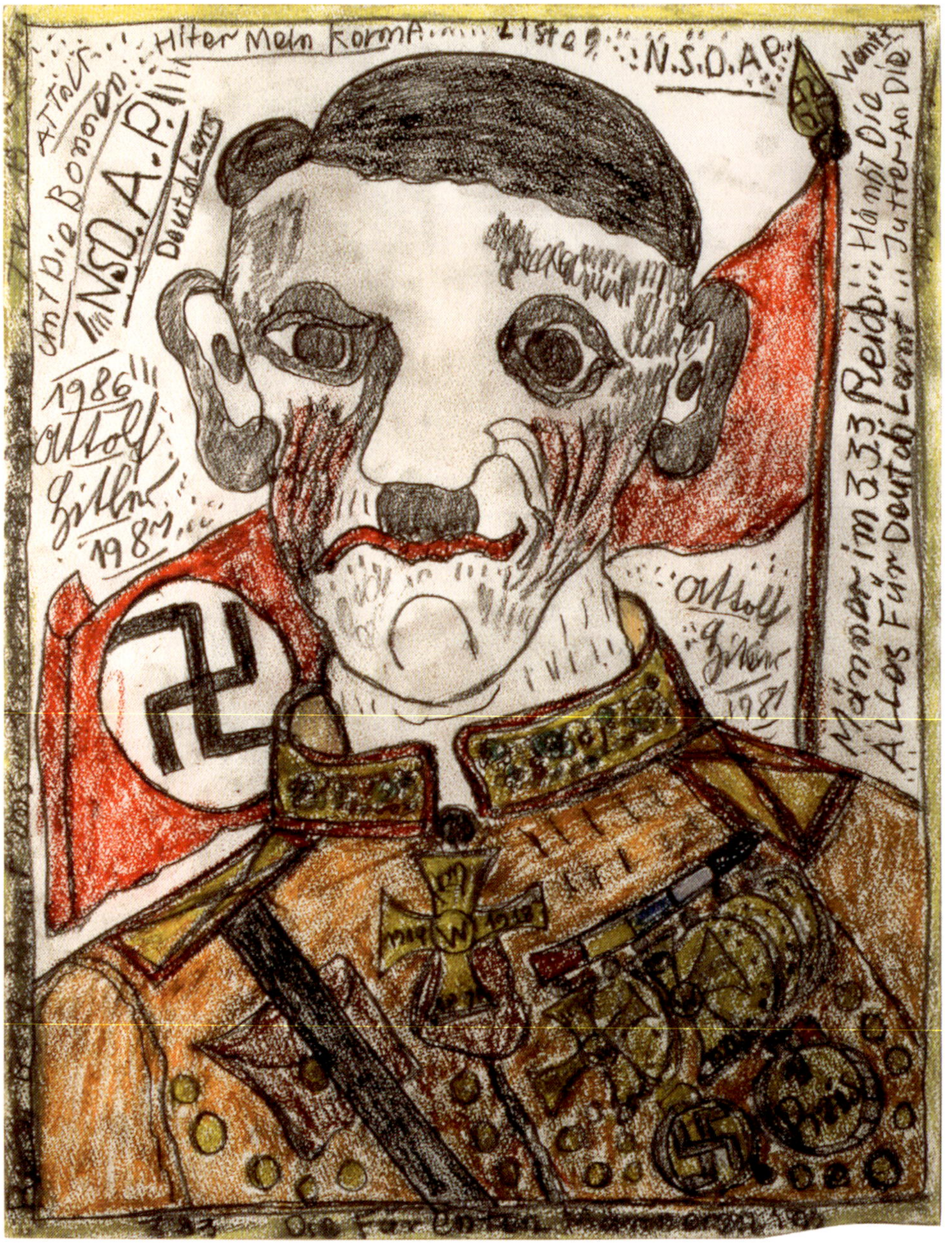

The German Theo or Theodore Wagemann (1918–1998) was traumatised at the age of 13 after being shot by customs officers when smuggling. From then on, he stopped speaking and was hospitalised several times. His mental condition endangered him in Nazi Germany of the 1930s, but his family and doctors managed to protect him against the T4 programme. He was, however, forcibly sterilised. In 1977, he was hospitalised in an institution, where he started to draw. Hundreds of portraits of Hitler and other dignitaries of the Nazis appear in felt-tip pen, to which he often adds xenophobic slogans, mixed with numbers related to the German Reich. These symbols were part of his personal mythology and do not have the significance that we generally give them.

Theo, **Untitled**, 1986, wax crayon, colour pencil on paper. De Stadshof Collection, Dr Guislain Museum, Ghent

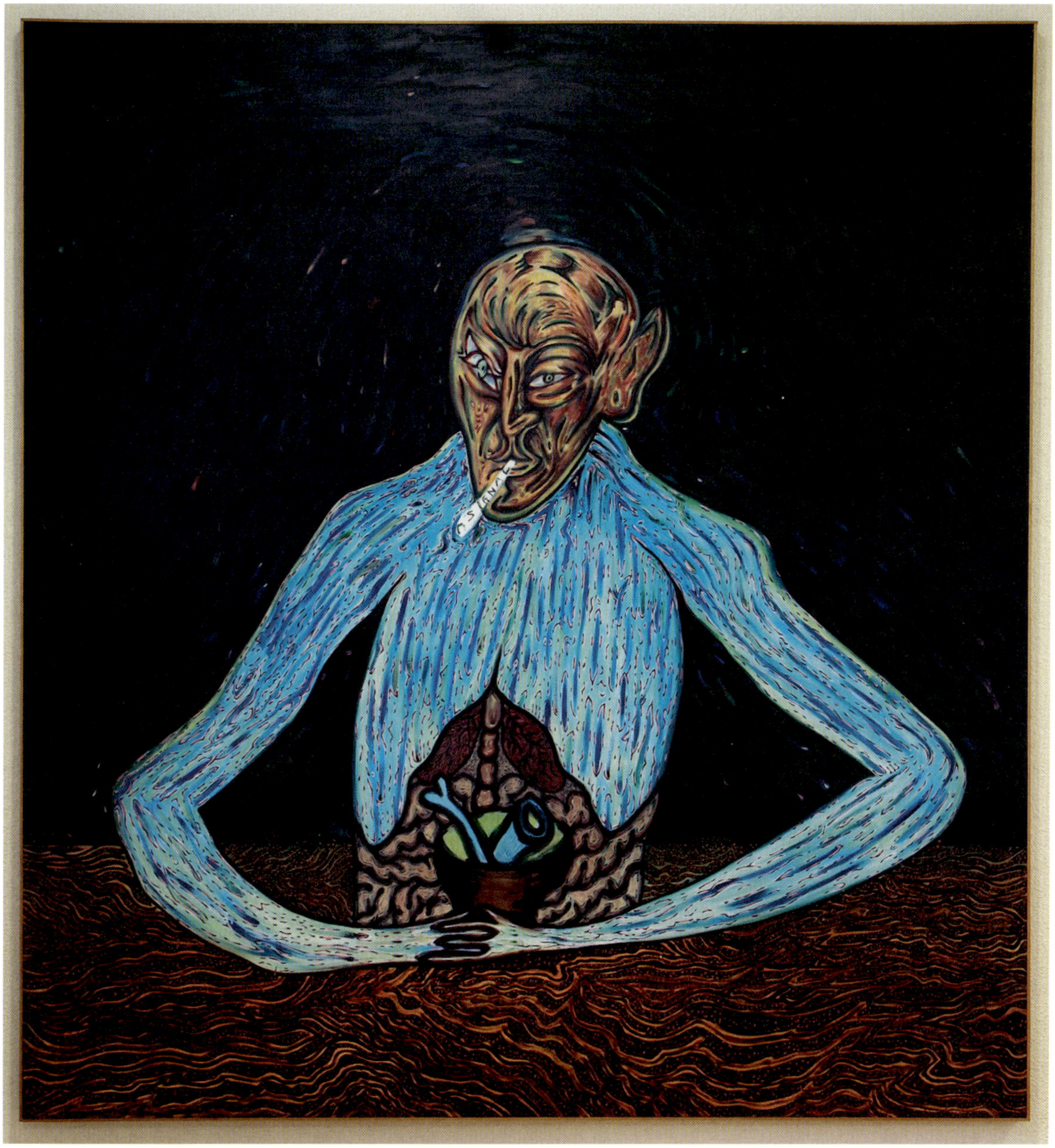

Man met vele eigenschappen [The Man With Many Qualities] is the opposite of Ulrich, the central figure in the novel *Der Mann ohne Eigenschaften* by Austrian author Robert Musil. Ulrich finds that it is impossible to choose a position or to support an ideology. In the painting by Pjeroo Roobjee (1945) there is, on the other hand, no doubt about the prevailing ideology: fascism. The second title, *De dichter in Nieuw Westerbork*, refers to the best-known concentration camp in the Netherlands. The table top at the bottom of the paintings is covered with the names of concentration camps and the cigarette reads 'Signal', the title of the Nazi's propaganda. Furthermore, the emaciated man with his exposed innards looks like a victim of the experimental drift of the sadistic Dr Jozef Mengele.
Pjeroo Roobjee, **Man met vele eigenschappen of de dichter in Nieuw Westerbork**, 1993, oil on canvas. Flemish Parliament, Brussels

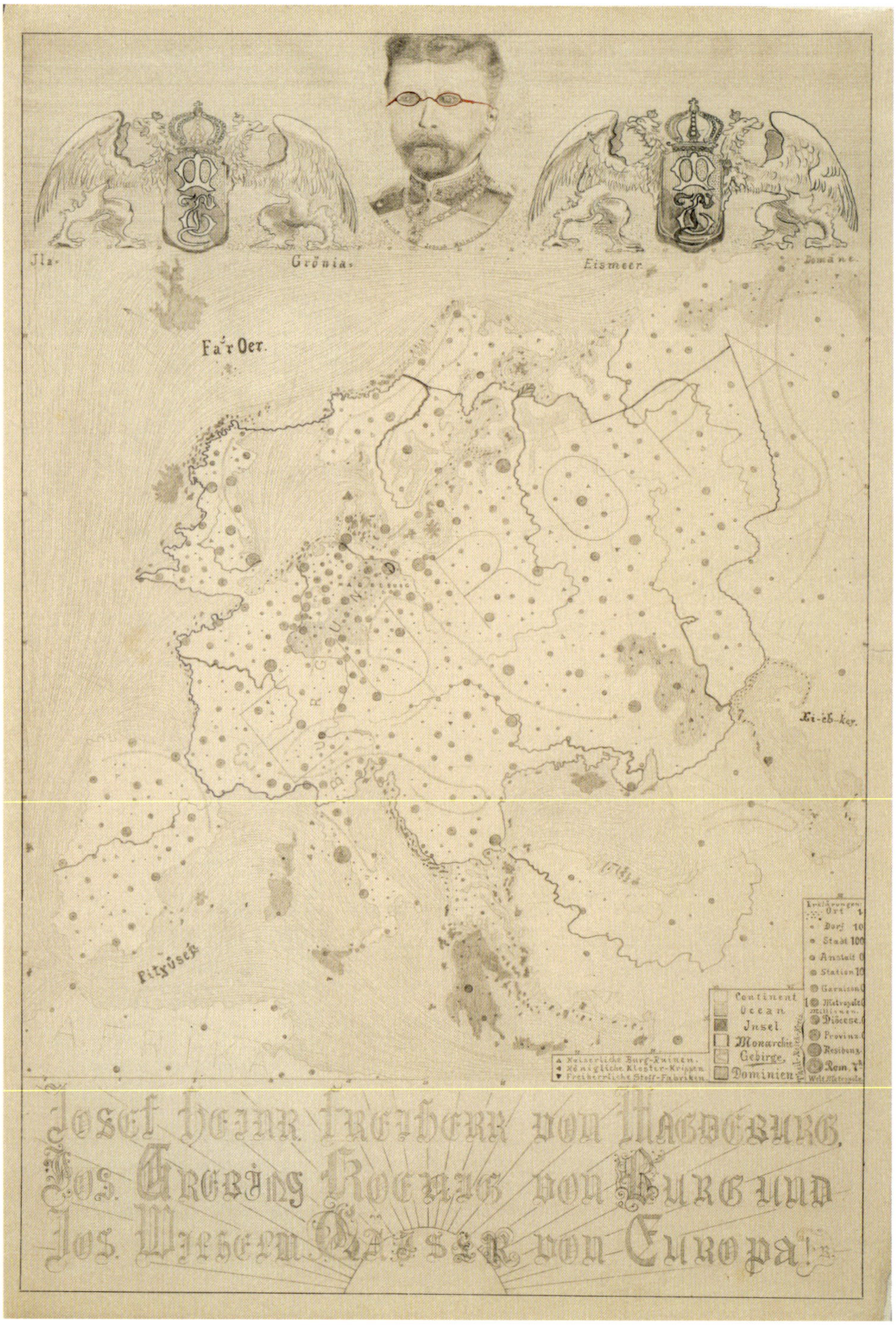

Calendars, lists of figures, collages and notebooks show the thoughts of businessman and artist Josef Heinrich Grebing (1879–1940). This artist first showed signs of mental illness during his imprisonment for fraud. In a brochure, he gave an account of his sentence and laid a complaint against the justice system of the time, which he believed required urgent reformation. He regarded himself as a martyr. After a failed suicide attempt, he was first hospitalised in a psychiatric institution and from that moment on he spent the rest of his life as a patient. Grebing was haunted by depression and a death wish. Apart from his collages and paintings, many of his letters have been preserved, which bear witness to his inner battle. After having spent many years in an institution, he died in the Grafeneck euthanasia centre in 1940.
Josef Heinrich Grebing, **Map of Europe**, 1920, mixed techniques on drawing cardboard. Sammlung Prinzhorn, Heidelberg

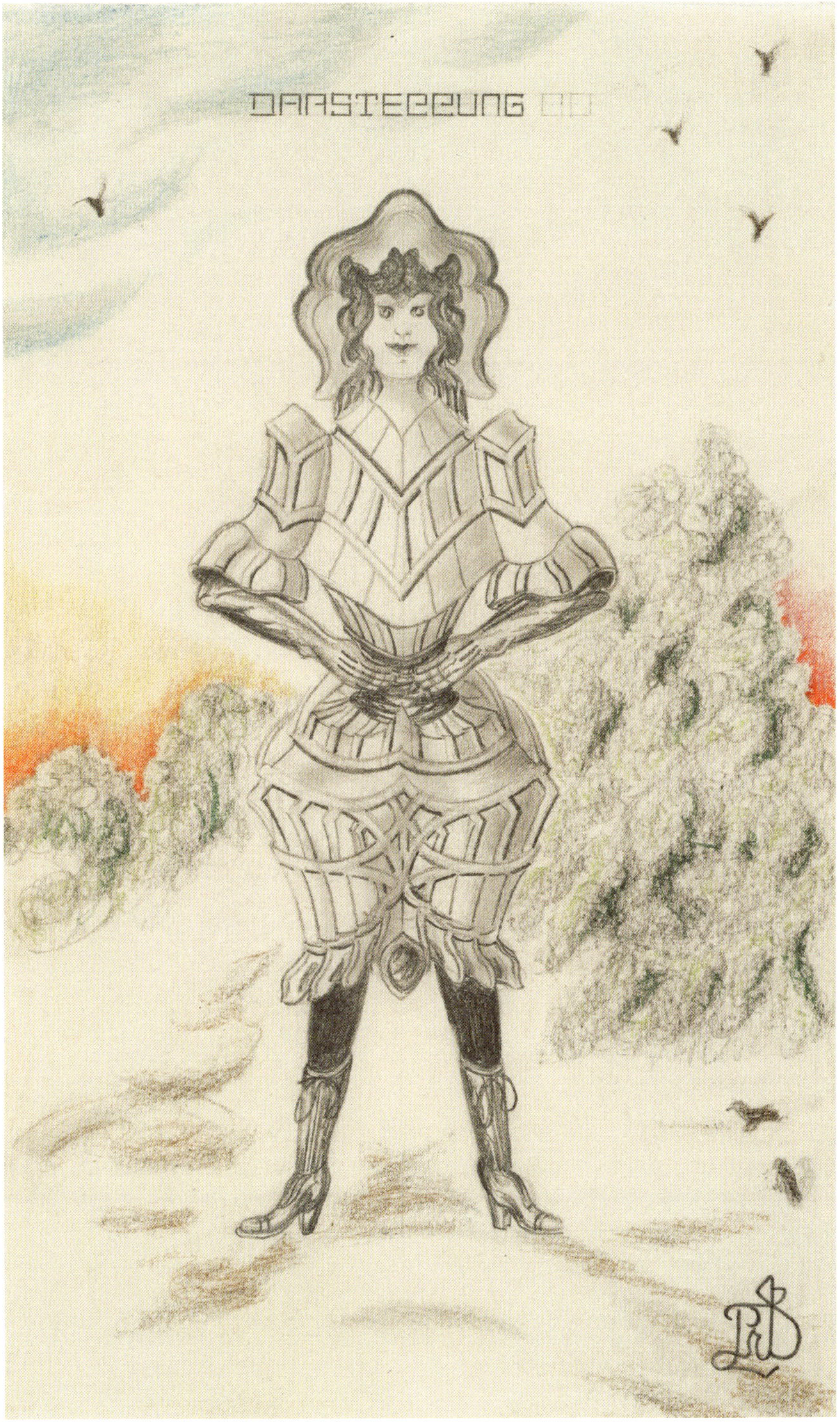

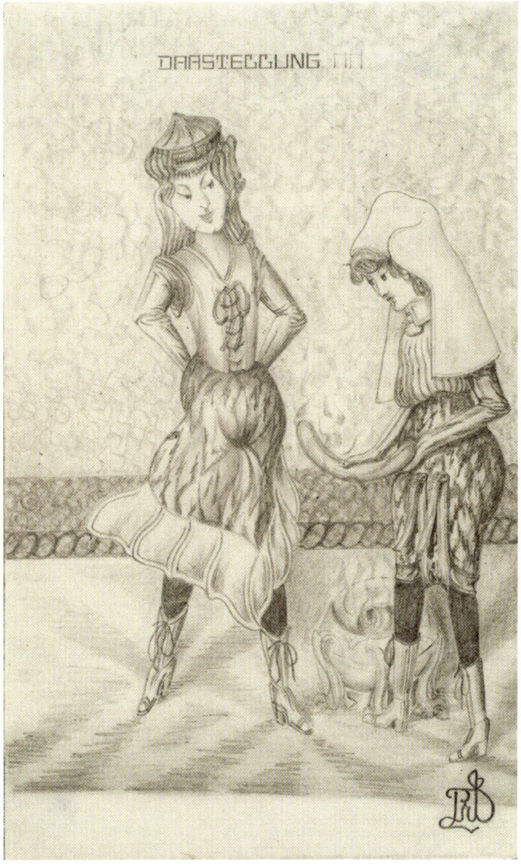

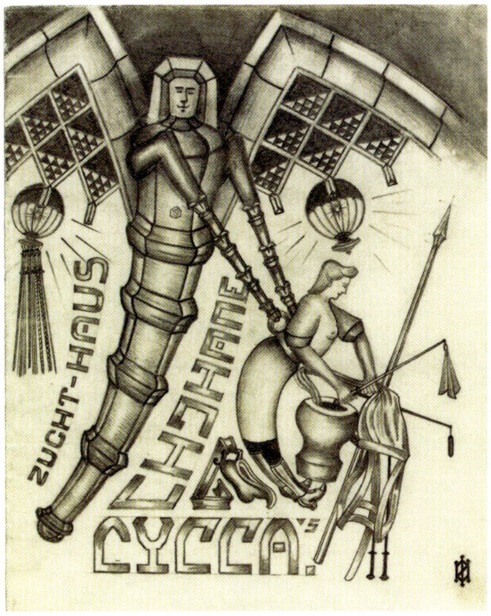

As a young child, Joseph Schneller (1878–1943) was already branded as a weak mummy's boy. He briefly worked as an architectural draughtsman, but had himself voluntarily committed to an institution. Schneller was diagnosed with catatonia. However, he suffered from delusions, heard voices and was convinced that conspiracies were plotting to kill him. In the psychiatric institution, Schneller was convinced that they tortured him in numerous ways: by putting urine in his coffee, serving him dog food, etc. His strongest conviction was that the physicians projected the suffering of others on to him and that he thus endured their suffering. Apart from architectural drawings, some sexually oriented drawings that he made have been preserved. His physicians also called him obscene. They believed his work indicated perverse sexual and sadistic ideas. Schneller died of TB in 1943.

Joseph Schneller, **Darstellung**, s.d., pencil, pastel crayon on paper. Sammlung Prinzhorn, Heidelberg
Joseph Schneller, **Darstellung**, s.d., pencil on paper. Sammlung Prinzhorn, Heidelberg
Joseph Schneller, **Zucht-Haus Chicane**, s.d., pencil on paper. Sammlung Prinzhorn, Heidelberg

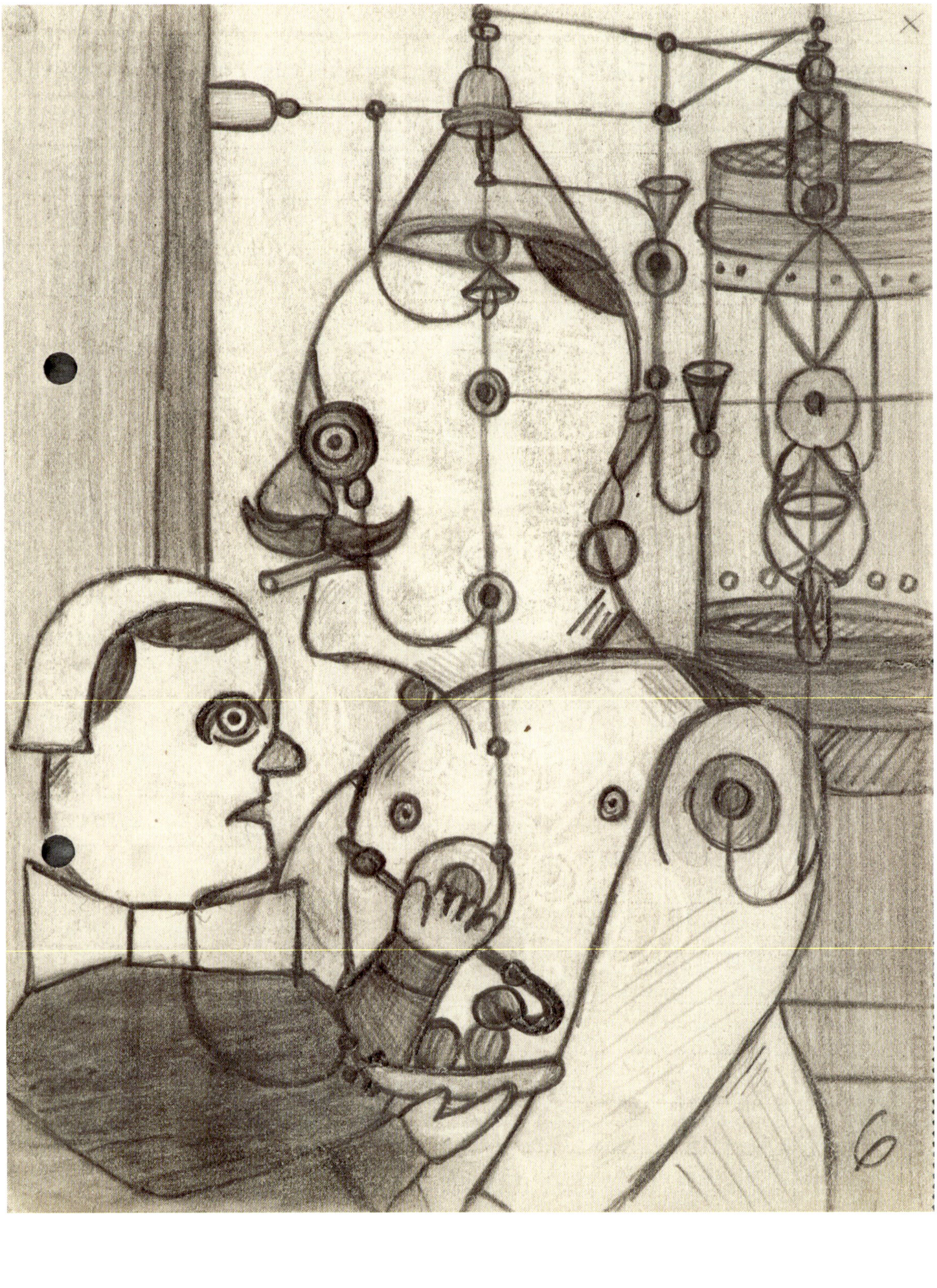

Wilhelm Werner, **Untitled**, ca. 1934–1938, pencil on paper. Sammlung Prinzhorn, Heidelberg

THOMAS RÖSKE & MAIKE ROTZOLL

Wilhelm Werner

'Siegeszug der Sterelation'

On 6 October 1940, Wilhelm Werner (1898–1940), who had been in a psychiatric clinic in Werneck (Unterfranken, Bavaria) since 1919 with the diagnosis of 'idiocy', was transferred to an 'unknown institution'. We now know that the latter was the T4 'euthanasia institute', Pirna/Sonnenstein. As most 'transferees' were already gassed on the day of their arrival, we know the probable date of his death. No data was preserved on the course of his psychiatric disorder. The notes in the institution's register in Werneck only teach us that he was Catholic, unmarried and unemployed[1].

Yet a number of unique testimonies of Wilhelm Werner himself were kept: an exercise book with *'44 Sterelationszeichnungen'* ('sterilation drawings', sic), which became part of the Prinzhorn collection in two phases, in 2008 and 2010. All drawings are probably from the period before 1938. A member of staff at the institution kept the exercise book and showed it to many friends and acquaintances, so the pages suffered heavily and even fell out. It was eventually perforated and rebound.

The pencil drawings are unique. They are the only preserved works of art on sterilisation of patients during the time of National-Socialism. We do know a number of poems in which the writers tried to deal with their experiences of germline surgery in the core of their personality, but there is almost no visual work. The drawings also indicate major complexity in how the experiences were dealt with, with the help of original models for people and things that are partly reminiscent of Bauhaus artist Oskar Schlemmer, which is only one of the reasons why the diagnosis 'idiocy' raises questions.

On the inside of the exercise book cover, Werner refers to himself. He calls himself 'orator of the people and theatre director'. His drawings indeed seem like puppet theatre scenes. The action takes place in a flat space and the figures generally act parallel to the frame. Their heads are usually depicted in profile, their arms and legs are only connected to the always voluminous bodies at one point, and the hands often have the shape of mittens. In nude figures, even the turning point at the shoulders can be seen, like the split pin of a jumping jack. Werner's drawings are populated by Catholic nuns in habits, men in suits, nude men, clowns with bulbous bodies, partly dressed, partly nude and nude boys.

Werner 'stages' meetings of doctors and nurses with the victims of surgery. The doctors here mainly play the part of observers and controllers, while the nurses manipulate the genitals of the men and boys in question. The drawer's sympathy is clearly with the helpless victims. The round clowns are striking. They are dressed 'cheerfully', but undergo surgery with a serious

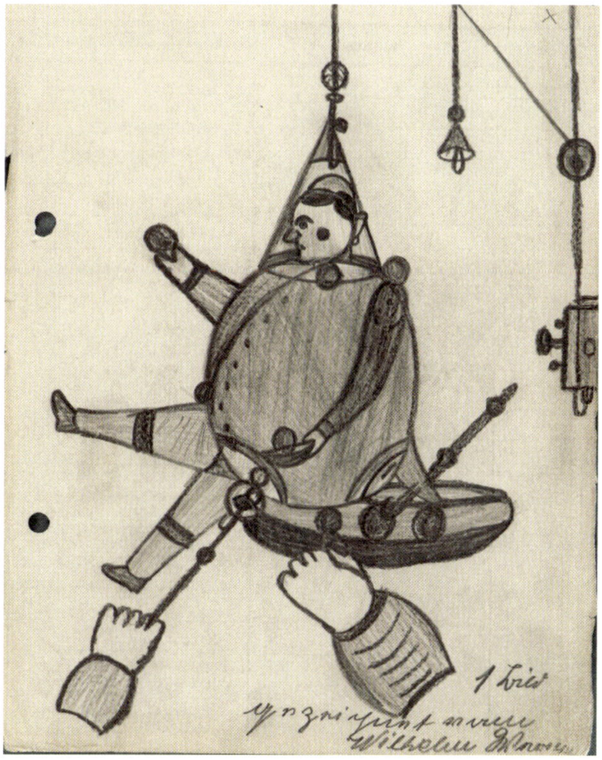

Wilhelm Werner, Untitled,
ca. 1934–1938, pencil on paper. Sammlung Prinzhorn, Heidelberg

face or juggle with testicles – 'balls'. Simultaneously, the 'perpetrators' are not simply presented as unambiguously evil. 'Portraits' – individual men and a nurse whom Werner shows from the knees up – exude a quiet authority. The only person whose name is mentioned in pencil, Dr Hans Weinzierl, was head physician of the surgical department in Schweinfurt[2] from 1920 to 1945. The fact that he cooperated on the forced sterilisation of patients in the institution cannot be proved. The page on *Der Siegeszug der Sterelation* ('The triumph of sterilation' - Werner always wrote the German word for sterilisation incorrectly) is rather ambiguous. Was it meant sarcastically or did Werner want to develop a humoristic fantasy about suffering for a 'good cause' and did he therefore refer to the propaganda vehicles that could often be seen in national-socialist Germany at the time?

Time and time again, Werner shows bulbous testicles being removed. This thus concerns castration, which was not common practice at the time. The *Gesetz zur Verhütung erbkranken Nachwuchses* ('Law for the Prevention of Genetically Diseased Offspring') in principle could only make the person in question infertile. Castration was prohibited, unless there were medical reasons or if the castration was justified by a sexual criminal act. Werner was probably not castrated in the medical sense of the word yet he apparently regarded the surgery as 'emasculation' which is why he chose the image of the removal of testicles to express his internal perception. It is a symbolic representation that may have been inspired by the Catholic tradition of symbols. The testicles, each time depicted on a plate or dish, are reminiscent of, for instance, Saints Agatha or Lucia who – to indicate their martyrdom – respectively carry their breasts or eyes on a tray.

In nine of his drawings Werner shows surgical instruments. Just like 'classic' images in surgical textbooks, they show surgical equipment Werner could have seen just before and during his operation. Two other pages show the various stages of how these instruments are used during testicular surgery. The people presented have been reduced to hands and the beginnings of arms. Did Werner see these images himself, e.g. in the operating room or in books? In any case, the serial representation of the surgical equipment could also be inspired by the Catholic tradition of symbols: in the Middle Ages, Christ's instruments of torture were also displayed in a similar way. Their use is also sometimes demonstrated through unattached hands, i.e. without a body, just showing the forearms.

The depiction of technical equipment in Werner's drawings is somewhat ambivalent. Twice, the space

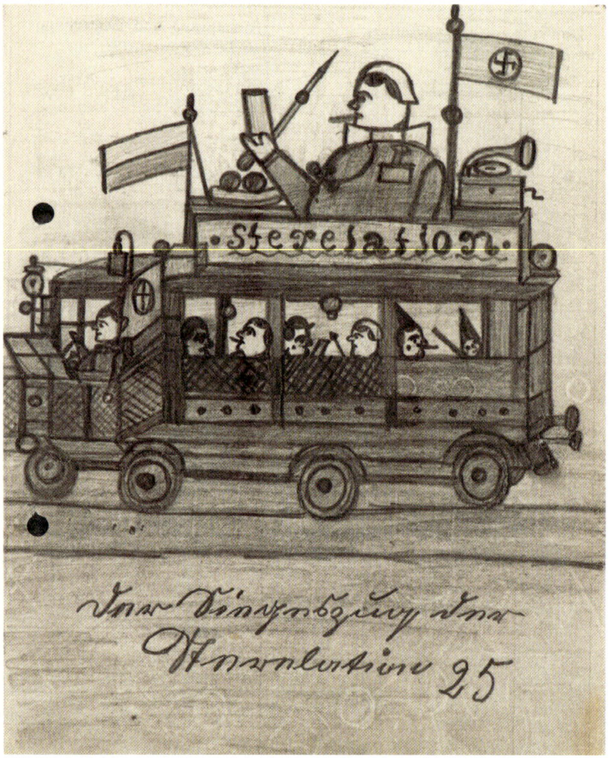

Wilhelm Werner, **Der Siegeszug der Sterelation**, ca. 1934–1938, pencil on paper. Sammlung Prinzhorn, Heidelberg

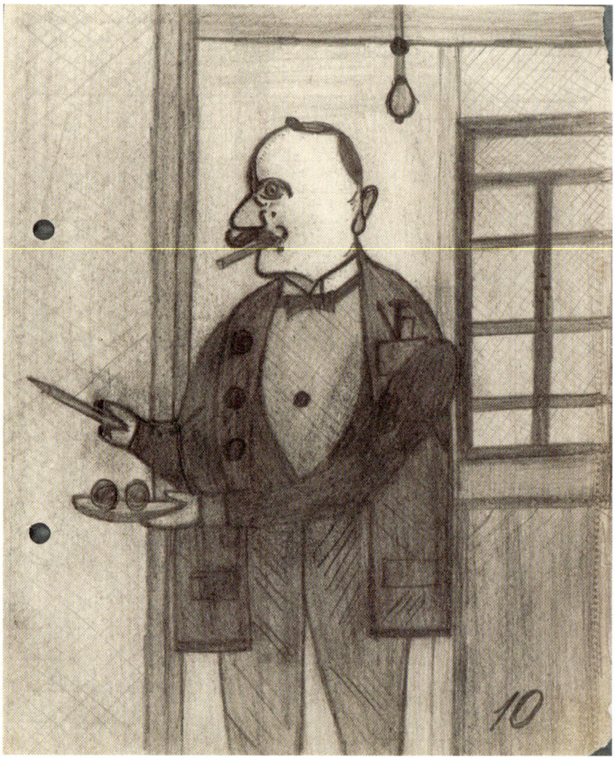

Wilhelm Werner, **Direktor Weinzier**, ca. 1934–1938, pencil on paper. Sammlung Prinzhorn, Heidelberg

around the figures is dominated by complex machinery with wires taking up almost the entire frame. The people in this drawing are powerless against technology, yet Werner does not demonise the machinery. On the contrary, he seems to have lovingly depicted the details of this equipment. This is also indicated in his fascinated view of a cabled roof construction.

Wilhelm Werner was a 'double victim': he was first forced into sterilisation and was then murdered. Is the killing of sick people a continuation of the negative eugenetics 'with other means'? In any case, there seemed to have been radicalisation: the apparently legal and often enforced intervention in the physicality of the people affected 'lowered the threshold for intervening in life itself'[3]. It was thought that the pursued economic benefit of the sterilisation policy lay in the future. The murder of sick people did, however, have immediate consequences on the division of resources. This concerned room in the institution, like in Werneck, staff and food. The war made the 'distribution battle' even harder.

Wilhelm Werner captured the dominance of the perpetrators and his own sense of powerlessness in *'Sterelation'* in images. In the same way, he was at the mercy of the killing of sick people, but there are no drawings of that.

NOTES

1 Compare: Röske T., Rotzoll M., 'Doppeltes Opfer. Wilhelm Werner, der „Siegeszug der Sterelation" und der Krankenmord im Nationalsozialismus', in: Westermann S., Kühl R., Ohnhäuser T. (eds.), *NS-'Euthanasie' und Erinnerung. Vergangenheitsaufarbeitung – Gedenkformen – Betroffenenperspektiven (Medizin und Nationalsozialismus 3)*, Berlin, 2011, pp. 169-194.

2 Town archive Schweinfurt, staff file Hans Weinzierl, PA 13406. We thank Dr Uwe Müller for his help in our archival research.

3 Bock, G., 'Nationalsozialistische Sterelisationspolitik', in: Henke K.-D. (ed.), *Tödliche Medizin im Nationalsozialismus. Von der Rassenhygiene zum Massenmord*, Cologne a.o. 2008, pp. 85-99, here p. 98.

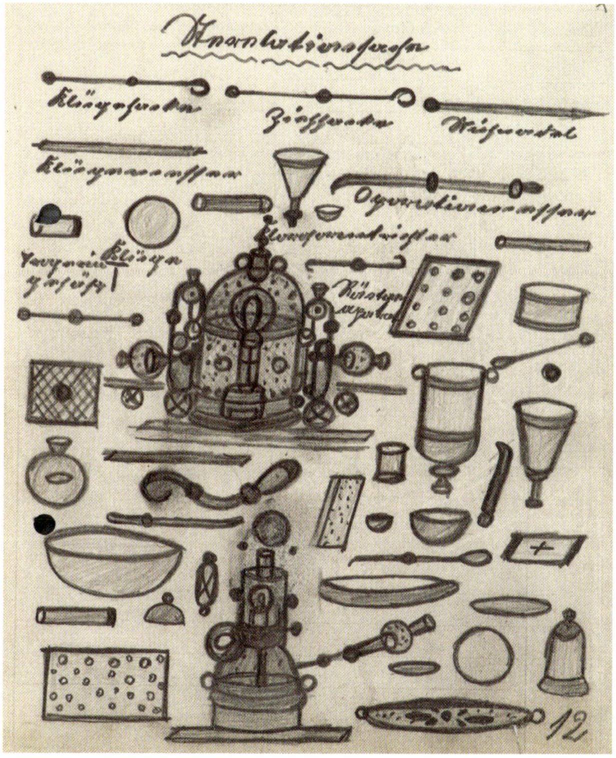

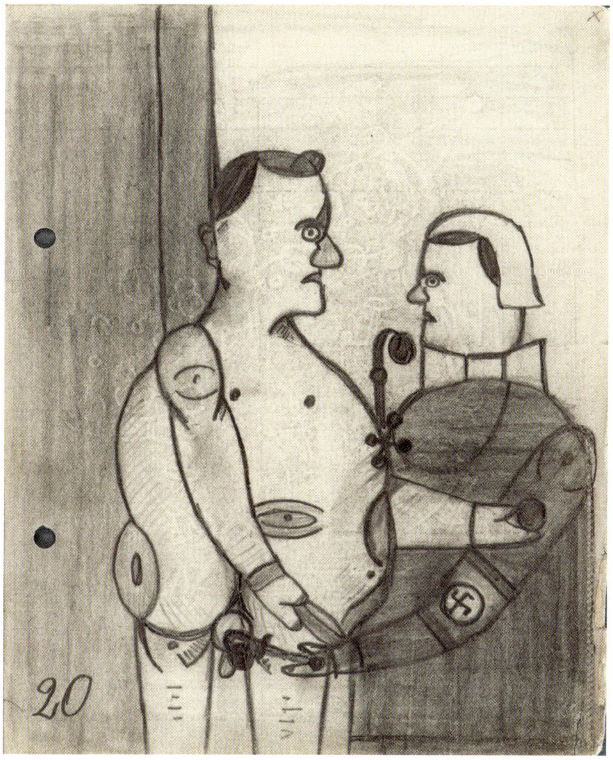

Wilhelm Werner, **Sterelationssache,** ca. 1934–1938, pencil on paper. Sammlung Prinzhorn, Heidelberg

Wilhelm Werner, **Untitled,** ca. 1934–1938, pencil on paper. Sammlung Prinzhorn, Heidelberg

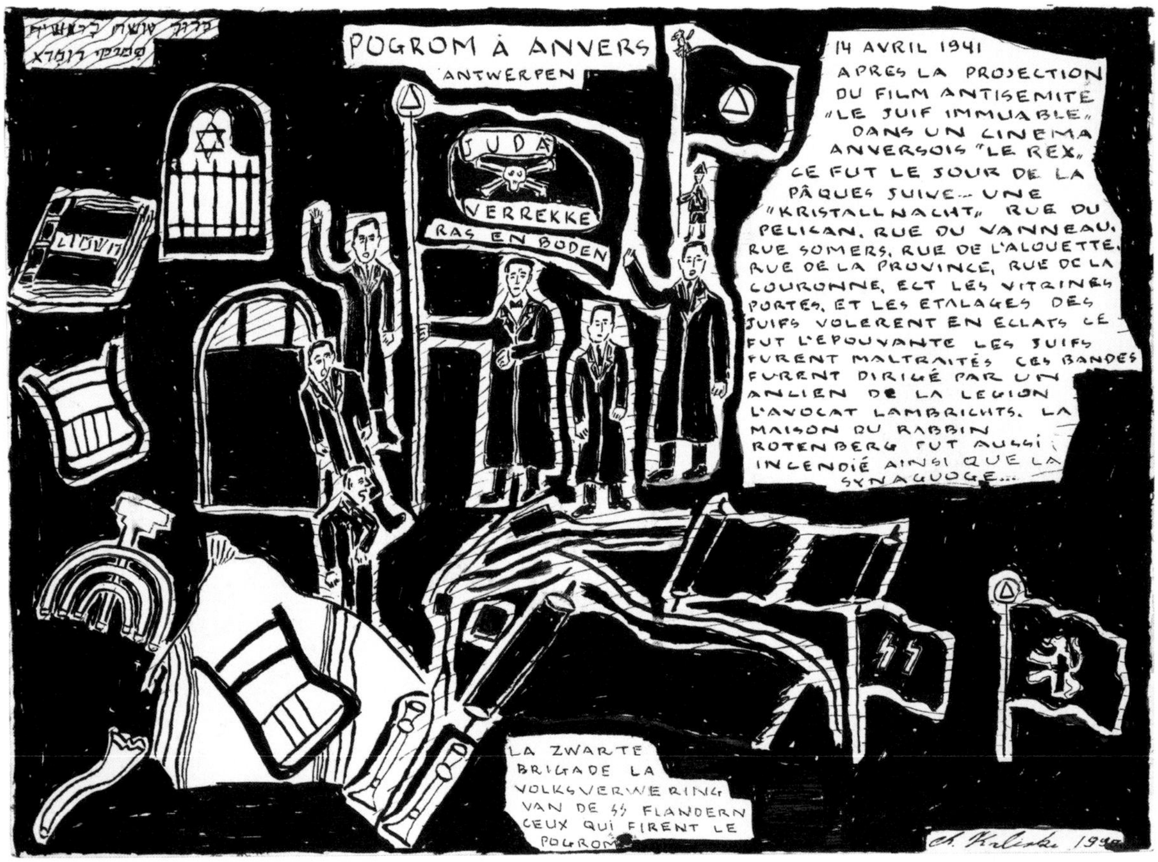

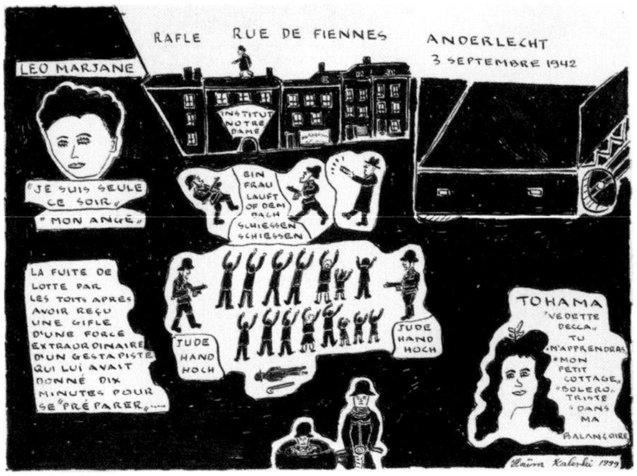

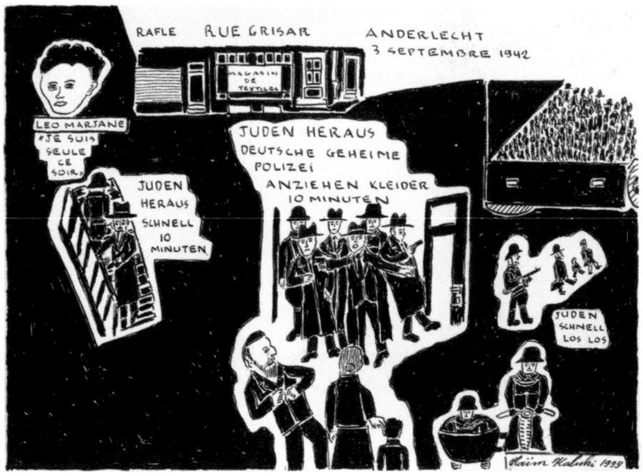

With his drawings about the Holocaust, Jim Kaliski submerges us into the lives of Brussels Jews, before, during and just after World War II. Kaliski was born in Brussels in 1929. Due to anti-Jewish laws, he was unable to finish his primary school education. He became the victim of bullying and discrimination. The family fled to Etterbeek. In 1944, his father was deported, a trauma from which he would never recover. Kaliski was 15 at the time. In 1989, at the age of 60, he began to make hundreds of drawings in Indian ink, without any artistic education and in a style that is similar to illustrations in children's books and comics. Kaliski does not draw his intimate history linearly. His fragmented memories follow the line of memories of the war and prosecution.

Jim Kaliski, **Progrom à Anvers**, 1999, felt-tip pen on paper. Jewish Museum of Belgium, Brussels
Jim Kaliski, **Rafle rue de Fiennes Anderlecht 3 septembre 1942**, 1999, felt-tip pen on paper. Jewish Museum of Belgium, Brussels
Jim Kaliski, **Rafle rue Grisar Anderlecht 3 septembre 1942**, 1999, felt-tip pen op paper. Jewish Museum of Belgium, Brussels

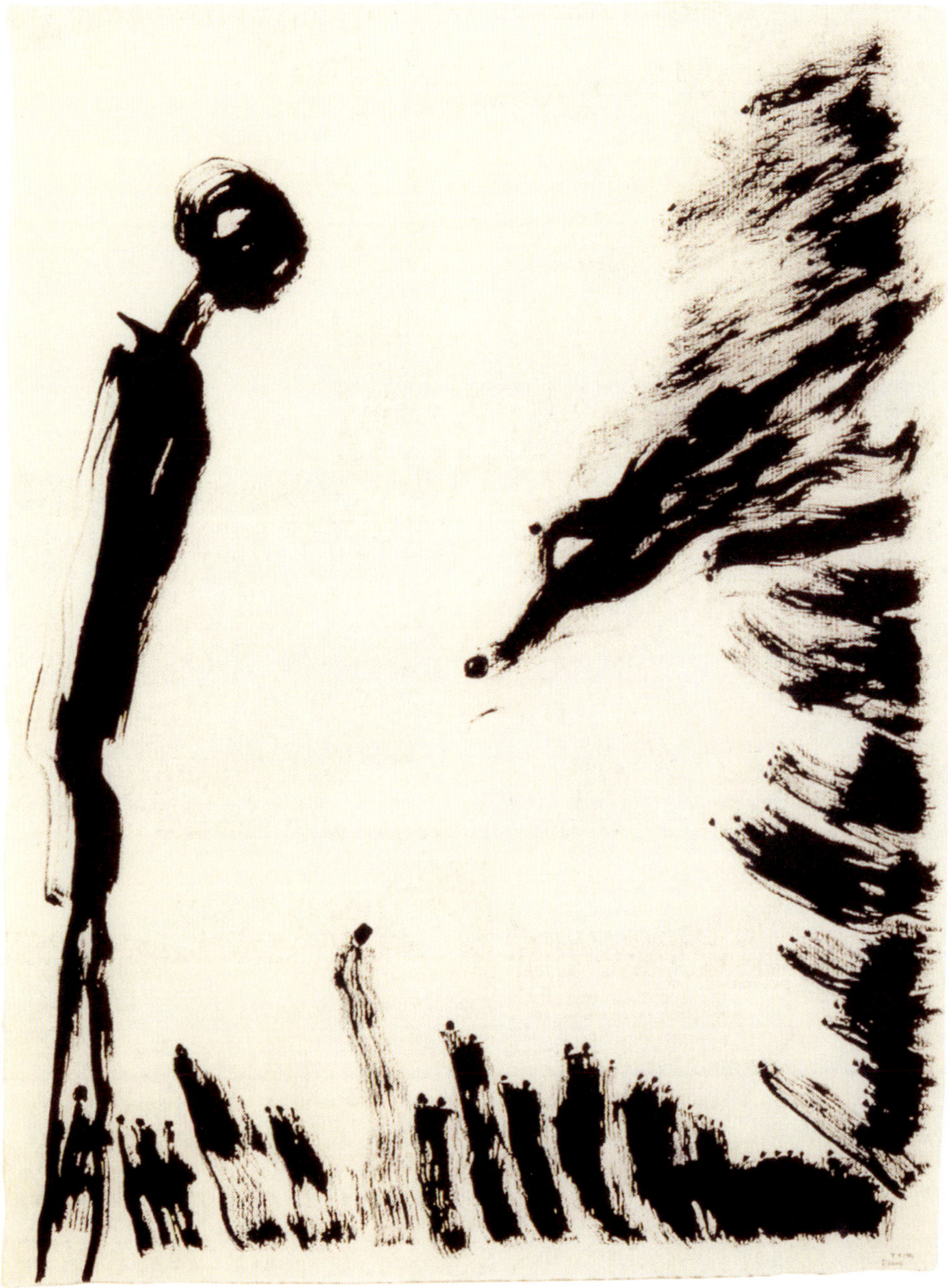

German Rosemarie Koczÿ (1939–2007) was three when when she was deported to the concentration camp in Traunstein, near Dachau. She survived two camps after which she was raised by her grandparents. After her grandmother's death, she ended up in an orphanage, where she had to work 15 hours a day. In 1959, she moved to Switzerland and studied at the école des Arts Décoratifs. Koczÿ became famous for her carpets, but from the 1970s she solely concentrated on the Holocaust. Her pen and ink drawings symbolise the victims, but her paintings and wood sculptures pay homage to "those I saw dying in the camps". Koczÿ did not consider herself an artist, but "as a labourer" working on the collective memory".
Rosemary Koczÿ, **Untitled**, 1986, ink on paper. De Stadshof Collection, Dr Guislain Museum, Ghent

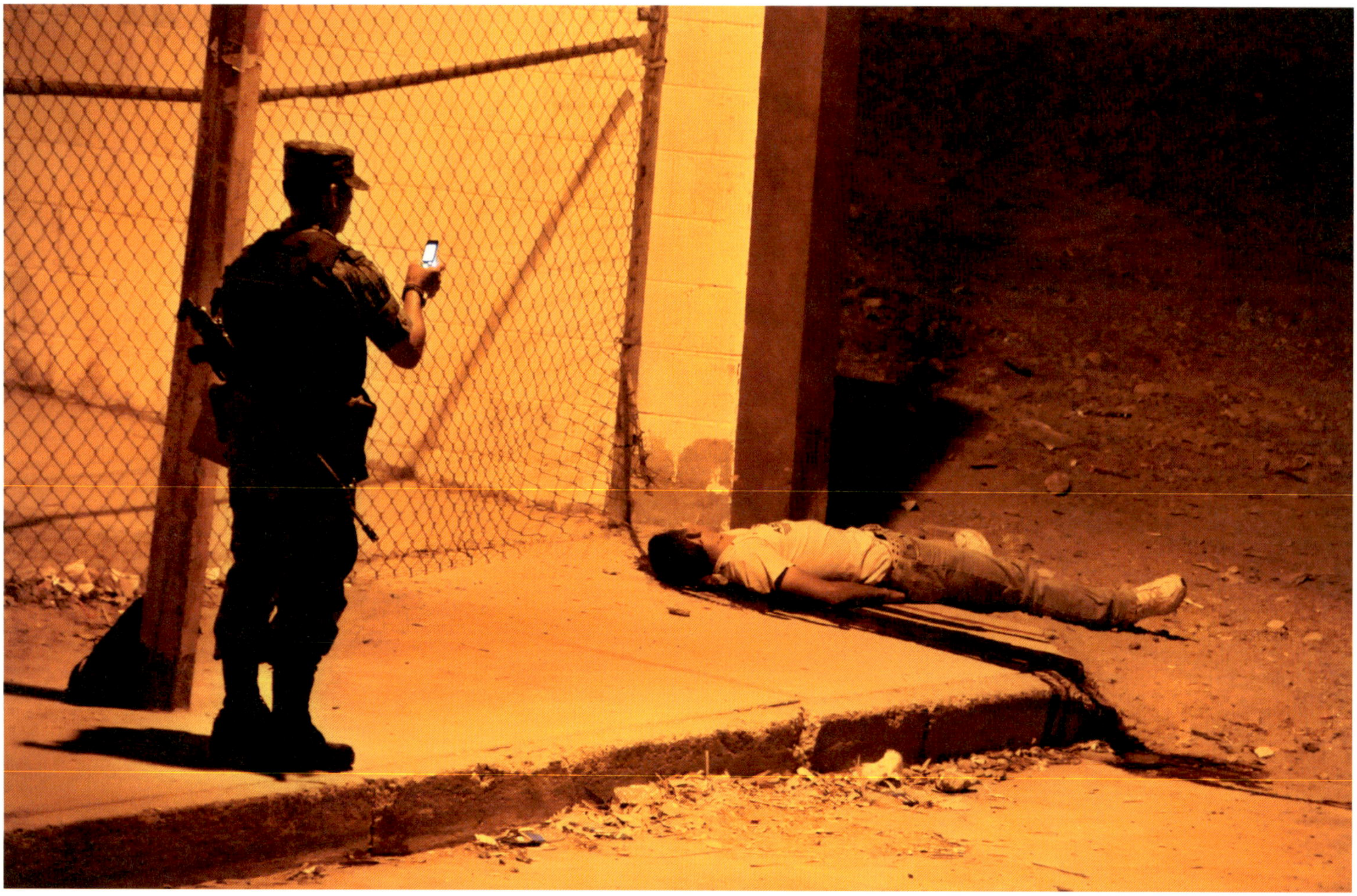

PATRICK ALLEGAERT & YOON HEE LAMOT

Between Macho and Mission

Teun Voeten, War Photographer

Dutch war photographer Teun Voeten is still tired from his journey back from Congo when we meet up in Brussels. Voeten has been covering conflicts in Bosnia, Rwanda, Colombia, Afghanistan, Iraq, Libya and other countries for over 20 years for media such as Vanity Fair, National Geographic, Newsweek and organisations such as the UNHCR (United Nations High Commission for Refugees) and the ICRC (International Committee of the Red Cross). He has also written books about, among others, the underground homeless in New York, the war in Sierra Leone and, recently, the Mexican drug war.

Teun Voeten is currently working on a doctorate on the 'new wars', a rather recent concept. For many centuries, war had the same pattern: several states declared war on each other with a clear purpose. The battle was fought by armies, each with their own uniform, and the outcome of the war was determined by the outcome on the battlefields. There was usually one winner and one loser, a truce and a peace treaty. "In the 1980s-1990s, we see the rise of new wars, with irregular armies without uniforms, without any clear purpose, without any clear declaration of war and without any clear ideology. These are wars to enrich a few war lords, where the war is no longer a means to an end but the actual objective", says Voeten. Today, war is waged on several levels and with varying intensities. The photographer believes this is without doubt a more dangerous form of war, where the civilian population is a target and where there is no more respect for neutral parties such as relief workers or journalists. Teun Voeten: "In the past, each camp benefited from showing journalists its side of the story, but if you rob diamonds from a country as a war lord you don't want journalists to take a look. Journalists are now considered as priers, as spies. This makes the profession of war photographer much more dangerous these days."

In 1998, Teun Voeten went to Sierra Leone to make a report about child soldiers. What was to be a simple assignment ended in disaster. He was robbed and threatened by several rebels of the Revolutionary United Front. While these frenetic teenagers held him at gunpoint, he felt his life hanging by a thread. He managed to escape, but had to hide for a fortnight to keep safe from his attackers. Voeten realises he had a narrow escape. He wrote down his experiences in *How de Body? Hoop en Horror in Sierra Leone*. "This book definitely helped me to process my experiences, but those terrible moments still surface sometimes", says Voeten. His disappearance was a major story at the time, but the photographer estimates that ten to twenty journalists have currently disappeared without a trace in Syria. "And this only concerns western journalists, because many more local reporters also vanish." Teun Voeten believes it all began with the execution of Daniel Pearl. The Wall Street Journal journalist was beheaded in Pakistan in 2002. The execution was filmed and released on the Internet. These days, films documenting the violence and cruelty of war constantly appear on YouTube, made by perpetrators as well as victims.

Why would anyone decide to become a war photographer? "As a child I dreamed of becoming a nature filmmaker, I didn't dream of war photography at the time. But I became interested in international politics, wanted to witness it, be in the field. Combine this idealism of wanting to reveal degrading situations with an adventurous nature and you get a war reporter." Teun Voeten does not deny that these experiences sometimes linger and are often never forgotten. Each war journalist develops his own processing mechanism. He

Teun Voeten, **Mexico**, 2009, photo. © Teun Voeten

finds it important to lead a normal life alongside his war work. His research on the 'new wars' gave him time to catch his breath. "Some colleagues do not give themselves a break, they run from one conflict to another. You then run the risk of losing the plot after about five years. They cannot put things into perspective in their lives, think they have a holy mission. Of course war photographers have a mission, but part of this mission should always be wanting to remain healthy." Sometimes he has had enough of photography and wants to write, sometimes he gets tired of always sitting at his desk and looks for action. This balance is essential to him. He finds it strange that some academics write about war without ever having been there. He believes that the academic world needs a constant interaction between theory and practice.

Contact with colleagues is equally indispensable in the processing act. Teun Voeten: "For a long time, war journalists were machos. Talking was regarded as a sign of weakness, but in the past decade so many horrible things have happened that it is now normal to speak openly about it. For instance, discussion groups are organised and many soldiers also dare to speak about their posttraumatic stress disorder."

Teun Voeten prefers to travel alone and rarely goes out and about with other journalists. This makes his undertaking all the more precarious. "You must dare to trust people. This can be very difficult, but otherwise you cannot come close enough to the conflict zone and you don't meet the people you want to meet." Voeten has, for instance, never been to Somalia because one has to hire bodyguards with Kalashnikovs – children of 16 years old you have to pay 600 to 700 dollars a day for protection and a car. "You can pay up to 3,000 dollars for five days of transport and a fixer, someone who arranges contacts for you, while you risk being kidnapped by the accomplices of that same fixer at the end of the day." A good portion of intuition is therefore indispensable, but your intuition can also be deceptive. "It is a profession without a hundred per cent safety guarantee. If you can't live with this, you have to choose a different career."

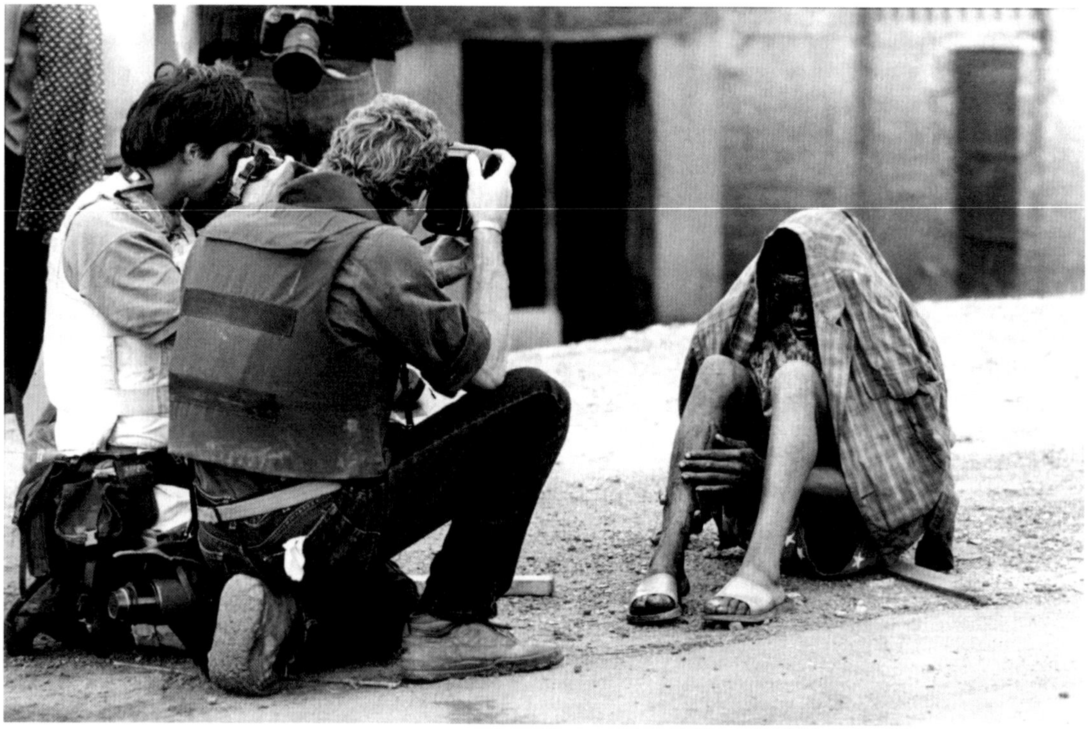

Teun Voeten, **Rwanda**, 1994, photo. © Teun Voeten

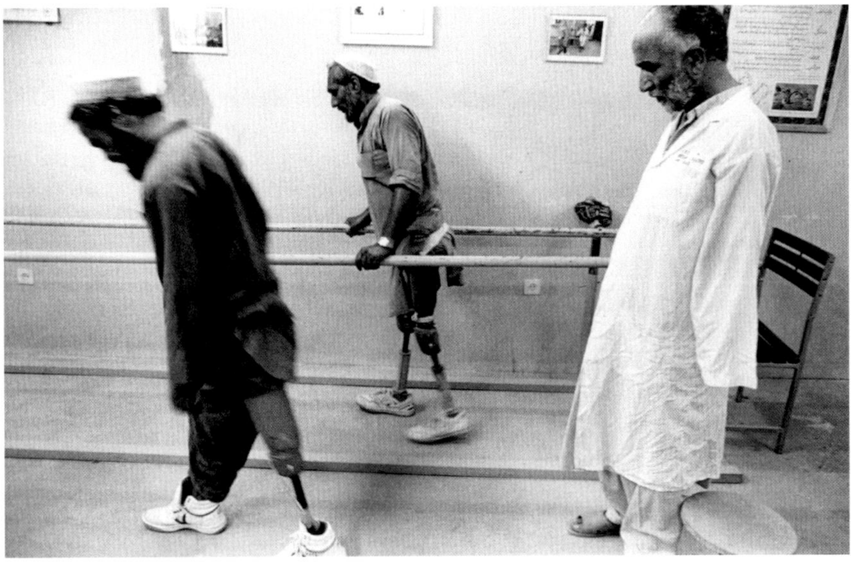

Teun Voeten,
Afghanistan,
August-November 1996,
photo. © Teun Voeten

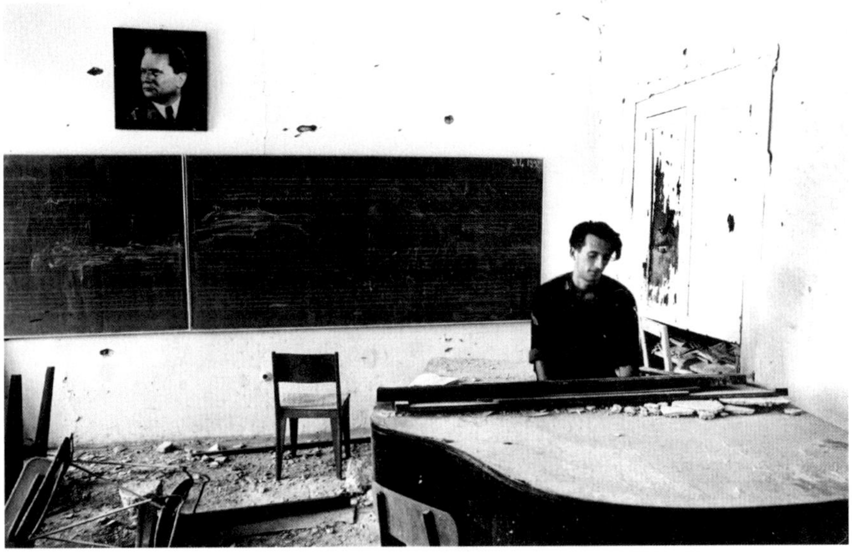

Teun Voeten,
Bosnia, 1992,
photo. © Teun Voeten

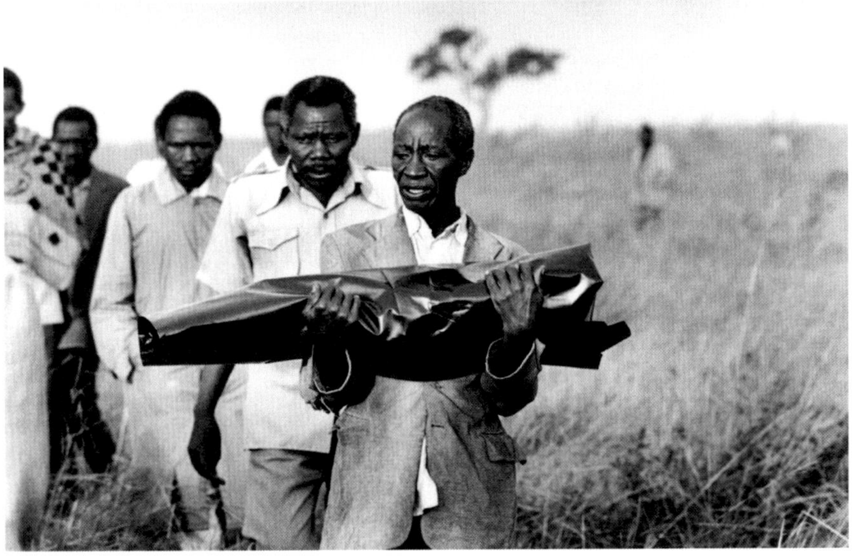

Teun Voeten,
Rwanda, 1994,
photo. © Teun Voeten

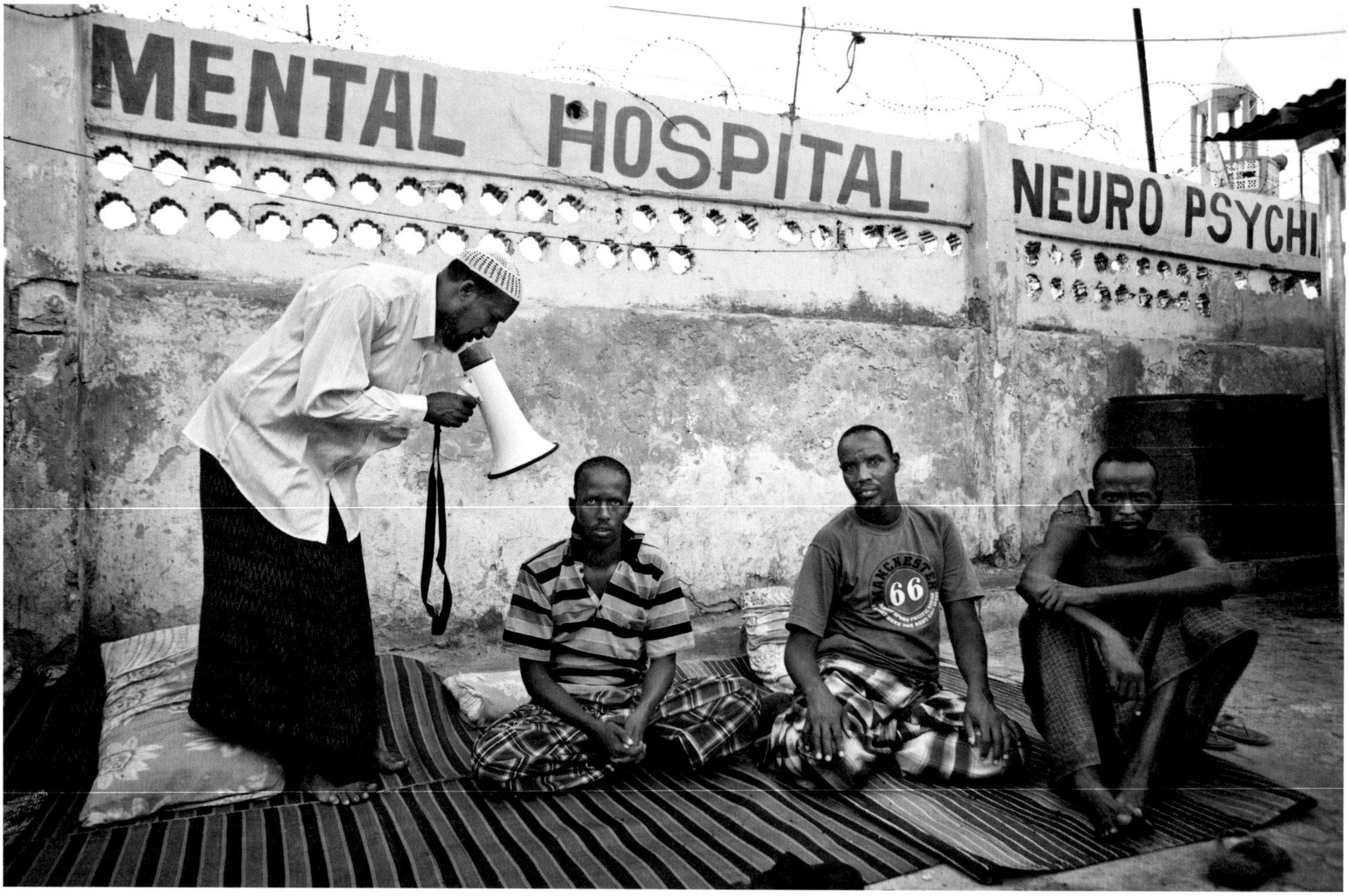

Not only do natural disasters, war and famine kill people, they also leave behind many survivors. Although many survive a crisis without any physical injuries, mental scars are no exception. During the past fifty years, black Africa has gone through more crises than any other region in the world. The price they pay for this, is large-scale mental illness and a lack of means for tackling these disorders. For this self-financed project, Robin Hammond went to the Democratic Republic of Congo, Sudan, Kenya, Somalia and Uganda. He saw people who had been let down by the government, aid organisations and society as a whole: a voiceless minority relegated into a forgotten corner in churches, chained to rusty hospital beds, doomed to spend their lives behind bars in dirty prisons. Many Somalis take mentally-ill family members to traditional or Koran healers.
Mogadishu, Somalia, May 2011
Robin Hammond, **Condemned**, photo. © Robin Hammond/Panos Pictures

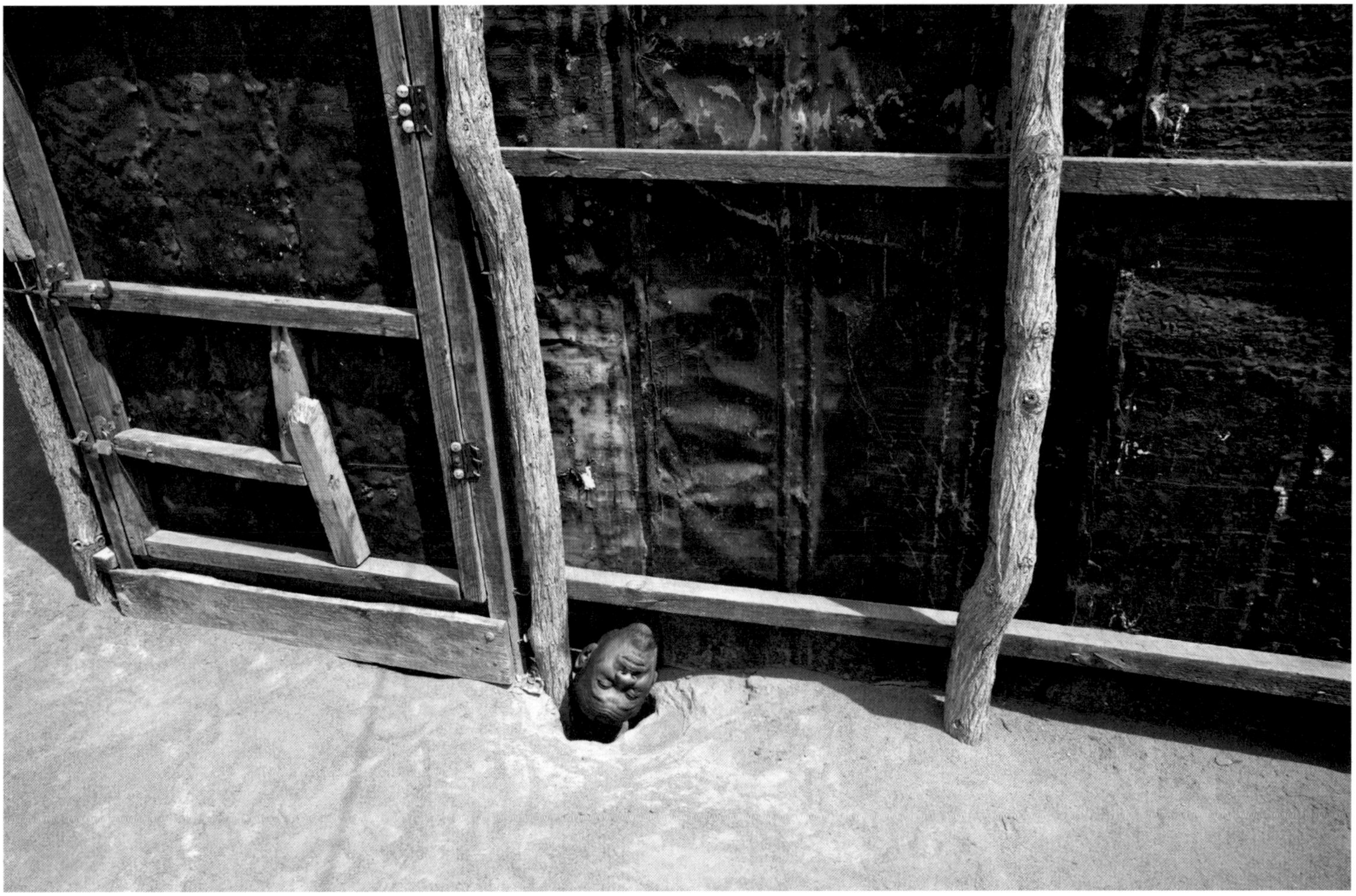

Abdi Rahman Shukri Ali (26) has been locked up in a corrugated iron hut for two years. He lives with his family in Dadaab, the world's largest refugee camp, where Somalis, uprooted by conflict and famine, seek protection.
Refugee camp in Dadaab, Kenya, June 2011
Robin Hammond, **Condemned**, photo. © Robin Hammond/Panos Pictures

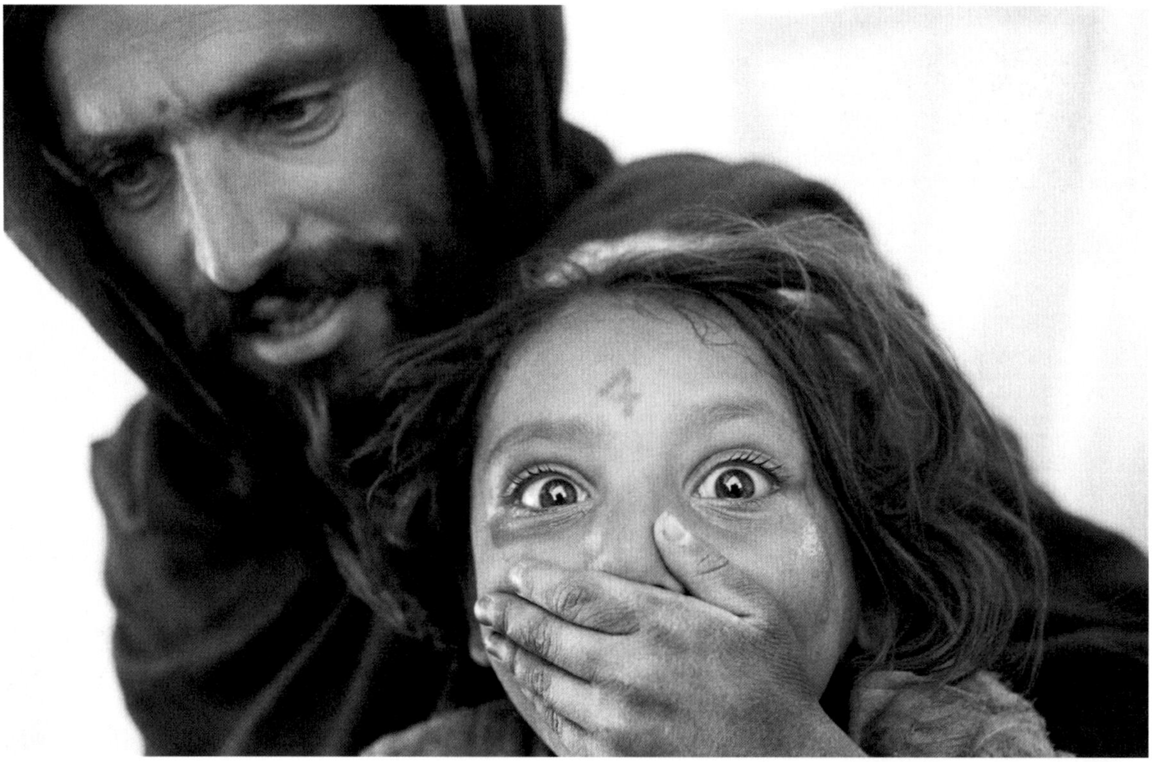

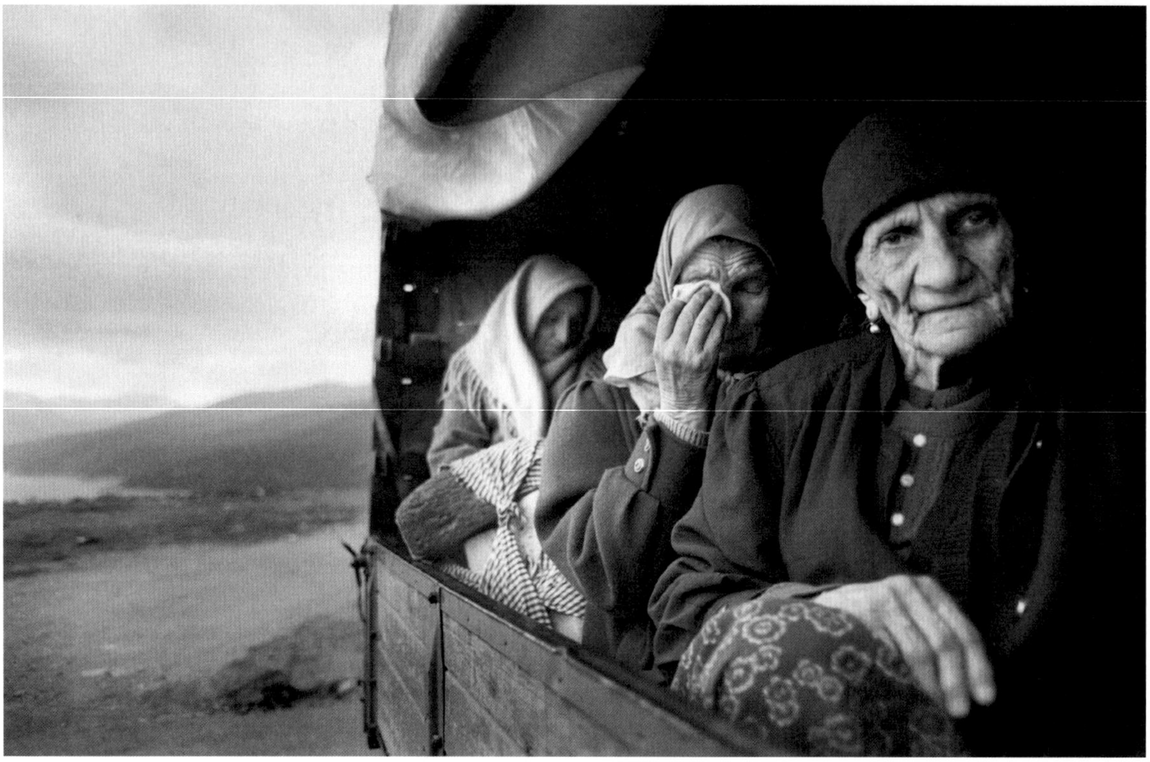

Apart from his intriguing and world famous portraits, the work of Belgian photographer Stephan Vanfleteren (1969) also consist of reports in conflict areas. His photos from, among other places, Afghanistan, Kosovo and Rwanda are characterised by his social involvement. People are always his subject of interest. Whether it concerns the war in Kosovo, the genocide in Rwanda or the Afghan battle, Vanfleteren always depicts refugees who survive in camps. Human suffering and the trauma of war are central here.

Above: Stephan Vanfleteren, **Afghanistan**, 2000, photo. © Stephan Vanfleteren / Below: Stephan Vanfleteren, **Kosovo**, 1999, photo. © Stephan Vanfleteren

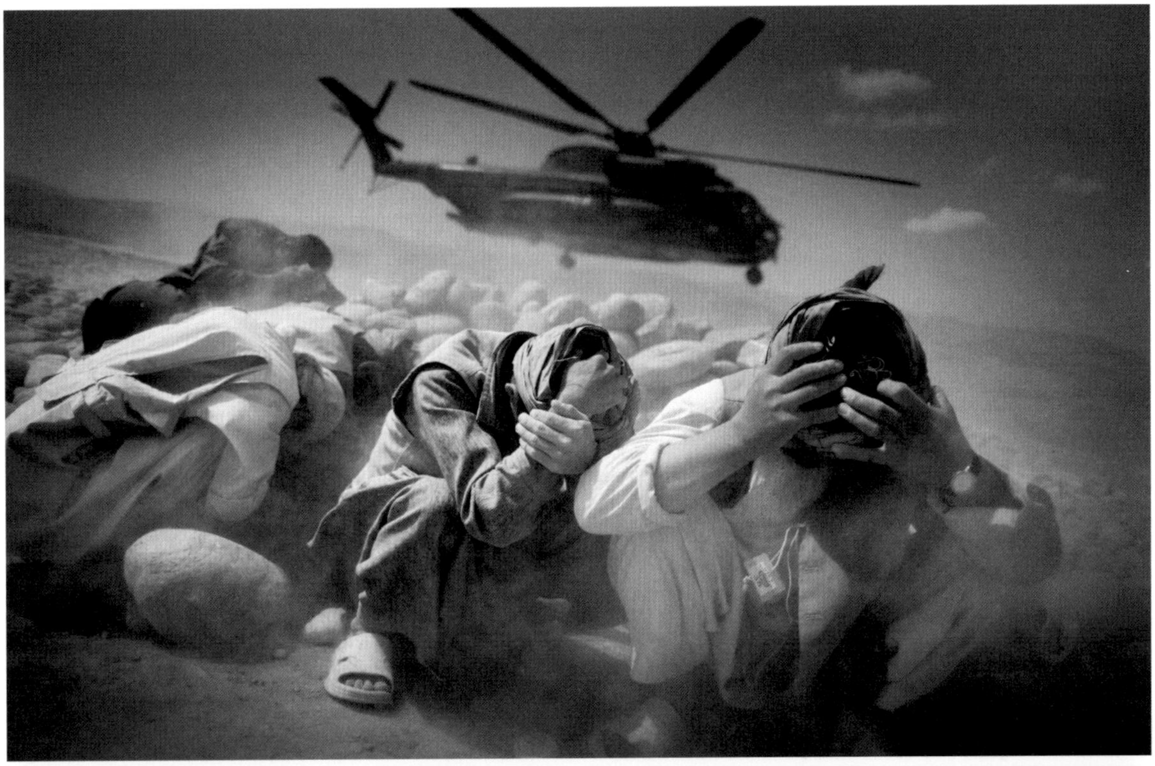

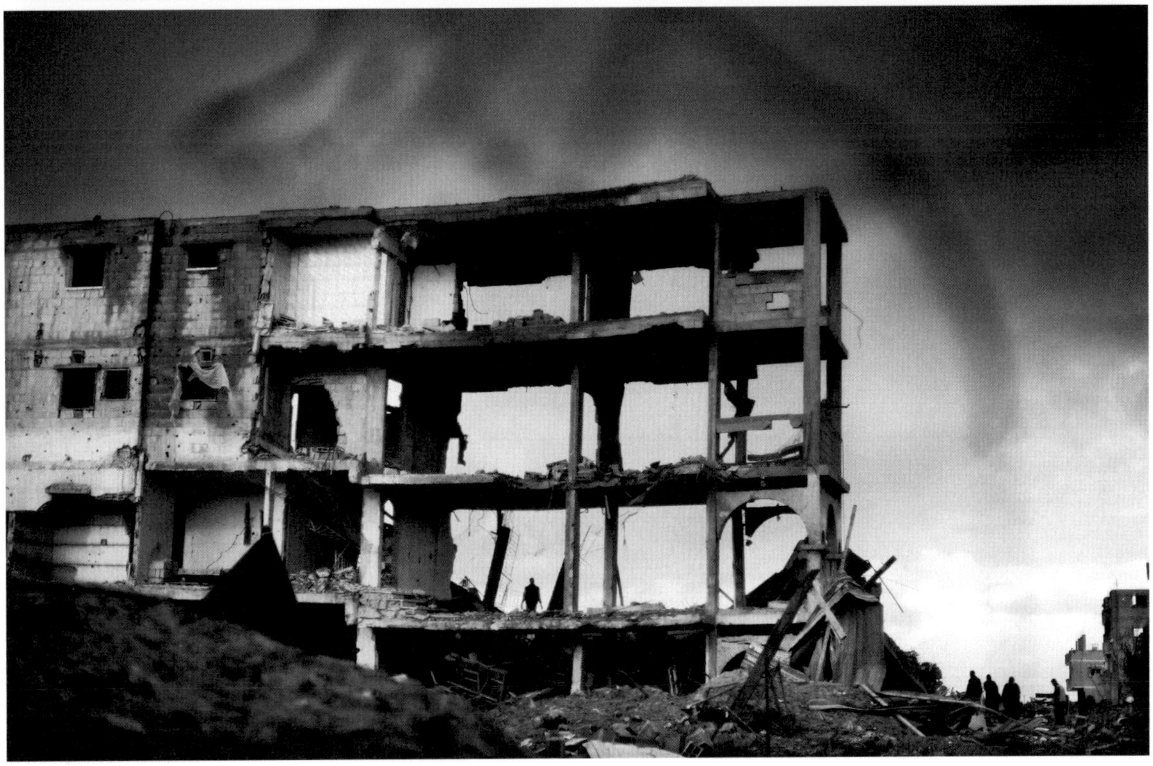

Danish photographer Jan Grarup (1968) has been documenting conflicts for over 20 years, including the Gulf War, the genocide in Rwanda, the conflict between Israel and Palestine, etc. He believes that a photo journalist has a major social role and is not merely someone who documents. He is a witness; he serves as a memory and is capable of making changes through his photos. He tells stories about those who are no longer able to tell their story themselves. Jan Grarup often depicted posttraumatic stress disorder, which he also fell victim to after many conflicts.
Above: Jan Grarup, **Afghanistan**, 2009, photo. © Jan Grarup / Below: Jan Grarup, **Gaza**, 2010, photo. © Jan Grarup

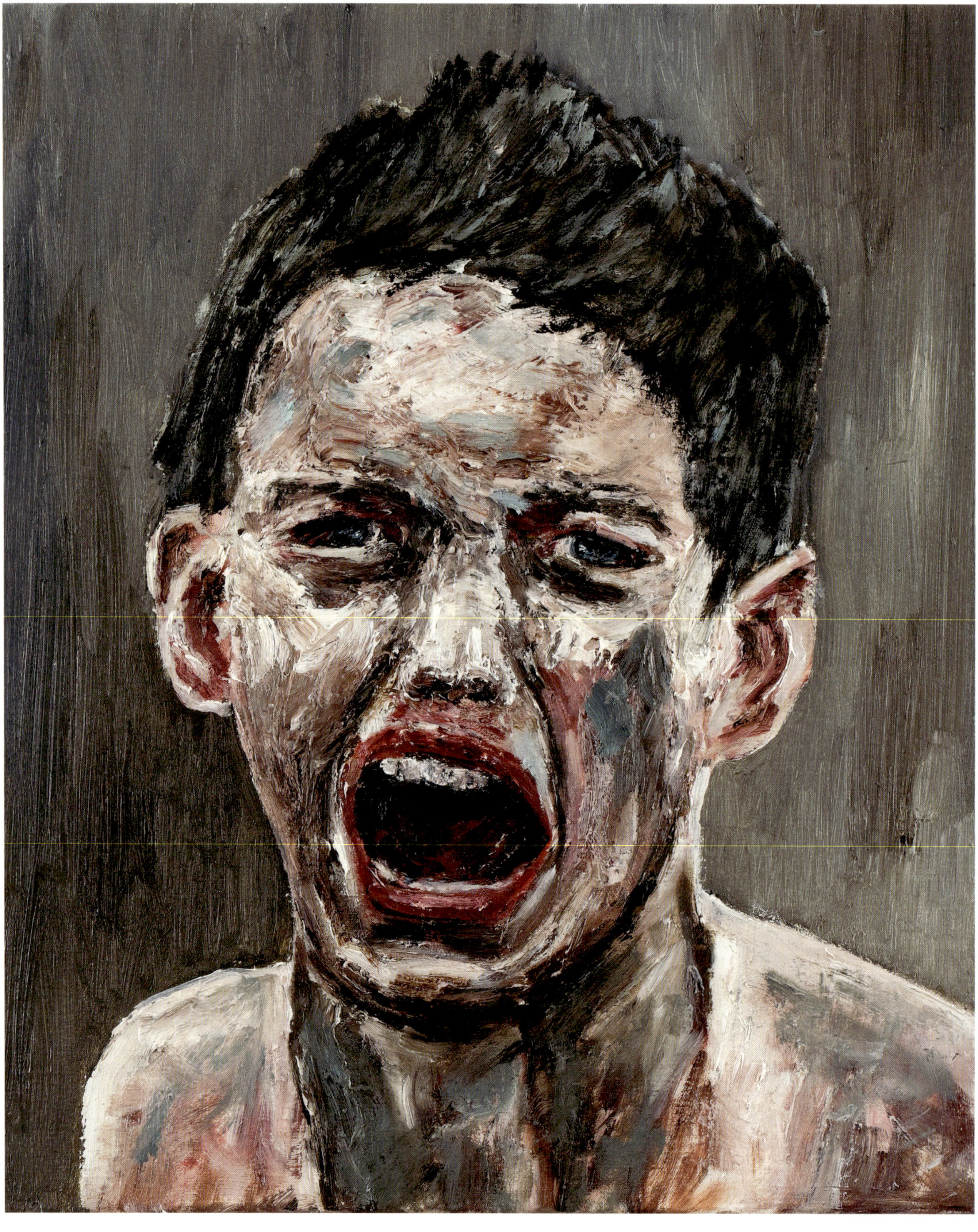

ERNST VAN ALPHEN

Acts of War in Paint

Ronald Ophuis mainly became famous for his paintings of acts of war. Even though he also depicted other forms of brute force, his paintings of Auschwitz and of wars in Srebrenica and Rwanda were those with which he made his mark. These paintings often gave rise to controversy. The scandal of the work of Ronald Ophuis, however, does not seem to come from the excessive violence it depicts, but from the refusal to convey an unambiguous message or judgement that makes the violence comprehensible and palatable. The reactions to Ophuis' work are symptomatic of what western spectators and readers expect from representations. A representation is much more than merely an image, a succession of events, a source of information. A representation is also expected to guide the spectator in how it must be understood, especially when it concerns a controversial issue such as violence.

In relation to the majority of the images of acts of war in the mass media, Ophuis' work is exceptional. Ophuis is not embodied in an artistic practice that has already been performed or is carried out much more adequately by 'new' photographic and cinematic media. Ophuis' 'realistic' representations of brutal scenes are equally shocking and controversial as the paintings of Manet and other realistic painters were to the critics of their time. The question thus remains how we can understand and legitimise this painterly project of depicting the brute force of war. In view of the omnipresence of mass media, what is the significance of the fact that Ophuis chose painting as a medium to depict this violence instead of, for instance, film, photography or opera? In other words, what does paint do in relation to the subject matter?

The emotional way of looking that is stimulated by Ophuis' paintings concerns more than the represented scene without a moral framework. If this would be the case, he could simply stage a *tableau vivant* and photograph it. Even though he uses actors for some of his paintings to perform the scene to then photograph them, he eventually transforms the photos into paintings. The material qualities of painting are very specific, in general of course, but especially in the case of Ophuis' work.

The medium of painting is typified as 'indirect', unlike the directness of photographic and filmic media. Painting is indirect because the representation in and with paint is explicitly mediated. The depiction is not transparent: we are fully aware of the paint of which the portrayal consists. Photographs, on the other hand, are still, in spite of the intolerableness of this assumption, regarded as immediate and transparent: we are looking at the photographed object without being aware of the material 'bearer', the medium.

Ophuis takes full advantage of this medium-specificity of painting. He transforms the indirectness of painting into a directness of a completely different nature. The skin of his paintings seems thin and raw. Not because he has only applied a thin layer of paint, but because the paint has been scraped away. The surface seems like skin that has been processed and torn open. This process of the surface induces the most intense physical associations with pain and rawness[1]. His treatment of paint intensifies the affective dimension revealed by his representations. But material has no object, no meaning. Because paint as a material has no object, the painted surface can as such not be transferred into meaning. However, the surface of the paintings of Ophuis attracts attention and evokes reactions. We are affectively moved and 'feel' it.

This brings us back to Ophuis' realism. Even though his work can be superficially regarded as realistically characterised, the spaces he paints are not real. A more accurate look makes the spectator aware of the construedness and artifice of the depicted spaces. The

Ronald Ophuis, Beslan II, 2008, oil on canvas. Private collection, courtesy of Aeroplastics Contemporary, Brussels

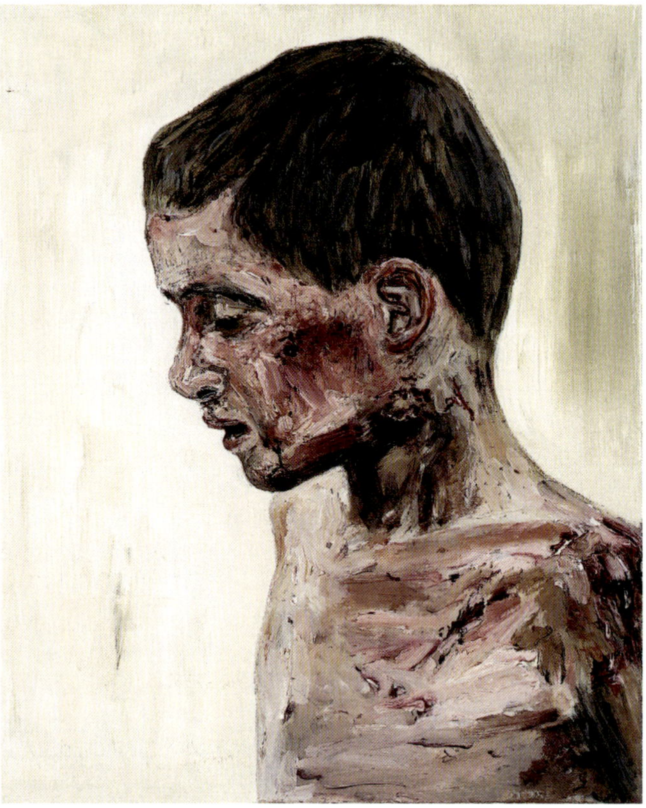

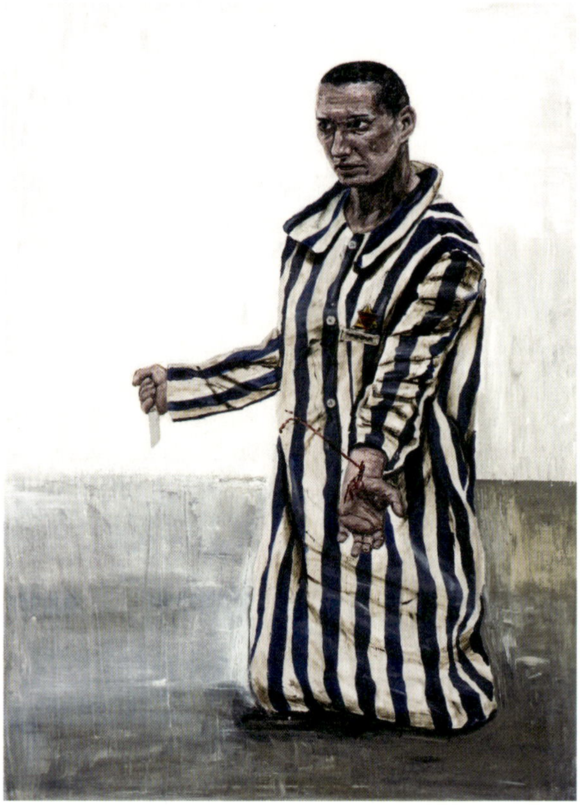

architectonic spaces in which the violent scenes are placed are perspectivistic. But there is often something strange, something forced, because of which the perspective does not look natural but explicitly construed. Add to this the fact that the figures in this space often seem wooden. In the end, Ophuis' representations are not realistic because the scenes do not form an entity. There is always friction between the represented scene and the way in which it is represented. Yet this is exactly the point. When the construedness of the image demands attention, the identification with the depicted figures is delayed. A reflexive moment is introduced in the affective way of looking, which prevents the identification from being blind.

In this regard, Ophuis' paintings can be compared to the huge photo Jeff Wall made in 1992, titled *Dead Troops Talk (A Vision After an Ambush of a Red Army Patrol near Moqor, Afghanistan, Winter 1986)*. Although the medium of photography is regarded as pre-eminently realistic, this photograph proves the contrary. The image shows dead or dying soldiers in a bombarded hilly landscape who are, however, explicitly posing. This landscape was staged by the artist in a studio. The paradox of this image is that the characters and the environment are realistic, but the image as a whole is not. This paradox clarifies that this photograph should not be regarded as a (botched) representation of the horrors of this war, but as an attempt of the artist to imagine this horror. The difference between these two qualifications is crucial. This image is not about war, but about imagining war.

His work does not depict brutal scenes but his attempts to picture such scenes. Instead of averting our eyes he suggests considering these scenes with an empathic look. Not to stimulate blind identification with the perpetrators (or victims), but to introduce affect to our thinking about perpetrators and victims.

While Jeff Wall enables a reflexive empathic vision through the artificial posing of his figures and by openly showing the construedness of the space, Ophuis has

Ronald Ophuis, **Boy of Sorrows, Beslan**,
2004, oil on canvas. Collection Vincent de Boer / Aliona Van der Horst,
courtesy of Aeroplastics Contemporary, Brussels

Ronald Ophuis, **De zelfmoord van Mala Zimetbaum**,
2006, oil on canvas. Private collection,
courtesy of Aeroplastics Contemporary, Brussels

even more means to realise such a vision thanks to the medium in which he works. The paint of his paintings embodies the violence and suffering he depicts simultaneously. Through this intensification through paint, in a different way to Wall, he is effective in activating an affective and empathic way of looking. His work thus shows that the art of painting is not dead, as some have claimed these past two decades. And more specifically and radically, that figurative, narrative painting is not dead. On the contrary, the new media have not at all taken over the function traditionally fulfilled by historic paintings. The continuous relevance of painting is possible because its function is not to inform or to represent, but to enable an emotional relationship with the events it represents.

1 A similar approach to painting can be recognised in the work of Francis Bacon. See van Alphen E., *Francis Bacon and the Loss of Self*, London, Reaktion Books, 1993

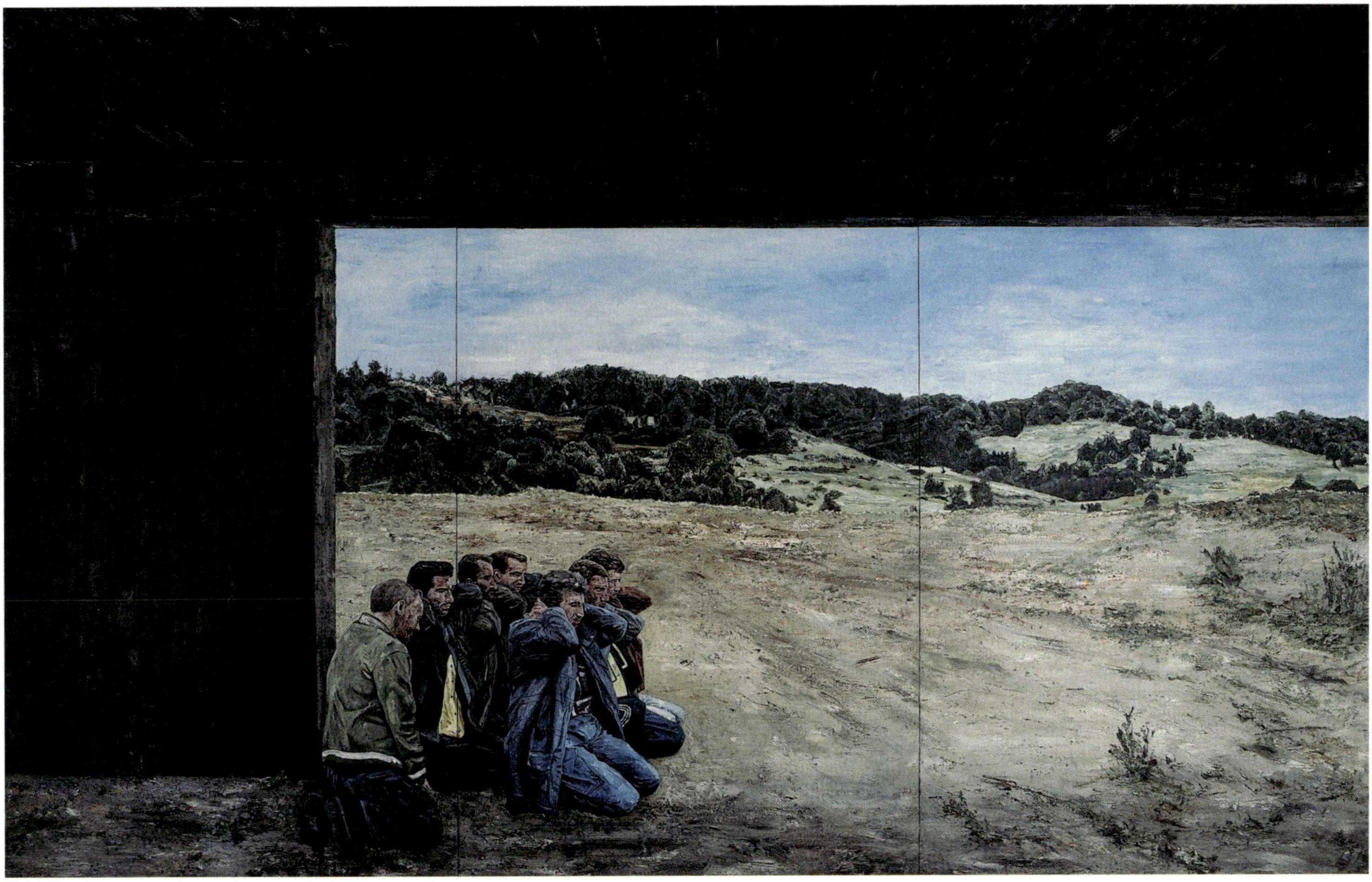

Ronald Ophuis, **Srebrenica I**,
2005, oil on canvas. Collection Bernard Massini, Nice, courtesy of Aeroplastics Contemporary, Brussels

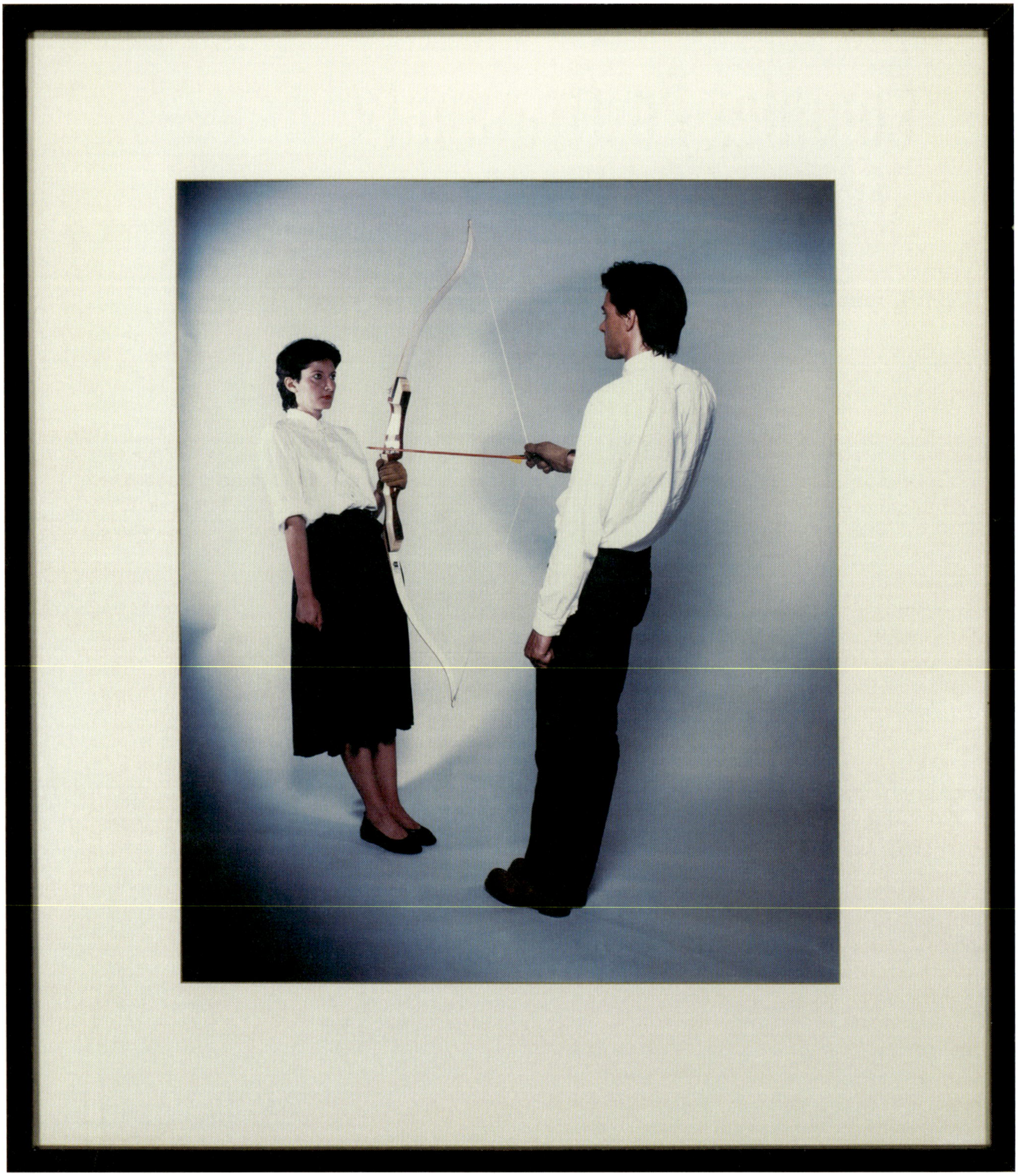

For fourteen years, Marnina Abramovic (1943) and Ulay (1943) lived and worked together as an artist couple. Between 1976 and 1981, they created numerous performances, *Relation Works*, with their artistic and romantic relationships as an object of research. In *Rest Energy*, made in 1981, Abramovic and Ulay face each other, leaning backwards slightly. Between them they hold a drawn bow and arrow.
The arrow points at the heart of Abramovic, who is holding the bow. Ulay draws the bow and arrow and thus decides the fate of his beloved.
Marnina Abramovic & Ulay, **Rest Energy**, 1981, photo. M HKA, Antwerp © SABAM Belgium 2013

JUDITH LEWIS HERMAN

Complex Posttraumatic Stress Disorder

A Syndrome In Survivors of Prolonged and Repeated Trauma

—excerpt from the *Journal of Traumatic Stress*, 1992

The current diagnostic formulation of PTSD derives primarily from observations of survivors of relatively circumscribed traumatic events: combat, disaster, and rape. It has been suggested that this formulation fails to capture the protean sequelae of prolonged, repeated trauma. In contrast to the circumscribed traumatic event, prolonged, repeated trauma can occur only when the victim is in a state of captivity, unable to flee, and under control of the perpetrator. Examples of such conditions include prisons, concentration camps, and slave labour camps. Such conditions also exist in some religious cults, in brothels and institutions of organised sexual exploitation, and in some families.

Captivity, which brings the victim into prolonged contact with the perpetrator, creates a special type of relationship, one of coercive control. This is equally true whether the victim is rendered captive primarily by physical force (as in the case of prisoners and hostages), or by a combination of physical, economic, social, and psychological means (as in the case of religious cult members, battered women, and abused children). The psychological impact of insubordination to coercive control may have many common tics or within the supposedly private (but equally political) sphere of sexual and domestic relations.

A preliminary formulation of this complex post-traumatic syndrome is currently under consideration for inclusion in DSM-IV under the name of DESNOS (Disorder of Extreme Stress). In the course of a larger work in progress, I have recently scanned literature of the past 50 years on survivors of prolonged domestic, sexual, or political victimization (Herman, 1992). This literature includes first-person accounts of survivors themselves, descriptive clinical literature, and, where available, more rigorously designed clinical studies. In the literature review, particular attention was directed

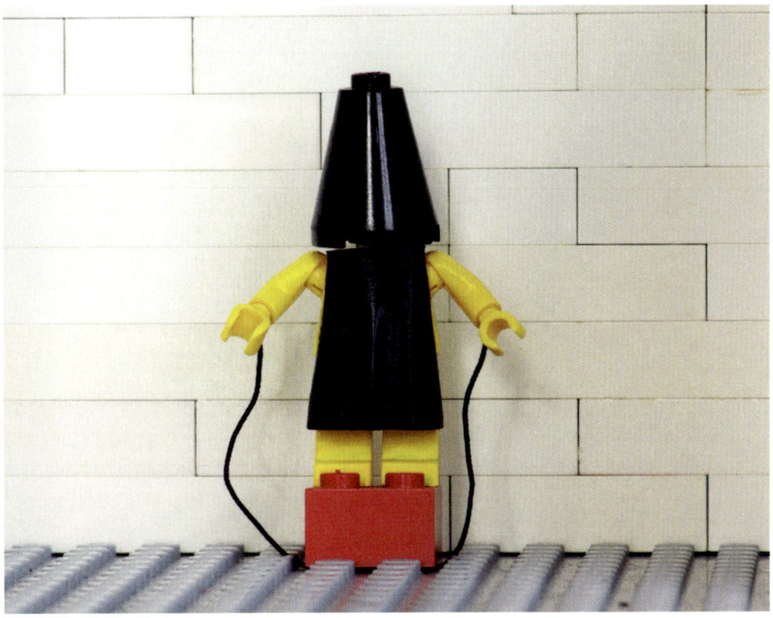

The anonymous English blogger Legofesto is fascinated by politics, current affairs and Lego. With her creations, for which she uses the famous blocks, she wants to depict injustice in the world, which is currently rampant, in a surprising way: the war in Iraq, the torture in Abu Ghraib, a bombardment on a refugee camp in Sri Lanka... Her Lego scenes are inspired by existing photos or testimonies, including children's drawings, making them extremely accurate. These days we are overwhelmed by images of war, torture, rape, etc. We see it daily on television, in newspapers and mainly on the Internet. We get 'used' to it. By staging these crimes with colourful building blocks, we suddenly see these horrific scenes in a new light and are again confronted with their inhumanity.
Legofesto, **Abu Ghraib**, 2005, Lego. © Legofesto

toward observations that did not fit readily into the existing criteria for PTSD. Though the sources include works by authors of many nationalities, only works originally written in English or available in English translation were reviewed.

The concept of a spectrum of posttraumatic disorders has been suggested independently by many major contributors to the field. Kolb, in a letter to the editor of the American Journal of Psychiatry (1989), writes of the 'heterogeneity' of PTSD. He observes that "PTSD is to psychiatry as syphilis was to medicine. At one time or another PTSD may appear to mimic every personality disorder," and notes further that "It is those threatened over long periods of time who suffer the long-standing severe personality disorganization." Niederland, on the basis of his work with survivors of the Nazi Holocaust, observes that "the concept of traumatic neurosis does not appear sufficient to cover the multitude and severity of clinical manifestations" of the survivor syndrome. Tanay, working with the same population, notes that "the psychopathology may be hidden in characterological changes that are manifest only in disturbed object relationships and attitudes toward work, the world, man and God" (Kristal, 1968). Similarly, Kroll and his colleagues, on the basis of their work with Southeast Asian refugees, suggest the need for an "expanded concept of PTSD that takes into account the observations [of the effects of] severe, prolonged, and/or massive psychological and physical traumata." Horowitz (1986) suggests the concept of a 'posttraumatic character disorder', and Brown and Fromm (1986) speak of 'complicated PTSD'.

Clinicians working with survivors of childhood abuse also invoke the need for an expanded diagnostic concept. Gelinas (1983) describes the 'disguised presentation' of the survivor of childhood sexual abuse as a patient with chronic depression complicated by dissociative symptoms, substance abuse, impulsivity, self-mutilation, and suicidality. She formulates the underlying psychopathology as a complicated traumatic neurosis. Goodwin (1988) conceptualizes the sequelae of prolonged childhood abuse as a severe posttraumatic syndrome which includes fugues and other dissociative states, ego fragmentation, affective and anxiety disorders, re-enactment and revictimisation, somatisation and suicidality.

Clinical observations identify three broad areas of disturbance which transcend simple PTSD. The first is symptomatic: the symptom picture in survivors of prolonged trauma often appears more complex, diffuse, and tenacious than in simple PTSD. The second is characterological: survivors of prolonged abuse develop characteristic personality changes, including deformations of relatedness and identity. The third area involves the survivor's vulnerability to repeated harm, both self-inflicted and at the hands of others.

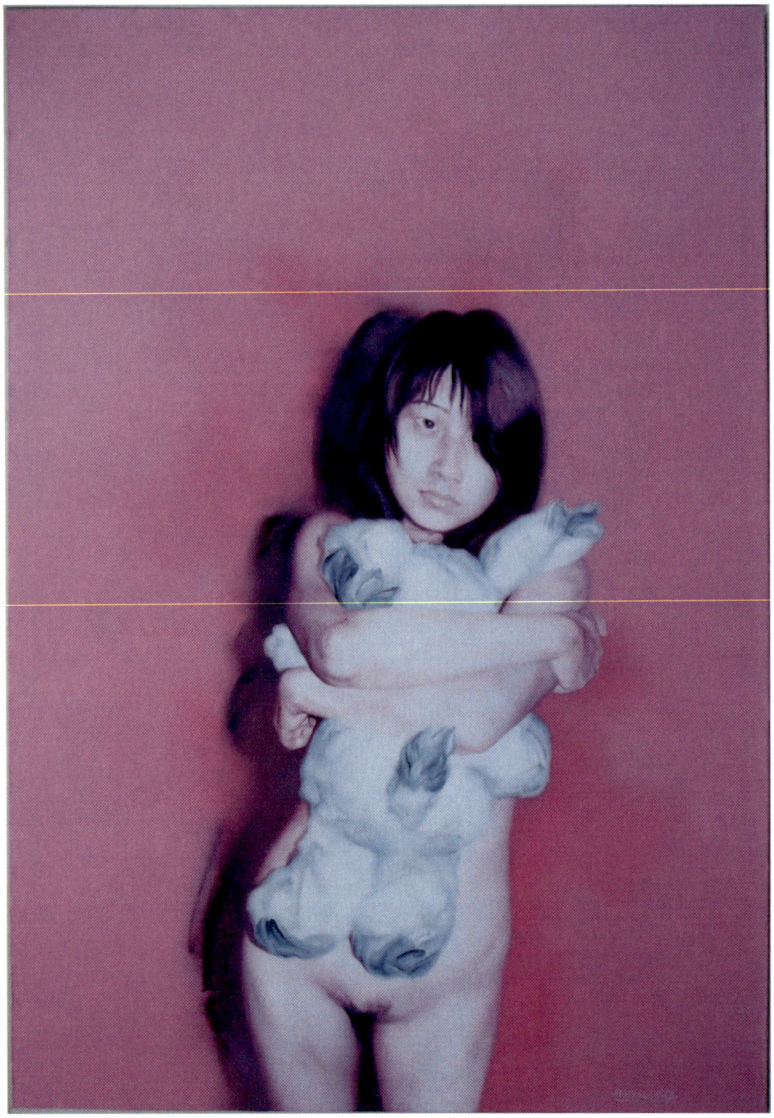

Since Chinese artist He Sen (1968) graduated in 1989, painting has taken hold of him. The central theme in his work is today's youth. In his early still-lives of cassettes, cigarette packs, etc., he referred to the world of adolescents and the increasing consumer society in which they are imprisoned. Later on in his work, figures start appearing, usually young girls in seductive poses and clothes. Smoking seems to be their favourite pastime. The paintings in which he combines girls with soft toys seem bizarre: the girl is neither a child, nor an adult. For now, she is in transition between both, but soon she will have to make a decision. The combination between sexuality and toys is reminiscent of prostitution, perhaps even abuse: a trauma that will mark the young girl's life.
He Sen, **Girl and Toy**, 2002, oil on canvas. Collection Gallery Adrian David, Knokke

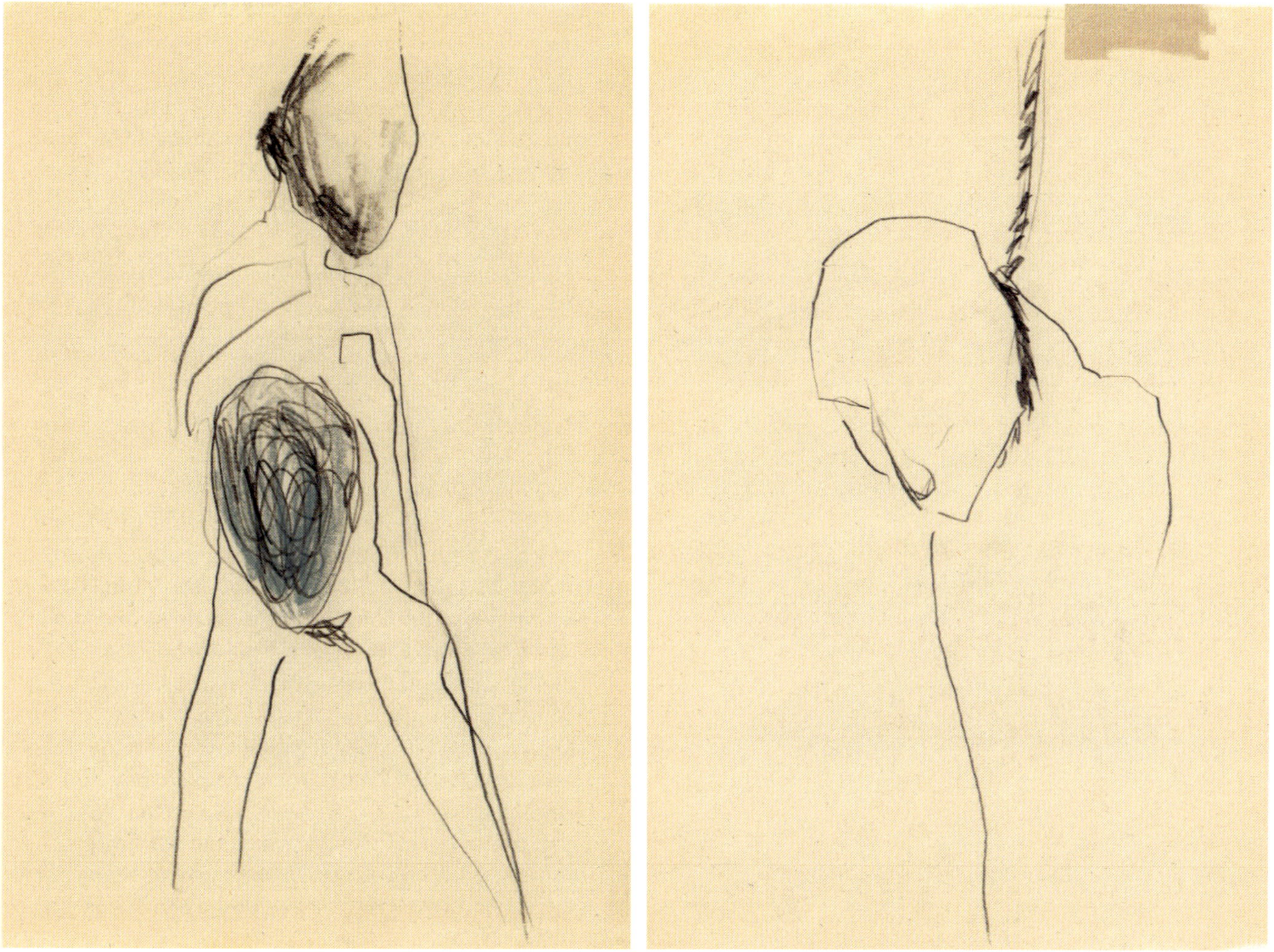

HISTOIRE from 1998 is a personal project of artist ARPAÏS du bois about her father, who was deported to Dachau during World War II. He did not speak about his war trauma for many years. When the stories eventually surfaced, ARPAÏS du bois made many drawings, visual notes, during their conversations of what she heard. This helped him process his war past. At the same time, the work reflects on the trauma of the bereaved, the children who have to live with the war-torn mother or father. For ARPAÏS du bois making *HISTOIRE* was necessary and a starting point for her later work.
ARPAÏS du bois, **Untitled, series 'HISTOIRE'**,
1998, graphite pencil on paper. © and courtesy ARPAÏS du bois

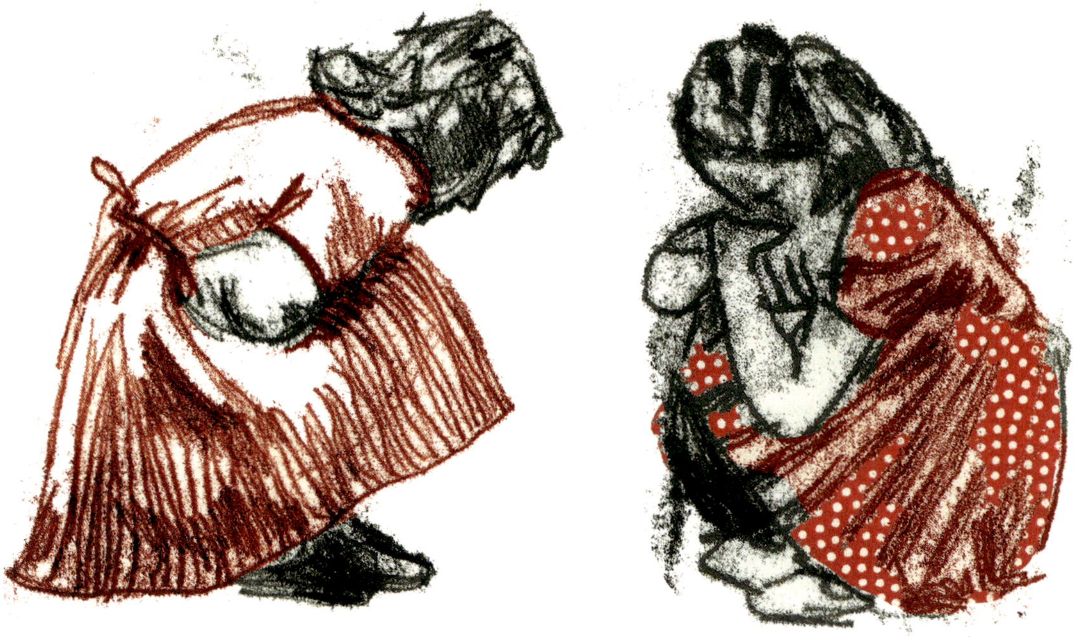

stilte meneer
dadiswaarekzoveelschrikvoorheb

krank van het oorlogstijdstramgerinkel
hoorek het geluidvanmijnentikker niemeer
tsoldatencircus maakte mij kapot
bevrorenbloed heeft mijn hart vastgezet
dagen en dagen diezelfde pijn
kben nevreemdelinginmijneigenvel
kloop verloren in de schotwonden van mijne geest
worde gij nooit is eenzaam
kijk naar mij alsk tegen u praat
aan den buitenkant bennek nenechtesnoepwinkel zeggen ze
maar in de bovenkamer ist stinkendenambras
omdak mijneneigenluchtnimeerkanrieken meneer

Astrid Van de Vijver, **Untitled**,
2013, monotype. Artist's collection

Matthias Hellemans, *Zij* (fragment)

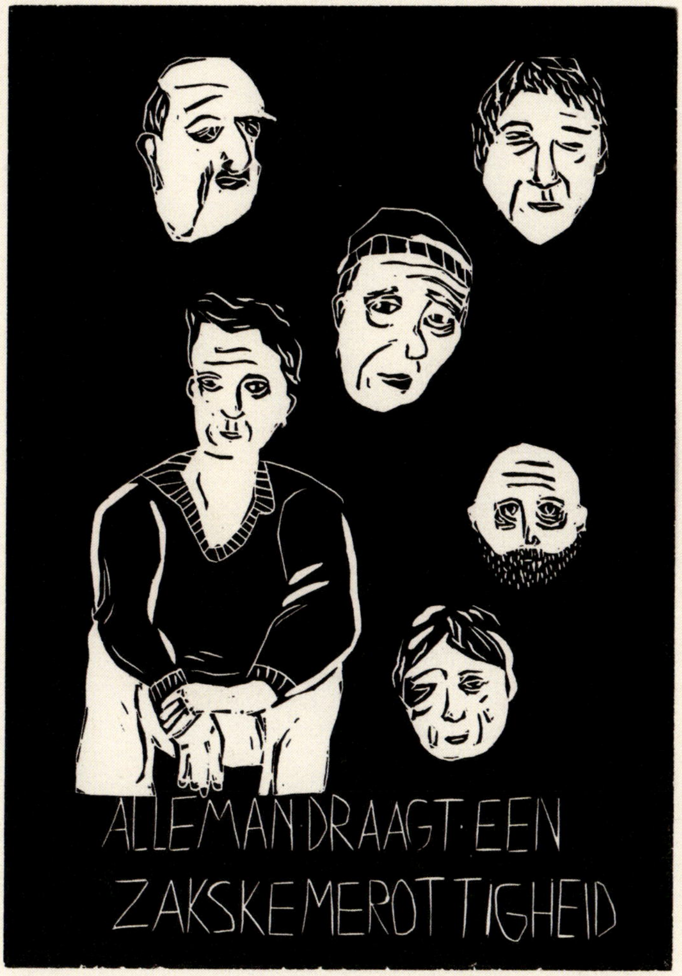

helden helden helden zegt u
ze waren allesbehalvedat
ze hakten op mekaar in
ze duwden mekaar van de weg als angstigebeesten
met de modder nog aan hun versplinterdebotten
wa gij leert uit uw geschiedenisboekskes
    is den buitenkant
kheb mijnbroekversleten tussen dingewanden
ge moogt dat letterlijk nemen
kheb deserteurs opgelapt
om ze mehakenenogen aanmekaargeplakt
tegen de muur te zetten
helden bestaan niet meneer
dat is wat wij ervan gemaakt hebben
in onze films en etalagepanden
sommige zijn gestorven in mijn armen
jankend als nepasgeborenbaby
met hun geweldige médaillemilitaire
    bengelend tussen hun ballen
anderen zitten vast in hunne zetel
    als ne kapotteplant totopteinde
maar kan ik het hun kwalijk nemen
nee meneer
niemand van ons hattervoor gekozen

Matthias Hellemans, *Zij* (fragment)

Lara Jakoba Breine, **Untitled**, 2013, woodcut. Artist's collection

Students of Bart Moeyaert' Creative Writing course (Royal Conservatory, Antwerp) have each written a text on the subject of *War & Trauma*. Students in the second bachelor year of Gerda Dendooven's Illustration course (School of Arts, Sint-Lucas Ghent) have been inspired by their texts.
The *Zij* text by Matthias Hellemans is based on the diaries of Ellen Newbold La Motte and Mary Borden, which were translated into Dutch by Erwin Mortier. In 1915, Mary Borden founded her own field hospital in Roesbrugge, near Ypres and Poperinghe; largely with her own means and donations from well-to-do people. It was soon a success, because of which she was also given other hospitals to supervise. Although the mortality rates were significantly lower there, there were still a large number of deaths. Mary Borden committed her experiences to paper in *Forbidden Zone*, a book that was heavily criticised and for which she did not find a publisher until after the war. One of the nurses, Ellen N. La Motte, also described the horror in her novel *The Backwash of War*, which was almost immediately banned.

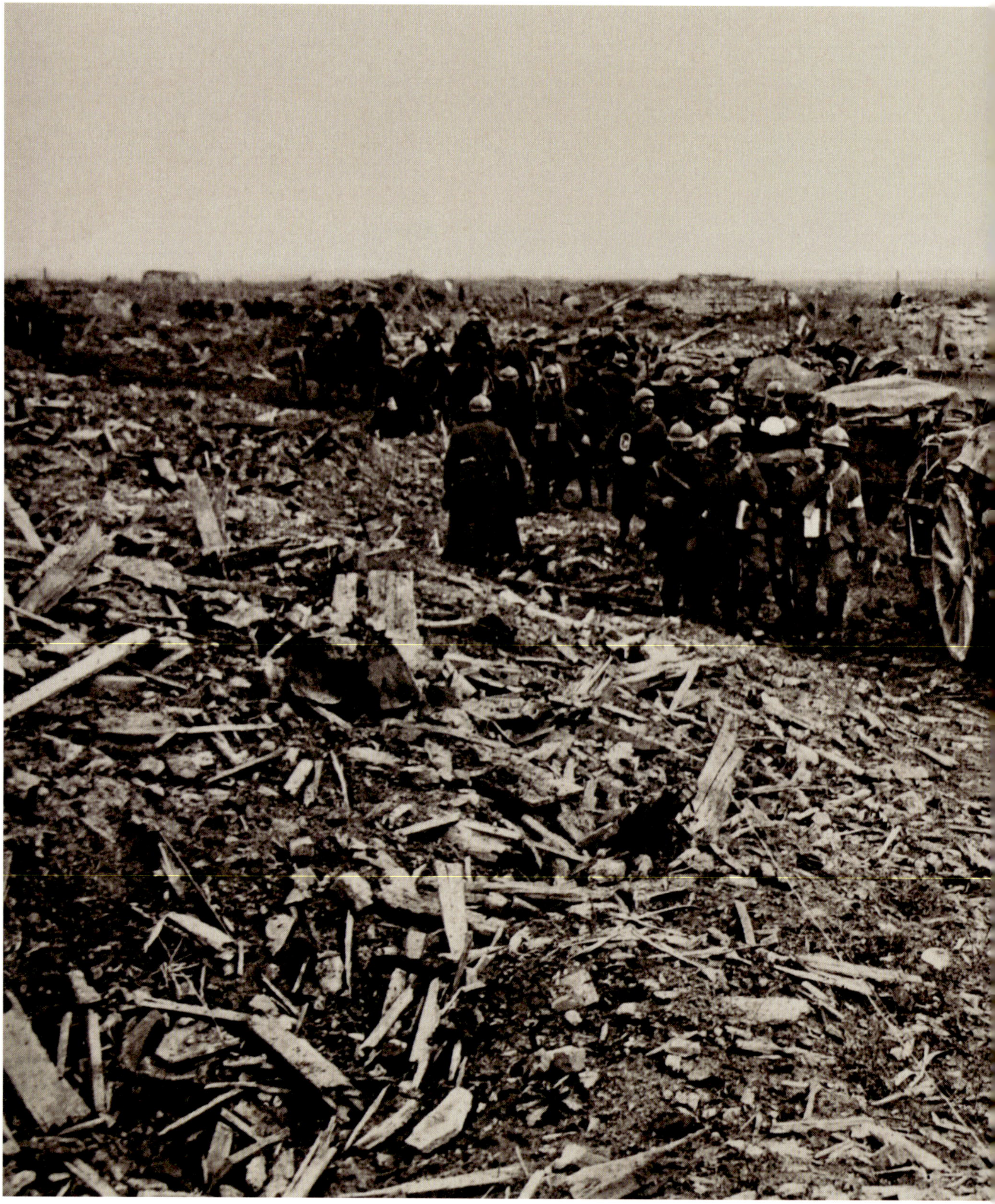

Service Photographique de l'Armée Belge, **Un Coin de Champ de Bataille près de Passchendaele**,
Oktober 1918, zilverbromidedruk. FotoMuseum provincie Antwerpen

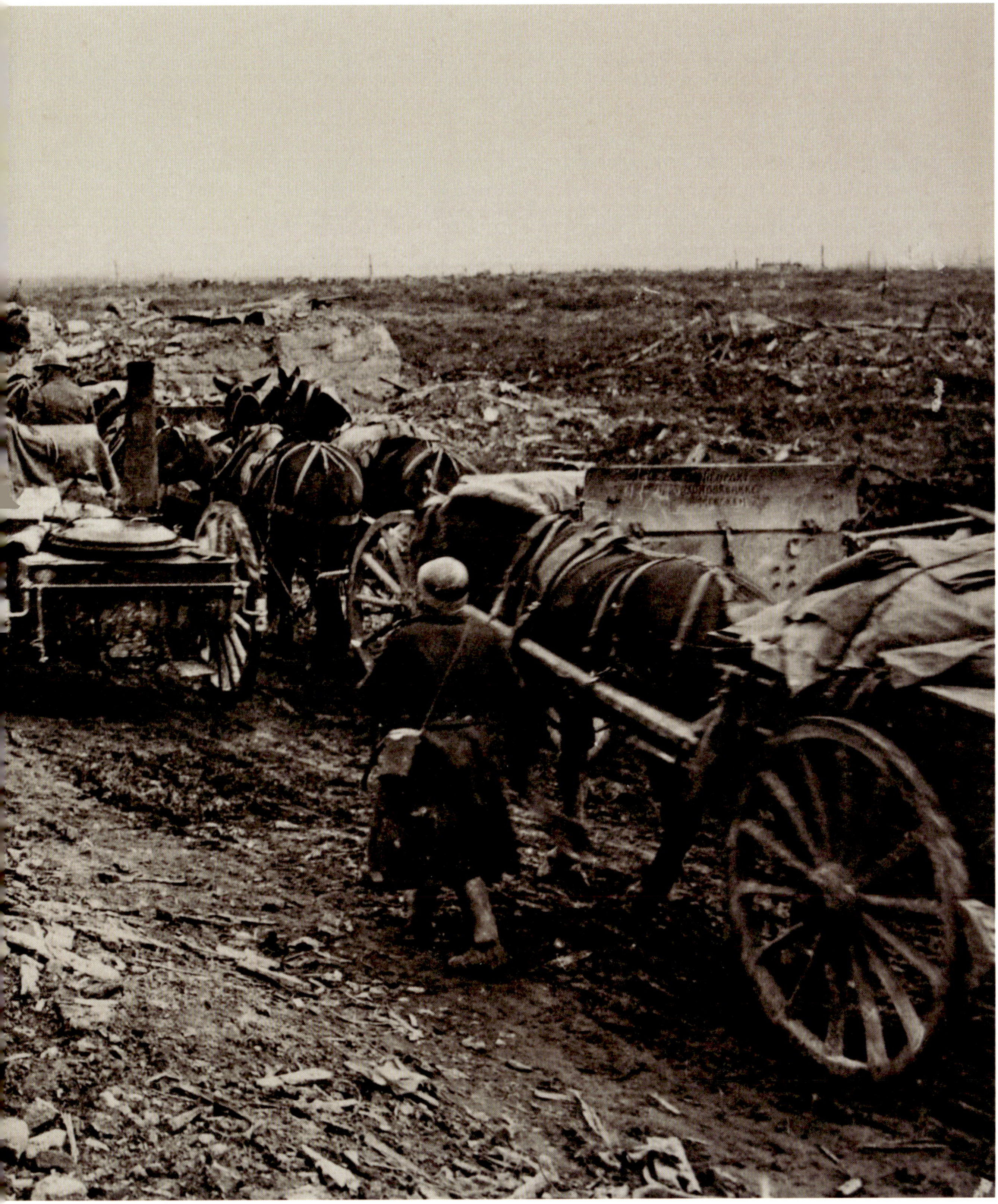

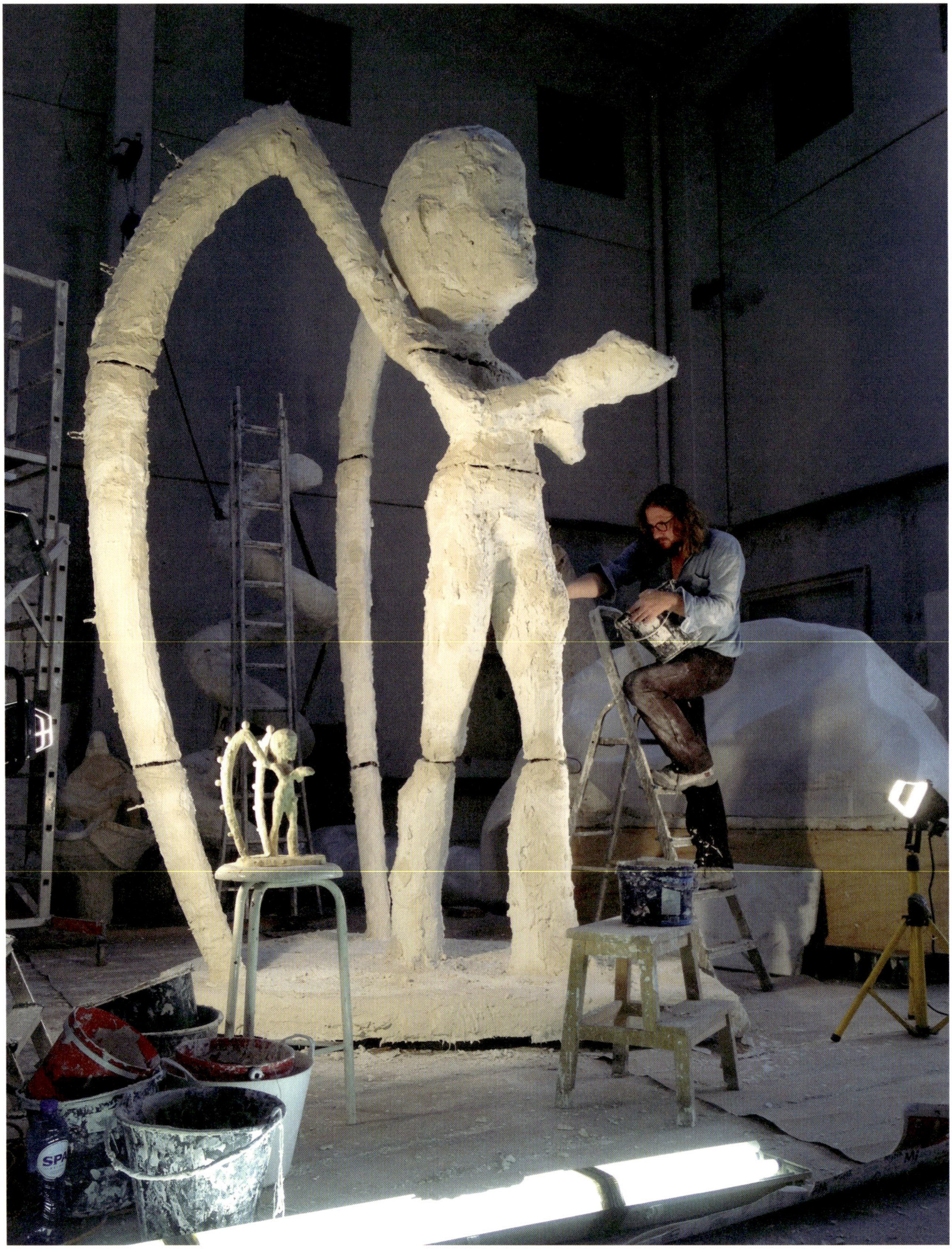

The oeuvre of Johan Tahon (1965) moves. Like no other he is fully aware of the impact of a personal history on his work and lets it seep in on purpose. In his studio in Oudenaarde the artist is surrounded by large, white plaster sculptures giving the place a shamanic serenity in both hellish summers and freezing cold winters. Tahon does his very best to fully master his own reality.
His sculptures are increasingly expanding and are taking on huge proportions. Each sculpture is a duel of physical and psychological matter. It is a trip through his deepest grievances and greatest joys: his own biography. Strictly separated from this is his library, the words are his very own Rilke and reveal the symbols in his work. The last part of this book and of the exhibition is a look back into the traumatic, an outsider's view of a traumatic childhood. By taking a step back, there is a possibility of seeing a positive future and casting off the burden of traumatising abuse.
Johan Tahon, **Lotus**, 2013, plaster

PERSONALIA

PATRICK ALLEGAERT is the artistic manager of the Dr. Guislain Museum. He also teaches art and heritage policy at the Catholic College of West Flanders (Vives) in Kortrijk and cultural policy at the Erasmus College Brussels. He is the chairman of the Cultural Heritage advisory committee (Flemish Community) and of Theater aan Zee (TAZ) (Ostend).

PIET CHIELENS is coordinator of the In Flanders Fields Museum where he is also responsible for public activities. He is the author and co-author of several publications on World War I.

DOMINIEK DENDOOVEN is a historian and researcher of the In Flanders Fields Museum.

PETRA FUCHS is a scientific staff member at the Institut für Geschichte der Medizin, Zentrum für Human- und Gesundheitswissenschaften in Charité – Universitätsmedizin Berlin.

JUDITH LEWIS HERMAN teaches psychiatry at the Harvard Medical School. She also holds a management position in an aid project for victims of violent crimes at the Cambridge Hospital, and at the Women's Mental Health Collective in Massachusetts, which she co-founded.

MARIA HERMES is a research fellow at the Staats- und Universitätsbibliothek Bremen. She is cultural historican and has written publications on the history of psychiatry in Germany during World War I and on the local history of Bremen in the 19th and 20th century.

YOON HEE LAMOT is a scientific staff member at the Dr. Guislain Museum. She is involved in developing temporary exhibitions.

PATRICK LOODTS was active as a military physician for many years. For some 15 years he has dedicated himself to studying Belgian military medicine during the Great War. This resulted in numerous conferences as well as a website (www.1914–1918.be) that is regularly completed and updated.

SUSANNE MICHL studied Modern History and French and was research assistant at different institutes. In 2011 she became an interim professor at the Department of Medical Ethics and History of Medicine, in Göttingen. Since April 2013 she is a research assistant at the Institute of Medical History, Theory and Ethics in Mainz.

THOMAS RÖSKE has been head of the Prinzhorn collection of the Psychiatric University Clinic in Heidelberg since 2002. He studied history of art, musicology and psychology at Hamburg University and obtained his doctorate in 1991 with a book about Hans Prinzhorn. He teaches at the Institute for European Art History of Heidelberg University and has published mainly on German Modernism and Outsider Art.

MAIKE ROTZOLL is a research fellow at the Department of History and Ethics of Medicine at the University of Heidelberg. She is a physician specialized in psychiatry and historian of medicine and has written publications on the history of psychiatry in the 20th century.

SANDRINE SMETS is an art historian and archaeologist. She has been working at the Royal Army and Military History Museum in Brussels since 2003 and in 2011 she became head of the scientific department that curates the collections from 1914 to the present. She is currently preparing a Ph.D. on Belgian artists in the Great War (ULB).

RENÉ STOCKMAN holds a Ph.D. in Public Health. He is the Superior General of the Brothers of Charity. As founder and curator of the Dr Guislain Museum, he contributes to the debate on the history of psychiatry.

PIETER TROGH is a historian and a researcher for the In Flanders Fields Museum.

ERNST VAN ALPHEN is a professor of Literature at the University of Leiden. He published, among others, *Francis Bacon and the Loss of Self* ((1993), *Caught By History: Holocaust Effects in Contemporary Art, Literature, and Theory* (1997) and *Art in Mind: How Contemporary Images Shape Thought* (2005).

ONNO VAN DER HART is a psychotraumatologist and Emeritus professor of the psychopathology of chronic traumatisation at the Department of Clinical & Health psychology at the University of Utrecht.

BESSEL A. VAN DER KOLK is affiliated with the Department of Psychiatry of the Harvard Medical School in Boston and is Medical Director of the Trauma Center at JRI in Brookline, Massachusetts.

CHRISTINE VAN EVERBROECK is head of the educational department of the Royal Army and Military History Museum in Brussels. Together with Pieter Verstraete, she is the author of the book *Verminkte stilte* (2013) [Mutilated silence] about Belgian invalids with physical and psychological problems caused by World War I.

DIRK VAN PEER is a philosopher and has been familiar with the work of Koen Broucke for many years.

VINCENT VERBRUGGE is a historian and director of the National Tobacco Museum in Wervik. Current research areas are the influence of smoking tobacco in military circles and a study of the role of the "black pope" in the years 1915–1919.

JEF VERSCHOORE is a civil engineer and active as a consultant and ICT architect from 1980 to this year. In 1989 he became a member of the Ypres town council. He has been a member of the Ypres bench of Aldermen since 1996. He is currently the first alderman authorised for, among others, coordinating the commemoration of the centenary of the Great War, for protocol and for tourism. He is also chairman of the IFFM vzw. In addition, he is a member of the provincial council, vice-chairman of Westtoer and member of the WVI management committee.

PIETER VERSTRAETE is affiliated with the Education, Culture and Society research unit of KU Leuven as a teacher of historical pedagogy. In his research, he focuses on the history and historiography of our association with and representation of people with a disability. Several of his publications are *In the Shadow of disability*, *The imperfect historian* and *Verminkte stilte* [Mutilated Silence].

LARS WEISAETH is affiliated with the Disaster Psychiatry Department at the University of Oslo in Norway.

COLOPHON

EXHIBITION

Soldiers and Ambulances 1914–1918
IN FLANDERS FIELDS MUSEUM, YPRES
1/11/2013–30/6/2014

Project exhibition: Piet Chielens, Dominiek Dendooven, Pieter Trogh, Annick Vandenbilcke (IFFM)
Irma Duim, Peter Van Lier, Sabine Van Velzen (Totems Architecture)
Scenography exhibition: Totems Architecture, Amsterdam (NL)
Production exhibition: Heijmerink Wagemakers, Nieuwegein (NL)
Composition exhibition: Dries Chaerle, Piet Chielens, Jack De Moor, Armand Deknudt, Isabeau Delaey, Dominiek Dendooven, Jan Dewilde, Christina Klein, Fleur Lamée, Hans Landler, Eva Langhals, Patrick Loodts, Philippe Oosterlinck, Sandrine Smets, Andy Tonge, Pieter Trogh, Annick Vandenbilcke, Frederik Vandewiere, Luc Van de Sijpe, Roger Verbeke, Vincent Verbrugge
Staff In Flanders Fields Museum:
Liesbeth Archie, Justine Blanckaert, Eva Blomme, Ann-Lore Braekeveldt, Liesbet Bryon, Ewout Catteeuw, Heidi Caulier, Ivan Claerebout, Ann-Sophie Coene, Petra Delvaux, Els Demuyt, Els Deroo, Anne-Marie Deschietere, Ingrid Lingier, Annick Louchaert, Michelle Martens, Elke Masschelein, Virginie Miniaïlo, Marjan Nachtergaele, Martine Platteeuw, Mietoe Schotte, Wouter Sinaeve, Peter Slosse, Femke Soetaert, Diederik Vandenbilcke, Fernand Vanrobaeys, Sophie Wicke, Roos Wildemeersch

LOANERS

Algemeen Rijksarchief, Brussel (BE)
Andy Tonge, Bromley (UK)
Anny Kerkhofs – Luc Van de Sijpe, Sint-Huibrechts Lille – Hasselt (BE)
Army Medical Services Museum, Mytchett (UK)
Australian War Memorial, Canberra (AUS)
BDIC–Musée de l'Histoire Contemporaine, Paris (FR)
British Red Cross Museum & Archives, London (UK)
Dr. Andrew Bamji, Gillies Archivist, Rye (UK)
Eric Monbel, Lille (FR)
Familie De Bruyker, Gent–Sint-Martems-Latem (BE)
Familie Dox, Wijnegem (BE)
Frankie Van Rossem, Gent (BE)
Imperial War Museum, London (UK)
In Flanders Fields Museum, donations Jack De Moor, George Luchies, Michel Rooryck, Familie Van de Craen–Van Bauwel
Institut Curie, Paris (FR)
Koninklijk Legermuseum, Brussel (BE)
Lucien Guillaume, Gédinne (BE)
Maureen Dennis, Taplow (UK)
Max Beckmann Archiv, München (DE)
Musée du Service de Santé des Armées au Val-de-Grâce, Paris (FR)
Order of St-John, London (UK)
Patrick Hilgers, Namur (BE)
Paul & Su Handford, Birmingham (UK)
Peter McGregor–Ambulance Heritage Society (UK)
Philippe Oosterlinck, Menen (BE)
Powel Cotton Museum, Quex Park, Birchington (UK)
Religious Society of Friends (Quakers), London (UK)
The Royal College of Surgeons of England, London (UK)
Union des Anciens Combattants d'Armentières, donation of Jacques and Colette Ulmann (FR)
Von der Heydt–Museum, Wuppertal (DE)
Wellcome Collection, London (UK)

EXHIBITION

Soldiers and Psychiatrists 1914–2014
DR GUISLAIN MUSEUM, GHENT
1/11/2013–30/6/2014

Project exhibition: Patrick Allegaert, Yoon Hee Lamot, Bart Marius
Scenography exhibition: Johan De Wit
Composition exhibition: Patrick Allegaert, Annemie Cailliau, Alexander Couckhuyt, Yoon Hee Lamot, Bart Marius, Annemie Sneijers, Kristine Timperman, Eline Van de Voorde, Saïdya Vanhooren, Vaast Vanoverschelde, Nele Vertriest
Staff Museum Dr. Guislain: Nadine Acce, Fatima Ammi, Fatiha Asghir, Peter Bosschaert, Lidwine De Buck, Eric Claeys, Kaat De Corel, Rudi De Graaf, Pieter Degroote, Henk Dewaele, Nico Deuninck, Olivier Hoge, Ann Huybens, Natasha Lahousse, Martin Lauwers, Benoit Lobos, Goedele Maes, Maurice Michiels, Ilse Milants, Mimi Pachova, Kristine Praet, Tim Reynaerts, Martin Riddle, Caroline Speeckaert, Anne-Marie Spanoghe, Stefanie Stragier, Sybille Van den Berghe, Dieter Vanden Bossche, Veerle Van Gaver, Geert van Pol, Marina Vanlierde, Mayke Vos, Hendrik Van Wordragen, Eric Verheedt

LOANERS

Belgium
Aeroplastics Contemporary, Brussels
Amsab ISG, Ghent
ARPAÏS du bois, Antwerp
Belgisch Museum voor Radiologie, Brussels
Chantal Pollier, Ghent
Collectie R.Q., Ostend
Dooreman, Ghent
Fifty One Fine Art Photography, Antwerp
FotoMuseum Province Antwerp
Galerie Adrian David, Knokke
Galerie De Zwarte Panter, Antwerp
Gery De Smet, St-Amandsberg
In Flanders Fields Museum, Ypres
In Situ Gallery, Aalst
Jan De Maesschalck, Courtesy Zeno X

Gallery, Antwerp
Jan Vanriet, Courtesy Roberto Polo Gallery, Brussels
Janpieter Chielens, Ghent
Johan Tahon, Zwalm
Joods Museum van België, Brussels
Kazerne Dossin, Mechelen
Koen Broucke, Boechout
Koninklijk Museum voor het Leger en de Krijgsgeschiedenis, Brussels
Koninklijk Museum voor Schone Kunsten, Antwerp
Korneel Detailleur, Ghent
Lucas Devriendt, Ghent
M HKA, Antwerp
Marge Monko, Ghent
Musée de la Photographie, Charleroi
Museum Dr. Guislain, Ghent
Mu.Zee, Ostend
Pascale Pollier, Brakel
Peter De Koninck, Antwerp
Pieter Vertraete, Leuven
Private collections
Rinus Van de Velde, Antwerp
S.M.A.K., Ghent
Stephan Vanfleteren, Veurne
Students 2nd Bachelor Illustration Sint-Lucas, Ghent
Students creative writing Royal Conservatory, Antwerp
Teun Voeten, Brussels
Tim Dirven, Laken
Universiteitsbibliotheek, Ghent
Vlaams Parlement, Brussels

Denmark
Jan Grarup

Germany
Galerie Susanne Zander, Köln
Harun Farocki, München
L.A. Galerie, Frankfurt
Sammlung Prinzhorn, Heidelberg
Stiftung Deutsches Hygiene-Museum, Dresden

France
Collection Bernard Massini, Nice
Contact Press Images, Paris
Fondation Francès, Senlis
Historial de la Grande Guerre, Péronne
Musée du Service de Santé des Armées au Val-de-Grâce, Paris
Robin Hammond, Paris
RTR Gallery, Paris

India
Dalit Foundation, New Dehli

Israel
Noam Omer, Hod Hasharon

The Netherlands
Cobra to Contemporary, collection Hugo and Carla Brown
Collectie Nauta, Leiden
Collectie Vincent de Boer / Aliona van der Horst
Stichting Collectie De Stadshof

UK
Annie Kevans, London
David Lewis-Hodgson
Eleanor Crook, London
Gillian Wearing, London
Legofesto, Liverpool
Mary Evans Picture Library, London
Wellcome Collection, London

USA
Alfredo Jaar, New York
James Nachtwey, New York
Juf Pictures Inc, Santa Monica

PUBLICATION

Editing: Patrick Allegaert, Georgina Boyes, Annemie Cailliau, Dries Chaerle, Piet Chielens, Alexander Couckhuyt, Dominiek Dendooven, Martin Lambert, Yoon Hee Lamot, Matt Leonard, Bart Marius, Freddy Rottey, Pieter Trogh, Annick Vandenbilcke, Eline Van de Voorde, Hadewych Van den Bossche, Jan Van Gansbeke, Nele Vertriest
Picture editing: Patrick Allegaert, Annemie Cailliau, Piet Chielens, Alexander Couckhuyt, Dominiek Dendooven, Séverine Lacante, Yoon Hee Lamot, Bart Marius, Rik Depraetere, Pieter Trogh, Annick Vandenbilcke, Nele Vertriest
Book design: Dooreman, design & Pieter Willems (pjotr.be), layout
Translation: Lode Demetter, www.ape-translations.be
Photography: Guido Suykens p. 54, 55, 127, 138, 140, 141, 143, 156, 164, 165
Photo cover: © Royal Army and Military History Museum in Brussels
Impression: die Keure, Bruges
Binding: Jansenbinders, Leiden

Hannibal Publishing is part of Cannibal Publishing.
www.hannibalpublishing.com

ISBN 978 94 9137 663 4
D/2013/11922/26
NUR 694

www.inflandersfields.be
www.museumdrguislain.be

Met de steun van:

Met ondersteuning van de Vlaamse overheid

Voor In Flanders Fields Museum:

Voor Museum Dr. Guislain:

Het museum is een realisatie van de Broeders van Liefde